Travel and Tourism in Europe

SECOND EDITION

Rob Davidson

LONGMAN

Pearson Education Limited
Edinburgh Gate
Harlow, Essex CM20 2JE, England
and Associated Companies throughout the world.

Published in the United States of America
by Addison Wesley Longman Publishing, New York

First published 1992
Second Edition 1998
Second impression 1999

ISBN 0 582 29224-7

Visit Addison Wesley Longman on the world wide web at
http://www.awl-he.com

British Library Cataloguing-in-Publication Data
A catalogue record for this book is available from the British Library.

Set by 35 in 10/12 Sabon
Printed in Singapore (PH)

To the memory of Eddie Jansen

Contents

Acknowledgements

A great many people have helped me in connection with this book, by giving me the information I needed for my research and by commenting on my analysis of that information. The case studies in particular could not have been written without the very substantial assistance I received from industry practitioners who were kind enough to provide me with the facts and figures, ideas and comments, upon which the case studies are based.

My heartfelt thanks are therefore due to all of those who very kindly responded to my numerous requests. I would particularly like to thank the following for supplying me with information and permission to use it in this book:

Gregory Alegi of Air One; Jeff Bertus of Europarks; Dirk Bochar of the Eurolines Organisation; Nick Brass of Air One; Terry Browne and Hugh Cade of Deloitte & Touche; Lisa Davies of the European Travel Commission; Natascha Crump of Madame Tussaud's; Richard Dickinson formerly of the DGXXIII Tourism Unit and now with the World Travel and Tourism Council; Sabine Faraut of Episodes; Frédérique Fau of Cahiers Espaces; J. Gilbert of Eurolines UK; Jiri Havlicek of Czech Railways; John Hume of the International Duty Free Confederation; Melissa Hutchings of Beehive Communications; Deborah Jepson of the International Union of Railways; Aline Legrand of the EFCT; Len Lickorish of the European Tourism Action Group; Louis Long of EMECA; Hamish McFall of Tavistock Communications; A. Martens, editor of Rail International – Schienen der Welt; Thierry Meeùs of Walibi; Marc Neciolli of EMECA; Marc Richter, editor of *AIT News*, Anna Ryland, editor of *Insights*; Bard Schjolberg of the DGXXIII Tourism Unit; Juliet Simpkins of Madame Tussaud's; Graham Todd of Travel & Tourism Intelligence; John Whitelegg of Eco-Logica Limited; Jane Williams of Cresta Holidays; and Sandra Woods of the International Road Federation.

Thanks are also due to two tourism students of the University of Westminster – Richard J. Maslen, for his assistance in connection with the chapter on air transport, and Iona McConnell, for giving up part of her summer holiday to act as my research assistant.

Finally, I would like to express my very special gratitude to Derek Robbins of Bournemouth University, for generously giving up his time in order to read – and make many extremely helpful observations on – the chapters dealing with transport issues and, in particular, for his very encouraging comments on my work.

Rob Davidson

List of figures

List of tables

List of abbreviations

AEA   Association of European Airlines
ATAG   Air Transport Action Group
ATC   air traffic control
ATK   available tonne kilometre
BALPPA   British Association of Leisure Parks, Piers and Attractions
BHA   British Hospitality Association
CAA   Civil Aviation Authority
CER   Community of European Railways
COR   Committee of the Regions
CRS   computer reservation systems
CTN   combined transports network
DG   Directorate-General
EAA   European Economic Area
EAGGF   European Agriculture Guidance and Guarantee Fund
EFCT   European Federation of Conference Towns
EIA   Environmental Impact Assessment
EIB   European Investment Bank
EIF   European Investment Fund
EMILG   European Meetings Industry Liaison Group
EMU   Economic and Monetary Union
ERA   European Regional Airlines Association
ERDF   European Regional Development Fund
ESF   European Social Fund
ETAG   European Tourism Action Group
ETC   European Travel Commission
ETM   European Travel Monitor

ETRF   European Travel Research Foundation
EYT   European Year of Tourism
FECTO   Federation of the European Cities' Tourist Offices
FFP   frequent flyer programme
GATS   General Agreement on Trade in Services
IAAPA   International Association of Amusement Parks and Attractions
IATA   International Air Transport Association
IHA   International Hotel Association
IRF   International Road Federation
IRTU   International Road Transport Union
ITs   fully inclusive tour packages
MEP   Member of the European Parliament
NTO   National Tourist Organisation
OECD   Organisation for Economic Cooperation and Development
OEEC   Organisation for European Economic Cooperation (now OECD)
PCO   professional conference organiser
TEE   Trans European Express
TENs   Trans-European Networks
UFTAA   Universal Federation of Travel Agents' Associations
UIC   International Union of Railways
VFR   Visiting friends and relatives
WTO   World Tourism Organisation
WTTC   World Travel and Tourism Council

EU Member States

Negotiations with these countries are underway and it is proposed that
they will join the EU before the year 2000

■ Headquarters of EU institutions
● Capital cities
National boundary
Region boundary
Regional boundaries extending around islands

Country/Region	Regional Capital
Austria	
1 Burgenland	Eisenstadt
2 Kärnten	Klagenfurt
3 Niederösterreich	Sankt Pölten
4 Oberösterreich	Linz
5 Salzburg	Salzberg
6 Steiermark	Graz
7 Tirol	Innsbruck
8 Voral-Lichensteinberg	Bregenz
9 Wien/Vienna	Wien/Vienna
Belgium	
10 Vlaanderen	Bruxelles/Brussels
11 Wallonie	Namur
Finland	
12 Hameen Lääni, Tavastehus Län	Tampere Tamerfors
13 Keskisuomen Lääni, Mellersta Finlands Län	Jyväskylä
14 Kuopion Lääni, Kuopio Län	Kuopio
15 Kymen Lääni, Kymmene Län	Kouvola
16 Landskapet Åland	Maarianhamina Mariehamn
* Lapin Lääni, Lapplands Län	Rovaniemi
17 Mikkelin Lääni, St Michels Län	Mikkeli St Michel
18 Oulun Lääni, Uleåborgs Län	Oulu Uleåborg
19 Pohjois-Kartjalan, Norra Karelens Län	Joensuu
20 Turun Ja Porin Lääni, Åbo Och Björneborgs Län	Turku Åbo
21 Uudenmaan Lääni, Nylands Län	Helsingfors/Helsinki
22 Vaasan Lääni, Vasa Lä	Vaasa/Vasa
France	
23 Alsace	Strasburg
24 Auvergne	Clermont-Ferand
25 Aquitaine	Bordeaux
26 Basse-Normandie	Caen
27 Bretagne/Brittany	Rennes
28 Bourgogne/Burgundy	Dijon
29 Centre	Orléans
30 Champagne-Ardenne	Châlons-sur-Marne
31 Corse/Corsica	Ajaccio
32 Franche-Comté	Besancon
33 Haute-Normandie	Rouen
34 Île-de-France	Paris
35 Languedoc-Roussillon	Montpellier
36 Limousin	Limoges
37 Lorraine	Metz
38 Midi-Pyrénées	Toulouse
39 Nord-Pas-de-Calais	Lille
40 Pays de la Loire	Nantes
41 Picardie	Amiens
42 Poitou-Charentes	Poitiers
43 Provence - Alpes - Côte d'Azur	Marseille
44 Rhone - Alpes	Lyon
Germany	
45 Baden-Württemberg	Stuttgart
46 Bayern	München
47 Berlin	Berlin
48 Brandenburg	Potsdam
49 Bremen	Bremen
50 Hamburg	Hamburg
51 Hessen	Wiesbaden
52 Mecklenburg-Vorpommern	Schwerin
53 Niedersachsen	Hanover
54 Nordrhein-Westfalen	Düsseldorf
55 Rheineland-Pfalz	Mainz
56 Saarland	Saarbrücken
57 Sachsen	Dresden
58 Sachsen-Anhalt	Magdeburg
59 Schleswig-Holstein	Kiel
60 Thüringen	Erfurt
Greece	
61 Anatoliki Makedonia Kaithraki	Komotini
62 Attiki	Athinai/ Athens
63 Dytiki Ellada	Patrai
64 Dytiki Makedonia	Kozani
65 Ionioi Nisoi	Kerkyra
66 Ipeiros	Ionnina
67 Kentriki Makedonia	Thessaloniki
68 Kriti/Crete	Irakleion
69 Notio Aigaio	Ermoupolis
70 Peloponnisos	Tripolis
71 Voreio Aigaio	Mytilini
72 Sterea Ellada	Lamia
73 Thessalia	Larisa
Ireland	
74 Connaught	
75 Leinster	Dublin
76 Munster	
77 Ulster	

Country/Region	Regional Capital
Italy	
78 Abruzzo	L' Aquila
79 Basilicata	Potenza
80 Calabria	Catanzaro
81 Campania	Napoli
82 Emilia-Romagna	Bologna
83 Friuli-Venezia-Giulia	Trieste
84 Lazio	Roma
85 Liguria	Genova
86 Lombardia	Milano
87 Marche	Ancona
88 Molise	Campobasso
89 Piemonte	Torino/Turin
90 Puglia	Bari
91 Sardegna/Sardinia	Cagliari
92 Sicilia/Sicily	Palermo
93 Toscana/Tuscany	Firenze/Florence
94 Trentino-Alto Adige	Trento
95 Umbria	Perugia
96 Valle d'Aosta	Aoste-Aosta
97 Veneto	Venezia/Venice
Portugal	
98 Alentejo	Évora
99 Algarve	Faro
100 Centro	Coimbra
101 Lisboa e Vale do Tejo	Lisboa/Lisbon
102 Norte	Porto
Spain	
103 Andalucía	Sevilla
104 Aragón	Zaragoza
105 Cantabria	Santander
106 Castilla la Mancha	Toledo
107 Castilla y León	Valladolid
108 Cataluña	Barcelona
109 Communidad Foral de Navarra	Pamplona
110 Communidad Valenciana	Valencia
111 Comunidad de Madrid	Madrid
112 Extremadura	Mérida
113 Galicia	Santiago de Compostela
114 Islas Baleares	Palma de Mallorca
115 La Rioja	Logroño
116 País Vasco	Gasteiz-Vitoria
117 Principado de Asturias	Oviedo
118 Región de Murcia	Murcia
Sweden	
119 Älvsborg	Vanersborg
120 Blekinge	Karlskrona
121 Gävleborg	Gävle
122 Göteborg Och	Bohus
123 Gotland	Visby
124 Halland	Halmstad
125 Jämtland	Ostersund
126 Jönköping	Jönköping
127 Kalmar	Kalmar
128 Kopparberg	Falun
129 Kristianstad	Kristianstad
130 Kronoberg	Växjö
131 Malmöhus	Malmö
* Norrbotten	Luleå
132 Örebro	Örebro
133 Öster-Götland	Linköping
134 Skaraborg	Mariestad
135 Söder-Manland	Nyköping
136 Stockholm	Stockholm
137 Uppsala	Uppsala
138 Värmland	Karlstad
139 Västerbotten	Umeå
140 Västernorrland	Härnösand
141 Västmanland	Våsterås
United Kingdom	
142 East Anglia	
143 East Midlands	
144 Northern	
145 Northern Ireland	Belfast
146 North-west	
147 Scotland	Edinburgh
148 South-east	London
149 South-west	
150 Wales	Cardiff
151 West Midlands	
152 Yorkshire & Humberside	

* these regions are not shown on this map

1

Europe and tourism

KEY OBJECTIVES

Reading this chapter will enable you to:

- Appreciate the extent and diversity of tourism in Europe.
- See European tourism in its historical context.
- Identify the main tourism flows into, out of, and within Europe.
- Understand contemporary trends in European tourism and the factors which are determining those trends.
- Anticipate the major features likely to characterise European tourism in the 21st century.

Introduction

Comprising no more than 7 per cent of the planet's land mass, the continent of Europe is more intensively visited by the world's tourists than all other continents taken together. As well as the 15 million tourists who arrive in Europe from other continents each year, a further 300 million European citizens visit another country in Europe apart from their own, and over 1 billion tourism trips are made annually by Europeans within their own countries of residence. In terms of international tourist arrivals alone, thirteen out of the world's top twenty destinations are European countries.

The great diversity of natural and cultural resources with which Europe is so abundantly endowed comprises the 'raw material' of this continent's tourism product. Many millions of years of geological activity and botanical evolution have created a varied and distinctive European landscape rich in mountain regions, forests, and plains, the whole punctuated by a matrix of streams, rivers and lakes flowing outward from the continent's core to its maritime periphery. In modern times, Europeans have shown themselves to be inventive and adept at using these natural resources for tourism purposes, imposing upon their landscape the infrastructure and superstructure necessary to create leisure facilities ranging from ski-fields and marinas to hiking trails and seaside promenades. Similarly, the products of Europe's 2,000 years of cultural heritage, intellectual development and tumultuous history have also proved to be major assets in encouraging visits not only by Europeans themselves but also by those from other continents, for many of whom a trip to Europe represents a cultural home-coming. Europe is the fountainhead of many ideas and attitudes which have become common denominators of global civilisation, and for this reason, for many non-Europeans, a trip to this continent is a return to the source.

Wherever they come from, tourists have now become simply part of the landscape in every European country and an inseparable element in the lives of most Europeans. Throughout the year, they stand four or five deep, clamouring for a glimpse of the Mona Lisa; the crowd at the Colosseum is far bigger than it ever was in the days of Trajan; the French medieval fortified city of Carcassonne, built to withstand foreign invasion now gladly throws open its gates to vast numbers of visitors from the world over, all year round; the Munich Oktoberfest has grown from a local celebration to become the world's largest international popular festival; and Prague's statue-fringed Charles Bridge has developed from a mere crossing point into a colourful and animated meeting place for the world's travelling public.

But for each of Europe's celebrated high-profile attractions, there are a myriad of simpler pleasures which help disperse visitors throughout the length and breadth of the continent. Irish country cottages, Austrian farmhouses and French *gîtes* provide access to Europe's rich rural heritage; mountain ranges such as the Alps and the Pyrenees are Europeans' chosen venues for winter (and increasingly, summer) sports, while the Mediterranean provides the playground for the many millions of pleasure-seekers who visit that region every year from all over Europe and beyond; the myriad of country churches and monasteries, medieval forts, and *châteaux* often hidden away in splendid isolation prove that the continent's historical heritage is in no way restricted to Europe's cities.

But Europe's attractions are not limited to its rich supply of natural and historic resources. In the twentieth century in particular, Europeans of imagination, vision and entrepreneurial ingenuity have enhanced and extended the range of facilities available to those travelling to or within this continent. Man-made attractions ranging from casinos to theme parks have added to the appeal of coastal, urban and rural destinations, while purpose-built conference and exhibition centres have provided the motive for the arrival of vast numbers of high-spending business tourists in many towns and cities throughout the continent. There have even been some valiant attempts to circumvent the dictates and vicissitudes of the European climate, with, for example, the construction of self-contained holiday villages offering year-round tropical micro-climates in the temperate northern European countries and the use of snow cannons and artificial slopes to extend the ski-ing season beyond the period determined by natural weather conditions.

Finally, the much less tangible but no less important element of Europe's human landscape has proved to be a major asset in encouraging Europeans to visit each others' countries and regions and in attracting visitors from other continents. For the natural and built landscape of Europe is constantly animated by its inhabitants' own culture, in the broadest sense of the word. Europe buzzes throughout the year with an abundance of events ranging from the simplest village *fêtes* and town carnivals, through arts festivals, large and small, to sports events of international renown and major centenary celebrations. But, on a more everyday level, what also makes Europeans a source of mutual fascination for each other and for others is nothing more or less than their day-to-day *mode de vie* as they get on with the simple business of living: for many tourists, the most memorable characteristics of a visit to a European destination are based on their quiet observation of such aspects as how the inhabitants dress, what they eat and drink, how they entertain themselves, and how they travel around. Seeing the Europeans at work, at rest and at play must rank among this continent's greatest – and certainly unique – attractions.

The innumerable attractions, man-made, natural and cultural, in which Europe abounds are made accessible to visitors by a vibrant transport sector. Many of the latest achievements of European transport engineers and planners are the envy of the world: an expanding network of inter-city rail links along which trains run at breathtaking speeds; a tunnel linking the United Kingdom with the continental mass; an array of bridges and mountain passes connecting regions previously separated by natural barriers; and a burgeoning network of air connections bringing growing numbers of Europe's smaller cities into national and international air transport systems. The vital accommodation component upon which Europe's tourism industry depends is supplied by a dynamic and responsive service sector building upon the best traditions of European hospitality. In all its diversity, this sector ranges from the many Europeans who make a living out of welcoming tourists into their own homes, be they humble farmhouses or grand palaces, to those running international hotel chains of worldwide renown. As is the case for the attractions and transport sectors, the accommodation sector is characterised in Europe by entrepreneurs of audacity and foresight, among whose more recent achievements is the creation of hotel chains which have managed to bring this form of accommodation within the reach of those on even the most modest budgets.

This book explores current and future developments in some of the most important aspects of Europe's tourism industry. This introductory chapter examines Europe in the global context of changing trends in tourism and presents a profile of the current and recent performance of Europe as a destination. In addition, Chapter 1 traces the history of tourism in Europe and makes a number of predictions for European tourism in the twenty-first century. Chapter 2 examines the role of one of the most important organisations for European tourism, the European Union (EU), whose policies have the potential to shape the development of the tourism industry in the countries which are its Member States. Chapter 3 focuses on air transport in Europe and includes an examination of the consequences of one of the EU's major policies, deregulation of the airline industry. Chapter 4 investigates road and rail transport in Europe, its importance for tourism and the impact of developments such as high-speed rail links and the Channel Tunnel. In Chapter 5, the importance of theme parks as tourist attractions in Europe is highlighted, with an investigation into developments in this dynamic sector of the industry. Chapter 6 provides a survey of recent and current trends in the different sectors of the business tourism industry: general business travel, conferences, exhibitions and incentive travel. The focus of Chapter 7, the final chapter, is the European short-break market, one of the most marked contemporary trends.

Although the main emphasis of this book are the developments in travel and tourism in Western Europe, and more particularly the Member States of the European Union, the countries lying to the east of the continent have not been overlooked.

In recent years, tourism throughout the continent of Europe has developed against a background of tumultuous political and economic events. The 1990s saw the development of an increasingly united Europe whose common interests were bound ever more closely together. The Berlin Wall was demolished and the Iron Curtain between East and West crumbled with it, reuniting the two Germanys in the process. In the transformed European scene, the whole of Eastern Europe and the former USSR have opened up to trade, development and investment. Eastern European nations are changing from having command economies with centralised controls to having market economies, with demo-cratic governments, private-sector industry and decentralised power.

Such changes are only proving possible because of the opening up of these countries to foreign investment. As a by-product of this new ease of access, cities such as Prague, Budapest and Warsaw have thrown open their doors to Western tourists and business travellers. To create the transport and infrastructural systems necessary for modern tourism throughout the newly reopened destinations of Eastern Europe, a superstructure of hotels, information and computerised booking services, well-managed attractions, a modern system of marketing, and market- and consumer-responsive skills and abilities are required. This represents an immense challenge and opportunity for the countries of Eastern Europe and for the Western countries prepared to invest there and share their experience and expertise. At the same time, for the new middle classes in countries such as Russia and the Ukraine, the chance to travel is an end in itself, and for the tourism industry in both Eastern and Western Europe, this new market represents an opportunity which no country can afford to ignore. Consequently, a theme common to all chapters is travel and tourism in the countries of Eastern Europe.

A brief history of tourism in Europe

How did tourism in Europe develop into the major activity it represents today? Before looking at the characteristics of contemporary tourism in this continent and future trends, it is worthwhile placing European tourism in its historical context.

Tourism in Europe is as old as the beginnings of civilisation itself in this continent. Its earliest origins may be traced back to those classical civilisations whose influence has so shaped the history and culture of Europe, and whose enduring architectural wonders, from Hadrian's Wall to the

Parthenon are now themselves the focus of considerable tourist interest.

Holden (1994) quotes the following sources demonstrating the presence of tourist activities in ancient times: Holloway notes that the Greeks hosted visitors during the first Olympic Games in 776 BC and that wealthy Romans travelled to the coast and as far as Egypt for holiday purposes; and Mill and Morrison (1992) also suggest that the Egyptians, Greeks and Romans travelled for pleasure purposes and identify the growth of a middle class with money from trading, combined with good communications, a single currency and common languages of Latin and Greek, as reasons for an expansion of travel in ancient times. Towner (1994) also cites various classical scholars, including Friedländer who, in his study of life and manners in ancient Rome, wrote extensively on travel and the emergence of second-home villas for wealthy Romans on the Bay of Naples.

Steinecke (1993) is among the many commentators who trace the origins of modern tourism in Europe back to the 'Grand Tours' of the seventeenth and eighteenth centuries, when the young aristocracy undertook extended journeys through the continent for educational purposes – to learn foreign languages, fencing, riding, dancing, the art of establishing connections of political or economic interest and manners befitting their rank. Lasting several years in some cases, the 'Grand Tour', for wealthy British travellers, began with a visit to France, followed by up to a year's touring of the historical and cultural Italian cities, finally returning through Switzerland, Germany and the Netherlands. The Grand Tour of Europe has been much studied, with research utilising the extensive range of journals, letters and guidebooks which have survived. However, as Towner (1995) points out, it is usually studied as an isolated event, only rarely being clearly set in the wider context of the life and leisure of the time. In the same article, Towner observes that tourism's history as it appears in the literature is largely concerned with the activities of the affluent and leisured elites of Europe.

Although other sectors of society undoubtedly did engage in some forms of travel for pleasure (most notably visits to friends and relatives), it was not until the late eighteenth and nineteenth century that tourism became accessible to other ranks of society in European countries. By then, the Grand Tour destinations had begun to attract the emerging merchant classes of Europe, who had the means to join the travelling aristocracy of the day. Meanwhile, throughout Europe, specialised tourist destinations were developing, as spa towns and seaside and Alpine resorts sought to establish themselves as health and leisure venues, first for the aristocracy, then later, for middle-class visitors. Spa towns such as Bath or Tunbridge Wells in the UK, Baden-Baden and Marienbad in Germany and Aix-les-Bains and Vichy in France developed specific leisure-related infrastructures and facilities for their visitors. After the turbulent decades following the French Revolution, many parts of the coastline of continental Europe began to emulate the British fashion for providing sea-bathing facilities in specialised resorts. The French Riviera and the north coast of France from Boulogne to Cherbourg were the first stretches of coastline to be developed in this way, initially in many cases by the British themselves (Berry 1992). By the middle of the nineteenth century, the changing perception of nature following the Romantic movement in European painting and literature, and the growing interest in mountain sports opened up the Alps as a tourist region for exploring, mountaineering and health treatment. Ski-ing was soon to follow as the alpine sport which would eventually eclipse all other forms of tourist activity in the region.

In the late nineteenth and early twentieth century, growth in tourist activities undertaken by Europeans was fuelled by two main factors: technological improvements in transport and revolutionary increases in leisure time and discretionary income. The advent of the railway was a major factor in accelerating the growth of tourism. The rail system made mass tourism a reality within a short time of its inception as a mode of travel and developed quickly, as shown in Figure 1.1.

In 1846, Western European countries had some 5,500 km of railways; a decade later, there were over 18,000 km, and by 1876, the network had quadrupled to more than 75,000 km.

The massive capital investment which railways required made it necessary for the railway companies to mobilise new markets in order to fill rolling stock with passengers. By the mid-1880s, most railway companies provided express train services

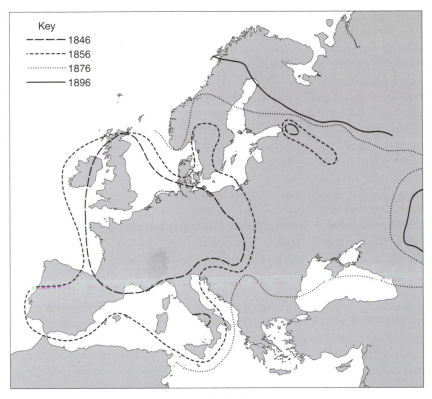

Figure 1.1 Railroad network service area, 1846–96
Source: Lundgren (1992)

on important links in the system which serviced some distinct tourist regions such as the French and Italian Riviera, the Atlantic coast, from Biarritz to the Channel coast resorts, as well as certain mountain areas including the Alps. The British tourist was able to cover the trip from the French Channel ports to Cannes or Nice in less than 24 hours; Russian aristocrats made the St Petersburg–Northern Italy run in less than 36 hours: two days and one night, in appropriate comfort (Lundgren 1992).

Before the end of the nineteenth century, the railway and the steamboat were firmly established as relatively high-capacity, low-cost and high-speed forms of transport in Europe. The reduced efforts and costs of travelling meant that not only were Europeans able to travel more widely and more easily, but that travel was open to a much greater proportion of them than previously had been possible. The twentieth century accelerated this process, culminating, after the Second World War, in the widespread adoption of aircraft as a means

of mass transportation. As an island nation, Britain in particular witnessed the tourism revolution which much more easily affordable air travel made possible.

> The technological breakthroughs in aircraft design during the war meant that air travel finally emerged as a viable, affordable alternative to sea travel. The large number of aircraft and pilots made available by the return of peace helped the growth of the major national airlines in Europe. Private airlines companies pioneered the development of charter services (an essential element in the Mediterranean package holiday business) which, by the early 1960s, had transformed the annual holiday pattern of the British holidaymaker. (Davidson and Maitland 1997)

However, the supply of cheaper transport facilities was not enough in itself to bring the majority of the population of European countries into the market for tourism. Significant changes affecting demand were also required before this could happen. From the beginning of the twentieth century, in all European countries, working people were accorded gradual reductions in the hours they had to work and increases in their holiday entitlements. Steinecke (1993) gives the example of Germany, where, during the Industrial Revolution period, industrial employees worked an average of 80–90 hours per week. By the First World War, the average number of working hours had decreased to 60 per week due to several factors, including mechanisation, technological progress, socio-political reforms, union activities and legal regulations. In 1975, a 40–hour working week was introduced in Germany. As the working week shrank, holiday entitlement in Germany grew. The Federal Holiday Law of 1963 set holiday regulations for the whole of the German population. In 1960, the number of days holiday for German workers had been 16. By 1990, holiday entitlement had risen to 30 days. In all Western European countries, the same pattern was followed. Holidays with pay now average about five weeks in Western Europe, which represent some of the most generous entitlements in the world.

Rising earnings and discretionary incomes also played an important part in stimulating demand for tourism in Europe. Particularly following the Second World War, there were substantial increases in income for ordinary working people, beginning with the industrialised northern European countries, which enabled them to participate in tourism activities.

Nevertheless, despite these significant socio-economic advances, universal participation in tourism is still some way from becoming a reality in Europe. As will be shown in the next section of this chapter, even by the 1990s, significantly large proportions of the populations of some European countries were still excluded from the tourism market.

A profile of contemporary European tourism

EUROPE AND INTERNATIONAL TOURISM

Destinations

International tourism in Europe takes two forms: long-haul visits from other continents and intra-European tourism, composed of Europeans visiting other countries in this continent.

Before focusing on Europe as a destination, it is necessary to set it in the global context of developments in international tourism. During the 1990s, tourism developed within a context of fluctuating economic performances and the persistence of relatively high unemployment rates in major industrialised countries. Yet, despite the, at times, recessionary economic environment within Europe and in several of Europe's main markets in other continents, spending on travel and tourism on a global basis has remained remarkably resilient. More and more people travel today, undeterred it would seem by terrorism, natural disasters, as well as economic and political difficulties at home or abroad.

On a worldwide scale during the period 1990–96, international tourist arrivals grew at an average rate of 4.5 per cent per year, and international tourist receipts (excluding transport) at 8.13 per cent (WTO 1997). Declines in the growth rate for international tourism were recorded only twice during that period: in 1991 as a result of the Gulf War and in 1993 under the influence of the severe economic recession in many industrialised countries (WTO 1996). By the late 1990s, all world regions were benefiting from the global expansion in tourism flows, although on an unequal basis.

Europe maintained its position of leadership in international tourism, absorbing around 60 per cent of international tourist arrivals. But although international tourism in Europe was continuing to grow in both volume and value, Europe's share of all international tourism had been in decline over the preceding few decades, a period of massive expansion generally in world tourism. Table 1.1 shows the respective shares of the world regions in international tourism for the 36 years leading up to 1996.

Europe's market share is clearly undergoing a process of steady erosion, in terms of both its share of total international arrivals and total international receipts. It is also relevant to note that this erosion of the European share of international tourism took place at a much faster rate in the period 1990–94 than in the preceding decade 1980–90: while in the 1980s the market share diminished at 0.3 per cent annually, during the first

Table 1.1 Share of each region in international tourist arrivals and receipts worldwide, 1960–96 (%)

	1960	1970	1980	1990	1991	1992	1993	1994	1995	1996
Africa										
Arrivals	1.1	1.5	2.6	3.3	3.5	3.6	3.6	3.5	3.6	3.6
Receipts	2.6	2.2	2.6	2.0	1.8	2.0	2.0	2.0	1.8	2.0
Americas										
Arrivals	24.1	23.0	21.6	20.6	21.0	20.7	20.0	19.5	19.6	19.5
Receipts	35.7	26.8	24.1	26.3	28.5	27.2	28.3	27.0	25.1	25.1
East Asia/Pacific										
Arrivals	1.0	3.0	7.4	11.7	11.9	12.5	13.4	13.8	14.1	14.7
Receipts	2.9	6.1	8.3	14.6	14.8	15.1	16.3	17.8	18.4	19.1
Europe										
Arrivals	72.5	70.5	65.0	61.8	61.0	60.4	60.1	60.1	59.5	59.1
Receipts	56.8	62.0	60.3	54.4	52.5	53.2	51.0	50.8	52.0	51.1
Middle East										
Arrivals	1.0	1.4	2.6	2.0	1.8	2.2	2.2	2.4	2.4	2.4
Receipts	1.5	2.3	3.3	1.9	1.6	1.7	1.5	1.6	1.8	1.9
South Asia										
Arrivals	0.3	0.6	0.8	0.7	0.7	0.7	0.7	0.7	0.8	0.8
Receipts	0.5	0.6	1.5	0.8	0.9	0.9	0.9	0.9	0.9	1.0

Source: World Tourism Organisation (WTO)

half of the 1990s, it fell at a yearly average of 0.75 per cent (CEC 1995b). Moreover, the World Tourism Organisation (WTO) predicted in the 1990s that Europe would continue to lose market share, down perhaps to 50 per cent of all international visits by 2010. What are the main reasons behind this downward trend?

Europe and North America no longer enjoy the comfortable virtual monopoly they had in the 1960s, when international tourism became a mass market. The arrival of new destinations, especially in Asia and the Caribbean has brought about a general diversification of world tourism and a marked regional redistribution of tourism flows on a worldwide basis. In the past few decades, these regions have witnessed growth rates for international tourism well above those for Europe. And in the global competition for the fast-growing segment of travellers who like to travel between continents for leisure or business, there is no doubt over which world region is winning.

East Asia and the Pacific's market share has made huge strides in both international tourist arrivals and world receipts. In terms of arrivals, that region's share tripled between 1960 and 1970 and increased five-fold over the following 26 years. Even during the 1990s, despite the Gulf War and the economic recession in the major generating markets, the East Asia Pacific region continued to gain ground, particularly at Europe's expense. In a single year, 1995, visitors to East Asia and the Pacific contributed to 35 per cent of the total increase of international tourist arrivals worldwide. That year, excellent performances continued to be recorded in most Southeastern Asian countries, including both established leisure destinations such as Indonesia, Malaysia, the Philippines and Thailand, and newly emerging destinations such as Cambodia and Vietnam (WTO 1996).

Much of this growth is due to intraregional travel within the East Asia and Pacific region, where rapid economic growth has created a new holidaymaking middle class, which is naturally making more journeys to other parts of Asia than to America or Europe. But long-haul visitors from other continents account for one in five arrivals to the East Asia and Pacific region, approximately twice the ratio of long-haul visitors to intra-regional tourists in Europe. What explains the attraction of the East Asia and Pacific region?

The WTO sums up the reasons for the spectacular success of Europe's competitors thus: 'This is due to the economic importance of the Asia/Pacific region in general, which encourages business travel, effective promotion by airlines and tourist boards, a good quality and varied products, high level of customer satisfaction and reasonable air fares' (WTO 1996).

More colourfully, *The Economist* suggests that: 'Falling [long-haul] air-fares have encouraged Europeans to forsake Margate and Marbella for more exotic locations in Thailand and Malaysia. Thanks to cheaper labour, guests in resorts outside Europe are pampered by battalions of uniformed staff, a heady change from a solitary, surly chambermaid' (Economist 1995a).

Nevertheless, Europe remains in pole position as far as international tourism goes, with still over half of the world's international tourism taking place there.

How are international arrivals distributed within Europe itself? At the level of individual countries, Tables 1.2(a) and (b) show Europe's top twenty destinations, both in terms of numbers of arrivals and receipts from international tourism. (These figures include both intra-European tourist trips and trips made to European countries by visitors from other continents.)

Classifying countries in order of tourist arrival share and tourism receipts highlights the strong geographical concentration of tourist flows in Europe. In 1996, the top five destinations, France, Spain, Italy, the United Kingdom and Hungary, between them took over half of all international tourist arrivals in Europe, a situation little changed throughout the previous ten years. However, a sig-

nificant trend is that during that decade, certain countries of Central and Eastern Europe rose considerably in the ranks of the top ten destinations. In this respect, Poland has made the most headway, but the Czech Republic and Hungary have also made significant leaps in terms of their numbers of arrivals.

Grouped according to tourism receipts, European countries show a slightly different pattern. First, receipts are even more concentrated geographically than arrivals in the top five countries, which account for around 55 per cent of total receipts. In 1996, Italy stood in first place, before France. Two reasons go some way to explaining why France's international visitors have a relatively low average expenditure: the fact that France's visitor statistics include the large numbers of tourists who briefly cross that country on their way to Spain and Italy from northern European countries; and France's growing role as a short-break destination, which boosts its visitor numbers but not the average expenditure.

The WTO divides Europe into five sub-regions, as shown in Figure 1.2.

With almost 40 per cent of all international tourist arrivals in Europe and over 37 per cent of receipts, Western Europe, as defined by the WTO, is the most visited sub-region, almost half of these visits being generated by movements between countries in the sub-region itself. Between 1985 and 1995, international tourist arrivals in Western Europe grew at an average annual rate of 3.2 per cent against 4.5 per cent for Europe as a whole. Tourism receipts, on the other hand, rose by an average 11.6 per cent in the same period, thereby matching the pace of the entire European continent.

Between 1991 and 1993, Southern Europe was hit by a slump in arrival trends, and this is reflected in the sub-region's share of total arrivals in Europe, which went from 34 per cent in 1985 to 29.6 per cent ten years later, despite an annual average growth of almost 3 per cent. Spain and Italy are the sub-region's main international destinations, accounting for 76 per cent of its total arrivals in 1995.

By way of contrast, Central and Eastern Europe's share of all international tourism in Europe rose from 13.5 per cent in 1985 to 21.8 per cent in 1995, for arrivals and from 4.6 per cent to

Table 1.2(a) Top twenty tourism destinations in Europe. International tourist arrivals (excluding same-day visitors) (thousands of arrivals), 1996

1985	Rank 1990	1996	Countries	Arrivals (000) 1996	% change 1996/95	% of total 1996
1	1	1	France	62,406	4.0	17.77
2	2	2	Spain	41,295	5.0	11.76
3	3	3	Italy	32,853	5.8	9.35
5	6	4	United Kingdom	25,293	7.5	7.20
8	4	5	Hungary	20,674	−0.1	5.89
16	18	6	Poland	19,410	1.0	5.53
4	5	7	Austria	17,090	−0.5	4.87
12 (1)	11	8	Czech Republic	17,000	3.0	4.84
6	7	9	Germany	15,205	2.4	4.33
14 (2)	12 (2)	10	Russian Federation	14,587	57.5	4.15
7	8	11	Switzerland	10,600	−7.8	3.02
11	10	12	Portugal	9,730	2.3	2.77
10	9	13	Greece	8,987	−11.3	2.56
19	16	14	Turkey	7,966	12.5	2.27
15	14	15	Netherlands	6,580	0.1	1.87
13	15	16	Belgium	5,829	4.8	1.66
17	17	17	Ireland	5,282	9.6	1.50
18	19	18	Romania	2,834	8.7	0.81
25	22	19	Bulgaria	2,795	−19.4	0.80
21	20	20	Norway	2,746	−4.7	0.78
			Total 1–20	329,162	4.2	93.72
			Total Europe	351,227	4.6	100.00

Notes: (1) Former Czechoslovakia. (2) Former USSR
Source: World Tourism Organisation (WTO)

8.4 per cent for receipts. In the same period, tourist arrivals in the Central and Eastern Europe sub-region rose by an average 10 per cent and receipts by 19 per cent. The WTO notes that these are the highest rises in receipts registered in any European sub-region and represent over double the continental average. Partly responsible for this growth in earnings from tourism is the high-spending German market: in the 1990s in particular the number of German arrivals in most of these countries escalated.

In the Northern Europe sub-region, the United Kingdom dominates, accounting for two-thirds of all arrivals in 1995. Northern Europe's market share of total international arrivals in Europe remained stable, at around 10 per cent between 1985 and 1995, while its share of receipts fell slightly, from 18 per cent to 16 per cent.

Although not one of Europe's tourism heavy-weights, East Mediterranean Europe, Turkey, Cyprus and Israel, increased its share of total arrivals between 1985 and 1994 from 2 per cent to

Table 1.2(b) Top twenty tourism earners in Europe. International tourism receipts (excluding transport) (US$ million), 1996

| Rank | | | | Receipts (US$ mn) | % change | % of total |
1985	1995	1996	Country	1996	1996/95	1996
1	2	1	Italy	28,673	3.4	13.20
3	1	2	France	28,357	3.0	13.05
2	3	3	Spain	27,414	6.7	12.62
4	4	4	United Kingdom	19,296	4.0	8.88
6	6	5	Germany	16,496	−2.7	7.59
5	5	6	Austria	14,004	−4.0	6.45
7	7	7	Switzerland	8,891	−5.1	4.09
28	27	8	Poland	8,400	27.3	3.87
9	9	9	Netherlands	6,256	8.6	2.88
11	12	10	Turkey	5,962	20.3	2.74
8	8	11	Belgium	5,893	3.0	2.71
10 (1)	14 (1)	12	Russian Federation	5,542	28.5	2.55
15	10	13	Portugal	4,265	−1.7	1.96
23 (2)	25	14	Czech Republic	4,075	41.7	1.88
14	13	15	Sweden	3,683	6.8	1.70
12	15	16	Greece	3,660	−10.9	1.68
13	11	17	Denmark	3,425	−6.7	1.58
20	18	18	Ireland	3,003	11.7	1.38
16	19	19	Israel	2,800	0.6	1.29
18	17	20	Norway	2,404	0.8	1.11
			Total 1–20	202,499	4.3	93.22
			Total Europe	217,216	4.6	100.00

Note: (1) Former USSR. (2) Former Czechoslovakia
Source: World Tourism Organisation (WTO)

3.1 per cent, while its share of receipts grew to almost 5 per cent in the same period.

Markets

Who are Europe's international visitors? Table 1.3 shows the origins of international tourist arrivals in Europe.

There are three major international tourist flows in Europe. The largest encompasses travel by residents of European countries to other countries in the continent – intraregional tourism. Intraregional flows eclipse other types by a long margin. In 1995, they accounted for almost 85 per cent of total international tourist arrivals in the region as a whole. (However, as many commentators have pointed out, the fact that Europe contains many small countries whose relatively wealthy inhabitants like to travel sometimes distorts the figures: in the WTO league tables, every German on a Greek beach counts as an international visitor, whereas a New Yorker on a Floridian

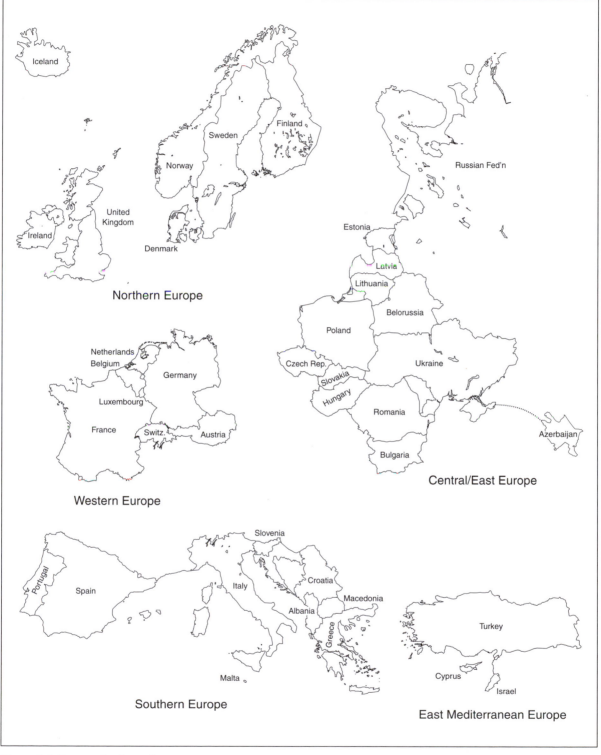

Figure 1.2 Europe – the five regions
Source: World Tourism Organisation (WTO)

Table 1.3 Tourist arrivals in Europe by main source market (arrivals in thousands, growth percentage and market share)

Source markets	Tourist arrivals in Europe (000s)		Average annual growth rate (%)	Market share (%)	
	1985	1995	1985–95	1985	1995
Europe	175,551	284,785	5.0	82.1	85.4
Americas	24,038	20,081	−1.8	11.2	6.0
Asia	6,024	10,865	6.1	2.8	3.3
Africa	2,879	2,565	−1.1	1.3	0.8
Middle East	1,627	2,010	2.1	0.8	0.6
Other markets	3,676	12,993	13.5	1.7	3.9
Total Europe	213,795	333,299	4.5	100.0	100.0

Source: World Tourism Organisation (WTO)

does not.) Regarding the outlook for intraregional tourism, the WTO study on *Tourism Trends to the Year 2000 and Beyond* forecasts that intraregional tourism in Europe will grow at an average annual rate of 3 per cent between 1995 and the year 2000. This would bring total intraregional arrivals to 311 million by the year 2000.

The second biggest tourism flow in Europe is composed of movements from the Americas to European countries. The Americas constitute a major tourist-generating market for Europe. Nevertheless, the market share represented by the Americas fell from over 11 per cent to 6 per cent between 1985 and 1995. The WTO forecasts that in the five years leading up to the year 2000, arrivals from North America will grow at an average annual rate of just over 3 per cent, which means that some 24 million North American tourists should visit Europe in 2000.

The remaining flow is mainly made up of arrivals from Asia, followed by Africa and the Middle East. Between 1985 and 1995, tourist flows from Asia to Europe showed a healthy growth rate of 6.1 per cent. These flows mainly spring from Japan and Australia, although the number of tourists arriving in Europe from new emerging markets in the East Asia and the Pacific

region is also on the upturn, albeit from a low base. Asia has perhaps the greatest potential for growth in foreign travel of all regions in the world. By the mid-1990s, the international travelling public of Japan, for example, represented just over 10 per cent of the population, leaving great scope for growth.

By 1995, the total outbound for the East Asia and the Pacific region for 1995 was estimated at 15 million (12 per cent of the population). A number of expanding markets in the region, such as Taiwan and South Korea, and emerging markets such as Indonesia and Thailand, are important by virtue of the sheer numbers of potential visitors they represent.

China is also capable of playing an important role in international tourism. The strong growth of gross domestic product (GDP) and real private consumption witnessed by China over the last few years, coupled with liberalisation of travel from China, could become a dominant influence in the region's travel and tourism industry.

EUROPEANS AS TOURISTS

The importance of the European market for domestic, intraregional and long-haul tourism is

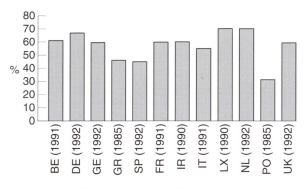

Figure 1.3 Holiday participation in EU countries (last available year; four+nights)
Source: National holiday surveys, European Commission

the subject of this section, which presents a quantitative and qualitative profile of Europeans as tourists.

National tourism surveys show that holiday participation, defined as the proportion of the population that takes at least one vacation of at least four overnight stays on a yearly basis, amounts to an average of between 55 per cent and 60 per cent for EU countries. However, there are marked differences between rates of holiday participation, the volume of holidays and the ratio between domestic and outbound holiday trips taken by the residents of those countries. Figure 1.3 shows the rate of holiday participation of some Member States of the EU.

In France and the northern European countries, holiday participation is above 60 per cent while levels for the Mediterranean countries are significantly lower, reflecting lower GDPs in general and less mature tourism markets.

However, the volume of holidaymaking by any one country is determined not only by the proportion of its citizens who take a holiday, but also by how often those citizens go on holiday each year. Taking this factor into account, only in the Netherlands and France is the number of holidays per capita on an annual basis higher than 1. The lowest scores are found in Portugal (0.3) and Greece (0.45). The remaining EU countries rank between 0.8 and 1 (CEC 1995b).

What are the destinations of European tourists? Eurostat has estimated that the amount of domestic tourism exceeds outbound tourism by a considerable margin: about two-thirds of all holidays generated by the EU population can be classified as domestic tourism, i.e. holidays taken within citizens' own country of residence; 22 per cent is international tourism within the EU region (intraregional tourism); and 13 per cent of all holidays are spent in destinations outside the EU (CEC 1995b).

The two categories of international tourism will now be examined in more detail, before returning to the issue of domestic tourism in European countries.

Europeans as international tourists

Just as Europe is the destination for the greater part of the world's international tourism, Europeans themselves are also major generators of international tourism spending.

In 1995, out of the 24 countries whose residents spent a billion or more US$ in the countries they visited, thirteen were in Europe. Two were in North America, two in Latin America and seven in other parts of the world. Germany, the UK, Italy and France, together with the USA and Japan dominate spending on international tourism, accounting between them for around 50 per cent of the world total.

Germany is by far the biggest spender in terms of travel abroad. Worldwide, it is only outpaced by the United States. At the European level, Germany is followed by the United Kingdom and France, whose combined spending on overseas tourism still falls US$6.5 billion short of Germany's (1996 figures). Moving down the list, a group of countries with a strong propensity to travel abroad emerges, made up of Austria, Belgium, Switzerland, Sweden, Denmark, Finland and Ireland. Moreover, certain traditional tourist-receiving countries, such as Spain, Greece and Portugal, now stand out as relatively high spenders on outbound travel. In 1996, the Russian Federation stood in seventh place in Europe's top twenty spenders on international tourism. (WTO 1997)

With their growing affinity for long-haul travel, European tourists themselves are partly responsible for the success of the 'new' destinations in other world regions. Table 1.4 shows the major destinations of European international travellers.

Table 1.4 Europe outbound

Destinations	Total (000) 1996	% change			Average annual growth rate (%) 1996/85	Market share % of world total	
		1996/95	1995/94	1994/93		1985	1996
Europe	275,385	1.0	1.4	6.5	5.1	91.3	87.2
Americas	16,750	6.2	7.7	−0.4	10.1	3.3	5.3
East Asia/Pacific	9,894	6.0	2.7	6.5	10.7	1.9	3.1
Africa	7,086	10.8	2.1	3.4	5.4	2.3	2.2
Middle East	4,598	24.2	37.6	13.7	13.3	0.7	1.5
South Asia	2,089	6.7	9.0	12.5	8.8	0.5	0.7
Total long haul	40,417	8.8	7.7	3.7	10.4	8.7	12.8
World Total	315,802	1.9	2.1	6.1	5.6	100.0	100.0

Source: World Tourism Organisation (WTO)

The growing popularity of long-haul destinations for Europeans clearly emerges from these figures, with only the continent of Africa losing some of its share of the European market between 1985 and 1996. Even during the recession of the early 1990s, long-haul travel by Europeans was on the increase.

This continuing predeliction towards long-haul travel is very clearly demonstrated by trends in overseas holidaymaking by the UK market. Towards the end of 1996, travel agents Thomas Cook reported that for the 1996 summer season the continuing appeal of the United States and the Caribbean for the UK holiday market saw their share of long-haul travel by British holidaymakers increase to 13 per cent by the end of August compared with 10 per cent at the same time in 1995. Regarding winter holidays, they too are increasingly taken by the British in long-haul destinations. For winter 1996, Lunn Poly recorded considerable increases in British visitors to the Caribbean (+95 per cent) and Florida (+49 per cent). Similarly, for long-haul ski-ing holidays, Lunn Poly, in late 1996, noted a rise in British bookings to Canada and the United States, mainly as a result of currency exchange making them more competitive than many traditional ski resorts closer to home (Times 1996). In the same report, the managing director of Thomson Holidays was quoted as saying that long-haul holidays were currently the most buoyant sector of the UK overseas travel market, with numbers growing at 15 per cent each year.

Nevertheless, as Table 1.4 demonstrates, the major destination for European international tourists is still, by far, their own continent. Visiting another European country apart from their own is how almost nine out of ten residents of Europe spend their holidays and short breaks, amounting to almost 300 million trips annually. *The Economist* gives some of the historic reasons for the high level of holiday-taking by Europeans in Europe:

> Frequent price wars have kept competition fierce. Package holidays have reduced both the price and the inconvenience of organising foreign trips. And charter airlines, which clock up roughly half of all the passenger miles travelled in Europe, have got around the high costs of the region's over-regulated scheduled flights. (Economist 1995a)

The European Travel Commission quotes European Travel Monitor data, on intra-European tourism, published in 1996, which estimates that Western Europeans made 195.4 million such trips in 1995 (up 1 per cent on 1994), Central/Eastern Europeans 23.8 million (up 12.8 per cent), Eastern Europeans 35.8 million (first ever survey figure),

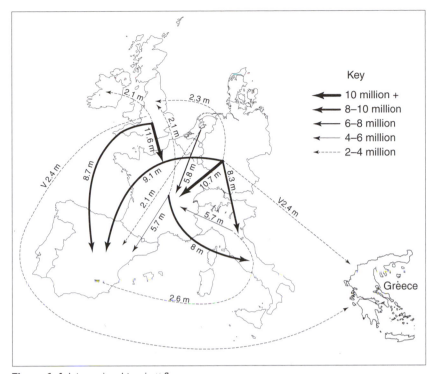

Figure 1.4 Intraregional tourism flows
Source: adapted from OECD (Tourism Policy and International Tourism in OECD Countries 1993–1994)
Figures represent tourists staying one night or more at the destination, except where marked with a V, where the figure includes day visitors

bringing the total for Europe to 255 million trips or 2.4 billion overnights, for a total expenditure of ECU 167 billion (ETC 1996).

This high degree of intraregional travel is dominated by a number of key tourism flows of outbound European tourists. Figure 1.4 shows that Germany and the United Kingdom are responsible for a significant proportion of the main flows, which have important implications for the tourism economies of origin and destination countries.

More generally, Figure 1.4 shows the importance of north-south intraregional tourist flows in Europe. Such flows have dominated holiday-taking patterns since the beginnings of mass tourism in Europe. About 70 per cent of international tourism with its origin and destination within the EU can be classified as 'north-south', principally directed to holiday destinations in France and the Mediterranean countries (CEC 1995a). For example, concerning the UK market, Spain alone accounts for four out of ten overseas holidays sold,

with Majorca alone welcoming nearly one million British holidaymakers in 1996; and for the British, the biggest winter market is the Canary Islands, which accounts for almost a quarter of all overseas winter holidays sold in the UK (Times 1996).

Domestic tourism in Europe

Lickorish (1992) draws attention to the difficulties involved in estimating European domestic tourism, for which statistics are very inadequate, yet which, he claims, quoting the European Travel Monitor, now exceeds one billion trips per year.

The scarcity of homogenous official data relating to domestic tourism trips and nights in tourism accommodation makes estimations of domestic tourism within Europe very difficult. Nevertheless, there is general agreement that, overall, domestic tourism has a far higher share of all tourism in Europe than international tourism has. Even taking as a measurement of this the number of tourist nights in hotels (the form of accommodation most likely to be used by international tourists), residents still account for the majority (55 per cent) of all tourist nights spent in the hotels of the fifteen countries of the European Union and Norway. When all forms of accommodation are taken into account, the share represented by residents as opposed to international visitors rises to 64 per cent (CEC 1995b).

What is clear is that fact that the ratio between domestic tourism and international tourism varies considerably between different European countries. Using as an indication of the relative importance of domestic tourism its percentage share of overall demand in the hotels of those different countries, Figure 1.5 highlights those differences.

Among the countries in which the greatest fre-quency of domestic tourism in hotels is found, is Germany (84.5 per cent) followed by a group of three Scandinavian countries. The geographic and climatic conditions of these countries explain. in part, the lower frequency of international tourism there. But a different reason explains the relatively high frequency of domestic tourism in Italy (65 per cent domestic hotel tourism): it is only recently that general tourism demand by Italians has begun to significantly consider international destinations. In last place come two different kinds of country: a number of relatively small countries (Austria and Belgium, for example) where a large proportion of the population live comparatively close to an international border; and countries where the overall domestic demand for tourism is still rather low (Greece and Portugal).

The relationship between domestic tourism

Figure 1.5 Domestic tourism in hotels (% on total tourist nights)

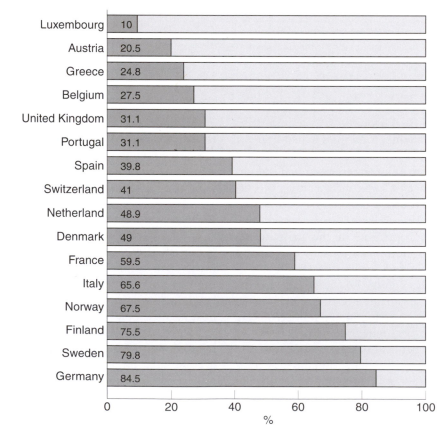

Source: Eurostat

and international tourism is therefore subject to various factors, including the proximity to international markets, the availability of a large pool of domestic demand, the development of a tourism policy, and the economic and cultural level of the population on which the propensity to international travel depends. All of these factors contribute to determine the type and volume of tourism which takes place in different destinations.

Current trends in European tourism

The European tourism industry operates within an environment over which it has little, if any, control. Powerful external forces and trends determine the conditions under which tourism operators must compete in the world market to hold on to, or improve, Europe's major share. This section reviews the prospects for tourism in Europe for the first years of the twenty-first century. It identifies and analyses the most important factors which should be influencing the European tourism market in the medium term.

In general terms, most commentators are optimistic concerning the future of tourism in Europe into the twenty-first century. Most base their positive expectations primarily on a combination of favourable demand-side and supply-side factors.

Jefferson, predicting the industry's prospects during the 1990s and into the twenty-first century wrote, in 1992:

> Europe will undoubtedly continue to dominate the international travel picture . . . Compared with the rest of the world, practically all Western Europeans enjoy above average standards of living and this is matched by longer than average holiday entitlement and higher than average disposable income. Europe offers the sort of cultural experience which is appealing to long-haul travellers. (Jefferson 1992).

Despite the effects of a damaging recession and the threat of growing precarity in the employment market, his observations generally still hold true today.

Europeans still enjoy substantially more favourable paid leave arrangements than either Americans or Japanese, for example. Six weeks of paid holiday are now not unusual, and these holidays are often accompanied by cash holiday bonuses over and above normal pay. Table 1.5 shows the extent of paid leave in Europe.

Regarding the future, the OECD (Organisation for Economic Cooperation and Development) is equally optimistic: 'Tourism is a very buoyant industry. Higher incomes, more leisure time and better education standards are inducing more people to travel and explore new regions. Communication networks – rail, road, air and sea transport – are much improved and facilitate travel' (OECD 1996). For its part, the European Commission (EC), in its 1995 Green Paper on tourism, invokes, first of all, demographic trends to justify its optimism: 'Conditions are favourable for further growth in the numbers of tourists, particularly at international level, because of the ageing populations in the industrialised countries, higher levels of education, more widespread paid

Table 1.5 Paid leave in Europe, 1998

	Collective agreements and practice	Paid public holidays (days)
Austria	5–6 weeks	13
Belgium	4–5 weeks	10
Denmark	5 weeks	9.5
Finland	5–6 weeks	12
France	5–6 weeks	11
Germany	6 weeks	9–13
Greece	4–5 weeks	12
Ireland	4 weeks	9
Italy	4–6 weeks	11
Netherlands	5 weeks	8
Norway	5 weeks	10
Portugal	22+ days	14
Spain	22+ days	14
Sweden	5–6 weeks	11
Switzerland	4–6 weeks	8 (varies)
United Kingdom	4–5 weeks	8

Source: Income Data Services Ltd., London

leave and shorter working hours.' In addition, the Commission's up-beat forecast is also based on a number of supply-side factors: 'the advent of the information society which involves more than just better reservation facilities using more sophisticated technology, together with improved transport systems and reduced prices for air travel' (CEC 1995a).

Finally, the WTO study on *Tourism Trends to the Year 2000 and Beyond* forecasts that intra-regional tourism alone in Europe will grow at an average annual rate of 3 per cent between 1995 and the year 2000. This would bring total intra-regional arrivals to 311 million by the year 2000.

The external market environment is a key element in determining the profile of tourism consumption in Europe in the first decade of the new millennium. This section examines some of the most important aspects of that environment.

THE DEMOGRAPHIC ENVIRONMENT

Demographic trends concerning population growth, life expectancy and age profile clearly represent a key change in the market environment to which tourism businesses must adjust. These trends will impact the tourism market in ways which might be defined as both quantitative and qualitative.

The quantitative changes have been widely predicted for some time. European tourism markets exist in a context of a declining rate of population growth, an increasingly aged population structure and smaller households with fewer children. However, the population of Eastern and Western Europe increased from 392 million in 1950 to 492 million in 1985 and is expected to grow to 512 million by the beginning of the twenty-first century (Page 1993). By the mid-1990s, the fifteen EU Member States between them had a population of 368.7 million inhabitants, compared to 258.3 million in the USA and 124.7 million in Japan, the world's other major tourism markets.

Within Europe, as in industrialised countries in other world regions, retired people will account for a larger share of the population. By the year 2001, about one in seven people in North America and Japan will be over 64, and one in four Europeans will be over the age of 55. These demographic developments, combined with the fact that in many European countries the average age of retirement is getting earlier, mean that in the opening years of the twenty-first century, a major part of the tourism market will be composed of record numbers of retired people, both within Europe itself and in its main long-haul generating markets such as the USA, Canada and Japan.

Although in the past, retired members of the public have tended to travel less than the young, in particular on foreign holidays, the elderly in contemporary society include large numbers of persons in excellent health, with the financial means and the spare time which gives them far greater opportunities to travel than those still in employment, with families to provide for and/or mortgages to pay.

The impact on Europe's long-haul markets will be considerable. It is estimated that the market composed of the 2 million mature (i.e. over 55 years old) American tourists who visited Europe in 1990 will have rocketed to 3.5 million by the early years of the twenty-first century. Similarly, 800,000 mature Canadians and 400,000 Japanese over 55 are expected to come to Europe by then, twice the numbers who visited in 1990 (Hart 1994).

The quantitative impact of this market will be considerable, not only because of the sheer numbers of potential visitors comprising it, but also because of their spending power. For example, in the all-important US market, where 50+ is the fastest growing population group, one commentator has said

> These new mature travellers are better travelled, more highly educated and in better physical and financial condition than their predecessors. They will be more demanding of the unique and more demanding of convenience. For these travellers, vacations are opportunities to pamper themselves with treatment and surroundings they have not realised in their day-to-day lives. This group controls over 50 per cent of the nation's wealth and more of the national expendable income. (Frenkel 1992)

But the main impact on tourism of these mature consumers is most likely to be qualititative. There appears to be general agreement that their tourism expectations will be very unlike those of their parents' generation, whose experience of travel and tourism was extremely different.

> With the twenty-first century just around the corner, the world belongs . . . to the 'babyboomers', to the generation born in the post-war baby boom, who grew up with tourism as a normal component of their existence and who have effectively changed every aspect of everyday life on which they have impacted up until now (hippies, flower power, the Pill, women's liberation, yuppies, test-tube babies, genetic engineering, etc.). We only have to look at Europe . . . to see how different the demographic profile is nowadays from when the first international tourists of 'mass tourism' embarked on voyages abroad in the 1960s. . . . Mature tourists of the future will be much more likely to be participating in polar bear safaris and white water rafting . . . than to be rocking themselves to sleep in a rocking-chair on the porch of the spa where they have gone to 'take the waters' . . . Mature tourists are experienced and discerning consumers who look upon international travel, not as an escape from the drudgery of everyday routine, but as a 'gateway to experience'. As such, they are more prepared to participate in the holiday experience and even to contribute to its success. The older people are, the less materialistic they become and the greater the value they attach to quality experiences: quality of service, for example, the personal touch and local hospitality. (Hart 1994)

Jefferson is equally convinced of the immense impact that this market will have on tourism demand:

> It is this mature and concerned segment, increasingly active in green issues and preoccupied with lifestyle, which is already impacting on tourism management. They were the mass travellers of the fifties and sixties. They were the ones who extended their horizons in the 1970s following the introduction of jumbo jets. They are today's sophisticated and discerning travellers with the means and the will to travel. But they expect high standards and, above all, they expect value for money. (Jefferson 1992)

THE SOCIO-CULTURAL ENVIRONMENT

It is difficult to generalise with much confidence about social trends affecting such a diverse and complex society as Europe, but there are, nevertheless, some indications of long-term trends of potential interest to the industry.

The move towards self-catering accommodation (holiday flats, timeshares, *gîtes*, for example) can be interpreted as a desire for more privacy and independence, away from the group and focusing on the individual. Such a thesis is consistent with the trend away from group consumption and towards private consumption which has been identified in other areas of consumer expenditure – from restaurants to take-aways, cinema to video, pub drinking to home drinking, for example. However, as has been rightly pointed out (TPR Associates 1991), the trend towards the use of these forms of accommodation can just as easily be explained as the consumer responding favourably to the offer of a new and convenient product – rented accommodation – which was not previously available on a mass-market basis for holiday purposes.

Arguments about a drift away from package tours and towards independent holidays may be somewhat simplistic. The possibility of this drift occuring became apparent at the end of the 1980s, and was interpreted largely as a sense of fatigue with the traditional beach holiday in the Mediterranean area, whose shocks and horrors were increasingly catalogued in the media. Many were too quick to extrapolate from this *malaise* to an imminent decline of package holidays in general. But the concept of a bundle of holiday services put together by a tour operator remains as valid as ever in Europe. As they have seen a fall in demand for their traditional product, the response of tour operators has been to put together packages which better meet the needs of their clients. The typical independent holiday has often been spent in a rented cottage, and such holidays are now being extremely successfully marketed by tour operators in many northern European countries in particular. Most British holidaymakers renting *gîtes* in France, for example, would not think of themselves as taking a package tour; but when they purchase a package which includes their ferry/tunnel transport, cottage accommodation, insurance and other services, that is what they are buying.

THE GREENING OF TOURISM

Concern for the state of the natural environment – the preoccupation which lies behind the interest in 'green issues' mentioned above – is a major element in the socio-cultural environment which partly determines tourism purchasing patterns. Those responsible for marketing tourism, and a host of other consumer products, have long realised that concern for the environment is no longer, as it was sometimes perceived, the province of the radical and the eccentric. For a growing number of people, the definition of a quality experience while away from home has come to include the need for tourism which respects the environment (and, increasingly, the quality of life of those who live and work at the destination), and this will certainly continue to grow as a theme.

Commenting, at the beginning of the 1990s, on customers' growing reluctance to buy holidays to destinations where beaches are polluted or where there are hazards of other types, TPR Associates remarked that: 'Such factors are however not new, and sensible people have always avoided booking into problem areas. What is new is that customers are being alerted to potential problems much more efficiently than in the past, are much better informed and more concerned than they were about water quality and similar issues. They are now insisting on higher standards than those they previously accepted' (TPR Associates 1991).

The problem that such consumer concerns present for the European holiday industry is that many of its products are based on the Mediterranean coast, where there is a shortage of destinations perceived by consumers as 'green'. Fact and consumer perception are, of course, not always in harmony, but it is certainly a reality that surprisingly few Mediterranean resorts can demonstrate conformity with EU norms for sea-water cleanliness.

The interesting question in respect of the standard Mediterranean high-rise resort is whether it can survive in its present form even if problems with, for example, beaches are resolved. If tourists are looking for a superior quality of life, of which clean beaches are but one aspect, then resorts will have to instigate a number of fundamental changes related to the physical environment: architecture,

town planning, traffic management, security, etc. The difficulty for such tourism destinations is that changes in consumer taste are now happening very quickly, but responding effectively to those changes takes considerable time and investment.

In the longer term, it is evident that Mediterranean beaches and Alpine ski resorts are sensitive to climactic conditions and depend on the right weather for success. Global warming and the greenhouse effect, if unchecked, have the potential to alter climactic conditions in Europe, as elsewhere and tourism purchasing patterns will change accordingly. The seeds of change are already there: there is a correlation between poor summers in northern Europe and residents of northern Europe holidaying at sun resorts the following year. Since there seems to be a new pattern of good summers being the norm in these northern countries, how much longer will it be before Mediterranean destinations feel the impact?

Medical considerations also enter the calculation. It is now recognised that ozone layer depletion increases the likelihood of skin cancer. Melanoma has doubled on average in Europe and the USA every ten years; sales of sun care products are increasing, sun protection factors are being stepped up. Many predict that sun and sand holidays may decline in popularity as a result of health concerns. Moreover, if hot summers in the north of Europe do become the norm, then this will accelerate the growth in tourist flows from south to north in Europe, which the European Travel Commission has identified as one of its 'megatrends' (ETC 1997).

Difficulties arising from ecological issues are not confined to Mediterranean and other beach destinations. In the longer term, European city tourism may also be threatened by an environmental problem – that of acid rain. This substance, which is very damaging to historic buildings and monuments, shows no signs of diminishing in Europe. Moreover, almost a third of Europe's forests are currently affected by acid rain to varying degrees.

ECONOMIC ENVIRONMENT

Among the reasons for the optimism of the European Commission's Green Paper on tourism is the fact that there is more widespread paid leave and shorter working hours in many European countries. But against this must be set the 1990s trend towards a greater casualisation of the work-force (not least in the tourism sector itself) and the significant fact of an intractable long-term growth in levels of unemployment, which may provide more 'free time' but also little money to fund tourist consumption. The European Travel Commission noted in its 'megatrends' report of 1997 that: 'Longer-term structural changes, notably in globalisation, affecting European economies, are leading to higher unemployment, poorer job security and lower economic growth, thereby reducing growth in disposable income for travel' (ETC 1997).

Consequently, the economic mood in Europe, and further afield, in the run-up to the twenty-first century is hardly one of reckless optimism. Since even those in gainful employment are too pain-fully aware that the vicissitudes of the global economy could mean a sudden change in their fortunes, spending well, as opposed to spending lavishly appears to be the main defining characteristic of the tourism market, as for most other areas of consumption. Value for money, combined with the quest for quality, is the order of the day.

The trend towards seeking greater quality and value for money in tourism products has been widely identified by industry watchers. Commenting on trends in tourism consumption in general, the OECD noted, in its 1996 review of international tourism in member countries, that 'Consumers have become better informed, and pay closer attention to the quality of tourism products, aiming for the best value for money' (OECD 1996).

In particular, tourists are increasingly adept at seeking out destinations where they will find the best product at the best price. The OECD emphasises the importance of this trend:

> Tourists from traditional major generating countries such as Germany and the United Kingdom showed a preference for destinations which had become more 'competitive' and thus reshaped market trends' (OECD 1996).

In France, too, the impacts of this trend are increasingly being observed by the industry:

The changing habits of European tourists are also making life harder for travel firms. Jacques Maillot, founder of Nouvelles Frontières . . . points out that, since the recession, consumers have begun to make sophisticated trawls to find the best combination of price and quality. This could easily become a permanent feature of industry. (Economist 1995a)

Moreover, as more Europeans travel further afield, they are increasingly exposed to standards of accommodation and levels of service in destinations such as Asia and America which cause them to revise their expectations about standards in European cities and resorts. As the competition to attract the international travelling public intensifies, there are many both inside and outside the tourism industry who believe that by comparison with a number of Europe's competitors, the European tourism product often seems dowdy and out of date. Some are of the opinion that the responsibility for at least part of the problem lies with European governments:

> Sometimes the trouble is a bolshie immigration officer. Too often, a shabby airport and a bumpy road is a visitor's first and last view of a country. Thanks to a combination of perennial strikes and fragmented air-traffic control, one in five flights is delayed by more than 15 minutes . . . Add poor signposting, parking and traffic jams around sites and it becomes clear that government-run infrastructure is also much in need of reform. (Economist 1995a).

But, it is clear that the main problem lies in the very nature of certain aspects of the European tourism product. Nowhere is this clearer than in some of the continent's outdated resorts:

> The broader problem dogging the European industry is the poor quality of much of its product. Too many European 'resorts' are euphemisms for polluted beaches, ageing, jerry-built hotels and erratic service. The tower-block hotels of the 1950s and 1960s have monopolised the best sites; pressure on water supplies and the need to maintain at least a few stretches of unspoilt coastline stop development elsewhere . . . Servicing the needs of today's more sophisticated and richer consumers with assets, products and attitudes designed for a 1960s mass market is a formula for failure. (Economist 1995a)

As is the case for any other industrial sector, the supply side of European tourism must adjust to the globalisation of the market by coming to terms with the increasing competitiveness of new destinations.

So how can the European tourism industry become more competitive? Occasionally, a country can acquire a temporary edge from a currency devaluation, as Spain and Italy both did in 1996. More often, competitiveness will depend upon training and investment and increased attention to certain aspects of the product. McIntosh is among those who are of the opinion that this already happening and that the European tourism industry is moving towards qualitative rather than quantitative growth – since this is where profitability is increasingly thought to lie:

> To emphasise only the quantity of tourists arriving . . . is to miss the indications that are increasingly pointing to a change in the type of demand from tourists. There is a stress now on improvements in quality, on relation to the environment, and on the degree of personal service offered. In economic terms, this may be seen as attention to increases in profitability rather than in quantity of tourism. (McIntosh 1995).

The implications of this for tourism are great. Rather than the emphasis on price and economies of scale typical of the traditional approach to competitiveness, this newer qualitative approach would suggest more attention to quality of service, specialised response in particular segments of the market to particular types and levels of demand, and less economising on staff.

To sum up, the EU Green Paper puts the challenge currently facing the industry as follows:

> Achieving the balance between quantity (particularly as regards mass tourism) and profitability (in particular the *per capita* profit expected) is basic to the future of the European tourism industry.

The foregoing review of market environments' relevance for tourism is clearly not exhaustive. Many other issues bearing on tourism decisions affecting Europe are dealt with in depth in the following chapters of this book: for example, the regulatory environment as it affects one aspect of tourism is covered in the chapters on transport, while EU fiscal and tourism policy is an element of Chapter 2.

Tourism in the twenty-first century

With so many factors operating on consumers' behaviour regarding their choice of destination and type of holiday, as well as other forms of tourism consumption, predictions about the precise nature of tourism in the twenty-first century have to be made with caution. Nevertheless, there is a fair degree of agreement as to what are the growth areas for tourism in Europe for the period following the year 2000.

SHORTER HOLIDAYS

The length of the average holiday taken by Europeans will continue to fall, as short breaks grow in popularity. As a result, cities, which are the focal points for a considerable proportion of European short breaks, will benefit. Chapter 7 deals with this market in detail.

GREATER VARIETY

Linked to the short breaks trend, second, third or even fourth holidays will be designed to meet 'lifestyle' needs and will be based more on culture, special interests and activities than the traditional formula of sun, sea and sand. Holidays will increasingly be about 'slimming bodies and broadening minds'. Patrick Lavery, quoted in *The Economist*, maintains that: 'the industry can only sell so much sun, sea and sand. Now that tourists take several holidays a year, they want variety.' For example, the German tour operator TUI has detected a move towards holidays based around an activity, such as golf or Spanish cooking, while others note an increasing demand for city breaks (Economist 1995a).

This theme is picked up by the European Commission's Green Paper on tourism, which states:

> The mobility of holiday makers in terms of changing destinations, seasonality and more active behaviour is increasing. Present trends indicate that holiday makers' preferences are shifting away from traditional products offered by sun resorts to more 'cultural' activities ('cultural' to be understood in a

broad sense) . . . Traditional holiday areas like the Mediterranean, providing sun and beaches as their main selling features, will experience stronger competition from . . . destinations offering a more diverse tourism supply. (CEC 1995b)

SHIFTS IN ORIGIN-DESTINATION FLOWS

One of the main trends in changing tourism flows has already been mentioned – the rise in the popularity of long-haul destinations for Europeans and for visitors to Europe. The European Travel Commission is among those predicting that long-haul holidays to and from Europe will increase faster than intra-European holidays. Technological advances in the production of 'Superjumbos' (see Chapter 3) can only intensify this trend.

Within Europe, some of the highest European growth rates outbound during the 1990s were from the south to northern European destinations. The European Travel Commission sees this trend continuing into the twenty-first century, outpacing growth in traditional north-south tourist flows. The European Commission concurs: 'It is evident that southern Community countries . . . in recent years have high growth rates in terms of international tourism inside the EU. Italy and Spain in particular became promising new markets for holiday destinations in the northern part of Europe' (CEC 1995a).

As mentioned earlier in this chapter, east-west and west-east travel is also a promising growth area, and it is clear that tourism from Western European countries is already having a strong economic impact on Eastern Europe, in particular in Poland, the Czech Republic, Slovakia and Hungary. Western European destinations, however, will have to wait longer to see such extensive tourist flows coming in the other direction: 'Tourist inflows by residents of Eastern Europe and more specifically the former East Germany . . . will continue. Nevertheless, the economic take-off which will be a condition before tourist flows from the east turn into mass tourism, will take some years' (CEC 1995b).

MORE AIR AND RAIL TRAVEL

Air travel, both short and long haul, will increase faster than other types of transportation due to various factors including new direct connections – although in Europe, crowded airspace and long waiting hours could be a deterrent until these problems are solved. Rail transport, however, will also show growth, in particular owing to convenient rail services in major population centres and the introduction of high-speed trains between many large European cities. More transport schemes based on intermodality of both air and rail will be developed for consumers (ETC 1997). These themes are taken up in Chapters 3 and 4.

CASE STUDY: the European Travel Commission's activities in the USA

Background

The ETC (European Travel Commission) was established in Norway in 1948, by a dozen European National Tourist Organisations (NTOs), with the aim of generating travel from the United States to the 'Old Continent' with funds from the post-war Marshall Plan. It was founded first as a part of the OEEC (the Organisation for European Economic Cooperation – now the OECD) then as a voluntary, autonomous organisation.

The ETC is now a not-for-profit organisation responsible for the worldwide promotion, in long-haul markets, of Europe as a tourist destination. Twenty-six countries are involved: most EU Member States (Austria, Belgium, Denmark, Finland, France, Germany, Greece, Ireland, Italy, Luxembourg, Portugal, Spain, Sweden, and the United Kingdom), as well as Norway, Iceland, Switzerland, Monaco, Malta, Cyprus, Turkey, Bulgaria, Czech Republic, Hungary, Poland, Slovenia.

ETC members are the Directors of European NTOs. They elect a Chairman, two Vice-Chairmen, a Steering Committee and a Planning Committee for revolving two-year terms. A Research Working Group regularly exchanges information and identifies market segments to be investigated. A small, permanently-staffed, Executive Unit ensures

continued

coordination from its headquarters in Brussels. A major reason for the ETC's move from Paris to Brussels in 1996 was given by the ETC Chairman Urbain Claeys as follows: 'In the years ahead, cooperation with the European Union is essential if we are to maintain market share. Strengthening these ties was one of the reasons why the organisation voted in 1995 to transfer its headquarters from Paris to Brussels' (ETC 1996).

The ETC operates in five major overseas markets where at least six NTOs are represented: USA, Canada, Latin America (Mexico, Brazil, Argentina), Japan and Australia/New Zealand – and occasionally elsewhere if opportunities arise. ETC never operates in Europe, where Members are in competition with each other to attract the intra-European market. The ETC's main remit is to create demand for European tourism in those five overseas markets. In order to do so, it uses a combination of three techniques: consumer promotion, trade promotion, and public relations. Prior market research determines the choice of activities, and all campaigns are harmonised with national campaigns.

How does the ETC function?

Outside Europe: the representatives of the European NTOs operating on the various long-haul markets join together to form an ETC Chapter and elect a Chairman. They decide on a programme of joint activities for the promotion of Europe in the year ahead, propose a budget and seek local industry support.

In Europe, the ETC's members meet twice a year in a General Assembly. After voting the organisation's overall budget, they allocate a budget for each of the overseas markets. They then approve or modify proposed programmes and review past activities.

The ETC is entirely financed by members' contributions, calculated according to a set of agreed criteria. Additional financial support for specific campaigns is raised overseas. Longstanding local industry support for ETC's activities is proof of its credibility in the field. ETC's seed money is annually multiplied by two, three or even four, through local contributions. These typically increase the ETC's

budget from around ECU 1 million to around ECU 4 million.

Who carries out the promotional activities? Each Operations Group may hire the services of a public relations agency which is also responsible for raising local industry support. One of ETC's strengths is that it has very low running costs and can therefore allocate the major proportion of its funds to overseas activities.

Expert knowledge of market conditions held by ETC representatives in the field ensures well-timed and well-targeted promotion. Consumer interest generated by magazine campaigns in the USA, Canada and Australia is systematically channeled by various mechanisms – reader response cards, toll-free telephone numbers – then satisfied by brochures giving practical information on travel and events in Europe, and finally measured by surveys determining conversion into actual travel. In Latin America, ETC booths at major trade fairs and workshops maintain vital links with the industry, while on-going press work promotes Europe's image as a desirable travel destination.

Other ETC activities

The ETC provides a forum for the Directors of European NTOs to meet regularly and exchange ideas. Over the years, this cooperation has led the ETC to take position on measures perceived as potentially detrimental to tourism on a Europe-wide basis. It is in constant touch with all international and multinational bodies working in tourism.

The EU participated actively in joint campaigns between 1986 and 1991 and has supported ETC market research projects. Joint ETC/EU action to promote Europe overseas is generally considered by those involved as the most cost-effective and practical means of ensuring this promotion.

Market research and statistics

The effectiveness of ETC's promotion depends on its prior knowledge of market conditions and expectations. High-quality market research and statistics are therefore essential to its operations.

Once a year, those responsible for market research and statistics in the ETC's member

continued

organisations meet to determine future research topics in view of marketing objectives.

Research is often carried out in partnership with local operators. For example, in 1996 the ETC completed a three-year cycle of field research into Brazilian, Argentinian and Mexican outbound travel to Europe. The Latin America chapter of the ETC managed to match the seed money provided by the ETC research budget with sponsorship raised locally and formed partnerships with university institutions to analyse original data collected at airports.

The Research Directors' Working Group has two other functions: first, avoiding duplication of research efforts, through the sharing of national statistics and the pooling of research funds to maximise results; secondly, commissioning research at the European level. For example, with the support of the EU and a number of other industry partners, first-ever investigations were undertaken by the ETC into the *European Senior Travel Market* in 1992 and the *European Youth Travel Market* in 1995. Research into the *Special Interest and Activity Holiday Market* in Europe is an example of a future research topic planned by the ETC.

A year of ETC activities in the USA

Despite fierce competition from destinations such as the Caribbean and Asia Pacific areas, Europe remains top of the league in the overseas US travel market. According to the ETC, departures by US citizens to Europe stood at 8.9 million in 1996, up from 8.7 million the previous year, making 1996 the fourth consecutive record year for arrivals in Europe from the USA. A major advantage of this market for European destinations is that off-peak (October to April) travel, consistently promoted by the ETC over the years, now accounts for nearly half of the annual US citizen's departures to Europe. New York, Washington and Boston metropolitan area residents between them account for 25 per cent or more of the off-peak total.

American expenditure in Europe in 1996 (exclusive of airfares) was estimated at more than US$18 billion, a rise of around US$4 billion over 1995. Increased consumer confidence, a growing economy, a stronger US dollar and increased

capacity on the trans-Atlantic routes presented a very promising outlook for 1997. Figure 1.6 shows the various world regions' respective shares of the US overseas travel market.

How does the ETC contribute to the success which Europe continues to enjoy in the US travel market? A profile of this organisation's activities in the USA during 1995 offers an insight into the ETC's role in stimulating tourist trips to Europe.

Consumer activities

1995 marked the third and final year of the ETC-sponsored 'Europe – Be a part of it' promotion in the USA. Designed and timed to encourage advance planning, issues of a full-page, four-colour advertisement appeared in February/March in leading upscale national magazines with reader demographics closely matching the profile of travellers to Europe. The advertisement offered free copies of the *Planning Your Trip to Europe* brochure featuring brief country-by-country profiles of ETC's 26 members, general travel information and a calendar of major events in Europe (Figure 1.7). A total of 400,000 copies of the brochure were printed. Total readership of the magazines involved was estimated at 30 million. Partners in 1995 were American Airlines, America Express and Rail Europe, each contributing US$250,000 to this one million dollar campaign.

To receive their free copies of the 60-page *Planning Your Trip to Europe* brochure, readers had the choice of filling in a Reader Service Card inserted in the magazine or calling a toll-free '800' number. Travel agents were also targeted in leading trade papers, with reminders that Europe was their prime overseas source of profit. Public relations to major consumer and trade media also backed up the promotion.

A Reader Service Card was also used to offer the *Planning Your Trip to Europe* brochure in the spring and autumn editions of *Your Invitation to Europe*. Some 2.1 million copies of this 40–page thematic magazine focusing on Europe's cultural, historical and natural attractions were distributed via *The New York Times*, *Chicago Tribune* and *Los Angeles Times* on Sunday, 2 April. The autumn issue was distibuted on Sunday, 8 October to readers of *The New York Times*

continued

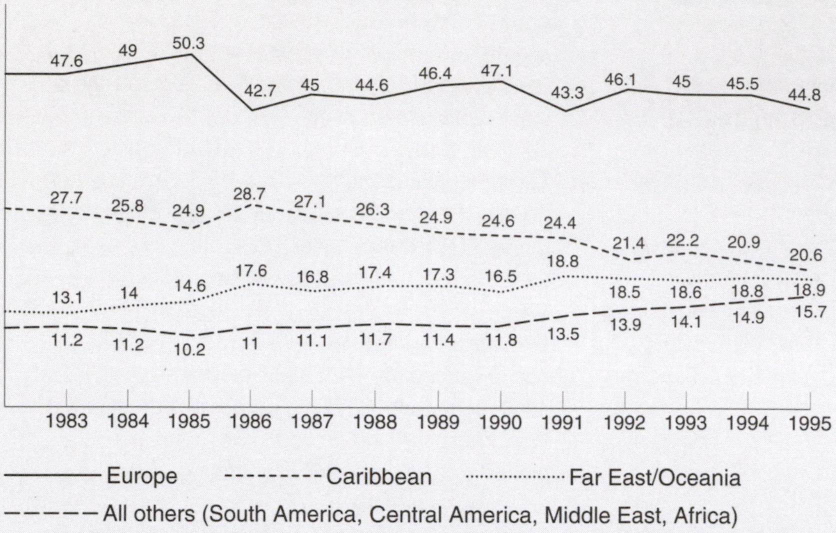

Data plotted in the chart (by year, 1983–1995):

Europe: 47.6, 49, 50.3, 42.7, 45, 44.6, 46.4, 47.1, 43.3, 46.1, 45, 45.5, 44.8

Caribbean: 27.7, 25.8, 24.9, 28.7, 27.1, 26.3, 24.9, 24.6, 24.4, 21.4, 22.2, 20.9, 20.6

Far East/Oceania: 13.1, 14, 14.6, 17.6, 16.8, 17.4, 17.3, 16.5, 18.8, 18.5, 18.6, 18.8, 18.9 / 15.7

All others: 11.2, 11.2, 10.2, 11, 11.1, 11.7, 11.4, 11.8, 13.5, 13.9, 14.1, 14.9, 15.7

——— Europe   -------- Caribbean   ·············· Far East/Oceania
— — — All others (South America, Central America, Middle East, Africa)

Figure 1.6 Percentage share of US market by destination (Canada and Mexico excluded)
Source: US Office of Tourism Industries

and for the first time to readers of *The Washington Post* and *The Boston Globe*.

The toll-free 800 numbers and the Reader Service Cards were the mechanisms for measuring the number of consumer and trade responses received and the relative cost of stimulating them. Final results show that the 1994 campaign generated 138,794 individual consumer responses as well as travel agent requests for an additional 30,000 copies (beyond the 190,000 copies initially distributed to the trade).

These results in themselves were highly encouraging, but a number of questions remained. Had the campaign reached its target audience? Was the proportion of first timers to repeat travellers reached? Did they actually go to Europe or make firm plans to go? What did they think of the *Planner*? To answer these questions, in March and April 1995, the US chapter of the ETC commissioned a Conversion and Activation Survey consisting of telephone interviews with 1,000 people who had responded to the 1994 'Europe – Be a Part of it' promotion and received the *Planning Your Trip to Europe* brochure.

Responders, the survey showed, were well educated, from professional/executive households in middle years, with comfortable incomes, ample holiday time and few children at home. The majority had multi-trip experience (correlated with a firm intention to travel again). One quarter were first timers, vital for market replacement. Of those surveyed, 49 per cent had gone to Europe in the 12 months after receiving the brochure. Another 41 per cent said they planned to go in the future, half of them taking action towards that end. Of those who received the brochure, 67 per cent considered it 'Very Useful' or 'Fairly Useful'. Media cost for magazine responses averaged a little over $6 per response, while PR-generated responses cost $1.15. The campaign had clearly stimulated an unusually high response from its target audience at a low cost per enquiry.

Trade activities

A total of 7,220 travel agents attended the new *European Roundtable and Supermarts* inaugurated at the beginning of 1995 and held in 20 cities in the USA. Designed to provide agents with essential information and brochures as well as with opportunities to meet suppliers, they also highlighted the profitability of selling travel to Europe.

Helping travel agents sell Europe was also the purpose of 'All-Europe' seminars with the American

continued

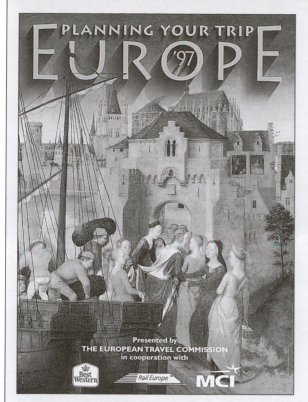

Figure 1.7 ETC brochure
Source: European Travel Commission

Society of Travel Agents (ASTA). The seminars took place at the annual ASTA World Congress and at each of ASTA's three regional meetings. After screening a motivational video on Europe, each panelist presented three special-interest travel topics, as well as information on new tourist developments and some important tips agents could pass on to their clients.

Taking a broader view, ETC's Trans-Atlantic Travel Marketing Conference on the theme 'Clearing the Hurdles for Continued Growth' attracted 324 delegates from the American and European travel industry and from consumer and trade media. Gathered at the Grand Hyatt Hotel in New York on 1 November 1995, they heard the European Union Commissioner for Energy, Small Businesses and Tourism address them on the theme of 'Tourism's rising prominence on Europe's agenda'.

In January 1996, the ETC opened its Web site on Internet, attracting 2,500 'visits' per day and 1,000 requests for brochures each week. By early March, 10 member countries had their own Web sites. This represents another way of prompting more Americans to take their first trans-Atlantic trip. Young people and students will be particularly targeted, but the babyboomers, the demographic heart of the American market, will not be neglected (ETC 1996).

THE EUROPEAN TOURISM ACTION GROUP

The European Tourism Action Group (ETAG) is an organisation formed in 1981 on the initiative of the European Travel Commission. ETAG comprises members from both the public and private sectors of the tourism industry, including the ETC itself as well as international federations and associations representing, for example, European hoteliers and restaurateurs, transporters, tour operator and travel agents, major city tourism authorities, travel journalists, youth hostels, conference organisers and theme park managers.

According to its own mission statement, the principal objectives of ETAG are:

- to encourage effective technical liaison between governments, national tourism agencies and the tourism operating interests in the public and private sectors;
- to promote the development of Europe's tourism;
- to help remove constraints on the growth of travel.

Despite its extremely small operating budget (ECU 25,000 in 1994), many commentators believe that ETAG acts as an effective liaison group between the secretariats of these different associations (Cockerell 1994).

ETAG aims to strengthen the collective voice of tourism by fostering cooperation and encouraging public/private sector partnerships essential to prosperous tourism development. It claims to provide a forum for all the key interests concerned with the provision of visitor services and facilities. And while each sector member interest has their own professional and trade concerns, ETAG seeks to identify and promote the common interest in tourism development which links all the sectors together.

There are three meetings a year and periodic industry liaison to ensure the exchange of information between members on issues of common concern and interest to all sectors of the industry in Europe. Once a joint position is reached and a course of action determined, representation is made to industry, governments or European agencies. Much of its time is taken up in lobbying the European Commission. On-going press and public relations ensure that ETAG's positions are made known to other agencies and the trade press.

What are the issues?

Three of the most pressing issues are:

Statistics: ETAG welcomed the EU's Directive on Tourism Statistics as an attempt to improve systems of measurement, but considered it too limited and therefore disappointing in its application. Its formal response to the Directive was:

> As a borderless Europe becomes a reality, there is a pressing need for a system of collection providing more reliable, harmonised, user-orientated tourism statistics. ETAG strongly recommends closer cooperation by the EU with the NTOs and the trade, as both have considerable professional experience in the research field. The establishment of a European Data Centre would help overcome the difficulties of collecting information from a wide range of sources.

Taxes: ETAG supports the OECD's work in recording taxes on individual travellers and WTO's in-depth survey. ETAG's message is that discriminatory taxes distort fair competition and erode Europe's competitive edge at a time when it is losing market share.

European legislation: The Group has been active in seeking amendments or change in a number of proposed items of EU legislation. ETAG's approach is to advocate voluntary environment and consumer protection programmes, rather than what it calls 'one-sided regulation and constraint'. Advice was given on proposals for a Single Currency, drawing attention to some problem areas and suggesting a technical study and trial period as a tourism currency.

ETAG has taken an active part in consultations on the future role of the Union in tourism and pressed for a high priority to be given to tourism in the revision of the Treaty in 1996 (see page 68), including support for overseas promotion.

But, on ETAG's own admission, the collective voice of the tourism industry in Europe is weak. 'Priority given in governmental policies to the industry's needs is low, resources devoted to future infrastructure development are inadequate, and fiscal, financial and regulatory framework of government affecting the industry are created without recognition of tourism's massive potential.' Many would argue that these problems are particularly acute at the European Union level of government. The impact of the European Union on tourism is the theme of the following chapter.

UPDATE

Undertake your own research to find out the answers to the following questions:

- Has Europe's share of all international tourist arrivals continued to fall?
- Has the East Asia/Pacific region continued to expand its share of international tourism?
- Are there any new 'rising star' destinations in Europe's top 20 countries?
- How much of the long-haul 'mature' tourist market has Europe managed to capture?
- Are there any signs that global warming is having a significant impact on European tourism?

References

Berry, S. (1992) The impact of the British upon seaside resort development in Europe, in *Proceedings of the 1992 Tourism in Europe Conference*, Centre for Travel and Tourism, Houghton le Spring.

CEC (1995a) 'The role of the Union in the field of tourism', Commission Green Paper, Commission of the European Communities, Brussels.

CEC (1995b) *Tourism in Europe*, Commission of the European Communities, Brussels.

Cockerell, N. (1994) 'The changing role of international travel and tourism organisations', in *Travel and Tourism Analyst (5)*, Travel and Tourism Intelligence, London.

Davidson, R. and Maitland, R. (1997) *Tourism Destinations*, Hodder & Stoughton, London.

Economist, The (1995a) 'A place in the sun', 29 July.

ETC (1996) *Annual Report 1995*, European Travel Commission, Brussels.

ETC (1997) *Megatrends of Tourism in Europe to the Year 2000 and Beyond*, European Travel Commission, Brussels.

Frenkel, T. (1992) *Proceedings of the 18th Annual Travel Outlook Forum*, Washington, DC.

Hart, M. (1994) How to use a mature tourism mix towards the healthy redevelopment of the traditional sun and sand resorts, in A. V. Seaton *et al.* (eds) *Tourism: The State of the Art*, John Wiley, Chichester.

Holden A (1994) Tourism: a commodity of opportunity for change, in A. V. Seaton *et al.* (eds) *Tourism: The State of the Art*, John Wiley, Chichester.

Jefferson, A. (1992) Speech, in *Proceedings of the 1992 Tourism in Europe Conference*, Centre for Travel and Tourism, Houghton le Spring.

Lickorish, L. (1992) Tourism in Europe, in *Proceedings of the 1992 Tourism in Europe Conference*, Centre for Travel and Tourism, Houghton le Spring.

Lundgren, J. O. J. (1992) 'Transport Infrastructure Development and Tourist Travel Case Europe', in *Proceedings of the 1992 Tourism in Europe Conference*, Centre for Travel and Tourism, Houghton le Spring.

McIntosh, S. (1995) *London and the Tourism policy of the European Union*, London and Europe Research Programme, London.

Mills, R. and Morrison, N. (1992) *The Tourist System: an introductory text*, Prentice Hall, Englewood Cliffs, NJ.

Page, S. (1993) 'European rail travel', in *Travel and Tourism Analyst (1)*, Travel and Tourism Intelligence, London.

OECD (1996) *Tourism Policy and International Tourism in OECD Countries 1993–1994*, Organisation for Economic Cooperation and Development, Paris.

Steinecke, A. (1993) 'The historical development of tourism in Europe,' in W. Pompl and P. Lavery (eds), *Tourism in Europe: Structures and Developments*, CAB International, Wallingford.

Times, The (1996) 'Greek islands lose their charm for Britons,' 3 October.

Towner, J. (1994) 'Tourism history: past, present and future', in A. V. Seaton *et al.* (eds), *Tourism: The State of the Art*, John Wiley, Chichester.

Towner, J. (1995) 'What is tourism's history?' in *Tourism Management*, Vol. 16, No. 5, pp. 339–43.

TPR Associates (1991) *The European Tourist*, Tourism Planning and Research Associate, London.

WTO (1996) *Tourism Market Trends: Europe 1985–1995*, World Tourism Organisation, Madrid.

WTO (1997) *Tourism Market Trends: the World, 1997 edition*, World Tourism Organisation, Madrid.

2

Tourism and the European Union

KEY OBJECTIVES

Reading this chapter will enable you to:

- Understand the role of EU institutions
- Understand the extent of and rationale behind EU involvement in tourism issues.
- See how tourism is indirectly and directly affected by a wide range of Community measures.
- Understand the background to the debate over a possible EU policy for travel and tourism in Member States.

Introduction

With its legislative, regulatory, fiscal and financial powers over an extensive and growing range of its Member States' activities, the European Union (EU) is an important inter-governmental body concerned with most aspects of life in Europe. By the late 1990s, the EU was composed of fifteen members, all sharing a common passport and heading towards a single currency. EU institutions legislating on a range of issues, from consumer affairs to trans-European transport networks, underlined Europe's emergence as a political and economic superpower, more than the sum of its parts, but with each part distinctly itself.

Policy and legislation developed at the European level are playing a increasingly important part in many aspects of the everyday lives of those living in EU Member States and are having a fundamental impact on the environment in which businesses operate. A growing number of the

important decisions which affect all EU citizens are now taken collectively by all of the Member States of the Community and are no longer the independent competence of national governments. Many of the rules and regulations implemented by national governments are thus of Community origin, even if they appear as national legislation.

This chapter traces the development of the European Union and examines some of its main policies affecting tourism demand and supply in Member States.

EU institutions

HISTORICAL BACKGROUND

The European Economic Community (EEC) was created on the signature of the Treaty of Rome on 25 March 1957 by the six nations which were already members of the European Coal and Steel Community: France, West Germany, Italy, Belgium, the Netherlands and Luxembourg. A third Community, the European Atomic Energy Community (Euratom), was established by a separate Treaty. For convenience, the three Communities were collectively known as the European Community (Forbes 1994).

The Community has come a long way since the European Coal and Steel Community was founded in 1952 to lay the basis for lasting peace and prosperity in what was then a continent deeply divided between contrasting political and economic systems. The following 40 years saw the Community transformed through a series of enlargements, from a six-member to a fifteen-member club, more than doubling its population to 370 million. At the end of 1997 enlargement continued as membership negotiations began with Poland, Hungary, the Czech Republic, Slovenia, Estonia and Cyprus. Key dates in the Community's development are shown in Figure 2.1.

Since the ratification of the Maastricht Treaty in 1993, the European Community has generally been referred to as the European Union.

There are now eight EU institutions employing 24,500 people, which, as they themselves like to point out, is less than half the number administering the city of Stockholm. The responsibilities of the main institutions affecting tourism are set out below.

The European Parliament

There are 626 European Parliament members (MEPs), who are elected every five years: Germany is represented by 99 MEPs; France, Italy, the United Kingdom by 87 each; Spain by 64; the Netherlands by 31, Belgium, Greece and Portugal by 25 each. Sweden has 22 MEPs, Austria 21, Denmark and Finland 16 each, Ireland 15 and Luxembourg 6. All of the EU's major political currents are represented in the Parliament, ranging from far left to far right, and numbering close to 100 political parties. These are organised in a limited number of political groups (currently eight).

The directly elected European Parliament is the largest multinational Parliament in the world (indeed, many believe that it is too large and unwieldy and that it would be more effective if the number of MEPs was limited). Representing the 370 million citizens of the Union, its primary objective is to pass laws and to scrutinise and control the use of executive power. Its responsibilities have been gradually widened and its powers strengthened, first by the Single Act of 1987 and then by the Treaty on European Union of 1993.

The European Parliament functions in three different places. It meets in Strasbourg for monthly plenary sessions, in Brussels for Committee meetings and additional sessions, while the 3,800-strong General Secretariat is based in Luxembourg. This arrangement has been much criticised for the time and expense it incurs, obliging MEPs to travel between the three locations and costing 100 million ECUs a year in rent and travel expenses.

The European Parliament sees itself as the guardian of the European interest and the defender of the citizens' rights. Individually or as a group, European citizens have the right to petition the European Parliament and can seek redress of their grievances on matters that fall within the EU's sphere of responsibility.

The main powers of the European Parliament fall into three categories:

Legislative power

Originally, the Treaty of Rome gave the Parliament only a consultative role, allowing the Commission to propose and the Council of Ministers to decide legislation. Subsequent treaties have extended Parliament's influence to amending and even adopting legislation, so that the Parliament and Council now share the power of decision in a number of areas. As a result, a wide range of legislation (including internal market, consumer affairs, trans-European networks, education and health) is adopted both by the Parliament and the Council.

Budgetary powers

The European Parliament approves the Union's budget each year. The budgetary procedure allows Parliament to propose amendments to the Commission's initial proposals and to the position taken by the Member States in Council. On agricultural spending and costs arising from interna-

Figure 2.1 Key dates in EU's development

Key dates in the EU's development

1951: Treaty of Paris on the European Coal and Steel Community
1957: Treaties of Rome on the European Economic Community and European Atomic Energy Community
1965: Merger Treaty on a single Commission and Council of Ministers for the three European Communities
1970: Luxembourg Treaty on budgetary matters
1972: Accession treaty for Denmark, Ireland and the UK*
1975: Treaty on various financial provisions
1976: Act on direct elections to the European Parliament
1980: Accession treaty for Greece
1985: Accession treaty for Spain and Portugal
1986: Single European Act
1992: Maastricht Treaty on European Union
1994: Accession treaty for Austria, Finland and Sweden*

* Also included Norway, which subsequently rejected EU membership in a referendum

tional agreements, the Council has the last word, but on other expenditure – for example, education, social programmes, regional funds, environmental and cultural projects – Parliament decides in close cooperation with the Council.

Supervision of the executive

The Parliament exercises overall political supervision of the way the Union's policies are conducted. Executive power in the Union is shared between the Commission and the Council of Ministers and their representatives appear regularly before Parliament.

Much of the work of Parliament is conducted in its 20 committees covering all areas of the Union's activities, ranging from Agriculture to Common Foreign and Security Policy, from Legal Affairs and Citizens' Rights to Overseas Cooperation and Development.

However, the European Parliament has often been accused of being remote and unfamiliar to a majority of the European electorate. It has been described as 'a body that few of the Union's 370 million citizens recognise, let alone love' (Economist 1997). Turnout for MEP elections tends to be low (57 per cent in the last round of polls) and the role of the European Parliament itself is widely misunderstood.

> Most voters expect an elected Parliament to produce a government and to act in an adversarial way. The European Parliament does neither. It is supposed to exert demographic control over the European Commission. But national governments still choose all the Commissioners. And the Parliament is far from adversarial: it needs consensus among its political groups to create absolute majorities to amend laws. It tends to work in cahoots with the Commission. (Economist 1997)

Tourism matters in the European Parliament are dealt with through its official Transport and Tourism Committee. In general, the European Parliament has been supportive of tourism and has campaigned for a higher profile for tourism as a EU concern and more active recognition of the tourism industry within EU institutions. Several of the Community's direct measures affecting tourism, including the European Year of Tourism and the Action Plan to Assist Tourism (see page 66) came

about as a direct result of initiatives of the European Parliament.

The Tourism Inter-Group coordinated by the Transport and Tourism Committee provides assistance with the task of liaising between the tourism responsibilities of the European Parliament, the Commission and the tourism industry operating in the countries of the Union.

The Council of the European Union

The Council of the European Union, usually known as the Council of Ministers, has no equivalent anywhere in the world. Its members are ministers of the Member States. Its presidency rotates every six months and it meets in Brussels, except in April, June and October, when all Council meetings take place in Luxembourg. It is within the Council of Ministers that the Member States legislate for the Union, set its political objectives, coordinate their national policies and resolve differences between themselves and other institutions.

Each meeting of the Council brings together Member States' representatives, usually Ministers, who are responsible to their national parliaments and public opinions. There are regular meetings covering more than 25 different types of issue: General Affairs (Foreign Affairs ministers), Economy and Finance, and Agriculture meet monthly; others, such as Transport, Environment and Industry, meet two to four times a year.

The Treaty on European Union established that Council decisions should mainly be taken either by qualified majority voting or by unanimity. In the vast majority of cases, the Council decides by a qualified majority vote, with Member States carrying the following weightings:

	No. of votes
Germany, France, Italy and the United Kingdom	10
Spain	8
Belgium, Greece, the Netherlands and Portugal:	5
Austria and Sweden	4
Ireland, Denmark and Finland	3
Luxembourg	2

When a Commission proposal is involved, at least 62 votes must be cast in favour. In other cases, the qualified majority is also 62 votes, but these must be cast by at least ten Member States. In practice, the Council tries to reach the widest possible consensus before taking a decision, so that, for example, in 1994 only about 14 per cent of the legislation adopted by the Council was the subject of negative votes and abstentions.

Community law adopted by the Council – or by the Parliament and Council in the framework of the co-decision procedure – may take the following forms:

- *Regulations*: these are directly applied without the need for Member States' national measures to implement them.
- *Directives*: these bind Member States as to the objectives to be achieved while leaving the national authorities the power to choose the forms and the means to be used.
- *Decisions*: these are binding in all their aspects upon those to whom they are addressed. A decision may be addressed to any or all Member States, to undertakings or to individuals.
- *Recommendations and opinions*: these are not binding.

The European Commission

There are twenty members, known as European Commissioners, who oversee the work of the Commission: two from France, Germany, Italy, Spain and the United Kingdom and one from each of the other Member States. Their term of office is five years. The headquarters of the European Commission is in Brussels.

The role and the responsibilities of the European Commission place it at the heart of the EU's policy-making process. With its staff of 15,000, the Commission is the largest of the Union's institutions and an important component in the EU institutional machinery. The Council and the European Parliament need a proposal from the Commission before they can pass legislation. EU laws are mainly upheld by Commission action, the integrity of the Single Market is preserved by Commission policing, agricultural and regional development policies are sustained, managed and developed by the Commission, as is

development cooperation with the countries of Central and Eastern Europe, Africa, the Caribbean and Pacific. Research and technological development programmes are also orchestrated by the Commission.

The activities of the Commission are divided into separate policy areas, in much the same way as, at national level, governmental responsibilities are divided between ministries. The Commission's basic units of organisation are its 26 Directorates-General (DGs), with an additional fifteen or so specialised services. Each DG is headed by a director-general, reporting to a Commissioner who has the political and operational responsibility for the work of the DG.

The work of the Commission

The Commission is not an all-powerful institution. Its proposals, actions and decisions are in various ways scutinised, checked and judged by all the other institutions, with the exception of the European Investment Bank. Nor does it take the main decisions on Union policies and priorities – this is the prerogative of the Council and the European Parliament. It has three distinct functions:

Legislative initiative

The legislative process begins with a Commission proposal – Community law cannot be made without one. In devising its proposals, the Commission has three objectives: to identify the European interest, to consult as widely as necessary and to respect the principle of subsidiarity. *The European interest* means that a legislative proposal should reflect the Commission's judgement of what is best for the Union and its citizens as a whole, rather than for sectoral interests or individual countries. *Consultation* is essential to the preparation of a proposal. The Commission listens to governments, industry, trade unions, special interest groups and technical experts before completing its final draft. *Subsidiarity* is enshrined in the Treaty on European Union and is applied by the Commission in such as way as to ensure that the Union only takes action when it will be more effective than if left to individual Member States. The idea is that decisions should be taken by those public authorities which stand as close to the citizen as possible. It is, therefore, a principle which resists unnecessarily remote, centralised decision-taking.

Once the Commission has formally sent a proposal for legislation to the Council and the Parliament, the Union's law-making process is very dependent on effective cooperation between the three institutions.

Guardian of the treaties

It is the Commission's job to ensure that Union legislation is applied correctly by the Member States. If they breach their Treaty obligation, they will face Commission action, including legal proceedings at the European Court of Justice. In certain circumstances, the Commission can fine individuals, firms and organisations for infringing Treaty law. Illegal price-fixing and market-rigging cartels, for example, have been a constant object of its attention and the subject of very large fines. The Commission also maintains a close scrutiny over government subsidies to industry and certain kinds of State aid must, by Treaty, receive its assent.

Manager and negotiator

The Commission manages the Union's annual budget (ECU 86 billion in 1996) which is dominated by farm spending allocated by the European Agricultural Guidance and Guarantee Fund and by the Structural Funds, designed to even out the economic disparities between the richer and poorer areas of the Union.

The Commission's executive responsibilities are wide: it has delegated powers to make rules which fill in the details of Council legislation; it can introduce preventive measures for a limited period to protect the Community market from dumping by third countries; it enforces the Treaty's competition rules and regulates mergers and acquisitions above a certain size.

The Union's effectiveness in the world is enhanced by the Commission's role as negotiator of trade and cooperation agreements with other countries, or groups of countries. More than 100 countries have such agreements with the Union, including the developing countries of Africa, the Caribbean and Pacific which are covered by the Lomé Convention, and those of Central and Eastern Europe and the former Soviet Union which

receive important technical assistance under the PHARE and TACIS programmes. The countries of the southern Mediterranean also benefit from a European development aid effort.

Within the European Commission, there is a small Tourism Unit (fewer than twelve members of staff) in DGXXIII, the Directorate-General with responsibility for Enterprise Policy, Tourism and Social Economy. However, the immense diversity of the Commission's activities in many fields means that tourism often becomes one of the focuses for the actions undertaken by other DGs under the various EU programmes. For example, DGVI (Agriculture) invests in the marketing of rural tourism within the Community; DGVIII (International Development) provides some 100 million ECU per annum in financial support to developing countries, under the Lomé Convention, to develop and promote their tourism industries.

The Tourism Unit's role is twofold: to coordinate the efforts of other DGs as they affect tourism; and to coordinate the national efforts of EU Member States in the field of tourism. However, the means at the disposal of DGXXIII's Tourism Unit are modest, reflecting in part the low priority which the EU has traditionally given to tourism. Moreover, the Tourism Unit has been the focus of considerable criticism, typified, at a low point of its history in the mid-1990s, by its being portrayed as 'ineffective and . . . now beset by allegations of fraud and mismanagement' (European 1995).

European Investment Bank

Membership of the European Investment Bank (EIB), which is based in Luxembourg, is composed of the Member States of the EU.

The EIB is the EU's financing institution. It provides long-term loans for capital investment promoting the Union's balanced economic development and integration. The EIB's ECU 20 billion volume of annual lending makes it the largest international financing institution in the world.

In the EU, EIB loans go to projects which fulfil one or more of the following objectives:

- Strengthening economic progress in the less favoured regions;

- Improving trans-European networks in transport, telecommunications and energy transfer;
- Enhancing industry's international competitiveness and its integration at a European level and supporting small and medium-sized enterprises;
- Protecting the environment and quality of life, promoting urban development and safeguarding the EU's architectural heritage;
- Achieving secure energy supplies.

Underpinning regional development is the Bank's priority task and well over half its total lending is for investment in regions which are lagging behind or facing industrial decline.

The EIB's financing for regional development often goes hand in hand with grants from the Structural Funds and Cohesion Fund. For example, the Bank has a role in financing for trans-European networks (TENs). It has set up a special lending 'window' with tailor-made financing facilities for priority TENs approved by the Essen European Council in December 1994.

Projects supported by EIB loans carry the lightest possible interest rate burden. This is because the Bank obtains the bulk of its resources on the capital markets, where its top (AAA) credit rating enables it to borrow on the best terms available.

Committee of the Regions

The Committee of the Regions (COR) is the EU's youngest institution. It has 222 members made up of regional presidents, mayors of cities and chairs of city and county councils, drawn from the fifteen Member States. It meets in Brussels five times a year.

Created as a consultative body by the Treaty of European Union, the Committee has emerged as a strong guardian of the principle of subsidiarity since its first session in March 1994. The creation of the COR reflects Member States' desire not only to respect regional and local identities and prerogatives, but also to involve them in the development and implementation of EU policies. For the first time in the history of the EU, there is now a legal obligation to consult the representatives of local and regional authorities on a variety of matters that concern them directly.

The members of the Committee are elected officials from the levels of government closest to the citizen. This means that they have a very direct experience of how the Union's policies and legislation affect the everyday lives of those citizens.

The Committee's work is based on a structure of eight standing Commissions and four sub-Commissions as follows:

1 Regional Development, Economic Development, Local and Regional Finances;
  Sub-Commission: Local and regional finances;
2 Spatial Planning (agriculture, hunting, fisheries, marine environment and upland areas;
  Sub-Commission: Tourism, rural areas;
3 Transport and Communications networks;
  Sub-Commission: Telecommunications;
4 Citizen's Europe, Research, Culture, Youth and Consumers;
  Sub-Commission: Youth and sports;
5 Urban policies;
6 Land-use planning, Environment, Energy;
7 Education, Training;
8 Economic and Social Cohesion, Social Policy, Public Health.

The Treaty requires the Committee to be consulted on matters relating to trans-European networks, public health, education, youth, culture and economic and social cohesion. But the Committee can also take the initiative and give its opinion on other policy matters that affect cities and regions, such as agriculture and environmental protection.

In its brief existence, the Committee has already grappled with a wide range of tourism-related issues including guidelines for a trans-European airport network and the development of rural tourism (COR 1995a). It also made a response to the Commission Green Paper on the role of the Union in the field of tourism (COR 1995b).

EU measures affecting tourism

THE DEVELOPMENT OF AN EU POLICY FOR TOURISM

Despite the importance of the tourism industry for Europe, EU legislators and policy-makers have been slow to direct their attention towards this sector, and there has never been a specific EU policy for tourism or any long-term tourism programme of direct funding. One reason for this is suggested by Lickorish: 'The Commission has never accepted a policy for tourism, maintaining in its principle of 'subsidiarity' that tourism is a matter for each member state, and that the Commission's intervention followed from other aspects of EU policy and was limited to a number of specific measures' (Lickorish 1991). The subsidiarity argument is a powerful one and is a very relevant concept in tourism, which is essentially a locally delivered activity requiring intervention at local and national government levels. (However, as a former head of the European Commission Tourism Unit has pointed out, subsidiarity has to work both ways. There is no reason why the Commission should not have a competence in tourism issues where the Member States are not effective: for example, in protecting the environment.)

Other explanations for the low priority given to tourism at EU level are suggested by Forbes: 'The failure of the EU to get to grips with tourism at all until the early 1980s is undoubtedly in part a reflection of the low status given to tourism by the public sector in some Member States, especially the more economically developed ones, and in part a result of the difficulty in identifying tourism' (Forbes 1994).

It is generally recognised that the Community makes its greatest impact on tourism *passively*, through its general legislation and measures which although not particularly designed with tourism in mind, nonetheless affect this sector substantially. Similarly, by far the greatest proportion of the EU's expenditure on tourism arises *indirectly* through its general funds and programmes rather than from its actions aimed specifically at tourism. For these reasons, the Community's general measures affecting tourism will be examined first, before turning to its specific interventions in this field. However, before examining these measures, two questions merit consideration:

1 What is the legal basis for EU intervention in tourism; and
2 What is the rationale behind EU intervention in this sector?

THE LEGAL BASIS FOR EU INTERVENTION IN TOURISM

The basis of all Community legislation is the Treaty of Rome, together with subsequent amendments to that treaty.

As a general rule, fully developed policy and supporting legislation at EU level is based upon specific provisions in the Community's founding treaties. The common agricultural policy, the common external trade policy, Community competition policy and the common transport policy are examples. As tourism and transport are interlinked, the EU's common transport policy inevitably affects tourism in Member States. However, when the EU was founded, the phenomenon of mass tourism was still unknown, and there were no specific provisions made for tourism in the Treaty of Rome. As a result, for more than 25 years, the Community took no action directly related to tourism, and there is still no common tourism policy.

Nevertheless, as tourism has grown in importance, EU institutions have become increasingly involved in measures directly relating to this industry. What is the basis in EU law for such measures? The validity of this involvement in the field of tourism was confirmed by a judgement of the European Court in 1984 to the effect that EU nationals travelling abroad within the EU are 'recipients of services'. As such, tourism is covered by Articles 48–73 of the Treaty of Rome concerning 'the free movement of persons, services and capital'.

The Maastricht Treaty on European Union acknowledged for the first time that the EC should take specific action on tourism. This reflected the economic importance of the industry and the need to introduce links between policies on tourism, consumer affairs and natural and cultural heritage.

In 1992, the Council of Ministers formally declared that it was appropriate to take action on tourism at Community level. 'The aim should be to strengthen the horizontal approach to tourism in Community and national policies and develop specific measures for promoting cross-border cooperation between all the players, both public and private, in the various sectors affected by tourism' (CEC 1996b)

RATIONALE FOR EU INVOLVEMENT IN TOURISM

Since the 1980s, EU administrators' and politicians' attention has been increasingly turned towards the tourism industry and the number of tourism-related measures flowing out of Brussels has been steadily growing. This increase in the amount of attention paid to tourism is explained by several economic and social factors.

Tourism's growing economic significance

EU expansion during the 1980s introduced a number of new member countries in which tourism is of major economic importance. With Greece joining in 1981, followed by Spain and Portugal in 1986, the relative importance of tourism to the EU economy as a whole suddenly increased. This coincided with a period of rapid expansion of tourism in other member states, including the five largest, France, Germany, Italy, Spain and the UK, each of which had between 1 million and 1.5 million workers employed in tourism by the end of that decade. The steady growth of this industry – at a time when many other sectors of economic activity in Europe were either experiencing difficulties or contracting – therefore attracted the attention of policymakers within the EU, for whom economic growth and employment creation are major objectives.

Other characteristics of tourism mean that it is regarded as a major factor of economic development and is often considered as an alternative to industries in decline:

- Tourism contributes positively to the balance of payments in Europe.
- It is estimated that 5.5 per cent of GNP in Europe can be attributed to tourism.
- It has been estimated that nine million are employed directly in the sector.
- Tourism generates major investment not only in itself but also in other areas of the economy. The dynamic and diversifying effect of tourism activity acts as a boost for other sectors of the economy (CEC 1996b).

The World Travel and Tourism Council (see page 72) offers an even more up-beat version of the importance of tourism for the economy of the European Union, taking into account the sector's indirect as well as direct impact, as shown in Figure 2.2.

Tourism's redistributive and regional development role

Since much of tourism's potential for economic development and job creation is realised in regions which would otherwise have difficulty in finding alternative sources of economic stimulus, the expansion of tourism is consistent with another major EU objective – that of regional development. Tourism is an important factor of economic development in many of Europe's less-favoured regions, rural areas and areas suffering various forms of industrial decline. This characteristic of the tourism sector in Europe is emphasised by Akehurst et al: '[Tourism] also accounts for a high proportion of employment in the poorer countries of the EU, such as Spain, Ireland, Portugal and Greece, and so to some extent in the poorer regions of the higher income countries such as France, Italy and the UK' (Akehurst et al. 1993).

Tourism can have the effect of encouraging economic convergence by redistributing income within the EU, when tourists travel from the richer densely populated industrial areas to poorer, more sparsely populated rural areas and the coast. In this respect, tourism has come to be regarded by the EU as a sector which offers great potential for helping it achieve its objective of increasing the level of economic activity and employment in the 'peripheral' regions. Tourism

> is an industry which is located in many areas which the EC would like to see further developed, because of long-standing problems of poverty and high levels of unemployment. That is, it frequently works against the tide of development, which draws labour and investment towards the established centres for manufacturing industry and financial services. (Barnes and Barnes 1993).

Tourism as a factor in European integration

Tourism may help achieve social as well as economic convergence in Europe, as it is an effective means of spreading awareness about the different European cultures, which in turn can lead to the

WORLD	EUROPEAN UNION
Travel and tourism contributes directly and indirectly more than 10% of GDP, jobs, capital investment and tax revenues	Travel and tourism is expected to directly and indirectly generate 13.4% of GDP, 13.2% of employment, 15.5% of capital investment and 15.1% of taxes in 1995
Travel and tourism is a high growth industry which is forecast to more than double in size over the next decade. Along with Telecommunications and Information Technology, Travel and tourism is poised to be one of three key components of the service-led economy of the 21st century	Travel and tourism is expected to grow its total output more than 37% in real terms over the next decade
1 in 9 jobs worldwide is directly or indirectly generated by travel and tourism	1 in every 8 jobs results from travel and tourism activity
Travel and tourism is a major exporter, with international visitors injecting foreign exchange directly into the economy	The industry is expected to earn ECU 142.1 billion in travel and tourism services exports and ECU 101.4 billion in travel and tourism merchandise exports in 1995
Travel and tourism is a major activator of small- and medium-sized enterprises. It is also a catalyst for construction, financial services and communications	The industry will spend ECU 192.2 billion in 1995 on infrastructure, plant and capital equipment from suppliers

Figure 2.2 Travel and tourism's economic impact on Europe
Source: WTTC (1995)

development of mutual respect for Europeans' different ways of life.

Since much tourist activity within Europe involves the movement of people across international borders, there are obvious social benefits to be reaped by the EU in terms of enhanced European integration through intra-EU tourism. Tourism has consequently come to be regarded as having a part to play in furthering the EU objective of promoting international understanding and strengthening EU citizens' sense of 'Union'. Barnes and Barnes recognised this characteristic of tourism and concluded that

> while the rationale for EC intervention in tourism is essentially driven by economic considerations, the industry does contribute towards the integration of people in a much deeper sense than a number of other industries. It involves contact between people and cultures. This can assist understanding and create a stronger feeling of European identity and citizenship. (Barnes and Barnes 1993)

Tourism also contributes to developing the social dimension within the European Union and is one way of combatting social exclusion. This is realised mainly through the encouraging of access to tourism of the less-favoured groups in society, such as young people and people with disabilities.

Tourism as a means of implementing sustainable development

Tourism can also be a vehicle for the application of sustainable development techniques aiming at preserving and respecting the environment in which it operates. Tourism's dependence on the quality of the environment means that much tourist activity in EU countries fits into the objective laid down in Article 2 of the Treaty on European Union: to promote 'a harmonious and balanced development of economic activities, sustainable and non-inflationary growth respecting the environment'.

The EU 1995 Green Paper on Tourism considers the tourism sector as a useful experiment in sustainable development, from which lessons may be drawn and applied to other sectors. 'Tourism is a field of action ready-made for implementing sustainable development. In addition, the foreseeable growth of tourism and the pressure which it exerts, allied to an increased demand for quality on the part of tourists, means that such an approach can no longer be delayed . . . This approach, which is essential and urgent for the tourist sector, could serve as an example for other activities, the future of which depends to an equal extent, but in a perhaps less directly perceptible way, on ensuring sustainable development' (CEC 1995).

General community measures affecting tourism

There are many more indirect than direct EU measures having a significant impact on how tourism is shaped and developed within Member States. This partly reflects the disparate and heterogenous nature of tourism itself, crossing into many different areas of policy.

Indirect support for tourism has come through Community programmes covering such fields as the environment, culture, consumer protection, structural funds, trans-European networks, educational and vocational training, common transport policy, policy for enterprise, research and development, establishment of the internal market and applying the rules governing competition.

Such measures may be divided into three main areas:

1 Measures affecting the tourist as a person living and travelling in a geographical space without physical or fiscal barriers. The tourist is protected by specific consumer legislation on health and safety as well as on economic and legal aspects.
2 Measures related to the economic and social environment which aim to provide common structures for economic and social activities, such as tourism, to develop within the Union. Such measures relate to various considerations such as the completion of the Single Market, competition and enterprise policy, economic and social cohesion, regional policy, trans-European networks, transport, employment, education and training.
3 Measures in the field of culture and the environment. These two aspects constitute the

broader environment within which tourism activity develops and with which tourism has a relationship of connection and mutual influence. Community measures aim to develop a sustainable relationship between tourism and architectural and cultural heritage, and the natural and built environment in Europe.

Some of the most significant general EU programmes affecting tourism are now examined.

THE SINGLE EUROPEAN ACT

The EU is based on the principle of free trade. In practice, this means ensuring that businesses in different Member States compete equally under the same conditions. The most obvious manifestation of this is the programme to create a single market in Europe.

In the mid-1980s, the Community embarked upon a programme to complete the Single Market in Europe by the end of 1992. In fact a Single Market, designed to create a favourable environment for the growth of trade between EU Member States, was one of the goals of the Community's founding treaty. It had not been truly brought to conclusion by the mid-1980's because technical, physical and fiscal barriers to trade persisted. Most of these barriers directly affected the tourism sector in one way or another.

In 1985, the EU Heads of Government committed themselves to completing the Single Market progressively by 31 December 1992. Their commitment was contained in the Single European Act of 1987. The purpose was to create an area without internal frontiers in which the free movement of goods, persons, services and capital was ensured. The result would be a single market of over 300 million people and the stimulation of economic growth by removing barriers and increasing competition.

The areas where the Single European Act has impinged on tourism are as follows:

The free movement of people and goods

EU citizens have the right to visit any Member State without restriction. A key element in the Single Market programme was the abolition of border controls between Member States in order to encourage greater mobility of people within

Europe for professional, educational and leisure purposes. The Single Market is supposed to make it as easy for EU citizens to move between Member States as it is to travel from one town to another in the same country.

The free movement of people also affects the tourism industry's workforce, since EU workers are guaranteed right of entry and residence in any Member State. This is a vital element for the tourism industry, which is a sector often requiring members of its workforce to relocate to another country. Hotels and restaurants in particular have a tradition of employing migrant labour. Furthermore, EU directives guaranteeing that a citizen's qualifications will be recognised throughout the EU mean that those working in the tourism industry should be able to pursue their profession without hindrance, whether for supplying services across borders or establishing themselves in other Member States.

The free movement of goods, another pillar of the Single Market programme, is also relevant to the tourism industry. This is particularly the case for exhibitions and trade fairs, which can involve the transportation of considerable volumes of equipment, often by road. The ability to transport such equipment without time-consuming controls at each frontier crossing represents an important advantage for exhibitors.

But while goods, services and capital have begun to move across borders with relative ease, the free movement of people has made much slower progress.

Full abolition of internal border controls has not yet been achieved, and passport checks still take place on some intra-EU passenger transport services. The reluctance of some Member States to abolish border controls (particularly the UK, Ireland and Denmark) stems from their suspicion that mushrooming illegal immigration would be the result, due to certain Member States being unable to control immigration effectively at the external borders of the EU. An effective system of controls at the EU's external frontiers would do much to re-assure Member States that passport checks are no longer necessary.

When fully implemented, the elimination of border controls at internal frontiers, and the saving in time and inconvenience which this will represent, will be an additional incentive for EU citizens to engage in intra-European tourism activities. For tourists from third countries, the same measure will do much to strengthen their perception of Europe as a single tourism destination. In practice, a Member State would not be able to refuse entry to a third country national holding a short-stay visa issued by another Member State on the sole ground that that person did not hold a visa issued by its own authorities. Residence papers for one Member State will also be recognised as equivalent to a visa (CEC 1996b).

Moreover, in general, the freedom of Europe's citizens to live and work in other Member States has been slow to develop. By 1997, EU citizens living in a country other than their own accounted for a mere 1.5 per cent of the Union's population (Guardian 1997b). Although the general workforce's lack of cross-border mobility partly represents language and cultural differences, some national governments are also to blame, for (illegally) continuing to place restrictions on the employment of foreigners.

When this is the case, the European Commission can, and does, use court action against the offending national government. An example from the tourism industry demonstrates the type of problem which arises when individual Member States fail to respect the Single Market rules. In 1994, the European Court of Justice ruled against Spain for restricting access to the profession of tourist guide and guide-interpreter to persons with Spanish nationality, and for failing to establish a procedure for examining qualifications acquired by a Community national who holds a diploma as tourist guide or guide-interpreter issued in another Member State and comparing them with those required by Spain (CEC 1996a). Similar abuses concerning the employment difficulties facing non-French ski instructors who want to teach on that country's slopes have also been taken to the European Court.

Harmonisation of Value Added Tax (VAT)

Harmonisation of VAT between Member States is regarded by EU policymakers as a key element of the Single Market vital to the creation of a 'level playing field' across Europe. But there are as yet no precise EU-wide VAT rules as such, and variations persist between Member States, affecting, for example, prices in hotels and restaurants and other tourism facilities.

Nevertheless, some progress towards harmonisation has been made. Transitional arrangements came into force on 1 January 1993, with all Member States being obliged to have a standard VAT rate of not less than 15 per cent and being permitted one or two lower, preferential, rates of not less than 5 per cent for goods and services on an agreed list. This list includes certain tourism-related products such as hotel, camp-site, and caravan accommodation, passenger transport, thermal spa services and admission to amusement parks.

The differences in the levels of VAT applied to tourism-related products by different EU Member States result in wide variations between the cost of, for example, a holiday in one country and an equivalent holiday in the neighbouring country. A 1996 survey undertaken by Deloitte Touche Tohmatsu (DTT 1996) showed that the total amount of VAT paid by a family of four on a typical two-week holiday varied from US$156 in Luxembourg to more than US$1,200 in Denmark, while in France and Italy, the amount paid in taxes was just over US$400.

Clearly, VAT represents a significant factor regarding the different terms on which European tourism companies compete in different Member States. Hotels, for example, apply VAT rates ranging from 3 per cent in Luxembourg and 5.5 per cent in France to 25 per cent in Denmark. On the other hand, France is one of the countries applying high VAT rates to restaurant meals and car hire (20.6 per cent in both cases).

The survey found that, of the 22 European states and fiscal areas studied, 14 levied reduced VAT rates on tourism products and services whereas 8 did not. A comparison of VAT rates applying to tourism and leisure services is given in Table 2.1.

In general, it is in the southern European countries, where tourism is a sector of considerable importance to the national economy, that the lowest rates of VAT for tourism-related products are found. The high proportion of countries levying a reduced rate of VAT on tourism appears to indicate that certain governments recognise that tourism is price sensitive and that a high level of VAT puts their country's tourism industry at a competitive disadvantage. It is not surprising that the tourism industries of many of those countries

Table 2.1(a) A comparison of VAT rates applying to tourism and leisure services[1] in northern European countries

	Standard VAT rate (%)	Hotel accom. (%)	Eating out (%)	Car rental (%)	Excursion (%)	Fun park (%)	Museum (%)	Theatre (%)	Night club (%)
Austria	20	**10**	**10**	20	**10**	10	10	10	20
Belgium	21	**6**	21	21	**6**	6	0	6	6
Denmark	25	25	25	25	0	25	0	25	25
Finland	22	**6**	22	22	6	6	0	6	22
Germany	15	15	15	15	15	15	0	7	15
Ireland	21	**12.5**	**12.5**	**12.5**	0	0	0	0	21
Jersey	NO VAT								
Luxembourg	15	**3**	**3**	15	**12**	3	3	3	15
Netherlands	17.5	**6**	**6**	17.5	17.5	17.5	6	17.5	17.5
Sweden	25	**12**	25	25	**12**	25	0	0	25
Switzerland	6.5	6.5	6.5	6.5	6.5	0	0	0	6.5
UK	17.5	17.5	17.5	17.5	0	17.5	17.5	17.5	17.5

Source: Deloitte & Touche

Table 2.1(b) A comparison of VAT rates applying to tourism and leisure services[1] in southern sun spots and two US cities

	Standard VAT rate (%)	Hotel accom. (%)	Eating out (%)	Car rental (%)	Excursion (%)	Fun park (%)	Museum (%)	Theatre (%)	Night club (%)
Canary Islands	4	4	4	4	4	4	4	4	4
Cyprus	8	8	8	8	8	8	8	8	8
France[2]	20.6	**5.5**	20.6	20.6	20.6	**5.5**	**5.5**	**5.5**	20.6
Greece	18	**8**	**8**	18	**8**	**8**	**8**	**8**	18
Italy	19	**10**	**10**	19	**0**	19	**10**	**10**	19
Malta	15	**10**	**10**	15	15	15	**0**	**0**	15
Portugal	17	**5**	17	17	17	**5**	**0**	**5**	17
Spain	16	**7**	**7**	16	**7**	16	**7**	16	16
Turkey	23	**15**	**15**	**15**	**15**	**15**	**15**	**8**	23
US: Orlando, Florida	6	11	6	6	6	6	6	6	6
US: LA County	8.25	14	8.25	8.25	**0**	**0**	**0**	**0**	**0**

Notes:

[1] In specific circumstances, variations in the above VAT rates may occur. For instance, a theatre or museum in some countries is exempt from VAT if state-owned. Some night clubs and theatres charge different VAT rates according to whether food and drink are consumed and some fun parks may vary in the same country according to sub-category. The VAT rate for lunch, when consumed as a take-away, can be different from that charged on the premises, and drinks consumed with a meal are often charged at a different rate than food

[2] We have included France as a southern country because, although there are tourism centres in the north, the bulk of French holidaymakers and visitors take their holidays further south

Source: Deloitte & Touche

with high levels of VAT are campaigning for a reduction. Comments from executive members of the tourism industry included in the Deloitte Touche Tohmatsu report indicate that most of them would prefer to operate in an environment where VAT rates applied to their industry are at least approximately the same across the continent. With this objective in mind, many tourist operators and National Tourist Organisations throughout Europe are actively campaigning for reduced rates for the major tourist services in their country.

Meanwhile, considerable differences persist among countries, regarding how much visitors pay in VAT. Figure 2.3 shows the VAT costs of a family holiday in a number of European destinations, with Orlando and Los Angeles included for comparative purposes.

The average amount of indirect taxes paid during a two-week family holiday in southern Europe is $293, as compared with an average of $562 in the countries of northern Europe. The high cost of a holiday in Denmark is not surprising: an overall 23.9 per cent of the total holiday cost is VAT. A holiday in neighbouring Finland, another Nordic country with similar prices, would save a family as much as US$600 in VAT costs alone.

Deloitte Touche Tohmatsu conclude that a harmonisation of VAT levels in Europe is necessary, preferably at lower levels than those being applied at the time of their survey. This is vital, they believe, in order to create a level playing field for the tourism industries in different European countries and to prevent some destinations using indirect tax levels to gain an artificial advantage over their competitors. Moreover, as many operating in the industry like to point out, a general fall in the level of VAT rates throughout Europe would help this continent remain more competitive on a worldwide scale.

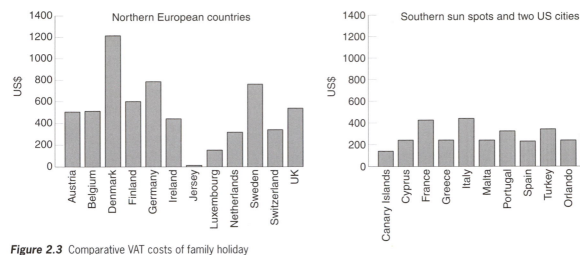

Figure 2.3 Comparative VAT costs of family holiday
Source: Deloitte & Touche

Background

Duty-free purchases are purchases exempt of excise duties. Those travelling internationally have become used to the right to buy duty-free goods for their personal use or consumption, within limits set by the authorities. This principle of selling goods tax-free has long been established in shipping, since liner passengers and crew have always been allowed to buy goods free of tax in international waters, and diplomats and military personnel have also enjoyed the same privilege. With the advent of travel by air, duty-free shopping began to assume far greater importance in Europe.

In 1947, the world's first airport duty-free shop was opened at Shannon in Ireland, when the Irish had the idea of offering transatlantic passengers on refuelling stops the opportunity to buy goods at reduced prices. At a small kiosk, passengers could purchase Irish linen, French perfumes, German porcelain and a few brand-name liqueurs.

When the tourist boom began in the 1960s, the principle spread first throughout Europe and then the rest of the world, when customs authorities agreed to grant travellers personal allowances up to clearly defined limits. The main reason behind the decision was that customs feared that, with such large numbers of people travelling for the first time,

smuggling would become an established pastime, since it was impossible to search every passenger. It was believed that travellers would be less likely to smuggle if they were permitted to bring in a reasonable quantity of goods legally.

By 1997, the duty- and tax-free retail trade had grown to be one of the most successful and dynamic industries of the post-war world. In the 50 years of its existence, it had grown from zero into a business with a worldwide turnover of US$14 billion representing sales in airports, airlines and shipping alone. US$5 billion of this total was put at risk by the decision to abolish intra-EU sales of duty-free goods.

Abolition

The abolition of duty-free shopping for those travelling within the European Union is possibly one of the most unpopular acts of the Single Market and certainly one of the most hotly debated. The controversial decision was taken unanimously by EU finance ministers at the end of 1992 and is due to take effect on 30 June 1999. If this goes ahead, it will mean the end of approximately 70 per cent of the duty-free industry in the EU. From that date, duty-free shopping in Europe will only be available to travellers entering or leaving the Community.

continued

The argument for abolition

The abolition argument is based on the fundamental idea of the Single Market, which is that EU citizens can travel within the Union as if it was a single country. The concept of duty-free, it is said, represents an anachronism in the Single Market. Moreover, the decision to abolish duty-free was taken democratically by political representatives of the Member States, who then left the Commission with the task of implementing their agreement in practice. Supporters of abolition back up their case with the following arguments:

Distortions in the market

As duty-free is only available to those travelling by air and by ferry, it is argued that this creates a distortion of competition against other modes of transport. It also causes a distortion in the market against other retailers, such as high-street stores, which are excluded from the lucrative duty-free system.

Paolo Buonadonna, writing in *The European*, quotes a Commission official as saying, 'At the moment we have a situation where only airline and ferry companies enjoy this advantage, while railway systems are excluded. Duty free works in effect like a huge state subsidy to airlines and ferries' (European 1996b).

However, in response to the subsidy argument, opponents of abolition have been quick to point out that in many EU Member States, the railways, including the high-speed trains, receive very substantial direct subsidies from governments, far outweighing the few subsidies still accorded to air transport, and the revenue this sector receives from duty-free. Regarding duty-free sales causing distortions in the market, the same commentators also argue that far greater distortions are caused by the massive traffic in duty-paid goods between EU Member States. This is best witnessed in the huge volume of goods purchased in northern French hypermarkets by day-trippers from the UK, leading to very substantial losses in duty for the British Treasury and badly affecting UK businesses selling cigarettes and alcohol.

Consumer protection

The travelling public's perception of how much money they are saving by buying duty-free may be inflated, according to certain defenders of consumers' rights. Clearly, duty-free operators are in the business to make money, not to provide a philanthropic service to travellers. According to the Brussels-based European Bureau of Consumers' Unions (BEUC), which supports the ending of the duty-free concession, travellers do not always get the best deal at airport and ferry shops. This organisation found that although prices for spirits and cigarettes were almost always cheaper than in the high street, that was not always the case with cameras, electronic gadgets and perfumes. The BEUC communications director has been quoted as saying: 'We find duty-free can often be misleading, and we don't like the way it is marketed. It is not the case that things are automatically cheaper' (European 1996a).

Consumption of valuable space

Many of those who support the abolition of duty-free do so because they believe that the space taken up by such shops, especially in airports, could be put to better use. Among these are Sir Michael Bishop, the head of the airline, British Midland, who has described duty-free as an 'anachronism'. He deplores the way in which, at many airports, travellers have to fight their way through a 'confusing clutter of camera and toy shops, food counters and sporting goods outlets to arrive at the departure gates'. Anti-duty-free campaigners believe that money and space which are at present set aside for duty-free would be better used to improve airport facilities. 'Airports are there to serve the airlines and airline passengers and are not designed to be shopping malls', is Sir Michael's conclusion (Financial Times 1997).

Airport retailing

Land-side retailing: Other supporters of duty-free abolition claim that even if abolition goes ahead, it will by no means signal the end of retailing at airports. Airports have a captive market of impulse buyers in the form of the many travellers who pass through them and who need to do something to while away the time in the limbo between check-in and departure. But 'non-travelling shoppers' – including those seeing off or welcoming friends and family or simply those visiting an airport for the fun of it – also represent a major market for airport land-side retailers.

Throughout Europe, airport shopping malls

continued

expanded considerably during the 1990s, as growing numbers of retailers expressed the wish to join in this highly profitable activity. In the UK, retail sales in airports were growing at three times the rate of high-street sales by the mid-1990s (Sunday Times 1995). Harrod's, for example, has a branch in Heathrow airport and other UK chains, such as House of Fraser, regard UK regional airports as possible showcases for local department stores.

Amsterdam's Schiphol airport's Plaza retail centre far exceeded expectations following its opening in 1995. Initial forecasts stated that 16 million visitors a year would come to shop at the airport, but in reality 25 million arrived in the first year of opening. The plaza is also used by the airport's 40,000 employees. With most Dutch shops closing at 5pm or 6pm, and the Plaza remaining open until 10pm, 365 days a year, it is not surprising that the Plaza's supermarket has the highest number of shoppers in the country (European 1996b). The largest airport currently under construction in Europe, Oslo's Gardemoen Airport, will also have substantial 'land-side' shopping facilities. Nevertheless, despite such expansion, it is undeniable that land-side sales earn far less revenue for airports than air-side retail operations.

Duty-free retail: Most duty-free retailers in airports have already diversified away from dependence on alcohol and tobacco, the two products most sensitive to duties. These traditional 'core' products have been overtaken by others, such as fragrances and other goods, where the duty paid (or saved) is far less as a proportion of the total costs of such goods.

Some brands also believe that duty-free abolition would mean more opportunities for them in airport retailing. Fashion, watch and confectionery companies are among those who could be the beneficiaries of space currently devoted to liquor and tobacco sales.

The argument against abolition

Ranged against the abolition of duty-free sales are powerful national industry lobbies, whose work is co-ordinated by the International Duty Free Confederation (IDFC) in Brussels. The European Travel Research Foundation (ETRF) provides much of the research which supports the lobbyists' arguments. The duty-free industry argues that the decision to abolish duty-free

sales was taken for purely doctrinal reasons, outweighing common sense and pragmatism. They say that the move will needlessly punish a flourishing sector, jeopardising many of the jobs which this sector provides and leading to severe consequences for EU transport infrastructure.

Supporters of duty-free trading maintain that it brings benefits not only to passengers but to the whole travel industry. They argue that the abolition of duty-free will have a detrimental effect on the provision of transport services and in turn the economies of several Member States and that by its very nature it will inhibit the movement of goods and people within specific parts of the EU.

A series of reports commissioned by the ETRF highlight the negative impacts which abolition could have on the following sectors of the travel industry.

Low-cost scheduled airlines

Liberalisation in Europe has opened the skies to a new generation of low-cost airlines, which are successfully competing with their more established conventional-cost airlines, whose costs tend to be 50–60 per cent higher (see Chapter 3). The report commissioned by the ETRF suggested that the financial impact of the loss of duty-free sales on low-cost airlines would entail:

- the loss of direct profits from duty-free sales;
- the loss or reduction of concessions from airports on landing and other aeronautical charges;
- landing charge costs would also rise due to the likely need for airports to make overall increases in charges as well as withdrawing discounts;
- airlines pay staff commission of duty-free sales, so withdrawal would mean that staff would need to be recompensed for the loss of that part of their income.

In money terms, it is claimed, this represents a direct cost/loss of revenue of up to around US$15 per passenger.

The study concluded that:

1 The loss of duty-free trading would result in 20 per cent of routes which are eligible for low-cost entry not having low-cost services by 2003, whereas with duty-free trading it is forecast that low-cost operations will have expanded to cover all such eligible routes by that time;

continued

2 Low-cost airline passenger traffic would be 25 million passengers per year by 2005 with duty-free, but only 20 million passengers per year without it;
3 Total air traffic on these routes would be 82 million passengers in 2005 with duty-free, but only 78 million passengers without it.

In addition, the report estimates that with the reductions in passengers and consequently the number of aircraft flying, the total loss of jobs in this sector caused by the abolition of duty-free sales would be 2,830 (ETRF 1997a).

Charter airlines

Total gross duty and tax-free sales on board intra-EU charter flights amounted to ECU 300 million in 1995. The impact on charter operators of losing the right to sell duty-free goods would be most concentrated in UK, German and Scandinavian originating passenger markets, which together account for nearly 90 per cent of total sales. The effect of abolition would be felt most acutely on the Scandinavian markets, where the average gross duty and tax-free sales per charter passenger is almost ECU 60. The net revenue is ECU 30 per passenger.

According to the report, user charges at different airports could increase, costing EU charter airlines an extra ECU 200 million per year and representing an average increase of almost ECU 8 per round trip passenger. Consequently, it is estimated that EU charter seat costs would rise by between ECU 8 and ECU 30 per seat, with an average of ECU 12 per seat. Charter airlines would be likely to pass on any such cost increases to tour operators, who would in turn pass them on to consumers over a two to three-year period. This would raise EU holiday prices by an average of over ECU 14 per passenger (including travel agents' sales commission).

The report estimates that such an increase in holiday prices would depress the underlying growth in intra-EU charter markets by nearly 3 per cent, to an annual rate of just 1 per cent in the years leading up to 2000. Such price increases could also have a significant effect on passenger choices, as they would give an automatic price advantage to non-EU destinations such as Turkey and North Africa.

Finally, the report estimates that up to 1,000 direct jobs would be lost within EU charter airlines, coming mainly from cabin attendants, but also from other airline staff involved in duty and tax-free operations (ETRF 1997a).

The ferry industry

On the North Sea ferry routes, tax and duty free sales on average account for almost 20 per cent of total ferry operator revenues. In the Western Channel, they contribute 30 per cent, and in the Dover Straits corridor, about 45 per cent (ETFR 1997b). Moreover, the contribution of such sales to profitability is much higher than the contribution to operator revenues. By the mid-1990s, many routes were said to be incurring large losses in carrying passengers and cars, which were wholly, or in many cases only partially, compensated for by the profits from tax and duty free sales.

Given the considerable importance of tax and duty free sales for ferry operators throughout the EU, it is claimed that it is particularly the island nations and those Member States with extensive coastlines that are likely to feel the most significant effects of the removal of such sales. Two initial responses to abolition may be envisaged: a certain proportion of ferry passengers will no longer travel, because their primary motive was to purchase duty and tax-free goods. More importantly, ferry operators will be forced to take measures to compensate for their loss of income from duty-free sales.

The chain of responses which could be set in motion by the abolition of duty and tax-free allowances is presented in Figure 2.4.

A review of several research studies into the impact of abolition on Europe's ferry services provides the following conclusions:

- Ticket prices rises will vary by market, according to particular conditions. The minimum rise is likely to be 10 per cent. On some Scandinavian routes, it is believed that price rises will be well in excess of 100 per cent. An average across Europe of 30 per cent would seem a reasonable assumption.
- 19 routes will be lost in the UK, Irish and German industry. Ferry capacity will be halved in Finland. As many as 25–30 of the current ferry routes around northern Europe could close.

continued

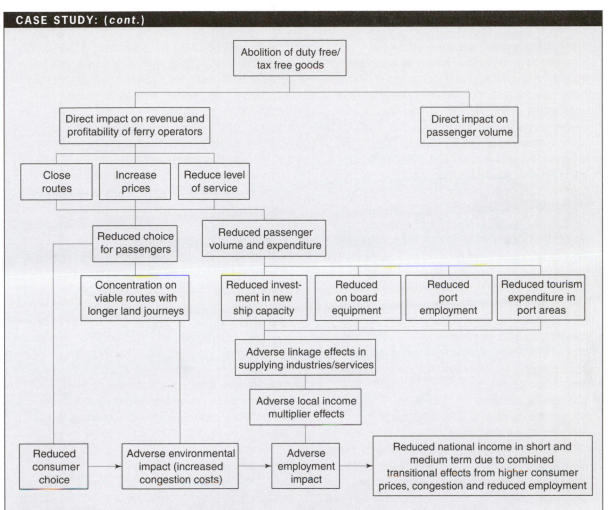

Figure 2.4 Impact of abolition of intra-EU duty and tax-free allowances upon the European ferry industry
Source: 'Impact of the abolition of intra-EU duty and tax-free allowances upon the European ferry industry', a report for the European Travel Research Foundation, by MDS Transmodal, Chester, June 1997

- A total of 18,000–20,000 directly related jobs will be lost following abolition.
- A further 5,000–7,500 jobs will be lost through linkages into the local region.
- Associated wider job losses particularly related to tourism have been estimated at 24,000 (excluding Finland and Denmark for which no estimates were produced). Estimating these at 2,000–3,000 would bring the total to 26,000–27,000.
- The above suggests that total job losses of 50,000 or more will result from the abolition of duty and tax free allowances (ETRF 1997b).

The decision to eliminate duty-free shopping within the EU has become another significant bone of contention on the bitterly contested cross-Channel market (see Chapter 4). With ticket prices and revenues depressed as a result of the competitive conditions in this market, the income and high profitability of duty-free and tax-free sales have become an increasingly dominant component of viability for both the ferry industry and Eurotunnel.

The cross-Channel ferry lines, and particularly those operating on the Dover Straits clearly have every reason to oppose the abolition of duty-free in

continued

1999. Already suffering from the impact of competition from the Channel Tunnel services, they regard the planned end to duty-free as a further blow. Passenger surveys have indicated that if abolition goes ahead as planned, over 20 per cent of passengers on the Dover Straits routes would not make the journey at all (ETRF 1997b). This figure reflects the relative importance of the day-trip market, for whom duty-free purchases represent a significant motivating factor in crossing the Channel for the day.

Eurotunnel, on the other hand, argues that duty-free should have been abolished at the time of the introduction of the Single Market on 1 January 1993, and opposes the Council's decision to postpone it until 1999. The Channel Tunnel operator claims that duty-free distorts the cross-Channel market by giving the ferry operators an unfair subsidy. This is because duty-free sales are not permitted on Eurotunnel's shuttle trains or on the Eurostar through trains – only at Eurotunnel's terminals at either end of the Channel Tunnel. It has proved to be highly profitable there, although the company still believes that it is at a competitive disadvantage from the continuing existence of duty-free sales.

If, as those lobbying on behalf of the ferry industry predict, abolition leads to a halving of the number of cross-Channel ferry routes, it is estimated that about 6 million passengers will switch routes to the surviving ferry ports and that the ferry industry will lose approximately 1.5 million crossings per year to the Channel Tunnel (ETRF 1997b).

Airports

The anti-abolition lobby also emphasise the extent to which airport economics depends on duty-free sales. The cost of retail rental space in airports is usually based on a percentage of sales made, which often means a lucrative source of revenue for airport operators. For example, income from retailers accounts for almost 50 per cent of the income of BAA, the former British Airports Authority.

Overall, around 75 per cent of all duty-free sales is intra-EU, and the loss of such sales will be a major blow, in particular to regional airports. Regional airports in particular are heavily reliant on this form of income, and since a greater proportion of their traffic is inter-EU, they stand to be more adversely affected by abolition than the major hubs serving destinations outside the EU as well as destinations in other Member States. Such airports, the anti-abolition lobby maintains, stand to lose high proportions of their revenues from duty-free, ranging from between 80 to 100 per cent in some cases.

As a result, landing charges, the other major source of revenue for airports, would most likely be raised to compensate for the loss of income.

Distortions in travel patterns

Since duty-free shopping will continue to be available to those travelling to non-EU destinations, it is argued that the ruling will create distortions in travel patterns within Europe. The argument goes that the continuing possibility of being able to buy duty-free goods on, for example, a flight to Berne or on a ferry trip to Oslo will give such countries an unfair advantage over Member States. Southern European states such as Greece and Spain are said to be vulnerable, since other Mediterranean destinations such as Morocco and Turkey will become relatively cheaper.

The reality of the internal market

Many of the opponents of abolition argue that the decision to end duty-free was taken on a theoretical view of the internal market. It had been presumed that rapid integration and progress towards the internal market would prove intra-EU duty and tax-free sales to be an aberration. However, the reality of the internal market was quite different. Clearly, the internal market had not evolved in the way expected back in 1992, nor at the pace intended.

By 1997, there were still wildly divergent excise duty rates being applied in the EU and no signs of any imminent move towards convergence. With 15 different tax regimes in existence, the idea of an EU in which all goods move freely, subject to the same duties and VAT rates, was still a long way from being realised. Since fiscal harmonisation still seemed a long way off, it was argued by opponents of abolition, there was no reason why duty-free could not continue to exist in such an environment.

continued

Decision in 1998?

In 1996, the European Commission reaffirmed its view that duty-free sales for intra-EU travellers should end mid-1999, following the publication of a report on this issue by the EU Commissioner for the Internal Market and Taxation. This report was commissioned by the EU finance ministers in 1992, at the time of the decision to abolish duty-free between their countries. It criticised travel operators and the duty-free trade for failing to comply with existing regulations on duty-free sales regarding the limits in force. The Commission subsequently accepted, however, that its assessment was out of date and that vendor control by operators was working satisfactorily.

Arguments for retaining duty-free tend to be stronger in countries on the periphery of the EU, and consequently, in 1997, at a meeting of Member States' transport ministers, Finland called upon the European Commission to initiate a study into the economic and social impact of the abolition of duty-free sales on intra-European ferry routes. Although the request was supported by ten transport ministers in all, it was turned down by the transport commissioner on the basis that this was a matter for finance ministers.

But the final decision on whether or not duty-free will continue within the EU will have to be taken by the EU Council of Finance Ministers (ECOFN). The views of Finance Ministers will therefore be crucial in resolving this issue.

The full implementation of the Single Market has taken much longer than many expected it to. After the expectations raised by the publicity surrounding '1992', many citizens, businessmen and women, as well as European politicans and administrators have become frustrated with the programme's slow progress towards full implementation. But EU administrators have stated that 'The Single Market in Europe is a 'process' not a finite number of actions tied to a deadline' (CEC 1996b).

In 1997, the EU's Single Market Commissioner promised to put forward a series of proposals aimed at truly completing the Single Market by the year 2000. He also called for the Commission to be given greater powers to enforce Single Market legislation, claiming that under existing procedures it could take years for the Commission to obtain court judgments against Member States that fail to respect the Single Market rules (Guardian 1996b).

EU CONSUMER PROTECTION POLICY

The EU recognises the principle that actions to complete the Single Market should not be at the expense of consumers. Hence the need to develop a more comprehensive transnational consumer protection policy. An important aim of Community action, therefore, is to ensure that the rights of the consumer (and access to redress) are not compromised by the fact that the service provider is in a different Member State.

Many tourism products, such as holidays and tours, are located at a distance from the point of purchase, very often in another country. Generally, these have to be paid for in advance. Thus, the consumer relies heavily on sales information provided about the product and on the integrity of the tourism operator supplying the product. Similarly, once at a tourism destination, tourists may be unfamiliar with the language and local selling practices, or may be unaware of their rights. This leaves scope for the consumer to be misled about the product on offer or, for example, for the operator to impose surcharges or unannounced cancellations.

The EU is well placed to legislate for this type of problem. Action at EU level can overcome the complexities which arise when consumers are confronted with problems such as differing conditions applying to contracts, the difficulty of understanding foreign legal systems, and the absence of legal aid in other states.

Tourism has therefore featured prominently in the EU's Consumer Policy, with several important items of EU legislation being aimed at improving the legal position of the consumer of tourist products. Such legislation has had a significant impact on the legal context within which tourism businesses operate in EU member states. There have been a number of tourism-specific directives of which the following are among the most important.

The 1990 directive on package travel

This sets minimum standards governing the selling and purchase of package holidays and package tours. It enables operators established in one Member State to offer services in another and consumers to benefit from comparable conditions when buying a package in a Member State. It requires that:

- detailed and comprehensive information must be supplied before departure;
- the holidaymaker should be protected by a contract which may not be changed unless this eventuality is made clear prior to signing;
- the operator guarantees not to leave tourists stranded at the holiday destination even in the event of bankruptcy;
- compensation must be made available in certain circumstances where the package has not met the operators' claims.

Some Member States have been slow to transpose this directive into their national legislation, even though the deadline for implementation was 31 December 1992. The main problem with implementation has been associated with the need to create guarantee schemes to protect consumers' interests. In the UK, the regulations have been accommodated by the outgoing travel industry without much difficulty, since there already was in place a regime (in the form of the Association of British Travel Agents' 1990 revised Code of Conduct) which incorporated much of what the regulations required. But, as Grant (1996) points out, the way in which the directive was implemented in the UK meant that the same regulations have not been enforced against UK *domestic* tourism operators.

The 1994 timeshare directive

Given the relatively recent arrival of timesharing – the buying of the right to own properties on a timeshare basis – national legislation on this activity is sparse. Accordingly, the EU timeshare directive aims to ensure harmonised European rules from the outset. The rules would protect the purchaser of timeshares from the potential abuse of power and the aggressive sales techniques used by some timeshare vendors.

Under this directive, consumers must be provided with the necessary information before signing a contract and must be allowed a set period of reflection and possible withdrawal from the contract and any associated credit agreements. During the so-called 'cooling off' period, no advance payments may be made. Contracts must be made available in the language of the Member State where the purchaser lives or is a national.

ECONOMIC AND MONETARY UNION: A SINGLE EUROPEAN CURRENCY

A key element of the Treaty on European Union was the decision to work towards economic and monetary union among the EU Member States. Economic and monetary union (EMU), if successful, would certainly have important macro-economic effects benefiting all sectors. But a clear, tangible advantage for transnational businesses would be the introduction of a single currency.

It is generally held that the substantial pan-European and international dimensions of much of the tourism industry would be greatly facilitated by a single currency. The Brussels-based European Association of Travel Agents and Tour Operators believes that the industry will benefit from the EMU, as the Euro will remove exchange rate volatility and should lead to sharper pricing through savings from the elimination of the exchange risk margin, which is usually added to holiday prices to take into account the possibility of exchange-rate fluctuations. Pricing policy would be simplified and even production of price lists, brochures and other promotional material would be made more straightforward.

However, the European Association of Travel Agents and Tour Operators anticipates that the European travel trade will also incur a one-off cost for changeover effects in technology and finance areas, amounting to approximately 1.8–3 per cent of turnover – a significant sum in what is in reality a low margin industry (Grieve 1997).

Many UK inbound tour operators are of the opinion that if the UK does not join the EMU in the first wave, then European tour operators will have to continue to price in the exchange risk margin on their British holidays, thus putting that country at a competitive disadvantage (Grieve 1997).

From the point of view of the tourist, especially those from other continents on touring holidays through Europe, the advantages seem evident. Jefferson (1992), for example, reports from British Tourist Authority research in Japan, which found that the difference in currency from one country to another causes inconvenience and confusion for visitors from that country. Another issue is the cost of changing money from one currency to another several times during one trip. The elimination of these costs should boost spending on tourism.

THE STRUCTURAL FUNDS

Strengthening the economic and social cohesion of the regions of the Community has been a major objective of the European Union since the 1970s, when a Common Regional Policy was first implemented and financed. The rationale behind this policy is the conviction that this type of cohesion will only be achieved where there is a better spread of economic activities and prosperity across the regions of Europe. At the end of the 1990s, the regions of the Community still varied enormously in respect of economic indicators such as average income, levels of unemployment and gross domestic product per employee. Figure 2.5 shows the extent of the economic disparities between European regions.

Subsidies distributed from the EU's Structural Funds provide the main financial support in the Community for the development of the less prosperous regions and the training and employment of Europeans at risk of exclusion from the labour market. No specific sectors are targeted in these aims, but tourism figures prominently in practice because of its potential for economic growth and employment.

Tourism development is one of the means selected for advancing the objectives of the Structural Funds in virtually all EU regions. As a result, by far the most substantial EU financial aid made available for tourism comes through the Structural Funds.

The Community has three Structural Funds:

1. The European Regional Development Fund (ERDF), which finances investment and infrastructure for regional development;
2. The European Social Fund (ESF), which finances human resources development;
3. The European Agricultural Guidance and Guarantee Fund (EAGGF), which supports rural development.

The Structural Funds are assigned according to a system of seven objectives. Some are regionally determined and others are 'horizontal' in character, meaning that they concern issues which are present across the entire Community. The former type of objectives target regions experiencing some kind of difficulty: Objectives 1, 2, 5(b) and 6:

- *Objective 1*: Promoting the development of regions whose development is lagging behind.
- *Objective 2*: Regenerating the regions or parts of regions seriously affected by industrial decline.
- *Objective 5(b)*: Developing economic activities in rural areas, in order to create jobs providing an alternative to employment in agriculture.
- *Objective 6*: Giving Objective 1 treatment to certain underpopulated regions in Sweden and Finland

Figure 2.6 shows those regions of Europe which are covered by Objectives 1, 2 and 5(b). Objective 6 regions are concentrated mainly in the region of the Arctic Circle.

The horizontal objectives are: Objective 3 (combating long-term unemployment and improving employment opportunities for young people), Objective 4 (adapting the workforce to industrial changes) and Objective 5(a) (adjusting agriculture, forestry and fishing).

Some 70 per cent of all Structural Funds go to the Objective 1 regions, amounting to aid totalling ECU 96,346 million for the period 1994–99 (CEC 1996b). How much of this can be expected to be spent on assistance for the tourism sector in the less-developed regions of EU Member States? In the funding period 1989–93, the amount of Objective 1 aid for the tourism sector was estimated by the Commission itself to be at least 5.6 per cent (ibid.). In the same period, tourism

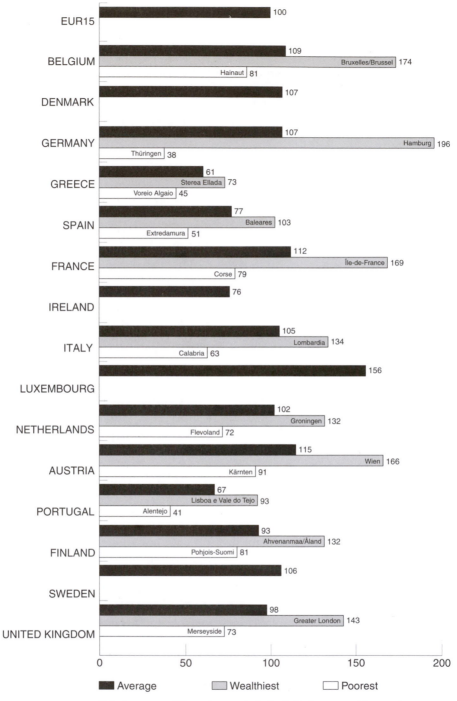

Figure 2.5 Gross domestic product per head of population in wealthiest and poorest regions of each EU Member State
Source: Eurostat, 1995

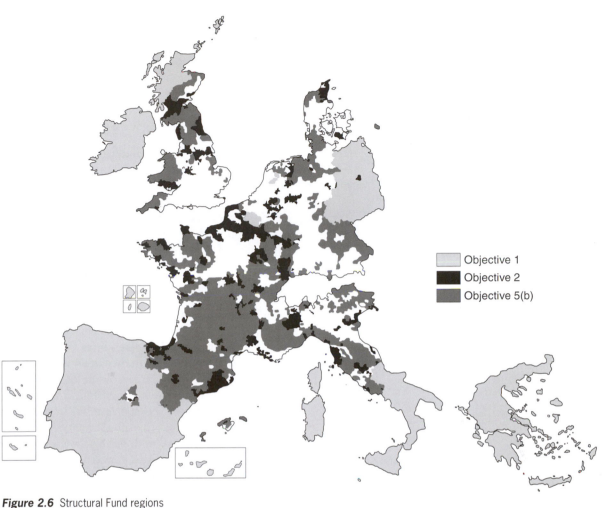

Figure 2.6 Structural Fund regions
Source: CEC

development also benefited from the Community support frameworks under Objectives 2 and 5b, through for example aid for the development of rural tourism.

The Structural Funds are used in three main ways to enable the underdeveloped regions to advance through their tourism industries:

- Direct investment in tourism facilities: co-financing projects such as marinas, conference centres, hotels.
- Investment in infrastructure directly linked to the tourism sector: co-financing transport, environmental and communications projects which improve the accessibility of undeveloped regions.

- Investment in projects to upgrade the cultural and historical resources of less developed regions, making them more attractive to potential visitors.

Of the three Structural Funds, the European Regional Development Fund, created in 1975 with the aim of contributing to the correction of regional imbalances within the Community, is the major source of subsidies for tourism development.

Table 2.2 shows ERDF contributions to tourism for Objectives 1 and 2 regions.

Of the total ERDF allocation to Objective 1 regions (5.6 billion ECUs approximately), 5.6 per cent can be clearly identified as contributing to tourism development. In Objective 2 regions (2.2

Table 2.2 Structural funds contributions to tourism based on Community Support Frameworks and the Single Programming documents for Objectives 1 and 2 regions (millions of ECUs at 1994 prices)

	Objective 1 (1994–99) ERDF	Objective 2 (1994–96) ERDF
Belgium	32	10
Denmark	not eligible	9
Germany	0	15
Greece	683	not eligible
Spain	538	0
France	99	147
Ireland	354	not eligible
Italy	775	66
Luxembourg	not eligible	0
Netherlands	4	34
Portugal	571	not eligible
United Kingdom	118	242
Total	3,174	523

Source: CEC

billion ECUs approximately for ERDF), 9.7 per cent will contribute to tourism. (CEC 1996a).

Aid provided by the Structural Funds usually reaches the user in the form of national, multi regional or regional schemes managed by Member State authorities. Lowyck and Wanhill (1992) maintain that one impact of this system of allocating of the Structural Funds is the growth in importance of the regional tourism structures in some Member States. Akehurst et al. remark upon this phenomenon in their discussion of tourism development funding:

> In some countries, there are close links with the EC's financial structure – Ireland, Portugal, Italy and Spain derive a large part of the financial assistance they provide to tourism from the EU's ERDF, and the regional structure of their tourism policy is either already organised according to EC regions or is in the process of being developed to such regions. There is a large degree of overlap between tourism policy and regional policy in the poorer EC Member States. Organisationally, there seems to be a shift to regional level . . . with the national structure becoming less important (e.g. in Spain, Portugal and Italy). It appears that generally, the EC and individual EC regions are gaining in importance at the expense of national organisations. (Akehurst et al. 1993).

THE EUROPEAN INVESTMENT BANK

As well as the subsidies available from the Structural Funds, loans to help reduce regional disparities within the EU are made by the European Investment Bank (EIB), the world's largest multilateral lender and borrower. Through the provision of loans for investments which promote balanced regional development in Europe, the EIB assists tourism in various ways. EIB assistance is mainly given in the form of loans/lines of credit to small or medium-sized hotels in regions which are in receipt of Community Structural Funds. The hotel projects are concerned to a great extent with business tourism, which throughout the year supports the economic expansion of regions less immediately attractive to tourists. A particularly large volume of investment of this kind has been made, since 1990, in the eastern regions of Germany, where such establishments were very rare. Most of the other investments cover very diverse establishments and serve to reinforce the tourist appeal of the regions concerned: camp sites, ski lifts, leisure areas and, particularly in Italy, buildings and sites of a cultural or architectural interest which warrant visits by tourists.

In addition to the regions receiving regional development aid, the EIB has financed a number of exceptionally large-scale projects contributing to the Community's tourist appeal, including infrastructure related to the construction of the Disneyland Paris theme park, and has advanced loans for investment in Europe's road and rail developments (see Chapter 4).

OTHER COMMUNITY FUNDING PROGRAMMES

Apart from the mainstream funding available to tourism through the Structural Funds, there are almost 60 other EU programmes and actions which may provide financial support to the tourism sector, even though they do not target the tourism sector specifically. Three of the most important of these are Rechtar, PHARE and Interreg.

Rechtar

Rechtar is a Community initiative providing financial assistance for the economic conversion of coal-mining areas. Tourism-related measures eligible for aid under this programme include subsidies for the promotion of tourism, especially in the area of industrial heritage, and environmental improvements in areas damaged by mining. EU funding for this initiative for the period 1994–97 was ECU 400 million.

PHARE

In Eastern Europe, the process of modernisation and the transition to market economies based on free enterprise and private initiative have created an extensive need for advice, foreign investment, technical expertise, training and exchanges.

Established in 1989, PHARE is an EU financial aid programme for the process of economic and social reform in Central and Eastern Europe. It provides non-reimbursable grants for programmes in key fields such as privatisation, agriculture, education and training. These are meant to finance the recipient states' own efforts to transform their economies. The funds are not dictated by the EU but are made in response to the restructuring priorities selected by the recipients. Potential applications to tourism include the financing of tourism-related studies, tourism action plans, policy advice, technical expertise and training. As the name suggests – Poland and Hungary Action for Restructuring of the Economy – PHARE was originally set up to provide assistance to just those two countries. But it has since been extended to include Bulgaria, the Czech Republic, Slovakia, the former Yugoslavia, Romania, the Baltic States, Albania and Macedonia.

Only Poland has a substantial tourism-related project in action, using PHARE funding. But, even there, Travis points out that tourism is a relatively lightly funded field, as compared to agriculture or manufacturing industry. He notes that Poland's PHARE allocation was about 200 million ECU and of that, approximately 2.5 per cent was allocated to the Tourism Development Programme (Travis 1994).

One explanation for this is suggested by the EIU who point out that 'although several countries offer potentially interesting (tourism) development opportunities, the selection of specifically defined tourism projects by receipient governments has been muted. It appears that most countries have so far considered tourism an inappropriate sector for their restructuring programme' (EIU 1993).

Interreg

Interreg is an initiative to encourage cross-frontier cooperation in the development of border regions within the Community. A broad range of cross-border measures is listed as being eligible for funding under the Interreg initiative, and these include tourism. The total Interreg budget for 1994–99 is ECU 2,900 million, of which three-quarters is earmarked for Objective 1 regions.

An example of Interreg funds being used for tourism purposes is in the marketing of the Region Transmanche, a joint campaign between the local authorities which include the Channel Tunnel terminals: Kent County Council and the Comité Régional de Tourisme, Nord-Pas de Calais in France.

EU ENVIRONMENTAL LEGISLATION

The environment has clearly risen up the list of priority policy areas within the EU in recent years, and the consequences have been felt across almost all sectors, including tourism. The Fifth Environmental Action Programme, established in 1992, selected tourism as a priority area for EU action, with the following aims:

- improving the quality of the planning, development and management of mass tourism, particularly in coastal and mountainous areas;
- encouraging the development of sustainable forms of tourism;
- attempting to raise tourists' awareness of environmental issues and persuading tourists to modify their behaviour accordingly.

To achieve these objectives, a number of initiatives have been introduced, including:

- asking national governments to prepare inventories of tourism resources and use these to shape new policies on tourism planning and development;

- encouraging cooperation between practitioners working in different regions which share similar problems, to share good practice;
- encouraging the establishment of information networks where hotels, restaurants and transport operators can share ideas on how to make tourism more environmentally friendly;
- funding research on sustainable tourism (Swarbrooke 1997).

A number of other environment-related EU measures have, however, significantly more immediate consequences for tourism:

The Blue Flag scheme

In 1987, the European Blue Flag scheme for recreational beaches was launched as one of the EU's measures dealing with the quality of the natural environment. It is based on 27 criteria and uses as its starting point the Bathing Water Directive criteria of 1977. This Directive set standards for officially designated bathing beaches. To meet these standards fully, the beach must be tested fortnightly during the bathing season and must satisfy 19 criteria. The most important of these criteria are bacteriological. In addition, the flag is awarded for the quality of beach management.

Blue Flag status is almost certainly commercially valuable, since the image of cleanliness is in tune with the spirit of the times. Whether the water standards are too stringent in terms of health risk is an issue on which scientists are still unable to agree

In 1994, the Commission proposed the revision of the Bathing Water Directive in order to better adapt it to contemporary technical and scientific knowledge and apply the principle of subsidiarity.

Environmental Impact Assessment (EIA)

The EIA Directive of 1985 affects the development of infrastructure in many tourism areas, introducing a set of criteria for the assessment of the impact on the environment of various large-scale tourism-related projects. Environmental assessment, in the form of a highly systematic quantitative and qualitative review, is now mandatory in all EU countries for proposed large developments.

Large-scale tourism-related projects (such as airports, motorways and ports) are now subject to an environmental assessment before being granted final approval (Davidson and Maitland 1997).

In April 1994, the Commission put forward a proposal for a Council Directive amending the 1985 Directive. According to this proposal, tourism and leisure have been considered as areas of application of the new Directive, focusing on:

- ski-runs, bob sleigh tracks, ski-lifts and artificial snow installations;
- golf courses and associated developments;
- marinas;
- holiday villages, hotel complexes and associated developments;
- camp-sites and caravan sites;
- leisure centres.

Other measures

The EU is also involved in conventions concerned with the environment in regions affected by tourism, for example, on the protection of the Alps and the Barcelona Convention on the protection of the Mediterranean.

EMPLOYMENT AND SOCIAL AFFAIRS

Community measures already implemented or being developed in the field of employment or social policy have a bearing on the millions of Europeans working in the tourism sector. The principles are set out in the Community charter of fundamental social rights of workers, adopted by all Member States. Through the charter, the EU sets the guidelines for measures to deal, notably, with the labour market and improvements in working conditions. The EU has taken a number of initiatives in the field of workers' rights which have implications for all industries including tourism. These include:

- enhanced maternity leave provision;
- more rights for young employees and part-time workers, both important groups within the tourism industry;
- the introduction of workers' councils;
- action on maximum weekly working hours.

Some EU directives, for example the one

dealing with maximum working hours, exclude certain groups of workers in the tourism industry (in this case, those in the transport sector).

While being generally welcomed by workers' representatives, many operators in the tourism industry maintain that the implementation of EU directives in the areas of employment and social affairs, as well as health and safety, imposes unacceptably high burdens on tourism businesses, many of which are SMEs. They claim that EU legislation is often framed with large integrated production plants in mind and that the different requirements of service industries are not sufficiently taken into account. For example, the British Hospitality Association (BHA) has argued that 'as a labour-intensive service sector, the hospitality industry is uniquely placed to create numerous jobs when the regulatory burden is low, but also to have to shed them when regulation rises and inhibits continued employment' (Voice 1995). In particular, the BHA claims that the seven days a week, 365 days a year and often cyclical work pattern necessitated by the nature of the tourism industry is incompatible with the EU's Working Time Directive.

The BHA gives as another illustration of its case against EU legislation the maternity leave rules, which it describes as potentially disastrous for small tourism-related businesses:

> Employers are faced with the additional cost of engaging someone on a temporary basis to cover for the pregnant employee while she is on maternity leave. There is often considerable difficulty caused by having to leave a position open in an industry with cyclical demand. (Voice 1995)

Similarly, many claim that in an industry where most businesses have proportionally large numbers of 'casual' staff and where many small companies operate on a seasonal basis only, the EU-imposed obligations to pay sick pay and maternity benefit to all employees may create an atmosphere of nervousness among employers and a reluctance to take on 'casual' staff – even when these are actually needed in the short term and even when many workers are only looking for this kind of work, e.g. students wishing to supplement their grants, mothers wanting to fit in a few hours'

work around their children's school day and school holidays.

In 1995, this kind of concern over the impact of cumbersome or bureaucratic legislation on business competitiveness spurred the European Commission to look at means of simplifying legislation, but many in the tourism industry regretted that the emphasis of the exercise was on the simplification of existing rules rather than less regulation as such.

TRANSPORT POLICY

Clearly, with the strong links which exist between tourism and transport, the EU's transport policy has a considerable potential impact on tourism within the EU. Indeed, the links with tourism are so strong that many believe that there is a case for combining these two functions within a single Directorate General. DGVII is responsible for transport policy.

Development of the Common Transport Policy

Whereas tourism was not specifically mentioned in the Treaty of Rome, the establishing of a Common Transport Policy was one of the Community's initial objectives, as provided for through Articles 3e, 74 and 75 of the same treaty. But, as Forbes (1994) points out, this objective reflected more the belief in the need for the efficient operation of freight transport in a free trade area, than any tourism-related transport considerations at that time.

The road towards a Common Transport Policy has been long and extremely turbulent, and such a policy is still incomplete. In 1961, the Commission submitted a memorandum to the Council outlining the principles of a Common Transport Policy, and this was followed in 1962 by an action programme, which had the following principal objectives:

- The removal of any obstacles which transport might represent on the establishment of the general common market.
- The creation of healthy competition of the widest possible scope.
- The development of a transport system which

would prove a powerful stimulant for the growth of trade and widening of markets.

The suggestions for achieving the above objectives, like the objectives themselves, apply to passenger transport, as well as to freight. But progress towards a Common Transport Policy was very slow.

Despicht (1964) identified three main reasons for this lack of progress:

- The Member States all saw their transport systems as special cases requiring exceptional treatment.
- The transport sector was characterised by a high level of public sector intervention (regulatory, ownership of transport operations and responsibility for infrastructure).
- Transport operators varied widely in their structure and regulatory environment, from state monopolies with no internal competition (the railways) to small road and inland waterway operators.

Within Europe, the transport policies developed by individual national governments have, in the past, been subject to changing attitudes, outlook and political ideology. Consequently, national transport systems have been characterised by a range of political approaches spanning the spectrum from a total free-market orientation to those entirely based on publicly planned resource allocation.

Those countries which support extensive state involvement in transport base their argument on market failure, a classical economic theory which recognises that in a free-market economy, supply imperfections result. They maintain that state intervention in the market economy is required in order to rectify supply imperfections on the grounds of social efficiency (to avoid inequalities in accessibility) and environmental considerations. For example, in situations where inadequate levels of demand exist to support an economically viable service (e.g. rail services in rural areas), state subsidies may be required to provide access for communities on social grounds.

By way of contrast, the market-orientated view has been pursued by some countries on the premise that centralised state control of transport produces an unwieldy and often unresponsive service requiring unnessarily high subsidies. According to this school of thought, introducing a greater degree of private-sector involvement and competition should result in improved services and less need for public subsidies (Page 1993). The emerging EU Common Transport Policy tends to veer towards this view, while not entirely embracing a pure free-market approach:

> the Commission believes that the concession system, where services are subject to open tender but within a defined operational framework, is well suited to providing an environment which gives incentives to operators to raise standards while safeguarding system integration which is particularly important in relation to urban and regional transport' (CEC 1996c).

Nevertheless, due to the wide differences of approach to the transport sector at national levels in EU Member States, by 1983, the only measures related to the CTP which were already in place related to less controversial issues such as harmonisation of matters including road signs and vehicle type approval, and the introduction of tachographs and drivers' hours regulations. Clearly, most of these related primarily to freight transport as opposed to tourism. Forbes (1994) remarks that by this time, the Commission had adopted a pragmatic approach to transport, no longer insisting on policy adhering dogmatically to the letter of the Treaty of Rome, but allowing a certain amount of flexibility.

Progress continued to be slow until 1985, when the Court of Justice partially upheld an action brought against the Council of Ministers by the European Parliament. The Court ruled that the Council had infringed the Treaty's rules on the freedom to provide international transport services.

This ruling, combined with the Community's commitment to the goal of a Single Market by the end of 1992, finally established a political momentum which delivered progress across a broad front.

Two of the most important areas of EU impact on transport are the liberalising of the transport of goods and passengers and the plans for a trans-European transport network. An overview of trans-European networks is given below. Chapters

3 and 4 examine how liberalisation has affected surface and air transport respectively.

Trans European Networks

'Transforming a patchwork into a network'

Those responsible for the formulation of EU transport policy point out that European transport networks were created at a time when European nations did not look far beyond their frontiers, but geared their planning to national transport requirements. This, they say, resulted in a European patchwork transport system of independent national infrastructure developments, instead of an integrated and rational Europe-wide transport network. On the continental scale, it is claimed, this has led to bottlenecks and congestion, leading to wasted resources and lost opportunities, not least for Europe's tourism industry.

Beginning in the 1970s, many international transport routes were established, but as the twentieth century drew to its close, many major rail, road and waterway links were still missing – particularly those connecting the newer Member States on the periphery of the Union and Central and Eastern European countries, many of which were preparing for accession.

In rail transport, there were still different operating and signalling systems; at some frontiers, trains could only continue after laborious shunting operations and a change of locomotives. Air transport in Europe was operating at the limits of its capacity because of insufficiently developed airports and because it was managed by 52 different air traffic control centres and 70 computer programming languages. And the road network included a number of motorways which came to an abrupt end at national frontiers.

In short, Europe's transport networks fell well short of the kind of integrated network required for a Europe without frontiers.

Moreover, EU policymakers predicted that by the year 2000, goods and passenger traffic within the Union would have doubled from its 1975 level, meaning more congestion, if no action was taken to avoid this (EC 1994).

The solution proposed by the EU is a network of rapid transport axes and corridors linking the national networks of Member States to form trans-European networks. It is claimed that these will:

- provide business with rapid and reliable transport services at competitive prices;
- give travellers a greater choice of rapid, punctual and safe travel within the Union;
- link major cities with high-speed trains; and
- reduce congestion and pollution by partly switching from road transport to rail, short ferry crossings, inland waterways and combined transport systems (EC/EIB 1996).

EU transport policymakers see such networks in terms of their strategic importance for Europe's future. They believe that just as the transcontinental railways of the 19th century were instrumental in uniting the United States of America, efficient trans-European networks are vital for the future of the EU.

Support for trans-European networks (for telecoms and energy as well as for transport networks) was formally adopted as a Community priority in the 1992 Maastricht Treaty on European Union, which underlined the need to develop trans-European transport networks in the interest of the Single Market and the Union's economic and social cohesion. That Treaty focused on the need to develop the trans-European networks for transport, energy and telecommunications as a common European objective and gave the Union three main tasks in this respect:

1. to lay down guidelines for the networks and identify projects of common interest;
2. to back projects by financing feasibility studies and providing loan guarantees or interest-rate subsidies;
3. to take the necessary steps for technical standardisation in order to ensure that the networks are interoperable.

The main priority for creating and implementing trans-European networks remains with individual European governments whose territory they affect, and with the operators themselves. The individual Member States are also responsible for the planning of the projects, including environmental impact assessments. However, the EU claims for itself an important role, that of acting as a catalyst. It does this in several ways:

- coordinating the work of Member States through the adoption of European master plans in key areas. These help governments identify and implement projects with a European as well as a national dimension;
- facilitating operational contacts between promoters, users, industry and research bodies;
- ensuring, through the creation of common standards, that the different parts of trans-European networks are compatible with each other and can be readily interconnected;
- taking policy initiatives to improve the internal market, especially in areas like telecoms, energy distribution and rail transport;
- encouraging private investors (through feasibility studies, pilot projects, loan guarantees, interest-rate subsidies, etc.). (EC 1994)

Trans-European networks are therefore the Commission's instrument for encouraging Member States to make their own investments in telecoms, energy and transport networks. Given the private sector's enthusiasm for the first two sectors, the EU's Trans-European networks plan in practice concentrates on transport and the creation of an integrated transportation system.

Following the 1992 Treaty, the European Commission presented its proposals for extensive trans-European networks, which were approved by the Council of Ministers and the European Parliament, with some amendments, notably on the need for closer environmental scrutiny of the proposed developments.

The proposals covered: 70,000 km of rail track, including 22,000 of new and upgraded track for high-speed trains; 15,000 km of new roads, nearly half in regions on the outskirts of the Union; corridors for combined transport; and the development of 267 airports of common interest and networks of inland waterways and seaports. The trans-European networks also included projects for a Europe-wide traffic management system for road, rail, inland waterways and air transport which is based on state-of-the-art telecommunications and information technologies. It was estimated that approximately ECU 400 billion would have to be invested to complete the trans-European networks for transport alone by 2010. The investment break-down by mode is roughly 60 per cent for rail, including high-speed rail, conventional rail and combined transport, 30 per cent for roads, and the remaining 10 per cent being distributed between inland waterways, port and airport infrastructure, traffic management and control systems (EC/EIB 1996 and http://europa.eu.int/pol/trans/en/info.htm#patch).

At the December 1994 Summit in Essen, the European Council acknowledged 14 major trans-European transport network projects to be of top priority and made an in-principle decision on their implementation. These are shown in Table 2.3.

The 14 trans-European networks projects chosen, costing a total of ECU 91 billion in total financing, underlined a clear priority for promoting alternatives to road transport. About 80 per cent of this sum is focused on rail links and a further 9 per cent on road/rail links, as opposed to only 10 per cent earmarked for new road building.

Since all trans-European network projects are very large-scale undertakings, rapid progress has been hindered by two main obstacles:

Member States' own priorities

The Member States attach different degrees of importance to the trans-European network projects, as they are seen in some cases as competing with other, more pressing, construction projects. Regional or national interests are often perceived as being more important than common European ones. Moreover, due to the very size of the projects, planning and approval procedures take a long time in all Member States, and international projects progress ultimately at the pace of the slowest country.

Overstretched public budgets

The trans-European networks programme was conceived at a time when national government budgets were very tightly stretched. The large debt burden resulting from the recession of the early 1990s and the need to balance public budgets meant that the large amounts of capital needed for TENs could not be covered just by Member States' public funds.

However, in connection with this second difficulty, four sources of Union funds are available for the development of the TENs:

1 *The Union budget*: ECU 1.8 billion is programmed until 1999 for feasibility studies and for the loan guarantees and interest-rate subsidies which can help unlock much larger sums of money;

2 *The Structural Funds*: non-refundable aid is available from the European Regional Development Fund for the least-favoured regions (ECU 15 billion programmed for transport projects for 1995/99) and from the Cohesion Fund (in the region of ECU 8 billion benefiting Spain, Portugal, Greece and Ireland only). Further, albeit more limited, funds are available from other Community initiatives to promote cross-border cooperation (Interreg for projects in EU border regions and PHARE for transport routes in Central and Eastern Europe).

3 *The European Investment Bank (EIB)*: as the Union's financing institution, the EIB provides long-term, specially-tailored loans for up to 50 per cent of the cost of infrastructure projects. From 1993 to mid-1996, the EIB lent ECU 8 billion for 9 of the 14 priority trans-European networks projects in the transport sector and ECU 10.5 billion for other non-priority trans-European network transport projects.

4 *The European Investment Fund (EIF)*: launched in June 1994 with a capital of ECU 2 billion, the EIF is 40 per cent owned by the EIB, 30 per cent by the EU and 30 per cent by 76 financial institutions in the Member States. It provides long-term loan guarantees when a project's promoter cannot arrange funding on a sufficient scale, thus facilitating the funding of trans-European networks by non-public finance. In the first two years, the EIF provided guarantees for fifteen trans-European network projects.

EU TRANSPORT POLICY AND THE ENVIRONMENT

The EU admits that despite its economic and social benefits, transport is increasingly seen as the source of often unacceptable damage to the environment. The most serious charges are laid at the door of road transport, whose growth in Europe over the last two decades of the twentieth century made it the dominant choice for the movement of people and goods. The energy consumption of the transport sector represents 30 per cent of total final energy consumption in the Union. Road transport is responsible for 84 per cent of this and contributes over 75 per cent to the total CO_2 output (contributions to the 'greenhouse effect').

The trans-European networks are designed to encourage the transfer of passengers and goods from road to other forms of transport, namely rail. This is a stated aim of EU transport policy: the need to strike a better balance in the use of the various transport modes so that passenger and freight transport is less dominated by cars and lorries. The development of the transport infrastructure through the trans-European network projects is supposed to serve this objective by strengthening the competitive attractions of more environmentally friendly alternatives.

Clearly, the trans-European network project cannot by itself deliver the objective of sustainable mobility and the Commission is active on a number of other fronts, with the aim of improving standards.

Disseminating examples of best practice in transport development and funding research are two techniques employed at Community level. An example of this approach was seen in 1996, when the Commission published a consultative Green Paper, 'The Citizens' Network', its first policy document on public passenger transport (CEC 1996c). This called for greater investment in public transport systems at the local, regional and national levels, as part of the approach to solving the problem of Europe's growing traffic gridlock. It listed examples of good practice in passenger transport planning as a means of disseminating suggestions of ways in which this form of transport could be made more attractive and usable. The document also listed EU-funded research and development programmes including transport-related studies designed to improve standards and efficiency in public transport systems.

Finally, the EU also has a role with respect to the regulatory framework which it creates and upholds. The scope for improving the quality, security and efficiency of public transport is, for example, partly defined by the EU's regulatory framework for transport equipment, which includes rules on technical harmonisation of equipment and on environmental standards. Regarding the latter, EU environment legislation

Table 2.3 The fourteen priority projects

	Coût estimé en milliards d'écus		Total écu billon		Insgesamt in Mrd. ECU
Trains à grande vitesse/ Transport combiné nord-sud Nuremberg-Erfurt-Halle/ Leipzig-Berlin Axe du Brenner Vérone-Munich	21.0	High speed train/ combined transport North-South Nuremberg-Erfurt-Halle/ Leipzig-Berlin Brenner Axis Verona-Munich	21.0	Hochgeschwindigkeitsverbindung Schiene/kombinierter Verkehr Nord-Süd Nürnberg-Erfurt-Halle/ Leipzig-Berlin Brenner Achse Verona-München	21.0
Train à grande vitesse Paris-Bruxelles/Bruxelles Cologne-Amsterdam-Londres	16.0	High speed train Paris-Brussels/Brussels Cologne-Amsterdam-London	16.0	Hochgeschwindigkeitsverbindung (Paris)-Brüssel-Köln Amsterdam-London	16.0
Trains à grande vitesse Sud Madrid-Barcelone-Perpignan Montpellier-Madrid Vitoria-Dax	13.0	High speed train south Madrid-Barcelona- Perpignan-Montpellier Madrid-Vitoria-Dax	13.0	Hochgeschwindigkeitsverbindung Süd Madrid-Barcelona Perpignan-Montpellier Madrid-Vitiora-Dax	13.0
Trains à grande vitesse Est Paris-Metz-Strasbourg Appenweier-(Karlsruhe) avec des jonctions vers Metz Sarrebruck-Mannheim et Metz-Luxembourg	4.5	High speed train east Paris-Metz-Strasbourg Appenweier-(Karlsruhe) with connections to Metz-Saarbrücken Mannheim and Metz-Luxembourg	4.5	Hochgeschwindigkeitsverbindung Ost Paris-Metz-Strasbourg Appenweier-(Karlsruhe), mit Anbindung an die Strecken Metz-Saarbrücken-Mannheim und Metz-Luxembourg	4.5
Trains à grand vitesse/ Transport combiné France/Italie : Lyon-Turin Turin-Milan-Venise-Triéste	14.0	High speed train/ combined transport France-Italy/Lyons- Turin/Turin-Milan Venice-Trieste	14.0	Hochgeschwindigkeitsverbindung/ kombinierter Verkehr Frankreich- Italien: Lyon-Turin Turin-Mailand-Venedig-Triest	14.0

Rail conventionnel/Transport combiné ligne de Betuwe-Rotterdam-frontière néerlando-allemande	3.3	Conventional rail/combined transport: Betuwe line Rotterdam-NL/D border-(Rhein-Ruhr) [FN 3]	3.3	Konventionelle Strecke Eisenbahn/kombinierter Verkehr: Betuwe Linie: Rotterdam-Grenze NL/D-(Rhein-Ruhr)	3.3
Liaison ferroviaire conventionelle Cork-Dublin Larne-Stranraer	0.3	Conventional rail link Cork-Dublin Belfast-Larne-Stranraer	0.3	Konventionelle Eisenbahnverbindung Cork-Dublin-Belfast-Larne-Stranraer	0.3
Liaison ferroviaire/principale côte Ouest	0.9	West Coast main line (rail)	0.9	Westküstenstrecke (Eisenbahn)	0.9
Liaison fixe ferroviaire/routière entre le Danemark et la Suède	3.4	Fixed rail/road link between Denmark and Sweden	3.4	Feste Verbindung Eisenbahn/Straße zwischen Dänemark und Schweden	3.4
Autoroutes grecques	6.4	Greek Motorways: Pathe and Via Egnatia	6.4	Autobahnen in Griechenland	6.4
Autoroute de Lisbonne à Valladolid	1.1	Motorway Lisbon-Valladolid	1.1	Autobahn Lissabon-Valladolid	1.1
Aéroport de Malpensa (Milan)	1.0	Malpensa airport (Milan)	1.0	Flughafen Malpensa (Mailand)	1.0
Liaison routière Irlande Royaume-Uni/Bénélux	2.7	Ireland/United Kingdom/Benelux road link	2.7	Straßenverbindung Irland/UK/Benelux	2.7
Triangle nordique	4.4	Nordic triangle	4.4	Nordisches Dreieck	4.4
Total	92.0	Total	92.0	Total	92.0
Conseil Européen (Essen, Dec. 1994)		European Council		Europäischer Rat	

attempts to maintain or improve air quality by setting limit values and objectives and by ensuring that policymakers and the public are properly informed about air pollution levels. For example, a Council directive on air pollution by ozone specifies procedures for monitoring ozone levels and for informing the public when certain values are exceeded. In addition, by 1996, the Commission had proposed a draft framework directive for air quality as the first step in the revision of existing air quality legislation.

However, many environmentalists believe that EU transport policy and the EU's environmental policy are fundamentally incompatible. Among these is Whitelegg (1995) who writes:

> Just as the penny is finally dropping about the futility of trying to keep up with the demand for passenger and freight transport through ever more roads, more airports and more car parking, the EU is embarking on its largest ever bout of road, rail and airport expansion as an agreed priority policy. The commitment to 'predict and provide' is dramatic and expensive. But more worrying is the enthusiasm for mobility and long-distance transport links against the background of commitments to sustainable development expressed in the Maastricht Treaty and in the Fifth Environmental Action Programme.

As an example of how transport priorities can overrule environmental considerations, Whitelegg describes how, in June 1995, the EU Environment Commissioner wrote to a number of environmental groups to justify the EU's approval of a new motorway in Germany. According to Whitelegg, the A20 motorway in Mecklenburg-Vorpommern crosses the Trebel and Recknitz valley and seriously damages areas of ecological and scenic value. His conclusion is that the motorway was approved by the German authorities and by the EU because of the overriding importance of economic development arguments in this region of the former East Germany. In other words, environmental matters were considered inferior to economic factors.

Many environmentalists believe that throughout Europe, major infrastructure projects are damaging the landscape, fuelling the growth in demand for transport and contributing to the growth in greenhouse gas emissions from transport. They maintain that environmental concerns are dealt with as afterthoughts or as mitigation tools, and are demoted to a lowly status from which they cannot challenge the search for international competitiveness. They point out that there has been no environmental assessment of trans-European networks or airport expansion schemes to raise questions about alternatives or about the achievement of sustainable development objectives.

Whitelegg believes that the reasons for this 'retreat from Maastricht, Rio and the Fifth Environmental Action Programme' are not difficult to find.

> When Jacques Delors, as President of the European Commission, wrote his White Paper, *Growth, Competitiveness and Employment* in 1993, he emphasised the importance of new transport infrastructure and 'faster, safer travel at lower cost' in creating a competititive economy and increasing the rate of job creation. This emphasis on lower cost is directly contrary to EU environmental policy based on the polluter-pays principle and on a commitment to 'internalise the external cost' of transport. (Whitelegg 1995)

Environmentalists believe that the consequences of trans-European networks could be dramatic:

> Trans-European links will have a devastating effect on the environment, both locally and on a wider geographical scale. The local devastation that can be expected can already be seen where major motorway projects have proceeded in sensitive areas like Twyford Down in England and the Aspe valley in the Pyrennees. More generally, carbon dioxide emissions will rise by 15–18 per cent above the existing forecast, which threatens to undermine attempts to meet greenhouse gas reduction targets.
>
> For the EU's Common Transport Policy, transport efficiency means more transport infrastructure and cheaper transport. It means higher levels of mobility, more freight transported long distances by road, and more passengers flying longer distances. Nowhere does EU policy address the underlying rationale and value of all this extra transport, and nowhere does it ask if our economic and social objectives can be served with less tarmac, less concrete and less fossil fuel consumption.
>
> This is a crude misrepresentation of transport policy and a narrow interpretation of its role in

Direct community measures affecting tourism

The impact on tourism of the above EU policies and measures, in particular the structural funds, is far more significant than that of the tourism-specific measures which follow. But the former type of measure gives little indication of EU tourism policy, as in the cases already covered in the previous section, tourism is merely an indirect beneficiary of a broader EU policy objective. In this section, the EU's actions deliberately aimed at assisting tourism are examined.

INITIAL APPROACHES TO TOURISM

Despite the low priority given generally to tourism within the structures of the EU, the European Commission, with the support of the European Parliament and the Economic and Social Committee has, since the early 1980s, intervened increasingly in this domain, bringing about a series of measures actively and specifically targeted at the tourism sector.

The Commission published its first guidelines for an EU tourism policy in 1982 and submitted them to the Council of Ministers for consideration. Areas were identified in which the EU could be effective: to stimulate harmonious tourism development, ensure freedom of movement and protection for tourists, and improve the conditions of tourism industry employees. Certain priorities for action were outlined, including combatting the problem of seasonality, the preservation of European heritage especially in disadvantaged areas, and the promotion of social, cultural and rural tourism.

Following this initial approach to the subject, a Community tourism programme was proposed by the Commission in 1986. In addition to some of the ideas contained in the initial guidelines, it included proposals for better use of EU development funding, better information and protection for tourists, and the establishing of consultation and coordination procedures between the Commission and Member States. Partly as a result of the last proposal, the EU's ministers responsible for tourism have met the Commission on a regular basis since 1988 to discuss Community policy and to exchange information on their respective national tourism policies. Other recommendations included in this programme, and subsequently adopted, are those on standardised information and fire safety for hotels, and the harmonisation of legislation on package travel. This last led to the 1990 Directive on Package Travel (see page 50).

THE EUROPEAN YEAR OF TOURISM

In anticipation of the Single Market in 1992, and with the purpose of stressing tourism's integrating role, 1990 was declared European Year of Tourism (EYT), by the EU's Council of Ministers. This, it was felt, would help to create the feeling of a 'people's Europe' and would stress the economic and social importance of the tourism sector, particularly in relation to regional policy and job creation. EYT was therefore a very public manifestation of the EU's growing interest in this sector.

This initiative proved to be the main inspiration behind the increased levels of Community activity which have been undertaken in support of tourism ever since (CEC 1996b). Many of the initiatives funded under this programme were concerned with spreading good practice, particularly in the fields of cultural, rural, youth and environmentally aware tourism. Activities also included the production of guide books, brochures and maps, and the organisation of seminars and partnership operations between regions and countries.

The success of EYT has frequently been called into question. Critics suggest that the relatively modest budget (ECU 4.6 million, plus an additional ECU 1 million from the Commission's general budget and ECU 2.5 million from the global budget for certain specific pilot projects) meant that the scale of operations was perhaps somewhat more limited than the breadth of the Council's vision. Also, as only a limited period of time – twelve months – was allowed for the preparation of the project, the standard of initiatives and their impact were, at best, mixed. Partly because of this, media coverage was poor (EIU 1993). However, Lickorish (1991) points to the positive outcomes of EYT, particularly to the partnership which was formed between the EU bodies and tourism's commercial sector.

COMMUNITY ACTION PLAN TO ASSIST TOURISM

In the early 1990s, the following emerged as the core challenges to be addressed by Community action for tourism:

- The need to take better account of the needs of the tourism industry at the appropriate levels to improve its operation and performance and the quality of its services;
- The need to increase the industry's competitiveness by promoting growth in the medium term while respecting the environment and local population affected;
- The need to take account of the tourism industry's requirements in other fields of policy directly affecting the sector, particularly those tackled at EU level (CEC 1996b).

The consensus that has emerged is that the Community's role within an overall framework to assist tourism must not take the form of heavy intervention. Rather it should be primarily aimed at:

- developing tourism by promoting information and mutual exchanges between the different parts of the industry;
- coordinating tourism activities within the Commission and with the Member States;
- encouraging and, in certain specific fields, supporting innovative demonstration projects

These challenges and objectives were addressed in the EU's Community Action Plan to Assist Tourism, which ran from January 1993 until the end of 1995, and which represents the most significant tourism-specific measure launched at Community level to date.

A budget of ECU 18 million was allocated equally over the three-year period at ECU 6 million a year for the Plan's associated measures.

There were three main axes of the Community Action Plan to Assist Tourism:

1 Gaining and improving knowledge about the tourism industry. This includes the development of reliable tourism statistics at the European level in order to monitor tourist/visitor flows, while relying on a 'common language' of understanding and comparison, and the publication of studies on subjects of interest to the European tourism industry and the public admininstrations.

2 Developing specific Community actions to assist the development of a diversity of quality tourism products and to promote transnational, cross-border cooperation between the public and private sector in various fields. In 1994, these fields included: tourist information, actions in Central and Eastern Europe, tourism and the environment, cultural, rural, social and youth tourism, and tourism education and training. (Most of the projects supported financially by the Commission were of a pilot nature and had a demonstratory character.)

3 Strengthening cooperation and coordination within the Commission, with other institutions (national and local public sector bodies, international or European professional organisations), with Member States and also with third countries to ensure harmonious and consistent tourism development.

Two different types of actions were undertaken under the Community Action Plan to Assist Tourism: some had a pan-Community dimension aimed broadly at improving Europe's tourism product and its competitiveness generally, while others had a more specific focus. An impression of the wide-ranging and varied nature of the projects selected for support by the Commission may be gleaned from the following examples of the initiatives arising from the Plan.

A series of publications intended to provide better information to both consumers and professionals in the tourism sector – for example, a manual providing guidance for tourism professionals on making Europe more accessible to tourists with disabilities; a 'European tourism and the environment prize' designed to raise awareness about environmental issues in the sector; the harmonisation of tourism statistics; a pilot programme to promote Europe as a tourist destination on distant markets, such as the USA; pilot actions for youth and cultural tourism; a conference on social tourism.

Some commentators have expressed disappointment at the Plan's lack of originality and lack of additional funding: 'Much of the Action Plan was simply restating ideas and initiatives that had been in place for some time . . . It could be argued that such initiatives are just a token, given that the Community funding for these purposes is available via the Regional Development Fund, the Common Agricultural Policy, and via programmes like LEADER and FORCE.' (Barnes and Barnes 1993).

Another industry reaction, from the World Travel and Tourism Council, expresses similar reservations: 'The Tourism Action Plan is inadequately funded at ECU 6 million (US$6,7 million) per year. The results are actions which are too small and fragmented to maximise the industry's potential contribution to growth and job creation. While the measures are worthwhile, the Plan lacks the top level policy commitment and financial support to achieve them' (WTTC 1995).

Specifically regarding initiatives for the development of rural, cultural, environmental and social tourism, the EU's Economic and Social Committee expressed its own reservations:

> There has not really been a structured policy in these areas. The projects supported, although agreeable, have been mostly on a small scale . . . The question is arising more and more of whether enough thought has been given to the way in which money from the Structural Funds is to be used for tourism in accordance with declared objectives. The ESC fears that the aims set out in the Action Plan will, in practice, have little or no influence over decisions on Structural Fund projects. Here too, it seems, there is little talk of co-ordination. (Economic and Social Committee of the EC 1994)

In fact, the principal value of both ETY and the Action Plan may not have been the strengths and weaknesses of their individual measures and proposals, but their giving further prominence to tourism in the EU decision-making process and further establishing tourism within the sphere of the EU's areas of activity. Both measures also provided a base for organising cooperation between Member States and stimulating dialogue within the industry, as well as a platform for comparing ideas and experience, building common projects and developing common strategies. 'The active participation of all the Member States in the actions tested as part of the (Community Action) plan has . . . given a real indication of the advantages of transnational cooperation as a tool for tourism growth and European integration (CEC 1995).

THE FUTURE OF EU TOURISM POLICY

What has been the result of over a decade of EU tourism-related initiatives? What remains to be done before a sound and effective framework for tourism planning and policy within the EU can be said to be established? Many commentators agree with Lickorish's opinion that tourism-specific measures undertaken to date amount to no more than 'an ad hoc and piecemeal approach with a very limited budget and programme of activity, with little attempt to fit tourism into the major policies of the Community' (Lickorish 1994).

Consequently, during the 1990s, there was growing pressure from the European Parliament, most of the southern Member States and many European trade associations for the EU to assume a much more important role in the field of tourism.

Their chief argument was that DGXXIII had insufficient influence over, and input into, the policies of other DGs which affect tourism. It was argued that, as a consequence, the tourism industry was vulnerable to the unintended negative effects of measures drawn up by these other DGs without due consideration of their potential impact on tourism. Since, as a multi-sectorial, horizontally structured activity, tourism is affected by the policies of a large number of DGs, it was argued that there was a need for an overarching tourism policy with a long-term outlook, known to and respected by all other DGs.

But the northern Member States in general (with the exception of Ireland) and the UK and Germany in particular were opposed to further powers being given to the EU in this area. Their argument was based either on a general opposition to governmental intervention in any form, or on a reluctance to accept a special status for the tourism industry, or both.

However, during the 1990s, supporters of greater EU intervention in tourism developed a specific claim to meet their objective. They campaigned for a legal basis for extended EU actions in the domain of tourism by including this in the Treaties which form the foundation of all EU legislation. Since the Treaty of Rome made no specific mention of tourism, all EU actions concerning tourism, including the Tourism Action Plan had been taken under a 'General Powers' section of the Treaty, the justification being that tourism is covered by those Articles in the Treaty of Rome, concerning 'the free movement of persons, services, and capital'.

During the discussions leading to the Maastricht Treaty the question arose as to whether tourism should be made a specific power or 'competence' of the EU. A tourism competence would raise the EU's actions in the domain of tourism to the same level of political legitimacy as, for example, its actions relating to transport and agriculture, other key EU competencies. Supporters of such a move argued that this was the key to political recognition for the tourism sector, and that, without this, the tourism industry would continue to be exposed to the negative effects of measures taken by other DGs without due consultation with this sector. A tourism competence would also bring with it an increase in staff and financial resources for DGXXIII.

Although a tourism competence was eventually not included in the Maastricht Treaty, a formal commitment was made to re-examine the matter in 1996, when the Treaty was to be revised (Garland 1995). Subsequently, those campaigning for tourism intervention to be given a legal basis set their sights on the revision of the Maastricht Treaty to be debated at the 1996/97 Intergovernmental Conference (IGC) negotiations in Italy, Ireland and the Netherlands.

In April 1995, a Green Paper on tourism (CEC 1995) was produced by DGXXIII, as a report and discussion document to form part of the debate leading up to the IGC. Its aim was to encourage discussion of the Union's future role in tourism, by stimulating a debate among all interested parties, both public and private, at the various levels of admininstration. It argued that in adopting a policy on tourism:

the European Union could reveal the true interlinkages between the means made available to tourist enterprises at Community, national, regional and local levels and improve the effectiveness of these by synchronising the various levels of public support in this field. (CEC 1995)

The paper's basic tenet is that it is vital to combine the three essential elements of tourism: the tourism industry, consumers, and the protection of the natural and cultural heritage. It proposes doing this through a partnership between the public and private sectors and by promoting initiatives at the European level. Through the Community's involvement in tourism, the paper claims, value is added to the measures carried out by national, local and professional bodies or various interests of the tourism industry.

The final part of the paper suggested four options for the future involvement of the EU in tourism:

1. *Reducing or eliminating direct action on tourism.* This option would be argued on the basis that existing EU policies under other headings already adequately cover the interests of tourism. For example, concerns of tourist satisfaction are dealt with by EU policy on consumer protection, environmental concerns are dealt with through environmental impact assessments in the Structural Funds, and issues of the growth of tourism are dealt with by EU policies on the creation of infrastructure, competition and the Single Market. However, adopting this option would mean that no effort would be made to coordinate tourism policy or encourage exchange of experience and best practice throughout the EU.

2. *Maintaining the status quo approach.* This would mean continuing action in a variety of policy areas, through measures impacting directly or indirectly on tourism, as described above. There is no doubt that this approach has a degree of usefulness. However, the lack of a legal basis would always limit the action taken. Options 3 and 4 envisaged a higher priority for tourism within the institutions of the European Union.

3. *Strengthening Community involvement within the framework of the present Treaty.* This

would mean increased support not only for specific actions on tourism, but also for other relevant areas of EU policy: for example, developing trans-European networks and advancing the Community's enterprise policy, especially in relation to small and medium-sized enterprises (SMEs) and the craft sector. The Community could also endeavour to ensure that greater account is taken of specifically tourist-related interests. There would be a recognised role within the Commission for the Tourism Unit as a coordinating body, reviewing the proposed actions and policies of all DCs, to ensure that they would not act against the general tourism interest.

4. *Creating a new tourism role for the Commission*, by which it would develop coherent tourism policies complementary to the policies of Member States. The Commission would, for example, take responsibility in the field of the environment and promotion of Europe in third countries. And where the Member States' activities needed to be coordinated, the Commission would work towards this common action. This would mean a specific tourist competence.

Within the tourism industry itself, most international professional associations and tourism lobby groups opted for Option 4, with supporters of this option including the European Tour Operators Association, the World Travel and Tourism Council (WTTC), Europarks, the Bureau International du Tourisme Social, and the Alliance Internationale de Tourisme. The WTTC's justification for their choice was that . . . 'An EU role for travel and tourism, enshrined in the Treaty on European Union, would help further the Union's goals of growth, employment and competitiveness. At the same time, the Union would also reap the social benefits of enhanced European integration which travel and tourism can uniquely provide as an industry which almost by definition promotes international understanding and strengthens EU citizens' sense of 'Union' (WTTC 1995).

However, within the tourism industry, others were deeply concerned at the prospect of additional restrictive regulation and intervention which could be the result of choosing Option 4. Even

some of the supporters of a tourism competency and the official EU tourism policy which this would entail, stipulated that this should not be interpreted as a wish for more regulatory measures for the tourism industry (Décision Tourisme 1995).

The EU's Committee of the Regions expressed the view that over and above the provisions of the existing EU policies, there was no need to establish a legislative basis for an EU tourist policy. Its members were of the opinion that the proposal to strengthen Community action via the existing Treaty (Option 3) constituted the soundest basis for the Commission's future work, since this option gave a clear political signal that the present legal basis (Article 3 in the Treaty of the European Union) is adequate for the Union to meet its goals in this field.

As for the positions taken on this issue by the Member States themselves, these were expressed at a European Tourism Forum held in Brussels in December 1995. Although all were in agreement as to the need for more coordination for tourism in the EU as well as to the need for a continuing role for the EU in this domain, there was no consensus as to what this role should be. Notably, no agreement was reached as to whether more EU staff and funds should be assigned to tourism matters or indeed whether there should be a tourism competence included in the future Treaty. The Options selected by the Member States are shown in Table 2.4

In June 1997, the European Parliament voted to accept Option 4, although the fifteen tourism ministers of EU Member States announced that they would not ask for a tourism competency at the IGC.

PHILOXENIA

In April 1996, the Commission submitted a proposal for a new Multiannual Programme to Assist Tourism 1997–2000, named Philoxenia – from the Greek meaning 'hospitality towards visitors'. This sought to 'ensure continuity of Community action in this field whilst, at the same time, rationalising it and deepening it by taking greater account of European tourism as a phenomenon with a major economic and social impact'.

Table 2.4 Member States' voting for or against a tourism competence

	Option 1	Option 2	Option 3	Option 4	Other
Austria			•		
Belgium				•	
Denmark					•
Finland			•		
France					•
Germany		•			
Greece				•	
Ireland				•	
Italy				•	
Luxembourg			•[1]		
Netherlands		•			
Portugal			•[2]		
Spain			•[2]		
Sweden					•
UK		•			

Notes:
[1] Luxembourg stated that it would not oppose option 4
[2] Spain and Portugal were said to be likely to move towards options 3 or 4 during the course of the negotiations
Source: Décision Tourisme, No. 4, February 1996

The rationale behind the Philoxenia Programme of action was based on a number of problems relating to issues of quality and professionalism. According to the proposal itself, these problems were principally due to:

- complacency owing to Europe's status as the predominant destination since the 1960s;
- historically, a lack of recognition within government of the importance of the industry;
- outdated facilities and poor infrastructure requiring wholescale regeneration of particular types of destination;
- a diverse and highly fragmented industry, most of which are SMEs, often resulting in less coherent policy formation and ineffective coordination at many levels;
- a large number of sub-sectors which have historically not worked together in the most effective manner;
- over-concentration in terms of both the products offered and the destinations served, leading to standardisation of the product, over-development of certain areas and under-development of others;
- limited use of strategic planning and tax development controls with consequent negative impacts on often fragile and built environments;
- a short-term investment culture which has served to reduce the ability to plan tourism strategically in the longer term;
- poor training provision and lack of an industry image.

The proposal claimed that the remedial measures it contained all had a common denominator: they were not, or could not be, satisfactorily undertaken at the local, regional or national level. In addition, they aimed to make more cohesive other Community measures which were relevant to tourism.

The proposal document claims that the Philoxenia Programme, with its emphasis on

Table 2.5 The Philoxenia Programme

Ultimate objective	Intermediate objectives	Immediate objectives	Actions
	A Improving knowledge in the field of tourism	1 Developing tourism-related information	• European statistical system for tourism
		2 Pooling tourism information from other sources	• surveys, studies and desk/field analysis • European research and documentation network on tourism
		3 Facilitating the assessment of Community measures affecting tourism	• establishment of a legal and financial watch
	B Improving the legislative and financial environment for tourism	1 Reinforcing cooperation with Member States, the industry and other stakeholders	• organisation and follow up of regular meetings (technical/thematic meetings, round-tables, European fora)
Stimulating quality and competitiveness of European tourism, in order to contribute to growth and employment	C Raising quality in European tourism	1 Promoting sustainable tourism	• local initiatives network • environmentally friendly management systems • European Prize
		2 Removing obstacles to tourism development	• identification of obstacles and development of appropriate responses
	D Increasing the number of tourists from third countries	1 Promoting Europe as a tourist destination	• support for multiannual promotion campaigns

Source: CEC (1996)

'partnership, cooperation, and consultation with the Member States and the tourism industry', responds to the needs of the tourist and the protection of the natural and cultural heritage. But it adds that the ultimate objective, however, was to stimulate the quality and competitiveness of European tourism, in order to contribute to growth and employment. The actions and objectives of the proposed programme are shown in Table 2.5.

The proposed budget was ECU 25 million, and although this sum is somewhat limited, given Philoxenia's wide-ranging scope, it was stressed by several trade associations that the four-year pro-gramme could be an important step towards achieving full recognition of tourism's importance for Europe. Conversely, many sectors of the European tourism industry believed that it would be a major step backwards if the programme was not agreed. By the summer of 1997, there was still no clear decision from the Member States over whether to accept or reject the proposal.

Industry influence on the EU institutions

The EU institutions cannot, by themselves, develop effective legislation, policies and measures for tourism or for any industry. Industry itself has a role to play in the process.

As an unelected body of civil servants, the European Commission has to be seen to be listening. Remaining open to lobby and special interest groups allows it to claim some democratic legitimacy, but also gives it a vital source of industry and special interest expertise in framing proposals. Lobbying has come to be recognised as part of the decision-making process in Brussels.

With every expansion of the European Commission's influence and the European Parliament's power, the number of lobbyists grows. Brussels is now home to an army of consultants and lobbyists, one of the European capital's biggest growth industries. Before preparations for the Single Market began, there were estimated to be between 300 to 500 lobby groups. The surge in legislation asociated with the 1992 project prompted a boom. There are now believed to be 10,000 lobbyists in Brussels (Guardian 1997a).

Clearly, the lobbying system is open to abuse, as interest groups can exert huge influence and can if they choose, put hurdles in the way of reforms by withdrawing cooperation. In March 1997, for example, the European Airlines Association faced accusations of trying to frustrate European Commission's attempts to cut air fares by encouraging their members to refuse to provide cost and price information. The growth in lobbying activity has therefore been accompanied by the establishment of codes of conduct to ensure that the lob-bying process remained to as great an extent possible free of suspicions of sleaze and favour-buying.

Most of the Europe-wide professional associations mentioned in the chapters ahead are actively engaged in lobbying EU institutions. Indeed, many have relocated to Brussels or have representation in Brussels to argue their case for special treatment or to keep a close eye on forthcoming EU legislation.

The lobbying role of one such cross-sectoral association, the European Tourism Action Group, was mentioned at the end of Chapter 1. Another cross-sectoral group is the previously mentioned Brussels-based World Travel and Tourism Council (WTTC). Active at both national and EU levels of government in Europe, the WTTC is a well-funded global coalition of Chief Executive Officers from all sectors of the travel and tourism industry.

The WTTC has identified a number of basic policy priorities, which would, it claims, help governments harness the travel and tourism industry's economic dynamism in order to increase overall growth and job creation. Its recommendations to the EU and its Member States come in the form of the following shopping list:

1   Make travel and tourism a strategic economic development and employment priority
    - Recognise the industry's economic and social contribution by including a role for travel and tourism in the Treaty on European Union – with due regard for the principle of Subsidiarity.
    - Include travel and tourism in mainstream programmes for job creation, export promotion and investment stimulation.
    - Establish EU and Member State Satellite Accounts for travel and tourism.
    - Strengthen the role of travel and tourism within the European Commission to ensure effective coordination and resources on key issues.
2   Pursue competitive and environmentally compatible markets
    - Implement the General Agreement on Trade in Services (GATS), liberalise air transport in line with the recommendations of the Comité des Sages, and deregulate telecommunications.

- Enhance promotion and encourage product improvements for international competitiveness.
- Establish a policy framework for sustainability and encourage industry environment initiatives.

3 Eliminate barriers to growth
- Expand infrastructure by increasing airport capacity, implementing a single satellite air traffic control system and introducing FAST for automated border clearance.
- Tax intelligently for growth and exports.
- Invest in human resource development.

While a number of the above demands would appear worthy and non-controversial, others involve additional public expense ('enhance promotion') and privilege ('tax intelligently'=reduce tax on travel) for the travel and tourism industry which other industries would most certainly oppose. *The Economist* even rejects the basis premise behind the WTTC's claims – that travel and tourism is now the world's biggest industry:

> European governments should treat such demands with a bucketful of salt. Far from being a single industry, travel and tourism are a bundle of separate and often unrelated businesses, operating in quite different, segmented markets. To lump together airlines, farmers who supply vegetables to resort towns, and the construction companies that build hotels is statistical sophistry rather than a basis for policy-making. And to use this as an argument for subsidy is special-interest lobbying at its most naked. (Economist 1995b)

UPDATE

Undertake your own research to find out the answers to the following questions:

- How has the debate over the abolition of intra-EU duty-free sales been resolved?
- What has been the outcome of Member States' move towards a single currency and how has this affected travel and tourism?
- What progress has been made concerning the setting up of trans-European transport networks and how successful has the environmental lobby been in having their concerns taken into account?
- Are we any closer to having a formal EU policy and/or a specific EU competence for tourism?

References

Akehurst, G., Bland, N. and Nevin, M. (1993) 'Tourism policies in the European Community Member States', in *International Journal of Hospitality Management*, Vol. 12, No. 1, spp. 33–66.

Barnes, I. and Barnes, P. (1993) 'Tourism Policy in the European Community', in P. Lavery, and W. Pompl, (eds), *Tourism in Europe – Structures and Developments*, CAB International, Wallingford.

CEC (1995) *The Role of the Union in the Field of Tourism*, Commission of the European Communities, Brussels.

CEC (1996a) *Report from the Commission on Community Measures Affecting Tourism*, Commission of the European Communities, Brussels.

CEC (1996b) *Tourism and the European Union: A Practical Guide*, Commission of the European Communities, Brussels.

CEC (1996c) *The Citizens' Network: Fulfilling the Potential of Public Passenger Transport in Europe*, Commission of the European Communities, Brussels.

COR (1995a) *Opinion on Policy for the Development of Rural Tourism in the Regions of the European Union*, Committee of the Regions, Brussels.

COR (1995b) *Opinion of the Committee of the Regions on the Commission Green Paper on the Role of the Union in the Field of Tourism*, Committee of the Regions, Brussels.

Davidson, R. and Maitland, R. (1997) *Tourism Destinations*, Hodder and Stoughton, London.

Décision Tourisme (1995) Le Livre vert entre consultations et négotiations, *Décision Tourisme*, No. 2, December, p. 29.

Despicht, N. S. (1964) *Policies for Transport in the Common Market*, Lambarde Press, Sidcup.

DTT (1996) *VAT: Its Impact on European Tourism*, Deloitte Touche Tohmatsu International, St Albans.

EC (1994) *Trans-European Networks*, European

Commission, Office for Official Publications of the European Communities, Luxembourg.

EC (1996) *Serving the European Union: A Citizen's Guide to the Institutions of the EU*, European Commission, Office for Official Publications of the European Communities, Luxembourg

Economist, The (1995b) 'Faulty Holiday Towers', 29 July, 1995.

Economist, The (1997) 'European Parliament: looking for legitimacy', 11 January.

EIU (1993) 'The European Community's tourism development programmes', in *EIU Travel and Tourism Analyst*, (5), Economist Intelligence Unit, London.

ETRF (1997a) Executive summaries of: 'Assessment of the impact of the abolition of intra-EU duty and tax-free allowances on low-cost scheduled airlines' (Symonds Travers Morgan), 'Assessment of the impact of the abolition of intra-EU duty and tax-free allowances on charter airline economics' (SH & E), 'Relative importance of duty and tax-free and explicit state subsidies on competition between rail and air travel on intra-EU routes' (Bipe Conseil), European Travel Research Foundation, Brussels.

ETRF (1997b) 'Impact of the abolition of intra-EU duty and tax-free allowances upon the European ferry industry (MDS transmodal)', European Travel Research Foundation, Brussels.

European, The (1995) 'Tourism needs to go places', 28 April–4 May.

European, The (1996a) 'Concession at odds with aims of Single Market', 1–7 August.

European, The (1996b) 'Say goodbye to a travel perk/An industry fights back', 17–23 October.

European, The (1996c) 'Tunnel holes ferry profits/Selling goods to the non-traveller', 17–23 October.

Financial Times, The (1997) FT guide to duty-free, 30 June.

Forbes, A. H. (1994) 'Tourism and transport policy in the European Union', in A. V. Seaton et al. (eds), *Tourism: The State of the Art*, John Wiley, Chichester.

Garland, S. (1995) 'VAT Harmonisation, Distance Selling Directive and other EU Legislative Issues: an update', *Insights*, May issue, English Tourist Board, London.

Grant, D. (1996) 'The Package Travel Regulations 1992: damp squid or triumph of self-regulation?' in *Tourism Management*, Vol. 17, No. 5, pp. 319–21.

Grieve, A. (1997) 'Budget blues for inbound industry', in *Tourism 94*, Tourism Society, London.

Guardian, The (1997a) The legions of lobbyists in the Avenue Louise, 6 March.

Guardian, The (1997b) 'Europe "needs migration"', 6 March.

Human, B. (1995) 'European paper takes a broader view of tourism', in *Planning*, 9 June, p. 10.

Jefferson, A. (1992) Opening address, Conference papers, *Tourism in Europe Conference*, Centre for Travel and Tourism, Tyne and Wear.

Lickorish, L. J. (1991) 'Developing a single European Tourism policy', in *Tourism Management*, Vol. 12, No. 3, pp. 178–84.

Lickorish, L. J. et al (1994) *Developing Tourism Destinations: policies and perspectives*, Longman, London.

Lowyck, E. and Wanhill, S. (1992) 'Regional Development and Tourism within the European Community', in C. Cooper, and A. Lockwood, (eds), *Progress in Tourism, Recreation and Hospitality Management*, Belhaven, London.

Page, S. (1993) 'European Rail Travel', *Travel and Tourism Analyst*, (1), Travel and Tourism Intelligence, London.

Sunday Times, The (1995) 'Retailers fly in to exploit airport shopping boom', 14 May.

Swarbrooke, J. (1997) 'The role of the European Union in UK tourism', in *Insights*, March, English Tourist Board, London.

Travis A. S. (1994) Scotland's role in Eastern Europe and the former USSR, in A. V. Seaton et al. (eds), *Tourism: The State of the Art*, John Wiley, Chichester.

Vellas, F. and Bécherel L. (1995) *International Tourism*, Macmillan, London.

Voice, The (1995) 'Europe presses the dereg button', February.

Whitelegg, J. (1995) 'Fast track to nowhere', in *Town and Country Planning*, November, 1995.

WTTC (1995) *European Union Travel and Tourism: Towards 1996 and Beyond*, World Travel and Tourism Council, Brussels.

3

Air transport in Europe

KEY OBJECTIVES

Reading this chapter will enable you to:

- Understand the importance of air travel for the European tourism industry.
- Identify the distinguishing features of Europe's airline industry.
- Understand the issues in the air transport liberalisation debate.
- Follow the development of the moves towards liberalisation in Europe.
- Appreciate the critical issue of developments in Europe's airport infrastructure.

Introduction

The rapid growth of tourism since the 1960s is one of the factors which have generated the huge increase in demand for the different forms of transport in Europe. Like tourism, passenger transport is a growth industry, growing faster than the economy in general. Between 1970 and 1993, passenger transport in the fifteen EU countries grew at an annual rate of 3.2 per cent, whereas the average growth rate of the GDP (in real terms) was 2.4 per cent. The average distance travelled each day by each European citizen, for all purposes, increased in that period from 16.5 km to 31.5 km (CEC 1996). This growth in demand for transport has been met largely by private cars, which now account for over 80 per cent of all kilometres travelled by Europeans. Figure 3.1 shows how the choice of mode of passenger transport for the fifteen Member States of the EU has developed since 1970.

Clearly, the growth in all forms of tourism, from day trips to holidays, is only partly responsible for this increased mobility on the part of European citizens. Continuing growth in urban sprawl and geographically dispersed family units, increasing the need to travel further to work and to visit relatives, are among the other contributory factors.

CHOICE OF TRANSPORT MODE

To what extent does the choice of transport for tourism purposes reflect Europeans' preferences for transport-use in general? Europe-wide research into this specific topic is rare. While most individual European countries undertake sample surveys of travel patterns, one of the few Europe-wide studies is the 1986 EU Omnibus Survey of *Europeans and their Holidays*. This documents travel patterns in Member States in relation to various aspects of tourism demand and, regarding choice of mode of transport, highlights the overwhelming importance of travel by private car, as shown in Table 3.1.

(Although the data in this table are for 1986, the EU Omnibus Survey remains an important source of information, since it allows EU-wide comparisons to be made, thereby serving as a baseline to future surveys.)

Scard (1993) compares travel patterns in Europe with those of the United States. The choice of mode of travel in the latter case is relatively straightforward: a drive by car is the preferred option for journeys up to four hours; over four hours, flying becomes the only practical choice (the one exception to this rule being the summer vaca-

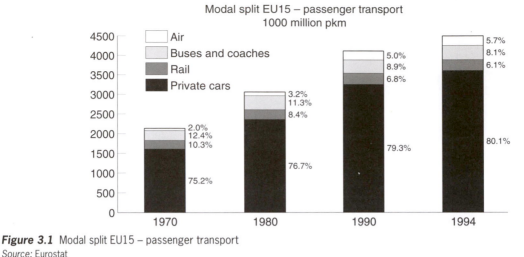

Figure 3.1 Modal split EU15 – passenger transport
Source: Eurostat

Table 3.1 Mode of transport used by European holidaymakers, 1986 (per cent)[1]

	Car	Train	Aeroplane	Boat	Bike/ motorbike	Coach
By origin						
Belgium	77	6	10	1	8	7
Denmark	59	14	18	11	3	4
France	81	15	6	2	2	7
West Germany	61	16	17	3	1	7
Greece	78	4	13	25	1	–
Ireland	51	11	31	18	1	6
Italy	73	15	5	5	2	11
Luxembourg	62	10	19	4	–	15
Netherlands	70	8	14	5	6	14
Portugal	76	17	3	3	1	16
Spain	70	16	5	2	–	12
UK	59	11	24	8	–	14
EC member states	68	14	13	5	1	10
By destination						
Own country	78	14	1	8	1	8
Other country	52	11	32	6	2	13
Non-EC Europe	53	15	29	17	–	18
Outside Europe	35	19	86	1	–	15

Note: [1] Totals exceed 100 owing to multiple responses
Source: EC Omnibus Survey

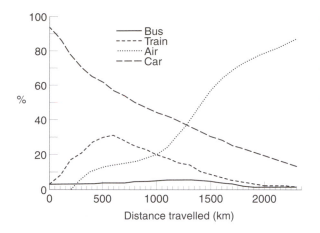

Figure 3.2 Current choice of transport mode in Europe by journey distance
Source: Insights, English Tourist Board, March 1993

tion period, when the Southern and Western States are the destinations for holidaymakers driving down from the North). Clearly, the American transport market is affected by the lack of a substantial inter-city rail network across much of the US and the significant demise of the coach market (eg Greyhound) in recent years. The situation in Europe is more complicated, as shown in Figure 3.2. A viable alternative in the form of train travel has developed, with the help of government subsidy, while cheap and efficient coach travel has also maintained a share of the market for all journeys up to 2,000 km.

This chapter and Chapter 4 examine the principal modes of passenger transport in Europe. This chapter examines current developments in Europe's air transport market, while in Chapter 4, trends in European surface transport are investigated.

Air transport

SUPPLY AND DEMAND

As recently as 30 years ago, air travel was still regarded as something of a luxury reserved for a privileged minority. In a relatively short period of time, air transport the world over has greatly increased in importance, with a fast-growing number of people using airlines for business and leisure travel.

Air transport is now one of the main forces driving tourism growth and development. In Europe, approximately one-third of international tourists arrive at their destination by air (WTO 1996). Although the airlines are in direct competition with other means of transport for intra-European tourism, air transport alone has made Europe accessible for long-haul markets, and facilitated the growth in the trend of Europeans making tourist trips to other continents.

Europe is one of the world regions in which international air transport demand is concentrated, along with North America, Japan and the newly industrialised countries of Asia. Air traffic between these areas accounts for 75 per cent of international passenger traffic. However, regarding domestic scheduled air travel, EU countries account for only 22 per cent of world domestic traffic, well behind the United States, which represents 56 per cent of the total (Vellas and Bécherel 1995).

Europe is the point of departure or point of arrival for the busiest international air travel routes, those over the North Atlantic and those between Europe and South East Asia. The latter in particular are experiencing substantial growth, due to the increasing popularity of Asian destinations for tourism and the general growth in international trade with this region. The busiest routes to/from/within Europe have London as their point of arrival or departure, and include London–Paris, the route with the most seats on offer in the world, London–New York and London–Amsterdam (Vellas and Bécherel 1995).

The EU airline industry is complex and heterogenous, with the national airlines of Member States varying enormously in terms of their sizes, economies, policies and structures. Two features distinguish the EU air transport market from markets in other parts of the world. First, the EU market is in reality an amalgamation of fifteen national markets, each dominated by one national airline, except in the case of SAS, which dominates both the Swedish and Danish national markets. Secondly, charter flights account for 30 per cent of the total airline output (expressed in revenue passenger kilometres–rpks) of the Community, a

Table 3.2 Major EU airlines in Europe. Scheduled services, international and domestic (million pkm)

		1982	1990	1993	1994	1995
Sabena	B	0.88	1.65	2.23	2.63	3.18
Lufthansa	D	4.25	7.81	9.95	10.80	11.98
SAS	DK+S	3.00	5.77	6.62	6.97	7.30
Iberia	E	4.47	6.59	5.57	5.28	6.59
Air France	F	3.89	6.08	5.73	6.33	5.88
Olympic Airways	GR	1.80	2.69	2.71	3.06	3.01
Alitalia	I	2.60	4.83	5.69	6.38	6.88
Aer Lingus	IRL	0.81	1.73	1.66	1.66	1.82
Luxair	L	0.09	0.25	0.29	0.36	0.38
KLM	NL	1.24	2.75	4.07	4.97	5.12
TAP-Air Portugal	P	1.11	2.45	2.99	2.81	2.95
British Airways	UK	5.10	10.22	12.65	13.74	14.42
Austrian Airlines	A	0.95	1.71	1.98	1.98	2.12
Finnair	FIN	0.95	1.86	2.05	2.88	4.37
Total of airlines		31.14	56.39	64.19	69.84	76.00

Note: average annual growth rate: 1982–94 = +7.1%
Source: Eurostat

much higher proportion than in other aviation markets around the world, notably the US. Non-scheduled traffic between member countries of the European Civil Aviation Commission represents 60 per cent of the world's total number of passenger kilometres. Most of this traffic is between tourism markets in the north of Europe and Mediterranean destinations in the south.

One thing which airlines of Member States have in common is dominance of their home markets and major hub airports. This dominance has often been built up over many years during which national airlines enjoyed positions of near or actual monopoly as a matter of government policy. For example, Lufthansa operated in a situation of near monopoly of international and domestic scheduled passenger services in West Germany and has been able to secure a similar position since reunification. Air France relied on a government policy which reserved to it all scheduled services to other European countries as well as those on most intercontinental routes. Even today, Air France accounts for 95 per cent of the French industry's output.

There is no one simple measure of airline size. Several measures of output can be used to determine the performance of an airline relative to other airlines. However, all such measures reveal striking differences in the sizes of the national airlines and the composition of their traffic. British Airways, Air France and Lufthansa are the three largest Community airlines on a variety of output measures, while at the other extreme, airlines such as Aer Lingus, Sabena and TAP are in some cases smaller than some of the independent airlines in Europe, such as Britannia, BMA and LTU. While some national airlines, such as Iberia and Olympic, depend heavily on domestic traffic, others carry a majority of international passengers. Intra-European international passengers outnumber long-haul traffic for each national airline. It is important to note, however, that the balance changes significantly if airline output is measured in terms of rpks, which is in many ways a more meaningful guide to airline output. In aggregate,

Table 3.3 Major EU airlines worldwide. Scheduled services, international and domestic (million pkm)

		1980	1990	1993	1994	1995
Sabena	B	4.85	5.91	6.49	7.50	8.62
Lufthansa	D	21.06	42.10	52.66	56.54	61.60
SAS	DK+S	7.53	11.52	18.14	18.47	18.51
Iberia	E	14.85	20.49	23.27	22.53	23.81
Air France	F	25.40	36.62	43.53	50.12	49.52
Olympic Airways	G	5.06	7.76	7.90	8.43	7.95
Alitalia	I	12.88	19.13	24.52	26.96	31.95
Aer Lingus	IRL	2.05	3.14	3.76	4.28	4.66
Luxair	L	0.03	0.20	0.29	0.36	0.38
KLM	NL	14.06	28.17	36.81	40.84	44.46
TAP-Air Portugal	P	3.43	6.84	7.87	7.59	7.72
British Airways	UK	16.08	44.66	80.09	86.23	93.86
Austrian Airlines	A	1.12	2.82	3.75	3.83	4.91
Finnair	FIN	2.12	4.71	5.32	6.49	8.34
Total of Companies		130.5	234.0	314.4	340.2	366.3

Note: average annual growth rate: 1980–94 = +7.1% (estimates in italic)
Source: Eurostat

some 69 per cent of Community national airlines' output in terms of rpks is on international routes outside Europe. Tables 3.2 and 3.3 show the outputs of the EU's major national airlines in terms of passenger kilometres.

OUTLOOK

Buoyant growth in air traffic is forecast for the years ahead. Vellas and Bécherel (1995) quote figures from Boeing's 1994 World Market Outlook publication which predicted that world air travel would grow at a rate of 5.9 per cent annually until the year 2000, and at 4.9 per cent from 2000 to 2013. This means that, in effect, worldwide passenger traffic will have almost tripled between 1994 and 2013.

Europe will share in this worldwide growth in air traffic. Despite the development of the high-speed rail network, forecasts indicate that air traffic there will grow faster than any other form of traffic in the fifteen years leading up to 2010. In

this period, it is claimed, the number of passengers is likely to double and the growth in air freight will be even greater (COR 1995).

In the late 1990s, healthy traffic levels were helping even the most troubled airlines make profits. European airlines together recorded US$1 billion in operating profit in 1995, after five years of losses totalling US$7.5 billion. However, director of airline consultancy Avmark International in London, was predicting that by the year 2000, European airlines would have to be ready for the next downturn (Business Week 1997).

Liberalisation

BACKGROUND

Deregulation of the airline industry first appeared in the US at the end of the 1970s and had far-reaching consequences on the policies and strategies of all airline companies in that country. During the

1980s and 1990s, it was the EU's turn to deregulate or liberalise its own airlines.

The Treaty of European Union conferred substantial powers on the EU, through the European Commission, to ensure that fair competition is maintained within the Community. These powers have been an important factor in the programme to liberalise air transport. In theory, these powers enable the Commission to enforce Community competition rules in order to block widespread restrictive practices in air transport within the EU. The moves towards liberalisation were welcomed by many in Europe, and not least by those hoping to have the opportunity to compete more effectively in a liberalised air transport market. Franco Mancassola, chairman of Debonair Airways, was quoted as declaring: 'It's like the birth of democracy in a dictatorial state' (Business Week 1997).

Prior to liberalisation, the European air transport sector was characterised by a system based on a cosy relationship between airlines, fully supported by their respective governments, rather than any form of free competition. The reasons for the substantial involvement of national governments in their airlines' operations are found in the historical development of airlines. Throughout the brief history of aviation, governments have owned airlines for the purposes of national defence and security, in order to be able to requisition aircraft in the event of war.

Consequently, the intra-EU air travel market was governed by bilateral agreements between governments of Member States, rigidly controlling route entry and capacity as well as ticket prices. Many international routes were single designation, so that only one airline of each country was allowed to operate, in effect leading to a system of formal duopolies. As each country had a single state-owned airline, it usually insisted that its own flag carrier should be guaranteed a minimum share of the capacity on any route, often 50 per cent.

Fares were almost entirely set by agreement between the airlines under the auspices of their trade association, the International Air Transport Association (IATA); indeed using IATA was a formal requirement of almost all bilateral agreements. Fare changes could only be made with the agreement of both governments concerned.

There were, however, a small number of exceptions to such restrictive agreements where governments had agreed bilaterally to be more liberal. The UK concluded a liberal agreement with the Netherlands in 1984 and similar agreements with Luxembourg, Belgium and the Irish Republic followed (CAA 1993). Nevertheless, the fact remained that most governments in Europe – and elsewhere – still adopted a highly restrictive and interventionist approach to civil aviation.

As a result of Member States' restrictive practices, air fares within Europe were high by world standards. According to a report (CEC 1994) commissioned by the EU, European airlines' operating costs were about 48 per cent higher than those of their US counterparts, measured by 'available tonne kilometre' (ATK). Total labour costs per ATK were nearly 37 per cent higher, leading to much lower levels of productivity than in the USA. Consequently, the cost of a scheduled carrier airline ticket in a regulated Europe was 35–40 per cent higher than for comparable routes in a deregulated USA (Mihalik 1992).

Before liberalisation, lower fares in Europe were only available through inclusive tour arrangements, mostly on charter flights and available only to major holiday destinations located outside the main axes of business travel. Thus, scheduled airlines, most of which were owned by their governments, retained control of the high-revenue, high-intensity and high-profitability routes.

In 1986, the EU Member States committed themselves to a gradual process of liberalisation of the Community air transport market. The decision to create, in effect, a Single Market in aviation formed part of the move towards a single internal market across the whole range of economic activity, as embodied in the Single European Act.

From 1987, the power of state airlines was gradually eroded by a series of measures with the aim of creating 'open skies' over the European Union. The EU did not attempt to introduce full-scale US-style air transport deregulation (which is what the Treaty of Rome implicitly required), but instead phased it in over three separate 'packages', designed progressively to eliminate protectionist barriers within the EU. This approach effectively represented a compromise between the more liberal EU Member States, who wanted all of the measures implemented immediately, and those, such as France, Spain and Italy, who favoured a long transition period.

THE THREE PACKAGES

The First Package, which took effect on 1 January 1988, relaxed some restrictions but essentially left the bilateral framework in place. The single designation provisions were largely removed, so that (subject to the availability of slots at airports and to being licensed by their own national authorities) any number of airlines were able to operate on the major international routes within the Community. The insistence of a number of Member States that their national airlines be given a 50 per cent share of the market was also overridden. Airlines were also given greater freedom to provide the capacity they wanted.

The *First Package* also made available for the first time an automatic right for airlines to operate so-called 'fifth freedom' services – services linking points in the territories of two or more Member States other than the airline company's own country (for example, a flight by a UK airline between France and Italy). This was regarded as a key condition for the growth of genuine international air transport competition.

Finally, new and more flexible procedures for the approval of fares meant that Member States could no longer simply block proposals for economic low fares.

The *Second Package* essentially took the process of liberalisation further, but did not add any significantly new dimension. It is only with the *Third Package*, applied from 31 December 1992, with the Single European Market, that a substantially liberalised internal Community market has been achieved. There are no longer any restrictions on which routes can be operated between Member States, Norway and Iceland, nor on the number of airlines which can serve each route. Community carriers holding an Operating Licence now have free access to virtually all international routes within the Community and are generally free to set fares according to their own commercial judgement rather than have them imposed by regulators (CAA 1993).

With the abolition of the regulatory distinction between scheduled and charter flights, which was another provision of the Third Package, governments of Member States are no longer able to prevent the sale of travel-only seats on charters or insist that such seats can only be sold several days or weeks in advance of departure.

However, it is the new common airline licensing rules which are potentially the most radical of the Third Package's features. Community airlines now need only one permission – an Operating Licence – from one licensing authority to be able to operate anywhere in the Community. Such licences must be granted to any airline which meets the uniform financial, safety and nationality requirements. These are:

- A minimum capital investment of ECU 100,000.
- The aircraft should be registered in the country that issued its certificate of airworthiness.
- At least 51 per cent of the company's capital should be owned by citizens of member countries of the EU.

This provision of the Third Package effectively means that Member States will no longer be able to favour particular airlines by issuing licences on a discretionary basis. In other words, there will be no more special status for flag carriers.

Furthermore, a UK airline, for example, which moves its principal place of business to, or sets up a company in, another Member State will be entitled to a licence from that Member State provided it satisfies the three common licensing criteria. This gives practical meaning for the first time in the air transport sector to the 'right of establishment' provisions of the Treaty of Rome. Thus, since 1993, all carriers in the EU have been able to trade from any EU country if they conform to the three conditions outlined above.

However, as a compromise gesture to the less liberal nations, the right of EU airlines to operate *cabotage* services was postponed until 1 April 1997. Cabotage was one of the most debated points in the whole issue of air transport liberalisation in Europe. It is the right of an airline company of one country to embark passengers, mail and goods in another country and carry them to another point in the same country. The cabotage right means that European carriers can now operate domestic flights in other EU countries. This is regarded as a fundamental step in European deregulation as it effectively introduces competition between international and domestic airlines.

THE IMPACT OF LIBERALISATION

To what extent have the objectives of liberalisation been achieved? Many believed that 1 January 1993, the date when the EU's Third Aviation Package came into effect, would be a significant landmark, and consequently, their expectations were high. It was widely believed that by sweeping away most of the old rules and regulations, many new opportunities would be created for innovative air services; it would be far more difficult for conservative governments to stand in the way of the establishment of new airlines in order to protect their flag carriers; and airlines would have more freedom to charge the fares they wanted to charge and react to market developments, without the constant threat of government interference.

But, other commentators, such as Humphreys, believed that the Third Package would not produce dramatic results overnight, especially in the UK. The reasons he gave were as follows:

- Europe had been engaged in an aviation liberalisation process for several years; as the name implies, the Third Package was simply the last in a series of measures designed to gradually reduce government control.
- Charters, which account for over half of Europe's air traffic, had been deregulated to a significant degree for many years.
- The UK had been pursuing a liberal aviation policy for some time and had successfully negotiated open air services agreements with several European partners.
- The long history of close cooperation between airlines, rather than open competition, would inevitably take some time to break down.
- Deregulation in itself would do nothing to remove the worsening problems of congestion, especially at certain key airports, which often severely restricted access to markets by new entrants (see page 91).
- There was still a tendency for governments to

over-control their air space, leading to excessive charges and inefficient use of airways. Some governments have protected airport monopolies, leading to inefficient and overpriced ground services (Humphreys 1994).

A 1993 report published by the United Kingdom Civil Aviation Authority (CAA 1993) sought to establish the facts about the extent to which liberalisation was actually working. Particular emphasis was placed on the experiences of deregulation in the United States, Australia and Canada, which it was thought might shed light on what could happen in Europe. It revealed a number of facts:

- Normal economy fares were still about 30 per cent higher on intra-Community routes than within the US, with only fares from the UK an exception.
- Community airline costs appeared to be significantly higher than those of US carriers.
- The largest US airlines, while owning more aircraft and carrying more passengers than their Community counterparts, were not significantly larger in terms of turnover.
- Most of the busiest international routes in the Community had a congested airport at one end, and on most routes, there were no more than two airlines.
- In the US, competition was taking place on long routes rather than short ones – and most intra-Community routes were short.
- Policies of allowing competition with minimum intervention in the US, Canada and Australia had led either to airline concentration or the complete elimination of weaker competitors in a short time.

The CAA report acknowledged that the Third Package had brought tangible, if limited, benefits. But it also argued that in the longer term, *an upsurge in active competition* (which it claimed was the fundamental objective since it is most likely to benefit users) would only occur if investors could feel confident that airlines which are efficient and responsive to their customers' needs would survive and be profitable.

According to the CAA, it was this consideration which should guide governments and the EU in implementing aviation policies in the Community. However, it states in the report that 'so far, competition in the scheduled sector has been largely absent and there is little sign of a change in the culture of collusion fostered in the past by many Member Governments'.

Turning to the future, the CAA produced a number of conclusions and recommendations, including the following:

1 Despite the progressive liberalisation of EC air transport since 1987, the great majority of international scheduled routes within the Community have only one or two airlines, and only 26 (only 5 per cent of the total) have more. Given substantial barriers to entry on many routes, the opportunities for competition will become reality only if positive long-term action is taken, going beyond the liberalisation already achieved in the Third Package.

2 In the leisure sector, the main priority should be to ensure that existing healthy competition in individual national markets is not diminished through unfair competition or by take-overs by the major carriers.

3 Given the distortions of the past, the reforms of the Third Package will be effective only if the central aim is to create an environment which maximises the opportunities and the incentives for competition from all the airlines, large or small, scheduled or charter, newly formed or long standing.

4 To secure this aim, the Community must have in place an effective aviation competition policy. It must embrace genuinely effective policies towards anti-competitive behaviour by large airlines against smaller ones through devices such as computer reservations systems, frequent flyer programmes, unfair commission structures and so on.

5 The misuse of state aid can be particularly damaging to smaller airlines, thereby jeopardising the prospects for future competition. A limit must be put on aid given for restructuring which should not be allowed to finance the acquisition of smaller airlines or inappropriate expansion. The Commission's methods, as applied in the aviation sector, must be tightened and made more transparent.

6 Airline mergers are inevitable as twelve markets become one. Mergers or alliances may, in the right circumstances, benefit competition, but this would not be so where the largest EU flag carriers seek to merge or build alliances with each other. Mergers policy should be aimed primarily at securing competition on routes within the Community. Two essentials are a firm refusal to sanction anti-competitive mergers and a competition policy that effectively stamps on anti-competitive practices.

7 Mergers or alliances between the Community's largest airlines are not needed for reasons of international competitiveness; the differences in size between the largest US and EU carriers have been much exaggerated and such arguments should be treated with great caution. Industry generally is not strengthened in international competition if it is sheltered from competition at home (CAA 1993).

The above conclusions reflect the CAA's views, which are by no means universally accepted by industry commentators. For example, many maintain that, regarding the first recommendation, there is simply not enough demand on a large number of European routes to support more than two airlines. Secondly, regarding mergers (recommendations 6 and 7), there is a widely-held alternative view that these are inevitable and essential if European airlines are to compete with their US rivals on long-haul routes.

The CAA report, however, was an important input to the on-going debate about the future of air transport in Europe. This debate particularly revolves around the status of the national flag carriers and the problems created by congestion, two issues which are now considered.

EUROPEAN MAJOR CARRIERS' RESPONSES TO LIBERALISATION

Clearly, the implementation of the three Packages constitutes a threat to the established positions of Europe's flag carriers. Understandably, given their privileged position in the past, some European airlines have shown themselves to be less than willing to engage in the truly free market economy which liberalisation is designed to bring about. However, most have developed strategies designed to enable them to ride the storm and even prosper under the new regime.

Cost-cutting

For many Member States' flag carriers, liberalisation has acted as a spur to reducing their costs. In the USA, fierce competition following deregulation forced US airlines to deeply reduce all costs, including labour. But many believe that costs will not come down so easily in Europe, where labour costs of the major airlines have been traditionally higher than in the US. 'Since the trades unions of Europe are stronger and have greater citizen support, it will be difficult for the European airlines to reduce their biggest single expense' (Mihalik 1992).

However, it has been shown that the established airlines can, when obliged to, adjust their bloated cost structures, and that the incentive to do so is often when a 'third carrier' (that is a third, non-flag carrier airline) begins to compete on a particular route.

The CAA highlights the role played by third carriers on routes previously dominated by national airlines: 'There is ample evidence where air transport markets have been deregulated that the presence of a third carrier on a route makes collusive or parallel behaviour more difficult and unstable, particularly where the new entrant is lower cost than the incumbents' (CAA 1993).

Much is at stake. It is generally expected that increasing competition will lead to a reduction in the number of European airlines operating in the future, reflecting the experience of liberalisation in North America. Most vulnerable are those flag carriers which have been sheltered by protected markets and government handouts. These include Alitalia, Iberia, Air Portugal (TAP) and Greece's Olympic Airways. The cost of keeping these airlines in the air has been enormous: since 1991, European governments have spent US$5 million per day keeping their planes in the air (Business Week 1997). In 1994, the EU declared a 'one-time, last-time' policy for letting governments bail out their airlines. But three years later, governments were still getting around this legislation with temporary subsidies targeted to specific restructuring goals. In March 1997, for example, Italy decided to double a 'one-time' state gift of US$2 billion to Alitalia. In summer 1996, Air France received a 'final' US$1 billion tranche of aid, prompting Lufthansa, on the road to full privatisation, to file a complaint with the EU.

Restructuring – within Europe

Before liberalisation, the flag carriers of Europe were principally preoccupied with strengthening their respective domestic market positions. However, the EU deregulation packages put enormous pressure on the industry to take advantage of wider market opportunities. As a result, competition between airlines on the international scale was intensified. The changed economic situation resulting from deregulation on both sides of the Atlantic has led European airline companies to reconsider their strategies for expansion. In the quest for increased market-share, various strategies have been pursued, leading to large-scale restructuring in the European air transport sector.

Since the 1980s, the number of mergers and acquisitions in the airline industry has increased considerably, in the airlines' pursuit of greater market dominance in Europe. However, experience has shown that this is far from being a 'quick-fix' response to the increasingly competitive environment engendered by liberalisation.

For example, in 1992 British Airways' strategy led it to acquire Dan Air, to buy 49 per cent of Deutche BA, 31 per cent of Air Russia and 49.9 per cent of TAT. The outright purchase of Dan Air immediately gave British Airways 39 aircraft and a number of valuable slots at London's Gatwick Airport. However, by 1997, BA's German and French subsidiaries, Deutsche BA and TAT had lost around ECU 140 million and industry watchers were forecasting a long haul to profitability (European Voice 1997a).

Air France's attempts, in 1992, to buy into other EU markets backfired. It was forced to sell its stake in Sabena, the Belgian airline, to Swissair, and, in 1994, it had to sell back its share in CSA (Czechoslovakian Airlines) back to the Czech government at the latter's request. Far from breaking into foreign markets, Air France was by 1997 engaged in a fierce rearguard action to protect its home turf from domestic and foreign interlopers.

Restructuring – intercontinental partnership agreements and alliances

With predictions that by the year 2010, international air traffic will reach 60 per cent of all air traffic, it is widely recognised that the relative strength of an airline may depend on its ability to compete in a global marketplace (Mihalik 1992 qu. Ruhnau).

One of the ways in which airlines can obtain a larger presence in the marketplace is by entering into a partnership or an alliance. Such agreements create competitive advantages for the partners by achieving economies of scale, through, for example, linking reservations, undertaking joint sales and marketing, offering special fares, sharing facilities and joint purchasing/maintenance agreements. At the same time, alliances, unlike mergers, enable all partners to maintain their independence.

For European airlines, alliances with North American partners brings the advantage that this gives them access to the lucrative domestic market in the US. Conversely, establishing links with European partners is regarded by US airlines and the US government as a way of spreading deregulation to all trans-Atlantic routes and within Europe itself, through the 'Open Skies' policy promoted by the US government. Therefore, before giving final approval to international alliances, the US government has insisted on there being an Open Skies agreement between the US and the home government of the European carrier concerned.

By 1996, three powerful alliances involving European and North American partners were already in place: Northwest and KLM; United Airlines, Lufthansa and SAS; Delta, Sabena, Swissair, and Austrian Airlines.

A fourth alliance, between British Airways and America Airlines, was unveiled in June 1996. It immediately met with a barrage of criticism from competing carriers and some regulatory authorities, many of whom objected to the open skies agreement between the US and UK which was required before the US government would grant anti-trust immunity to the BA/AA deal.

Regulatory delays forced British Airways and American Airlines to push back the timetable for fully implementing their controversial alliance.

It has been predicted that early in the twenty-first century, there will be only a handful of megacarriers which will serve all parts of the globe. Mihalik, for example, has forecast that consolidation, friendly partnerships and mergers may produce as few as three European supercarriers (Mihalik 1992). The race is now on among the major airlines to be one of those megacarriers.

CHARTER SERVICES AND LIBERALISATION

Since deregulation is widely expected to lead to lower fares being charged by the scheduled airline industry, many believe that charter services have a reason to worry about their role as a competitive force in leisure travel in Europe. If prices fall as expected, it is inevitable that liberalisation will have an impact upon charter operations. In the early 1990s, one representative of Lufthansa stated that he expected a trimming of charter carriers because of greater fare flexibility and competition in the commercial airline sector. His opinion was that liberalisation would prompt the beginning of the demise of charter flights for tourist travel' (Mihalik 1992 qu. Huff).

If this turns out to be the case, it would mirror the US experience of liberalisation. In that country, price differentials between scheduled carriers and charter airlines quickly evaporated because of competition from scheduled carriers offering more discounted fares such as supersaver rates. The presence of large US charter carriers is a thing of the past since the deregulation of 1978.

Two solutions seem to point the way towards the survival of the charter carriers, however: they need to make maximum use of their labour cost advantages over the national carriers with their high labour costs; and they need to remain a strong niche market player and not try to compete head-on with major carriers.

NEW ENTRANT AIRLINES

One of the goals of liberalisation was to loosen the grip which Europe's flag carriers – many still state-owned – have on their respective markets,

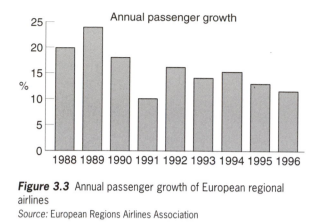

Figure 3.3 Annual passenger growth of European regional airlines
Source: European Regions Airlines Association

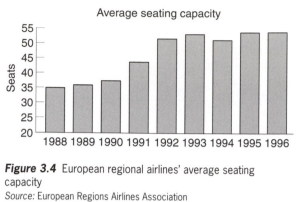

Figure 3.4 European regional airlines' average seating capacity
Source: European Regions Airlines Association

by creating the conditions within which new airlines might prosper, thus increasing consumer choice.

The increased freedom of pricing and market access which came into force with the three liberalisation packages prepared the ground for a number of new entrant airlines. Accordingly, some of the most striking initiatives among European airlines since the beginning of the liberalisation process have come from Europe's new entrant airlines including regional services and the new generation of European budget carriers.

REGIONAL AIRLINES

The creation of the European liberalisation programme has had a massive effect on the regional air transport sector. To the European Regional Airlines Association (ERA), the organisation which lobbies on behalf of regional aviation in Europe, a regional airline is one that flies from a regional point to either another regional point or to a major hub airport. By 1997, 50 per cent of all air routes in Europe were *only* operated by such airlines.

Throughout the 1990s, regional carriers witnessed average growth rates approximately double those of their major airline counterparts. Regional airlines were carrying over 50 million passengers a year by 1997 and were operating 1.5 million flights annually to over 340 destinations in 26 European countries (ERA 1997). According to the ERA, annual passenger growth for its members is as shown in Figure 3.3.

The ERA now has over 50 member airlines ranging in size from Vienna-based Eurosky Airlines (with 30 employees and two tiny Metro SA-227 aircraft offering commuter services to Trieste, Verona, Debrecen, Wroclaw, Ostrava and Kosice) to Air Littoral in Montpellier (with 790 employees and 24 aircraft on routes such as Nice–Naples, Montpellier–Rome, Biarritz–Geneva and many other innovative city pairings).

Between them, these pioneering companies operate more than 750 aircraft of all sizes on 750 routes throughout the length and breadth of Europe. Of the 36 aircraft types they use, the Fokker F100, British Aerospace's BAe 146 jets (usually configured for around 100 seats) and the 50–seat Franco-Italian ATR 42 turboprop are the most popular.

However, a significant trend in the regional aviation sector is the ever-increasing size of aircraft being utilised. Figure 3.4 shows the growth in average seating capacity of aircraft used by European regional airlines.

This growth in aircraft size is caused by a number of different pressures. Foremost is the increasing popularity of regional services. At peak times, the smaller aircraft are not large enough to serve the level of demand from passengers. A more negative factor is the lack of runway capacity in Europe, which causes the twin problems of a shortage of available slots for more frequent services and also the use by airports of higher charges to force out smaller aircraft (see page 91).

The level of the saturation at major airports is such that much of this growth in domestic and intra-European air services has come on unusual but innovative new routes which previously enjoyed few, if any, air connections. The ERA believes that the air links that its member carriers operate are becoming vital components in the economic prosperity of Europe. It points out that regionally-based businesses must have regular and efficient air links allowing local business travellers to access national and international markets, while allowing all-important inward investment.

Concentrating on linking cities through routes not served by the major airlines avoids head-on competition with the mighty flag carriers. But the relationship between regional airline and flag carriers need not necessarily be a conflictual one. Another option is for the regional airlines to cooperate with the flag carriers (even if the net result is to reinforce the dominance of the latter). By feeding into capital and major city hubs, many small airlines – some operating under franchise agreements with their national 'big brothers' – are finding significant niches as regional feeders, positioning themselves as the only economically viable short-haul partners of Europe's major airlines.

Bringing efficient air services to business and leisure travellers flying between European cities is what these small and medium-sized airlines are gradually achieving. Given adequate access to airports (as well as some regulatory protection from the dominant airlines), they would appear to have a vital role to play in intra-European air transport.

BUDGET AIRLINES

Among the many airline start-ups in Europe in the 1990s have been a number of low-cost, 'no-frills' or 'low-frills' carriers which have modelled themselves on the cut-price US carriers launched in the 1980s following liberalisation in that country.

European budget airlines such as Debonair and EasyJet based at Luton, Spanair and Air Europa based at Palma de Majorca and Dublin-based Ryanair have attempted to follow the examples of US airlines such as Southwest and ValuJet in providing low-cost air travel. Low-cost airlines' fares undercut very substantially those of conventional airlines, typically being 60 per cent to 85 per cent lower than the cheapest unrestricted fares offered by conventional airlines (ETRF 1997). Table 3.4 shows details of six airlines operating low-cost scheduled international services in Europe.

How have these airlines been able to offer such attractive rates to their customers? French (1996b) notes how US no-frills airlines have shown that concentrating on a few key business basics can lead to a powerful customer franchise and consistent profits:

- keeping a tight rein on overheads;
- boosting staff efficiency;
- paring aircraft and training costs by sticking to one type;
- maximising aircraft utilisation;
- retaining a niche market philosophy however big the overall operation;
- keeping growth within manageable bounds;
- not treading too directly on more powerful competitive rivals;
- exploiting developments in information technology to move into cheaper ticket distribution methods such as direct selling and ticketless travel;
- reducing in-flight service to the minimum;
- never blurring the product perception and brand image. (French 1996b)

European budget airlines have borrowed many of these techniques from their US forerunners. The budget airlines' most visible cost-saving measure is their dispensing with in-flight 'complimentary' food and drink. They offer no meals, although often, drinks may be purchased, as on a train.

But there are a number of other, more subtle, ways in which these airlines have been able to cut costs. For example, most of them have dispensed with the traditional ticketing system, selling through travel agents and computer reservation systems (CRSs). Customers, usually having booked by telephone using their credit cards, simply turn up at the airport with identification and obtain a boarding pass. This form of direct selling and ticketless travel cut costs enormously: in Europe, the associated costs of producing a traditional ticket, in labour, printing, distribution and travel agency commissions, is between US$15 and US$30 per ticket (French 1996b).

Table 3.4 Summary of low cost airline market and frequency shares

Airline	Route From/to	To/from	Frequency share (%)	Estimated/actual load factors (%)	Estimated market share (%)
Air Europa	Barcelona	London	9.7	88.0	17.0
	Madrid	London	5.7	88.0	9.9
Easy Jet	London	Amsterdam	7.1	75.0	6.8
	London	Barcelona	11.3	75.0	9.0
	London	Nice	17.5	75.0	15.1
Debonair	London	Barcelona	11.3	50.0	4.2
	Barcelona	Munich	25.9	50.0	17.5
	Barcelona	Rome	14.3	50.0	6.5
	London	Copenhagen	10.0	50.0	4.4
	Copenhagen	Munich	25.0	50.0	17.8
	London	Dusseldorf	9.2	50.0	4.9
	London	Madrid	6.6	50.0	2.5
	London	Munich	5.5	50.0	2.4
	London	Rome	8.1	50.0	2.6
	Munich	Rome	20.0	50.0	10.5
Ryanair	Dublin	Birmingham	50.7	82.0	65.6
	Dublin	Bournemouth	100.0	82.0	100.0
	Dublin	Cardiff	100.0	82.0	100.0
	Dublin	Glasgow	63.0	82.0	58.5
	Dublin	Leeds/Bradford	55.6	82.0	79.2
	Dublin	London	36.7	82.0	40.4
	Dublin	Liverpool	100.0	82.0	100.0
	Dublin	Manchester	49.2	82.0	59.6
	Connaught	London	100.0	82.0	100.0
	Cork	London	34.5	82.0	42.9
Spanair	Madrid	London	0.9	92.0	1.2
Virgin Express	Brussels	Barcelona	27.3	75.0	34.9
	Barcelona	Rome	14.3	75.0	16.9
	Brussels	Copenhagen	18.7	75.0	25.5
	Brussels	Madrid	21.2	75.0	23.2
	Brussels	Milan	10.3	75.0	13.4
	Brussels	Nice	25.9	75.0	33.7
	Brussels	Rome	18.0	75.0	20.5
	Brussels	Vienna	12.7	75.0	17.3
	Madrid	Rome	13.2	75.0	11.5

Source: *Assessment of the impact of the abolition of intra-EU duty and tax-free allowances on low-cost scheduled airlines*, by Symonds Travers Morgan, commissioned by the European Travel Research Foundation, London 1997

The availability of cheap labour and aircraft have also been key factors driving the start-up of low-cost carriers in Europe. However, the supply of both of these is thought by many to be cyclical in nature. French notes that in the first half of the 1990s, Europe's major carriers shed around 40,000 jobs, supplying a pool of already trained talent prepared to accept lower salaries and more flexible, productivity-driven payment packages. For example, the cabin crew may be required to do the tidying-up at the end of each flight, thus cutting both turn-around time and cleaning bills. Such savings meant that a new entrant airline was likely to enjoy a 50 per cent unit labour cost advantage over an unrationalised major carrier (French 1996).

Regarding aircraft acquisition costs, from 1990 onwards the aircraft over-supply cycle meant that start-up airlines could negotiate highly advantageous lease rates for the aircraft they needed – in many cases the bargain-basement Boeing 737s. However, according to the same author, the longer-term outlook for the continuing availability of relatively low-priced aircraft was much less encouraging. As Europe entered a new upward cycle in air travel in the mid-1990s, the over-supply of aircraft shrank and lease rates turned sharply upwards, forcing some carriers to turn towards a more traditional outright purchase of aircraft to support expansion.

The budget airline market

A strong consumer expectation of cheaper air travel within Europe has prepared the way for the budget airlines and provided them with a ready market. Most of them have established a core market of leisure travellers, and many operators believe that the availability of low-cost flights within Europe will eventually change the pattern of holiday-taking and short breaks, leading to significant growth in second foreign holidays and exotic weekends away. Richard Branson, whose business empire includes the Brussels-based budget carrier Virgin Express, expressed the opinion that the growth of such airlines would cause the number of people flying in Europe to treble in the last three years of the twentieth century. 'At these prices, shopping trips in Milan and do-it-yourself holidays in the south of France and Spain will all

become possible for a much larger group of people' (Sunday Times 1996).

However, the business market has also responded positively to the advent of no-frills flights in Europe, in particular to the fact that operators do not insist on a Saturday night stay-over to qualify for their cheapest tickets. As a result, the proportion of business customers in this market is higher than might be expected. The new airlines estimate that around two-fifths of their customers are business travellers, attracted chiefly by price but also by the punctuality and speed through the terminal that small carriers using less-congested locations can achieve (Daily Telegraph 1996). Interviews carried out in the UK in November 1996 for the annual Carlson Wagonlit Travel/MORI business travel survey indicated that 81 per cent of business travellers, decision makers and bookers agreed that they would be happy to use no-frills flights for short-haul routes within Europe, a rise of 5 per cent over the previous year's survey (Carlson Wagonlit 1997).

How much additional demand has been generated by the advent of budget airlines? Drawing conclusions as to generated growth is difficult, partly because a number of routes have not been operated for very long and are therefore growing rapidly from small bases. However, consultants Symonds Travers Morgan assessed the growth stimulus provided by Ryanair, a more established low-cost airline, as being in the order of 15–20 per cent more than underlying UK to Ireland growth.

Figure 3.5 EasyJet jet aircraft
Source: Courtesy of Richard J. Maslen

The experience on the Ryanair routes can be regarded as an important indicator, since most Ryanair services have been operated for at least 3–4 years with the airline in its current form. This length of service gives us a firm basis for assuming that Ryanair's traffic growth is not a temporary aberration, and we can see no reason why it should not be replicated by other low-cost operators which are managed equally effectively. (ETRF 1997)

A similar picture of additional demand created by the arrival of new low-cost airlines emerges when the EasyJet services from Luton to Scotland are considered (Figure 3.5). Services to Edinburgh and Glasgow began in November 1995. The first full year's figures amount to over 146,000 and 128,000 passengers respectively. Traffic on the overall London to Edinburgh and Glasgow markets grew by 16.6 per cent and 21.6 per cent respectively, compared to overall growth within the UK domestic market of 7.9 per cent. In this case, the low-cost effect appears to be between 8.7 per cent and 13.7 per cent in excess of underlying growth (ETRF 1997).

OBSTACLES TO SUCCESS?

What are the prospects for budget airlines in Europe? There is no doubt that the demand for such services exists, but there is some scepticism that even a liberalised European air transport system will be able to accommodate that demand. A number of obstacles to the continuing growth of any new airlines in Europe, including budget airlines, still stand in the way despite full airline liberalisation.

High infrastructure costs and fuel charges

In Europe, where monopoly state ownership is still the norm for most airports and for the provision of en-route navigation, a combination of inefficiency and overmanning keeps user charges for airlines – mainly take-off and landing fees – relatively high. Inefficiencies and tax differentials also mean that European carriers pay more for aviation fuel than US airlines do. Table 3.5 illustrates these differences in infrastructure and fuel costs.

Table 3.5 Fuel and handling costs

(a) Fuel costs, mid-February 1996 (US cents per gallon)

USA	
Atlanta	56
Dallas	58
Detroit	58
Washington/Dulles	58
Miami	59
Orlando	61

Europe	
London/Heathrow	63
Paris/CDG	65
Frankfurt	65
Athens	72
Copenhagen	73
Gibraltar	100

(b) Handling costs, mid-February, 1996 (US$)

	MD DC-9	Airbus A320
USA		
Atlanta	700	800
Detroit	700	800
Dallas	750	850
Washington/Dulles	750	850
Orlando	800	900
Miami	800	900
Europe		
Gibraltar	765	1,148
London/Heathrow	1,071	1,530
Copenhagen	1,754	2,632
Athens	1,758	3,823
Frankfurt	2,721	4,286
Paris/CDG	3,175	4,762

Source: French, T. H. E. (1996a)

High handling costs and landing charges in Europe's main airports mean that low-cost airlines are forced to go where low infrastructure-related charges take them, and that usually means using less expensive secondary airports. For example, Ryanair's service between Dublin and Brussels does not arrive at Zaventem airport, but at Charleroi, 55 km away from the capital. But at less than ECU 100 for a flexible return fare, compared with state-owned rival's tariff of almost ECU 685 for an open ticket, Ryanair's passengers do not complain. Similarly, when passengers take Debonair's flight to Düsseldorf, they actually land at Mönchen-Gladbach, and Ryanair's flights to Paris use Beauvais airport instead of Orly or Charles de Gaulle.

Europe's second-tier airports have welcomed this trend. In return for having life breathed back into them, many of them have taken steps to make life easier for passengers and to minimise the disavantages for the airlines. Thus, for example, Debonair passengers travelling to Mönchen-Gladbach get free return rail tickets to Dortmund, Düsseldorf, Cologne and Bonn. In the UK, Luton Airport, used by EasyJet, will soon be more easily accessible when a train line is extended to the terminus (European Voice 1997a).

But low-cost carriers' use of second-tier airports may mean that they incur substantial increases in landing charges if the decision to abolish intra-EU duty-free sales proceeds as planned. As such airports tend to have significantly fewer flights to destinations outside the EU (for which duty-free sales will continue to be allowed), they are likely to suffer disproportionately more from the abolition of duty-free trading than major airports are. In turn, since airports will have to make up for the loss of revenue from duty-free, the airlines serving the second-tier airports will be more at risk of increased landing charges than their counterparts at larger airports.

However, the European Commission is doing its best to improve the general situation regarding infrastructure costs, by attempting to introduce competition and value for money into the system. For example, in December 1994, the Commission adopted a proposal for a directive to facilitate access to the ground handling market and to improve fair competition. Similarly, in April 1997,

a proposed directive was presented to the Commission giving airlines greater powers to check on and challenge the prices they are charged by airports. This directive was designed to put an end to discriminatory pricing practices which continued even after the arrival of full EU airline liberalisation. For example, airlines are often charged higher take-off and landing fees for intra-European flights than for national flights, even though, airlines claim, the same type of aircraft is often being used and there is very little difference in the administrative costs involved for the airport. There is also evidence of potential discrimination against airlines using smaller aircraft: since fees are normally related to the aircraft's weight and the number of passengers carried, some managements, especially those at Europe's most congested airports have floated the idea of imposing significantly heavier fees on smaller regional aircraft, effectively pricing them out of the market and making way for larger, more lucrative aircraft (European Voice 1997a).

The three-pronged measure proposed by the Transport Commissioner called for non-discrimination, transparency in pricing and a 'reasonable relationship between charges and costs'.

Access to the market

Difficulties in achieving effective access to the market, is regarded by many as the most serious problem for new airline services. At a time when European air travel continues to be plagued by congestion both in the sky and on the ground at main airports, the issue of access to the market is one which threatens to undermine effective competition in European air transport.

The key to access to the market is having sufficient take-off and landing slots at Europe's airports. The traffic management of Europe's air space depends on the allocation of slot schedules, a vital element in the system which regulates departures and arrivals at Europe's busy airports. Slots, not planes, are an airline's most important asset, and take-off and landing slots have become even more prized possessions as the system has become increasingly congested.

However, as slot restrictions have become a more acute problem throughout Europe, it is clear that smaller airlines get a poor deal in the system by which slots are shared out between airlines. Most slots at EU airports are in the gift of coordinators employed by national flag carriers, a situation which ensures that these airlines continue to dominate their home markets. Even in the UK, where an independent body makes allocations at Heathrow, BA still has 41 per cent of slots at that airport.

As a result, their growing frustration at slot restrictions prompted smaller carriers to seek changes in the way in which slots are distributed. In 1992, EU transport ministers tightened the rules so that airlines would lose slots they did not use, but many smaller carriers complained that this regulation did not go far enough. They wanted slots to be confiscated from large carriers in order to make way for new airlines. In this, they had the support of the UK Civil Aviation Authority, which in 1993 suggested a policy of positive discrimination in slot allocation, favouring new third carriers:

> All newly created, unused or otherwise available slots should be placed in a pool and earmarked for new competing third carrier services. Slot coordinators should allocate these to prospective third carriers on a route using agreed Community criteria, the principal one being an applicant's past record as an effective operator. By adopting such a policy of positive discrimination in slot allocation, more effective competition on many currently duopoly routes should be possible in a relatively short time. At those important EC airports where congestion is not yet acute, this would reduce the risk of existing flag carrier dominance becoming as entrenched as it is now at the most congested airports. (CAA 1993)

The problem is far from being solved to the satisfaction of the new entrant airlines. The European Commission has introduced regulations to ensure that new entrants are given the opportunity to operate services out of congested airports, through a system based on giving them priority on new slots when these become available. But new entrant airlines complain that the so-called 'grandfather rights' – effectively the allocation of slots to the airline which had them first – mean that the established carriers are still entitled to automatically claim the same slots from

one season to another. Naturally, the big carriers will fight tooth-and-nail against surrendering slots, since no slots means no service. They are a heavyweight lobby and many of them argue that their sizeable share does not inhibit fair competition.

Failing a sweeping upheaval of the slot allocation system, availability can only be increased either through piecemeal improvements in Europe's air traffic control and growth in terminal capacity (but efforts in these fields are handicapped by frustratingly long lead times – see page 97) or by extending the working day at airports. The CAA has pointed out, for example, that by adding an extra half hour in the morning and in the evening to the time available at airports for take-offs and landings, an extra 74 movements would be produced (Financial Times 1993). However, such moves would clearly give rise to earlier morning and later evening noise, to which environmentalists would strongly object.

Safety concerns

There is also considerable apprehension among the new airlines over the possibility of growing public concern over safety standards. The US airline ValuJet, often considered a model for the new European low-fare carriers, was grounded after one of its DC-9s crashed into a Florida swamp on 11 May 1996, killing all 109 passengers and crew. The crash reignited an intense debate over the safety of budget airlines. ValuJet had been under close scrutiny by the Federal Aviation Administration after a string of accidents and the company had already agreed to cut back on expansion and to recruit more experienced pilots and technical staff. By 1997, the airline was operational again, but its planes were barely half-full, against an industry average of around 70 per cent (Economist 1997).

However, Europe has some of the toughest safety inspection standards in the world, and there are few signs that Europeans are overly anxious about this issue, or at least not enough to prevent them using low-frills flights. Shortly after the ValuJet crash, Richard Branson gave this reply to the suggestion that new airlines were in any way less safe than their established rivals:

There is no question of new companies cutting corners on safety. Some of the larger players may like to make that argument, but the truth is that their higher prices have nothing to do with better safety. They have allowed their sales and distribution costs to fly out of control. (Sunday Times 1996)

The reaction of Europe's major carriers

However, even if the preceding problems can be resolved or avoided, another serious potential obstacle to the success of low-fare new entrants remains: the reaction by European major carriers if any attempt is made to move into key markets in strength. As French (1996b) points out, many new-entrant airlines have been reluctant to move on to the major routes, fearing a hostile, repressive reaction from the large airlines who dominate these. In theory, the European Commission's own rules governing concerted price-fixing, predatory pricing and the abuse of dominant positions would provide budget airlines with sufficient protection against such practices. But such rules are still largely untested and most new entrant airlines, including low-fare carriers, have been unwilling to take the risk.

Moreover, as the major carriers attempt to reduce their own costs over time – often using techniques tried and tested by low-fare carriers themselves – they will be able to compete more effectively with the new entrants. For example, by the mid-1990s, all of Europe's major carriers were investigating direct selling, mostly on high-yield business markets. It seemed that direct, ticketless selling would not be the sole preserve of low-cost new entrant airlines for much longer.

The widespread adoption of direct selling by Europe's major airlines would bring Europe more into line with the USA, where over 60 per cent of airline bookings are direct by telephone. In Europe, by comparison, over 90 per cent of bookings are still made through the CRS/travel agent system (French 1996b).

By cutting their own costs in such ways, the major carriers will increasingly be able to offer more capacity at lower fares, narrowing the difference between themselves and the low-fare airlines. There have already been casualties. In 1996, Air Liberté opened 23 new cut-rate routes in France,

offering full-service flights, with even more champagne than Air France. Such generosity meant that their costs spiralled and when Air France cut its fares, Air Liberté was forced into bankruptcy and then was bought by British Airways.

It could be a bitter battle, with few winners. In Germany, for example, where fares are 20 per cent above the EU average, Lufthansa was already facing tough competition from companies such as Eurowings and Deutsche BA, British Airways' German subsidiary, even before Debonair arrived on the scene in 1997. Lufthansa's response was to slash fares in order to protect its 80 per cent share of the German market. But, as a senior member of their staff was quoted as saying at that time: 'We will not make any money, but no-one else will either' (European Voice 1997a).

By 1997, it was clear that some new-entrant airlines were already driving down fares on formerly monopolised routes. Ryanair had taken 40 per cent of Dublin-London traffic from Aer Lingus, resulting in a price drop to US$94 return trip, 44 per cent lower than Aer Lingus' fares ten years

Figure 3.6 Round-trip prices on popular routes
Source: Business Week

Round-trip prices on popular routes		
	Lowest fare	Unrestricted
FRANKFURT-BERLIN		
LUFTHANSA	$153	$494
EUROWINGS	$140	$469
ROME-MILAN		
ALITALIA	$130	$278
AIR ONE	$82	$211
PARIS-TOULOUSE		
AIR FRANCE	$88	$350
AIR LIBERTÉ/TAT	$70	$286
STOCKHOLM-OSLO		
SAS	$244	$455
BRAATHENS SAFE	$130	$486
LONDON-BARCELONA		
BA	$358	$816
EASYJET	$165	$261

previously. When Norway's Braathens SAFE started flying the Stockholm-Oslo route in autumn 1996, it offered a US$263 return trip with no restrictions. Scandinavia Airlines System (SAS), which was charging US$500 at that time, responded by offering an express check-in, a Travel Pass allowing ten trips without pre-booking, and a matching fare. And when Italy's Air One (see page 101) introduced its Rome–Milan flights in 1996, it forced Alitalia to cut off-peak prices by 42 per cent (Business Week 1997).

Figure 3.6 compares return air fares on some popular routes within Europe.

Instead of struggling to match the lower fares of their lower-cost rivals, other options remain open to national carriers. Since many of them lose money on short-haul routes, these could be sub-contracted. By 1997, Belgian's Sabena World Airlines had given its flights between Brussels and London, Barcelona and Rome to Virgin Express. High-cost Sabena thus shed unprofitable routes, Virgin gained Sabena's precious airport slots, and passengers got prices 50 per cent lower than Sabena's former fares.

Another strategy the national carriers are pursuing is to franchise shorter routes to start-up carriers, yet insist that they carry the national brand name. By 1997, British Airways already had eight franchisees, mostly under the umbrella name BA Express flying throughout the UK and into Scandinavia, South Africa and the Middle East. Similarly, Lufthansa had three German franchisees flying domestic flights as Team Lufthansa.

With so many factors militating against them, what are the prospects for the survival and success of low-cost, no-frills operations in Europe? French is among those commentators who tend towards taking a pessimistic view of these airlines' chances against the entrenched European air transport system. He believes that 'Not even a period of sustained airline growth is likely to offer security for cheap travel operators, while the next recession in the airline industry will cut away the last inefficiencies in the major airline sector, leaving them leaner and more competitive than ever' (French 1996b).

Others are more up-beat in their analysis. Consultants Symonds Travers Morgan, for example, while acknowledging that the principal limit on growth for low-cost airlines is the capacity they are able to offer, nevertheless foresee considerable opportunities for expansion in this sector. Assuming that such airlines can maintain their price differential compared to their high-cost competitors, Symonds Travers Morgan believe that any intra-European route which already has

Table 3.6 Top ten eligible routes for new carrier entry

Route	Passengers (1996)	Economy fare (ECUs)	Sector distance (kms)	Fare (ECU) (per km)	Load factor (%)
Milan–Paris	919,727	358.28	621	0.577	57.4
Paris–Rome	892,584	524.67	1,106	0.474	68.9
Amsterdam–Paris	864,102	261.40	417	0.627	61.4
Copenhagen–Stockholm	861,756	271.83	534	0.509	59.0
Madrid–Paris	827,035	460.98	1,049	0.439	60.9
Frankfurt–Paris	811,654	287.84	460	0.626	60.4
London–Munich	809,762	328.98	912	0.361	61.9
London–Vienna	744,581	337.35	1,255	0.269	70.9
London–Stockholm	659,856	359.65	1,432	0.251	67.9
Helsinki–Stockholm	633,333	254.66	404	0.630	58.4

Source: Assessment of the impact of the abolition of intra-EU duty and tax-free allowances on low-cost scheduled airlines, by Symonds Travers Morgan, commissioned by the European Travel Research Foundation, London, 1997

150,000 passengers per annum or more and which does not already have a low-cost carrier could be regarded as an eligible route for low-cost carrier entry. There are 90 such routes in Europe, the ten largest (by traffic density) of which are shown in Table 3.6.

The 90 eligible routes between them accounted for an estimated total passenger volume in 1996 of 32.9 million passengers.

Many commentators are of the opinion that the best opportunities for budget airlines will come on an opportunistic basis, and in closely defined niche markets, rather than competing head-on with the major, established carriers. Budget carriers, like the regional airlines, may finally find their niche through concentrating on secondary routes within Europe and feeding passengers into the hubs of the established carriers, who will continue to dominate the long-haul market. This arrangement would, however, bring with it two disadvantages: it would further aggravate congestion at busy hubs, and it would firmly tie the smaller airlines into the major carriers.

WILL LIBERALISATION LEAD TO LOWER AIR FARES?

From what has already been discussed on the subject of air fares in this chapter, it is clear that the pressure on fares during most of the 1990s has been a downward one. The increased competition arising as a result of deregulation is one of the factors driving prices down and, linked to this, customers' expectations of lower fares is another. Nevertheless, in sharp contrast to the downward trend in economy tariffs for weekend returns and leisure flights, fully flexible business travel fares have remained stubbornly high since European airline deregulation began.

In 1997, this situation attracted the attention of the European Commission, which made efforts to assess whether airlines were charging inflated prices for business travel. EU transport officials have powers, granted by a 1993 regulation, to force cuts in fares. Under these rules, ticket prices amounting to 130 per cent of the airline's costs are regarded as excessive. The regulation has never been used, partly because of a lack of complaints from passengers and of information on which to proceed. However, the Association of European Airlines (AEA) refused to supply the information on fares and costs which the European Commission requested.

The AEA's argument was that since liberalisation was supposed to give airlines the freedom to set their own fares, it was ironic that the Commission now appeared to want to turn the clock back to the days of regulation. A spokesman was quoted as saying that it should be left to the market to decide prices. He added that the Commission had contributed to high costs by failing to do enough to attack airport monopolies and introduce more competition for services used by airlines (European Voice 1997b).

But commentators had predicted that even if fares fell, there were other factors which could cancel out any temporary reductions. Some of those factors were indeed a direct result of EU policies. For example, Jefferson (1992) expressed the view that 'new [EU] labour laws, the removal of duty-free and the imposition of VAT will push airfares up, so it is doubtful if liberalisation will result in cheaper fares'. The possible imposition of taxes on aircraft fuel is another EU-related factor to be taken into account in the calculation of the direction air fares are likely to take in the future. Lickorish (1997) also warned that transport price reductions may be negated by increased taxes, especially port or exit taxes imposed by national governments.

Airports

The expectations of many providers and users of passenger air transport that liberalisation would lead to extensive growth of air services in Europe have not yet been realised. For it has become clear that the major impediment to the expansion of air services in many parts of Europe is no longer government regulation but airport congestion. This is particularly the case at Europe's major airports, where the vast majority of traffic is concentrated. In all, Europe has a total of 537 airports, but 85 per cent of all passenger traffic goes through only fifteen of them (Time 1997c). Table 3.7 shows how traffic at Europe's twenty busiest airports has increased since 1970.

Table 3.7 Traffic at selected major airports (total passenger movements; million passengers)

		1970	1980	1990	1994	1995
1 London Heathrow	UK	15.6	27.5	43.0	51.7	54.5
2 Frankfurt Rhein-Main	D	9.4	17.6	29.4	35.1	38.2
3 Paris Charles de Gaulle	F	2.2	10.1	22.5	29.6	28.4
4 Paris Orly	F	10.4	15.7	24.3	26.6	26.7
5 Amsterdam Schiphol	NL	5.2	9.4	16.5	23.6	25.4
6 London Gatwick	UK	3.7	9.7	21.2	21.2	22.5
7 Rome Fiumicino	I	6.5	11.4	17.7	20.3	21.1
8 Madrid Barajas	E	4.8	10.1	16.2	18.4	20.0
9 Manchester	UK	1.9	4.3	10.1	14.8	15.0
10 Palma de Mallorca	E	4.8	7.3	11.3	14.1	15.1
11 Düsseldorf	D	3.6	7.2	11.9	14.0	14.9
12 Copenhagen Kastrup	DK	6.5	8.6	12.1	14.0	14.7
13 München	D	3.6	6.0	11.4	13.5	13.5
14 Stockholm Arlanda	S	2.6	4.3	14.0	13.4	14.7
15 Bruxelles Zaventem	B	2.8	5.1	7.1	11.3	12.6
16 Barcelona	E	4.0	5.8	9.0	10.6	11.7
17 Athens Hellenikon	GR	3.7	9.2	10.1	10.5	10.5
18 Milano Linate	I	2.9	6.2	9.5	10.1	10.8
19 Vienna	A	1.5	2.7	5.5	7.7	8.5
20 Dublin	IRL	1.9	2.6	5.5	7.0	8.0
Total of Airports		97.6	180.8	308.3	367.5	386.8

Note: average annual growth rate: 1970–95 = +5.7% (estimates in italic)
Source: Eurostat

The problems of airport congestion are familiar to anyone who has flown from or to a European airport. Major hubs in particular are increasingly saturated at peak times and delays are more widespread as a result. A study by the Association of European Airlines noted that 18.5 per cent of scheduled departures in 1996 were delayed more than fifteen minutes, the figure rising to 21.1 per cent in January 1997 (Time 1997a).

During the late 1980s and early 1990s, many of the problems of severe congestion and delays were created by Europe's disparate air traffic control (ATC) systems. But during the 1990s, Europe scored a signal success in improving the efficiency and capacity of its ATC systems by pro-ducing a single, harmonised system and improving facilities. Much of the investment required to do so was underpinned by loans from the European Investment Bank (EIB), which totalled some ECU 404 million between 1990–94. About a quarter of this sum was used to support centralisation of Eurocontrol's operations in premises close to Brussels airport plus a test centre at Bretigny-sur-Orge near Paris, where investment was made into new research and digital equipment (EIB 1995).

But in many ways, such improvements only added to the continuing problems caused by lack of capacity at European airports, by increasing pressure on their already overstretched infrastructure. It has become clear that the major constraint to growth now lies in the area of infrastructure: Europe's top 30 airports are all either full or very close to it; check-in times are stretching longer and longer, and passengers encounter congestion in and around the airports. Many argue that without expansion of Europe's airports, liberalisation remains a sham, and that one of Europe's most notable growth sectors, air transport, risks stagnation.

Progress on improvements to Europe's airports, and in particular on the construction of new runways has been painfully slow. It has become clear that the ability of existing airports to add runways is severely circumscribed, usually because land is not available, or because environmental factors – primarily aircraft noise and emissions – can make projects politically controversial. Even where new runways can be added, the process is proving so time-consuming that, when finished, they are likely to be used immediately at their full capacity, again leaving the system with no space to accommodate subsequent growth.

French (1996a) has predicted that by the first few years of the twenty-first century, most of Europe's main hubs will be capacity-limited despite expansion plans and efficiency improvements.

In summary, unless air transport reverses its historic tendency to grow faster than forecasts suggest, the first decade of the twenty-first century will see real problems in system capacity for the first time in the history of civil aviation. Something will have to give: either airport development will be speeded up, against the wishes of environmental campaigners, or the real costs of air travel will start to rise because there will be no choice but to ration demand by price.

The problem is worldwide, but data show that the two world regions which are giving most concern on airport capacity – Europe and the Pacific – are also those in which the demand for air passenger transport and air freight transport are growing the fastest.

There has been some considerable investment in airport capacity improvements throughout the 1990s, but those in the industry are almost unanimous in their belief that this is not enough. A 1990 study by consultants SRI International indicated that the then level of investment in infrastructure for commercial aviation activities in Europe was insufficient to support the existing levels of traffic or permit significant growth. Since 1990, several airport capacity improvements have been implemented or planned. Amsterdam Schiphol, Copenhagen, Dublin, Frankfurt, Hamburg, London Heathrow, Manchester, Munich, Paris Orly and Charles de Gaulle are examples of airports where produced or planned measures to increase runway or terminal capacity or to reduce general aviation and commuter activity should ease the situation. Despite these improvements, however, capacity increases have barely kept up with increased demand (French 1996a).

Against this background, air transport and airport managers are becoming increasingly concerned about the lack of significant progress in laying the groundwork for the construction of new airports, especially as the possibilities for expanding existing key hub airports are increasingly limited. At the beginning of 1996, there were only three all-new airports under way in Europe:

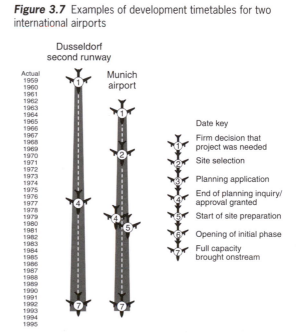

Figure 3.7 Examples of development timetables for two international airports

Source: French, T. H. E. (1996a)

at Oslo, Athens and Berlin. These are in fact replacement airports, where the capacity of the current airports will be lost when the new ones open.

French (1996a) reports how in Europe, industry lobbyists are becoming increasingly vocal in objecting to the length of time it is taking to get major infrastructure projects through the process of approval, planning and construction, and commissioning. He gives as examples the new airport at Munich and the construction of a second runway at Düsseldorf both of which took a full generation to come to fruition, as shown in Figure 3.7.

Scard (1993) maintains that lead times of this sort can be greatly reduced in Europe and elucidates:

> Airport development lobbyists remain acutely aware that the due democratic process must be followed; what they object to is not that each project is stringently weighed up against the environmental and social disruption it will bring, but that the process of doing so is often clumsy, vulnerable to political interference, and hard to conclude.

Nevertheless, in the on-going battle between pressures for and against development, many of those responsible for Europe's airports find it hard to reconcile demands for expansion with cries for restraint. In an article for *Time* magazine, the president of the International Air Carriers Association was quoted as complaining that the Dutch authorities have given Amsterdam's Schiphol Airport permission to handle up to 44 million passengers, even while accepting a noise-abatement programme proposed by environmentalists – which, he claims, will make it impossible to meet that traffic target (Time 1997c).

Efforts to build a second runway at Manchester Airport were, by 1997, literally undermined by protesters squatting in tunnels around the construction sites. At the same time, the British Airport Authority, wishing to build a fifth terminal at London's Heathrow by 2003 to handle up to 35 million additional passengers within twenty years, was fighting environmental and resident groups for planning permission. The same *Time* article quotes Heathrow's managing director as saying:

'We are just about at capacity. If we cannot meet the passenger demand, the airports at Frankfurt, Paris and Amsterdam would love to take our place' (Time 1997c).

The Air Transport Action Group (ATAG) is a coalition of commercial interests (airports, airlines, aircraft manufacturers, chambers of commerce, etc.) which acts as a pro-airport lobbying group. French (1996a) describes ATAG's two-part strategy to press for what they say are urgently needed improvements in aviation infrastructure:

1 convincing planning authorities, governments, politicians and the public of the progress which the air transport industry has made in reducing the environmental impact of aircraft noise and emissions and demonstrating their willingness to make concessions such as agreeing to night curfews;
2 countering the claims of environmental and social disruption by pointing out the economic benefits in terms of employment and wealth creation which airports, and the air services they support, can bring to a region or its chief metropolis.

Time will tell whether this strategy will prove to be effective enough to persuade decision-makers that airport developments are necessary and capable of being implemented without unacceptably compromising the quality of life of those living near such termini. What is certain is that it is the current debate between the needs of the air transport industry and those of the population which is affected by its proximity which will set the scene for the first decade of the new millennium.

THE ROLE OF THE EU

Europe's central planners in Brussels, at the European Commission, are aware of the problem of limited airport capacity, and have included airport developments in their policy directives. Their approach consists of a plan to establish a European airport network as an integral part of a trans-European transport network.

In this context, the European Commission, working in cooperation with the Member States, has defined a trans-European airport network to meet the growth in demand for air transport. Such a network, according to the Commission, is based on the need to ensure that:

- airport capacity in the Community is able to meet current and future demand, taking into account the expected effects of the Third Civil Aviation Package adopted by the Council;
- capacity development remains compatible with environmental requirements, particularly with regard to how the quality of life of the population living in the vicinity of airports is affected by air traffic as well as the land-side access to airports and the ensuing growth of land-side traffic;
- airport development contributes to the economic and social cohesion of the Community, with special emphasis on the links between peripheral and core regions.

The general aim of the European Commission report on guidelines for the trans-European airport network (SEC 94) is, first and foremost, to make better use of the existing capacity of the network and individual airports and – only if required – to develop new capacity to meet the growing demand. It states that the development of a European airport network should focus on (in this order):

- the enhancement of existing capacity;
- the development of new capacity;
- the enhancement of the environmental compatibility of airports;
- the enhancement and development of access to the airport.

However, this preferred solution of the European Commission – making the demand fit into available infrastructure rather than pushing development at key central hubs – is increasingly coming under fire as an unrealistic and unworkable solution.

In dialogue with the European Commission on this issue is the Association of European Airlines (AEA), the representative body for Europe's main carriers. In a 1995 report, the AEA made a firm plea for more action to tackle congestion, existing and future, at the continent's key hub airports. The AEA, stressing that traffic in Europe is expected to double in the next twelve years, pointed out that 85 per cent of scheduled and freight traffic goes through the top 15 per cent of airports by number. According to AEA lobbyists, of Europe's 29 largest airports, 26 will need more terminal capacity and 25 will need more runway capacity by 2005, over and above the expansion plans currently in place. This will be needed to cope with 1.2 billion passenger movements in 2005, compared with 600 million in 1993 and over 16 million aircraft movements compared with 9 million in 1993.

Throughout the AEA's report, it warns that the problems are and will be worst at the major hub airports which offer a comprehensive global coverage of destinations. These are: London/Gatwick and Heathrow, Frankfurt, Paris/Charles de Gaulle, Amsterdam, Rome, Madrid and Zurich. Of these, only Amsterdam has firm plans for another runway (its fifth) while Madrid is in the early stages of planning its third runway. All these airports except Gatwick have plans for significant terminal capacity enhancement.

French (1996a) points out that the entry into service of Munich's new airport in 1992 left only three airports – Oslo, Athens and Berlin – under any sort of firm planning, although the Milan/Malpensa 2000 project is a development on such a scale that it almost amounts to a new airport. Of the three projects currently in planning, only one – Berlin – is sited at what will, in future, become a major hub. The other two are more peripheral airports, and as such will have less effect on the continent's major pressure points.

He adds that the chief difficulty within Europe is that fairly small variations in passenger growth assumptions – say 4 per cent low growth, 4.6 per cent medium growth, and 5.9 per cent high growth – result in large differences in the likely timing of traffic-limiting congestion. For example, taking planned enhancements into account, the number of runway-constrained airports in Europe in 2010 could be only five at low growth, but could reach 23 at high growth. This variation appears to allow some breathing space, but air transport's actual performance has always at least matched, and often exceeded growth forecasts. Given the long lead times of airport projects in Europe, especially all-new airports, the conclusion is that plans are lagging far behind the likely needs of the continent.

Table 3.8 World airport traffic growth,[1] 1990–94

	1990	1991	1992	1993	1994
Aircraft movements[2] (m)	41.98	42.11	43.21	43.71	45.14
Passengers[3] (m)	1,879	1,843	1,979	2,055	2,224

Notes:
[1] Data cover 385 airports
[2] Movement=take-off and landing of an aircraft
[3] Passengers=arriving and departing passengers counted twice, direct transit passengers counted once.
Source: French, T. H. E. (1996b)

ALTERNATIVES TO AIRPORT EXPANSIONS?

Given the often intractable nature of the expansion versus environment question surrounding airport development in Europe, other possible solutions to accommodating air transport growth have been considered with interest by both sides in the debate.

Use of larger aircraft

During the 1990s, some of the growth in demand for air transport services was absorbed by the use of larger aircraft. This emerges from the data contained in Table 3.8, which shows that the rate of growth in aircraft movements during the first half of the decade was less than half the growth rate of passenger traffic.

There is further scope for limiting the number of aircraft movements through using aircraft with more carrying capacity. On some intercontinental routes, in and out of Europe, for example, there is potential for using new very large aircraft, such as the double-decker A3XX currently under development in Toulouse. The 550-seat jet could be ready for delivery by 2003. But the world's two main commercial jet makers, Airbus, the European consortium currently developing the A3XX, and the Seattle-based Boeing disagree on whether or not the need for the Superjumbo actually exists. Airbus claims that a continuing surge in tourism, crowded airways and environmental limits on new airport construction all mean that 1,400 Superjumbos will be required during the first two decades of the twenty-first century. Boeing (who abandoned their own version of a 550-seat jet in 1997) argues that airlines are increasingly flying point-to-point routes with smaller aircraft, bypassing the congested hub airports where huge planes may make sense (Time 1997b).

What must also be taken into account is the argument that, in general, given the choice, customers – in particular business clients – prefer a high frequency of service to a concentration of services into more occasional flights.

European high-speed train network

A strong body of opinion exists among European regulators that air transport congestion can be solved by encouraging the development of a European high-speed rail network (see page 128). Their belief is that fast trains could attract so much of the short-haul air market that flight frequencies could be cut, easing the pressure on the infrastructure (and on the environment). The case rests on the evidence of Paris–Lyons, a busy 400 km route which experienced a 35 per cent drop in frequency when the TGV link was opened.

But, others argue that there are few busy air transport connections in Europe with similar characteristics to the short distance, high-volume Paris–Lyons route. Three-quarters of intra-European air transport capacity is on longer connections than this example, and therefore less likely to be significantly affected by high-speed rail services. For example, if total journey times between London and the south of France are compared, it becomes clear that there is a vast difference between them: approximately three hours by plane, as opposed to nine by rail.

Background

Air One is a private Italian airline operating scheduled services on domestic and European trunk routes and international charter flights, with a fleet of Boeing 737s and DC-9s (Figure 3.8). The company started operations on Italy's primary trunk route, Rome–Milan in November 1995. The network now includes London (since summer 1997), Turin, Naples, Bari, Crotone, Reggio Calabria.

Established in 1983 under the name Aliadriatica as a light aircraft training school in the city of Pescara, the company has, since 1989, been a part of the Toto Group, which is one of Italy's main civil engineering firms and general contractors. Among the group's operating companies is European Avia Service, which provides passenger handling services for Air One.

The company's acquisition of its first Boeing 737 in June 1994 signalled the stepping up to medium-sized commercial jets, which are considered optimal for both scheduled and charter operations over medium-range routes.

In April 1995, Aliadriatica started scheduled services between Milan and Brindisi, Reggio Calabria and Lamezia Terme. In November of that year, the new Air One identity and the Rome–Milan route were unveiled together. This meant that for the first time, this route, the fifth busiest in Europe, with over 2 million passengers carried each year, was open to competition, with passengers being able to choose between the national carrier Alitalia and the new alternative, Air One. Until then, this

Figure 3.8 Air One jet aircraft

Source: Aeronews

continued

route had been one of Alitalia's few sources of profit.

As early as 1990, Air One's chairman had wanted to operate this route, but, in those days before full liberalisation, the company's application to do so was turned down. But in 1993, after the EU had issued its Third Package of reforms, requiring Member States to open up competition at least to domestic airlines, Air One decided to re-apply. This time, despite the three law suits filed against the company by Alitalia, Air One succeeded in gaining authorisation. The airline was also able to take advantage of an increase in take-off and landing slots at Milan's Linate airport.

Air One's products

By 1997, Air One was operating 430 flight sectors a week, including 26 daily on the Rome–Milan route, spread out through the working day to best meet the needs of the users on this major, mainly business, route. On the Milan–London route, Air One's twice daily schedule of early morning and evening services is supplemented through an agreement with Air UK, which flies London Stansted–Linate three times a day, offering Air One customers a total of five flights daily.

The Air One strategy is to match quality service, both on the ground and in the air, with affordable rates and a simple price structure. For example, while Alitalia's domestic passengers get little more than peanuts and a drink, Air One serves sandwiches and sparkling wine and distributes free copies of the *International Herald Tribune*.

Air One sells tickets at peak and off-peak rates. The company also offers a 'Carnet' of eleven flights for the price of ten on any given route and a 'Carnet Plus', which also includes six Hertz car rental vouchers at special low rates.

All flights enable passengers to earn miles in Qualiflyer, the Swissair frequent flyer programme, in which fourteen different airlines participate. All domestic flights are operated in single-class configuration. A Business Class service is also offered on the London route. Air One is also active in the charter field, which accounts for about 5 per cent of its business.

All flights are operated from primary airports, namely Linate for Milan and Fiumicino for Rome. Air One's reservations system is connected with the major international and domestic distribution networks via the main CRSs (computer reservation systems) operating in Italy: Galileo, Sabre, Amadeus and Worldspan.

Cost-cutting measures

Price is the main reason why Air One's customers choose to fly with this company. Young staff, no trades unions and no override commissions, together with fewer overheads and more outsourcing than other airlines means that Air One's fares are consistently cheaper than those of their rivals. For example in 1997, Air One's full, unrestricted one-way fare from Rome to Milan was US$105, compared with US$140 on Alitalia. Direct sales account for 20 per cent of the total tickets sold, and the company feels that there is scope for more direct selling, as the airline's products are relatively simple ones.

Regarding operating costs, because Air One's route network is mainly a short-haul one, its largest operating cost are the handling charges it pays, followed by maintenance, fuel and crew. In order to control costs, Air One provides its own ground handling where it can, particularly at crucial points such as Rome and Milan.

The market

The market for Air One's flights is overwhelmingly one based on business travel. A typical Air One passenger has been described as 'the midlevel executive who pays for tickets out of his own pocket' (Air Transport World 1996).

In 1996, Air One carried over 713,000 passengers, two-thirds of whom were on the Rome–Milan route. On 14 March 1997, the airline carried its millionth scheduled passenger. By that year, it was already the third largest of Italy's ten non-charter airlines, after Alitalia and Meridiana.

Expansion prospects

In February 1997, Air One's expansion continued when it was given permission by the Italian Ministry of Transport to absorb the scheduled airline operations of Noman, a smaller domestic carrier that had just suspended service. Under the terms of the

continued

agreement, Air One obtained permission to utilise Noman's two DC-9/15 aircraft and its Rome-based engineering division. The agreement also included seven slots (fourteen movements: seven landings and seven take-offs per day) at the congested Milan–Linate airport. With these, Air One planned to increase frequency on some key trunk routes from Milan and also to expand its international services.

The future

In an environment characterised by acquisitions and franchising, one possible future role for Air One could be that of Alitalia's low-cost domestic partner. In other words, Air One could link up with Alitalia, providing domestic services and leaving Alitalia to concentrate on long-haul routes. The trade publication, *Air Transport World* asked both airlines in 1996 if Air One might end up as the lower-cost domestic arm of Alitalia.

At the time, Alitalia's reply was that it seriously considered Air One as a possible domestic partner. But, the Air One response was that while a link-up with Alitalia might look good on paper in the short term, in the long term Air One was confident that alone it could surmount the formidable barriers posed by Italy's notorious bureaucracy, and succeed by itself (Air Transport World 1996).

Moreover, it is also the case that, even where there exists a high-speed rail link as an alternative to travelling by air, many passengers will still want to fly. These include those making onward air connections and those having a final destination more conveniently served by the airport than the train station.

Offshore airports

An imaginative idea, already tried out in Asia, could be applicable in some European centres: offshore airports linked to city centres by high-speed rail. Hong Kong, for example, has plans to divert traffic from its airport in heavily populated Kowloon to a huge new facility on one of the region's islands. Tokyo, too, may establish its third airport away from its built-up zone by building it on an artificial island (Time 1997c). The combination of air and high-speed train travel is already operating successfully in some European airports.

High-speed train services are available to and from airports serving Amsterdam and Frankfurt, as well as London's Gatwick; and Heathrow will have a similar rail connection before the twenty-first century.

References

Air Transport World (1996) 'Booting up competition: Air One is challenging Alitalia for executive power as well as the domestic Italian market', October.

Business Week (1997) 'Flying cheap', 31 March.

CAA (1993) *Airline Competition in the Single European Market*, Civil Aviation Authority, London.

Carlson Wagonlit (1997) *1996 Business Travel Survey*, Carlson Wagonlit Travel/Mori, London.

COR (1995) *Opinion on the Commission Report on the Guidelines for the Trans-European Airport Network*, Committee of the Regions, Brussels.

CEC (1994) *Comité des Sages report on the Privatisation of the European Airline Industry*, Commission of the European Community, Brussels.

CEC (1996) *The Citizens' Network: Fulfilling the Potential of Public Passenger Transport in Europe*, Commission of the European Community, Brussels.

Daily Telegraph, The (1996) 'The heavens open with bargain fares', 21 November.

Economist, The (1997) Fasten your safety belts, 11 January.

EIB (1995) 'EIB financing for telecommunications', in *EIB Information No. 86*, November, European Investment Bank, Luxembourg.

ERA (1997) Regional air travel for quality and safety, European Regional Airlines Association, Chobham.

ETRF (1997) Assessment of the impact of the abolition of intra-EU duty and tax-free allowances on low-cost scheduled airlines (Symonds Travers Morgan), European Travel Research Foundation, Brussels.

European Voice (1997a) 'Fresh bid to end "unfair" airport fees', 'The days of open skies are dawning', 'Airlines cut out the frills to fit into the slots', 20–25 March.

European Voice (1997b) 'Airlines snub bid to cut excess fares', 27 February–5 March.

Financial Times, The (1993) 'Increasingly hostile dogfight', 19 April.

French, T. H. E. (1996a) 'World airport development plans and constraints', in *EIU Travel and Tourism Analyst (1)*, Travel and Tourism Intelligence, London.

French T. H. E. (1996b) No-frills airlines in Europe, in *Travel and Tourism Analyst (3)*, Travel and Tourism Intelligence, London.

Humphreys, B. (1994) 'Deregulating Europe's skies', *Insights*, May, English Tourist Board, London.

Jefferson, A. (1992) Speech in *Proceedings of the 1992 Tourism in Europe Conference*, Centre for Travel and Tourism, Houghton le Spring.

Lickorish, I. J. (1997) 'The European perspective – a need for coordination', in *The ATTT Tourism Education Handbook*, The Tourism Society, London.

Mihalik, B. J. (1992) 'An American Perspective of EC92 and Tourism', in *Proceedings of the 1992 Tourism in Europe Conference*, Centre for Travel and Tourism, Houghton le Spring.

Scard, L. (1993) 'Transport changes in Europe – a time for hubbing?' *Insights*, March, English Tourist Board, London.

SEC (1994) *Report on the Guidelines for the Trans-European Airport Network*, European Commission, Brussels.

Sunday Times, The (1996) 'War in the skies', 25 August.

Time (1997a) 'The coming rail revolution', 16 June.

Time (1997b) 'A sky-high poker game', 16 June.

Time (1997c) 'Sky unlimited', 16 June.

Vellas, F. and Bécherel, L. (1995) *International Tourism*, Macmillan, London.

WTO (1996) *Tourism Market Trends: Europe 1995*, World Tourism Organisation, Madrid.

4

Land-based transport

KEY OBJECTIVES

Reading this chapter will enable you to:

- Understand the importance of Europe's road network for tourist traffic.
- Be familiar with the role played by the coach transport industry.
- Identify the key factors in the development of Europe's rail network, including the impact of high-speed lines and the Channel Tunnel.
- Understand the impact of EU legislation on both forms of surface transport.

Introduction

The fact that, within Europe, surface transport in general and road transport in particular are the predominant modes of travel for journeys of less than 1,000 km means that changes to Europe's surface transport infrastructure can have wide-ranging implications for tourist flow patterns. When time for leisure and holidays is limited and when, for the business traveller, time is money, it is clear that an efficient transport infrastructure plays a critical role in encouraging people to travel.

The Channel Tunnel is an obvious example of a major infrastructure development with the potential to radically alter travel flow patterns, in this case between the United Kingdom and the European continent. But the proposed Baltic Straits Bridge link is another example of a project with major geopolitical consequences, with its potential to radically alter the travel flow characteristics between the northern rim of central Europe and the Scandinavian peninsula.

Lundgren (1992) demonstrates how earlier additions to Europe's surface transport infrastructure have affected travel flows. The Brenner Pass and other Alpine motorway connections built in the past decades have seen Alpine pass traffic flows increase at rapid rates. The Brenner Pass motorway, opened in 1972, now records traffic flow volumes ten times higher than those of the old highway pass. Similar examples of unprecedented increases can also be found in the more peripheral and less populated areas of Europe: for example, when Europe's longest bridge was inaugurated between the Swedish mainland and the touristically popular island destination Oland in 1972, all expert traffic forecasts became obsolete after only a few months as traffic skyrocketed.

Two of the land-based transport modes which have over the past 150 years played a major role in shaping travel movements in Europe are the roads and the railways. Both play a role not only in influencing tourist flows, but also in triggering the establishment and development of new destinations, by establishing effective transport links between the market and the destination. This chapter examines both modes from the point of view of their relevance for passenger transport and ends with a review of the Channel Tunnel's impact on travel and tourism.

Road passenger transport

EUROPE'S ROAD INFRASTRUCTURE

As shown in Chapter 3, the modal split of European passenger transport is dominated by the

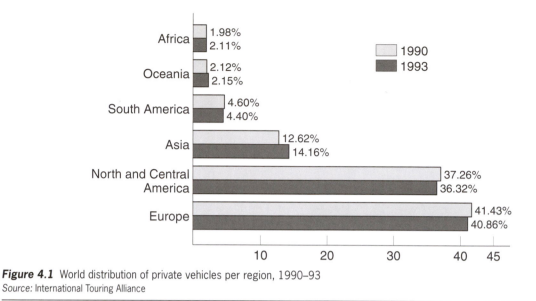

Figure 4.1 World distribution of private vehicles per region, 1990–93
Source: International Touring Alliance

car, and tourism contributes to this widespread use of road transport.

Europe has a greater share of the world's motor vehicles than any other continent, including North America, as shown in Figure 4.1. The data shows, however, that the relative shares of these two world regions are falling slightly as other continents, notably Asia, experience increasing rates of motorisation.

Road transport plays a vital role within the overall European transport infrastructure, carrying some 90 per cent of passengers (IRF 1995). The road network connects all major cities and regions of Europe and, as such, contributes to its economic and social cohesion. Moreover, in many places, especially on the periphery of Europe, road transport is the only available option. Roads also provide an essential link to other transport modes such as rail, air and water. Figure 4.2 shows the road traffic map of Europe, with traffic density.

Naturally, use of Europe's roads is not confined to tourism-related purposes. Commuting and the transport of freight are also important activities placing demands on the network. Nevertheless, roads of all categories within Europe, from the single-track routes across the Scottish highlands to the twelve–lane *autobahn*, play a vital part in providing transport for visitors. As they carry vehicles ranging from the humble bicycle to the luxury coach, roads are an important element of both

domestic tourism and intra-European travel and touring.

But the layout of Europe's roads was not, of course, originally constructed for the transporting of tourists. The European highways system was originally planned, first of all by the continent's Roman invaders, then by individual nation states for strategic, geopolitical reasons and as communication channels. However, the significance of Europe's roads for tourism grew with the advent of continental leisure travel. Lundgren (1992) notes, for example, that the Alpine pass roads later became important for tourism, as obvious passages for the first flow of tourists from the north towards the Italian lake region, the cities of Tuscany, the Riviera and for the first tourist wave arriving in Venice.

It was not until the introduction of the motorway that long-distance travelling by car achieved a competitive edge over rail travel. Figure 4.3 shows the development of Europe's motorway network during from the 1970s to the 1990s, with the principal tourist regions superimposed.

The expansion of Europe's motorway system has made possible a very broad mobilisation of the car-travelling public, facilitating efficient long-distance motoring in a manner comparable to US holiday travel behaviour – not simply within the confines of the nation state but also between countries. The system provides for comfortable and

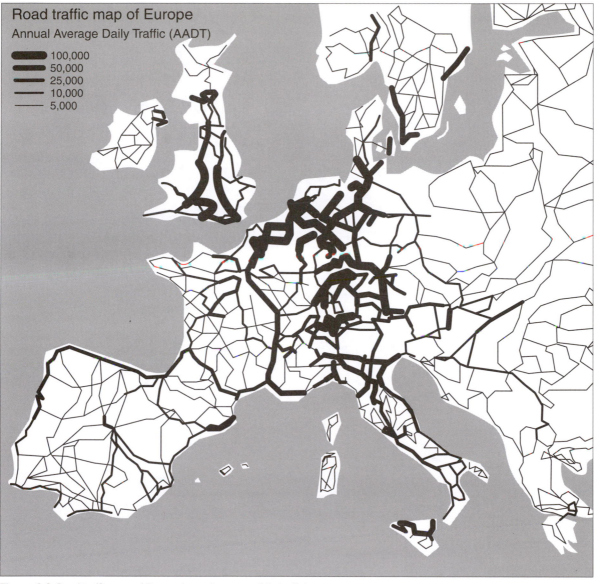

Figure 4.2 Road traffic map of Europe (annual average daily traffic)

Source: Cedre – Albert Serratosa, Courtesy of International Road Federation (IRF)

rapid travel by car and coach from the core to the very extremities of the European continent, responding to, and at the same time creating, the demand for travel to peripheral areas.

Over the years, some critical bottlenecks in Europe's traffic flow arrangement have been removed. North-south motorways in particular meet important natural barriers, in the form of the major mountain backbone of Europe stretching from west to east, from the Alps to the Balkans, in the centre of Europe. These barriers are clearly not unsurmountable but the obvious construction difficulties of tunnels and bridges impose huge financial burdens. Since the 1960s, Alpine motorway links have facilitated north-south flows in a manner which makes for very effective linking of major travel-generating regions with destination zones on a continental scale.

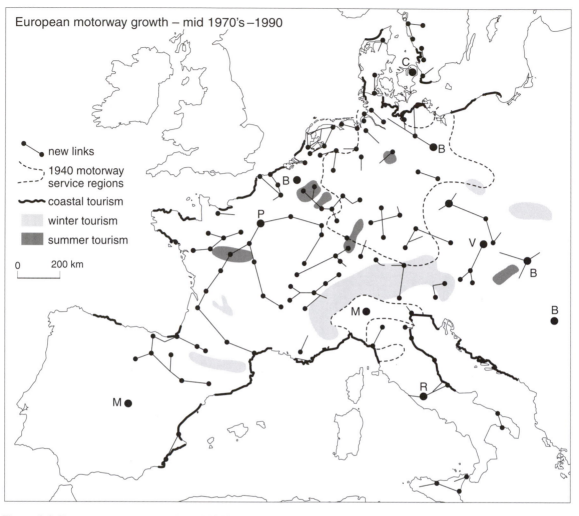

Figure 4.3 European motorway growth, mid-1970s–1990
Source: Jan Lundgren (1992)

Starting in the 1960s, a truly continental motorway network began to develop in Europe, as inter-country links were constructed, resulting in effective linkages such as that from Flensburg at the Danish-German border to the Messina Straits opposite Sicily. The Mediterranean coastline also became entirely motorway-serviced, from Valencia/Barcelona in Spain along the whole French section to La Spezia in Italy in the east, with a high density of entry/exit points where the route travels through important tourist zones such as the Côte d'Azur and Liguria. Figure 4.4 shows how individual EU Member States have extended their motorway infrastructure over the years.

As long as the built-in geopolitical divide between Eastern and Western Europe continued, the north-south orientation in the transport network was naturally dominant. However, with the opening up of the former Communist countries of Europe, several of which are candidates for a future enlarged EU, and the addition of vast expanses of new 'tourist destination space' to the east, the geographic thrust of future road transport infrastructure development in Europe has been reassessed.

The East European tourist region, from the Baltic States and the Polish sandy coastlands across the Carpathians and the Danubian river

	B	D-W	D-E	DK	E	F	GR	I	IRL	L	NL	P	UK	A	FIN	S	EU15	Index 70 = 100
1970	488	4461	1600	184	387	1553	11	3907	0	7	1209	66	1073	478	108	403	**15 935**	100
1975	1018	6207	1600	345	1135	3401	91	5431	0	25	1530	66	2026	651	180	692	**24 398**	153
1980	1192	7538	1687	516	1933	5264	91	5900	0	44	1773	132	2573	938	204	850	**30 635**	192
1985	1456	8350	1850	603	3170	6150	92	5955	8	58	1975	183	2838	1261	204	897	**35 050**	220
1990	1666	8959	1850	601	5126	6824	190	6193	26	78	2092	318	3181	1445	225	939	**39 713**	249
1991	1650	9084	1871	653	5801	7080	225	6301	32	84	2118	474	3211	1450	249	968	**41 251**	259
1992	1658	9135	1878	696	6988	7408	280	6306	32	95	2134	520	3246	1554	318	1005	**43 253**	271
1993	1665	9185	1895	737	7404	7614	300	6401	53	100	2150	579	3252	1557	337	1061	**44 290**	278
1994	1666	11 143	{1}	786	7736	7956	*300*	6940	72	121	2167	587	3286	1559	388	1125	**45 832**	288

km

Note: {1} includes in D-W

Estimates in italic

Figure 4.4 Motorway development in EU Member States
Source: Eurostat, IRF, National Statistics

plains to the mountainous coastlands of northern Greece and the Bosphoros may well represent the new Europe's 'last tourist frontier' (Lundgren 1992). However, in the countries of the former Soviet Union, the problems facing road development in the post-Communist era are staggering. Since 1989, there has been an overall rush to private motoring and trucking. The highway system, totally neglected under Communist regimes, was not fit for this explosion of road traffic, especially on West-East axes such as Berlin–Warsaw, Vienna–Budapest or Dresden–Prague. The need to rehabilitate existing links and build new ones will require not only significant investment but also considerable technical knowledge and experience not readily available in the countries of Eastern Europe. The final solution which has been applied to solve this problem is, in many cases, that of building roads by private sector concessions and financing them by tolls.

But this financing formula is not restricted to Eastern Europe. As late as the 1980s, the idea that the construction and maintenance operations of road infrastructure should be directly paid for by users was unthinkable in most European countries. But with government cutbacks in road investment during the 1990s, many of them have recognised that the privatisation option offers added support for publicly funded networks. Throughout Europe, West as well as East, almost all new road

projects are partly or entirely to be built by private sector concessions and financed by tolls. The French and Italians have had toll motorways for many years, and most of them are extremely profitable for operators. But even in Germany, until recently one of the countries holding out most resolutely against tolled networks, the government announced in the mid-1990s that it was ready to franchise seventeen new highway projects as toll concessions and was to introduce electronic tolls for trucks on all of its roads by the year 2000 (IRF 1997).

EXPANSION PLANS

Not only is road passenger transport currently the clear first choice of mode of travel for all purposes, including tourism, but the demand in Europe for road systems and vehicle use is constantly increasing. The DRI Study undertaken in 1994 on behalf of the European Commission predicted that by 2010, road passenger transport would have increased by 55 per cent over its 1990 volume. Can supply keep up with this level of growth in demand? Indeed, should it even try to?

It is clear that the situation in many European countries is already critical. Traffic congestion regularly brings a number of major conurbations to a virtual standstill. The OECD estimates that vehicle speeds declined by 10 per cent over the twenty years leading up to 1996 in member countries' major cities. Since 1971, inner London transport speeds, for example, have fallen to less than 18 km/h. Estimates indicate that in some European cities, average traffic speeds at peak times are lower than in the days of the horse-drawn carriage (CEC 1996b). Whole areas of Germany, the Benelux countries and the Paris region witness an almost endless 'rush hour'. Road building continues, but to take the UK as an example, for every fifty additional vehicles on the roads, the government constructs extra capacity to accommodate just one of them (Scard 1993). Moreover, British roads, with 67 cars for every kilometre are the most congested in Europe, where the average is 44 (Sunday Times 1996).

The solution proposed by industry lobbying bodies such as the International Road Federation (IRF) and International Road Transport Union (IRTU) is more roads and, in particular, more motorways.

EUROVIA is the name given to the IRF's project for a mostly private-sector funded and developed trans-European motorway network to be completed within the EU's trans-European road network (TERN). In 1996, the IRF and the European Transport Commission (DGVII) agreed to fully integrate EUROVIA into TERN. Together, TERN and EUROVIA aim to modernise the existing 43,000 km of EU motorway networks and complete them with 15,000 km of new links between national motorway systems to create a fully integrated system. The motorway sections constructed under the EUROVIA project will be built by the private sector on the basis of the 'user pays' concept.

Europe's pro-motorway lobby claims that expanding and rehabilitating Europe's motorway system can help the environment. The argument is that if, as expected, technology eliminates a large part of the undesirable engine emissions from new or modernised vehicles early in the twenty-first century, the greatest damage to the environment will be caused by congestion. As slow-moving heavy traffic pollutes and burns up fossil fuels unnecessarily, they argue, the most important priority is to make sure that motorway traffic flows freely. Road builders also maintain that in the modern world, there is no need for road networks to be regarded as being incompatible with a protected environment. They say they have both the technology and the will to provide maximum noise and environmental protection in their planning and implementation of new road systems and their rehabilitation of existing networks – although, of course, this type of environmental protection comes at a price.

ENVIRONMENTAL AND SAFETY ISSUES

Environmentalists in Europe see things differently, and accuse the road-building lobby of needlessly wanting to 'pave the world'. Their arguments are familiar: that roads consume too much land, often enter intrusively into ecologically delicate regions, and that they encourage the use of vehicle transport, with all the damage that entails for air quality and the ozone layer. They also argue that all motorway and trunk road traffic has an end destination and that free-flowing motorways, for example, simply bring more cars into already congested cities.

Undeniably, the environmental consequences of road traffic are considerable. It has been estimated that transport causes 62 per cent of carbon monoxide, 50 per cent of nitrogenoxide, 33 per cent of hydrocarbon and 17 per cent of carbon dioxide, thus fuelling concerns over both local and global air pollution. It has also been calculated that 20 per cent of Europe's citizens suffer from unacceptable levels of noise from road traffic (CEC 1996b).

Safety is also an important issue in Europe, where more than 45,000 people are killed each year and 1.6 million injured on Member States' roads. Experts say that one in four of those deaths could be prevented if speeds were cut by an average of only 3 mph (Guardian 1997a). But national legislation differs considerably from country to country. For example, Germany has no speed limits on its motorways, and the Scandinavians impose far tougher penalties on drink-drivers than do other Member States.

Many environmentalists insist that stringent measures ought to be taken to reduce the harmful impact of the road transport. Not only would these include moves to address the problem of pollution but also legislation to introduce punitive 'traffic calming' measures designed to slow vehicles down to speeds of 30 mph or less in cities.

EU INVOLVEMENT

At EU level, the future development of road infra-structure is a political football and the winning team usually tends to be the one most influenced by environmentalists and rail lobbies.

Environmentalists' demands in particular are generally heeded in Brussels, where the actions of many EU institutions suggest that they share the same concerns. In early 1997, for example, the EU Transport Commissioner put forward proposals for increased road safety, including a coordinated effort to reduce road speeds, set uniform drink-driving levels and improve safety standards for cars. At the same time members of the European Parliament pressed for tougher limits on exhaust emissions. This was a reaction to plans put forward by the Commission in 1996 to reduce pollution in the years leading up to 2010 by tightening vehicle emis-sion standards. MEPs claimed that the reductions were less stringent than the controls in Scandinavia and would have little effect. For their part, car manufacturers and the oil industry said that the proposals would be too costly (Guardian 1997a).

However, despite having a sympathetic ear in Brussels, many environmentalists, as stated in Chapter 2, are far from satisfied with EU transport policy, in particular as it relates to road transport. The Commission has been accused by the environ-ment lobby of needlessly 'carpeting Europe with motorways' as part of its plan for trans-European networks.

Coach travel

Coach travel plays an important part in Europe's tourism industry. However, until recently, it has been difficult to appreciate just how important a contribution it makes to the day-trip, short break and longer holiday market. Many statistical sources simply use the blanket category 'road travel' and do not distinguish between modes of road travel for tourist arrivals. Coach travel is somewhat neglected in official data sources, often because it it not seen as worthy of expensive research, which is made all the more complex due to the complexity of surveying a large number of small operators and companies.

Nevertheless, an important and timely study undertaken on behalf of the Economist Intelligence Unit (Page 1994) reveals a number of significant trends in coach usage during the 1990s, with par-ticular reference to international coach travel.

A presentation of this study's findings follows. However, in order to avoid confusion, a few defini-tions are first of all required. The 1987 European Conference of Ministers of Transport classified the coach travel market as follows:

International coach travel

Scheduled services

Scheduled services transport passengers at speci-fied times, often based on a timetable, over speci-fied routes. They involve the picking up and setting down of passengers at established stops. Such services are provided under a licence for a prescribed period for which the service is offered. Timetables, tariffs and the vehicles to be used are also specified. These services are often referred to as *European Express Coach Services*, such as those operated by a consortia of companies (for example Eurolines) and those run by individual operators.

Shuttle services

Shuttle services consist of repeated trips for the transport of groups of tourists from the same point of departure to the same destination. The group is also transported back to the original departure point and the service usually involves accommoda-tion for the group at the destination. The services are often referred to as *holiday shuttles*, such as those formerly operated by Coach Europe.

Occasional services

Most notably, these include: *closed-door tours* (where one vehicle is used throughout the journey for the same group and the tour returns to the orig-inal point of departure), which are often referred to as *continental coach holidays* or *continental coach tours*.

Domestic and day-trip coach travel

This market segment includes: *day excursions*; *extended tours* (coach holidays); *private hire* (including the market for group travel and educational trips) and *airport shuttle services*.

The market segments to which coach travel appeals are far from homogenous, ranging from the youth travel market for express domestic and international services to the elderly markets which dominate coach tours.

COACH SERVICES AND THE EU

As has already been emphasised, within the EU, despite attempts to develop a common transport policy, national transport policies tend to take priority for Member States. This is particularly the case for the regulation and operation of international road transport. Although national governments have acknowledged the importance of removing restrictions to the free movements of goods and people across Member States if the EU is to remain competitive, transport policy in the EU remains fragmented. Many transport operators complain, accordingly, that the absence of real free market competition in road transport diminishes the benefits of economic integration for the EU as a whole.

As Page (1994) notes, the national transport interests of Member States are often defended using the public service obligations argument – that state subsidy is needed to operate uneconomic services for the public good. However, such arguments do not readily hold true in the case of inter-urban and international coach services which compete directly with state railway networks. Such policies run contrary to the principles of the Single Market, putting international and domestic coach transport at a disadvantage.

An example of discrimination against coach operators was seen in 1990, when the Danish licensing authority, the Passenger Traffic Council, refused to grant licences to express coach operators, in order to protect the state railways and bus network. Such licensing constraints have limited the growth of long-distance express services as a direct result of national government policy.

Yet the Single Market legislation suggests that by deregulating road transport and introducing more competition, transport costs will fall. This will then lead towards the objectives of achieving a common market in transport. So what is the posi-

tion of coach operators *vis-à-vis* the Single Market?

Page (1994) quotes from a 1992 study in *Modern Transport Geography* which stated that 'any carrier will have the right to provide transport services freely throughout the Community as long as a number of conditions are met'. The most important of these are:

- that national and international road safety requirements are met;
- that companies are established in a Member State in conformity with the national regulations of that state;
- that companies are authorised by that state to carry out the international carriage of passengers; and
- that the carrying company must belong to, or have the majority of its shares with, nationals of Member States.

In the context of international coach services, the operation of any scheduled or shuttle service requires the provider to consult the Member States through which services pass and the destination country served. The former need only be consulted, but the Member State in which the destination is situated needs to authorise the service for it to operate. Should permission be refused, the matter is then referred to the EU for arbitration. In contrast, for those operators seeking to offer occasional services, no authorisation procedure exists. New services to be offered by coach operators within a national context have to prove that there is a demand for the product and show what areas of existing markets will be affected (for example, competition with rail and air). This system, therefore, provides national railway companies with the automatic opportunity to object to licensing authorities over proposed services which may affect their market share.

Among EU Member States, it is only the UK which has positively embraced the principles of competition in coach travel, coinciding with the ideological stance of the UK government to embrace greater competition and reduce state subsidy for public services. In most other countries in the EU, the provision of coach services has evolved from centrally planned bus operations which have diversified into providing coach services.

Table 4.1 European bus and coach travel, 1975–90 (billion pkm)

	1975	1980	1986	1987	1988	1989	1990	% change 1975–90
Belgium	9.6	9.1	9.5	10.0	10.2	10.5	n/a	9.4[1]
Denmark	5.7	7.3	9.0	9.0	8.9	8.9	8.9	56.1
West Germany	58.7	65.6	53.1	52.9	52.4	53.0	55.5	−4.5
Greece[2]	4.8	5.8	5.0	4.8	5.1	5.1	n/a	6.3[1]
Spain	26.9	28.1	33.5	35.2	37.5	39.0	38.7	43.9
France	28.9	38.0	39.8	42.2	41.9	40.3	41.3	42.9
Italy	42.3	57.8	70.5	72.7	77.2	79.8	84.0	98.6
Netherlands	11.8	13.2	12.1	12.8	12.8	12.8	n/a	8.5[1]
Portugal	5.2	7.8	8.3	10.0	10.0	10.1	10.3	98.1
UK	55.0	45.0	41.0	41.0	41.0	41.0	41.0	−25.5
EC 10	248.9	277.7	281.8	290.6	297.0	300.5	n/a	20.7[1]

Notes: [1] 1975–89, [2] 1988 data used again for 1989
Source: Page, S. (1994)

TRENDS IN INTERNATIONAL COACH TRAVEL

Despite the difficulties facing coach operators wishing to establish scheduled services, the coach is still widely used for tourism-related purposes.

The use of coach transport for international tourism is one of the elements highlighted in the 1986 Omnibus Survey of *Europeans and their Holidays* referred to in Chapter 3. Table 3.1 (page 77) shows the degree of variation in the use of coaches, rising to 16 per cent in Portugal.

Since the 1986 survey, the European coach market has undergone rapid change, with increased opportunities for international travel, especially to and from Eastern European countries. Major improvements in comfort and price competitiveness to new destinations, such as Disneyland Paris, have also led to a revival in domestic and international coach travel in many European markets. Table 4.1 shows that bus and coach travel in most of the EU Member States grew considerably between 1986 and 1990. Spain and Italy experienced substantial rises, due in part to growth in their general prosperity, creating a new market for coach-based holidays.

PAN-EUROPEAN EXPRESS COACH SERVICES

Although the state authorisation procedures for international coach services in the EU are complex, the development of services targeted at the extremely price-sensitive youth market can be dated back to the 1970s. London was at the hub of the emerging network. In 1975, the first EU international service was authorised to operate on a seasonal basis between London, Dublin and Galway, provided by the Irish company CIE. This was followed by the development of the London–Munich service operated by a consortium of operators in Belgium, Germany and the UK under the Eurobus brand. In February 1982, National Express and Magic Bus in the UK also entered the European market, carrying 500,000 passengers in its first year of operation. The market for youth travel and economy continental coach services was focused on Victoria Coach Station in London, and developments in the 1970s laid the foundations for the pan-European network that now exists (Page 1994).

In 1984, the Supabus brand was launched by a consortium of UK, Irish and continental operators, after the collapse of Magic Bus offered a number of market opportunities for additional services. Greater international cooperation between operators evolved, as the tickets were sold through the network of National Express agents in the UK and ticket agents in continental European cities. Services were based on the cheapest form of travel to and from mainland Europe, with few comfort improvements over and above the standard service offered on express services in the domestic market. In 1985, the Supabus product experienced major growth and in 1986, the Eurolines consortium was formed, expanding the original nine Supabus operators to 33 European partners (Page 1994).

CASE STUDY: the Eurolines organisation

Background

The formation of Eurolines Organisation marked a new era in the operation, development and coordination of a European network of express coach travel. It has grown to become Europe's largest operator of scheduled coach services. The Organisation comprises 27 partners, who work together to provide a comprehensive network of services linking over 400 destinations throughout Europe. Established European coach operators such as the UK's National Express, Deutsche Touring of Germany and Spain's Julia are leading partners in the consortium of operators. Figure 4.5 shows the network covered by the Eurolines Organisation's members.

The role of the central office

The objective of the Organisation is to 'develop an integrated pan-European network of international lines capable of competing with other means of transport and to promote the interest and prosperity of the undertakings making up the Eurolines Organisation'. To this end, the name 'Eurolines' is used as a commercial brand name.

From its central office in Brussels, the Eurolines Organisation undertakes a range of technical, administrative and policital tasks aimed at achieving its objective.

Technical tasks

The central office makes efforts to work towards a complete standardisation of the Eurolines products, so that the same level of quality, safety and service to clients is available on every route. For example, in order to provide the public with a clear and unified image of Eurolines products, a Eurolines identity manual provides a clear definition of the conditions under which the Eurolines logo may be used on all relevant materials: vehicles, tickets, coach stations, etc.

Administrative tasks

The central office is responsible for the international promotion of the Eurolines products. One such product is the Eurolines Pass, which offers unlimited travel for a month between 21 European cities served by members of the Eurolines Organisation. This product is offered as a competitor for the existing rail products in Europe.

The central office is further responsible for the organisation of Working Committee meetings among the Eurolines members and the implementation of decisions taken within the Standardisation, Quality and Marketing Committees.

Political/policy tasks

The central office is also responsible for the defending of the interest of the member companies towards international bodies such as DGVII of the European Commission and the International Road Transport Union, of which the Organisation is an associate member. Conversely, the Brussels office also disseminates information from such organisations to its members. In this way, member companies have prior notice of, for example, changes in regulations, and can take the necessary actions without waiting to be informed by their own national transport federations or governments.

Eurolines (UK) Ltd

The services which link the UK with this network are provided by Eurolines (UK) Ltd, Britain's largest

continued

Figure 4.5 Europe's express coach network
Source: Eurolines (UK)

continued

operator of scheduled coach services to Continental Europe and Ireland, which is a separate company within the UK's National Express Group. Eurolines (UK) Ltd itself owns no coaches, but contracts Department of Transport-approved coach operators to carry out its services, which, in the majority of cases, depart from and arrive at Victoria Coach Station.

The majority of services from London operate direct to key destinations throughout Europe. In addition, a number of services are operated on a 'hub and spoke' basis, with key interchanges at locations such as Paris, Frankfurt, London and Amsterdam. This allows Eurolines (UK) Ltd, for example, to offer regular departures from London to Morocco, a destination which in itself would be unlikely to support a high volume of passengers from the UK. This service interchanges in Paris because, given the high ethnic population from North Africa in France, Eurolines France can easily attract a viable number of passengers to support the service.

Since 1992, Eurolines (UK) Ltd has also operated services to Eastern Europe, as changes to licensing following the demise of Communist rule in many states led to new market opportunities.

Service details
All coaches contracted to Eurolines (UK) Ltd have 49 seats, on-board washroom facilities and reclining seats. No-smoking coaches are provided on services to the Netherlands, Scandinavia, Ireland, the Czech and Slovak Republics and Northern Germany. There are no-smoking seating areas on all other services. Smoking is not permitted on any overnight services between 10pm and 6am, with the exception of services to Spain, where the law prohibits this ban. Services to the South of France, Italy and Spain have air conditioning, and Eurolines (UK) Ltd is extending this feature to other routes.

With the exception of Channel Link services, all services to the Continent are 'through' services where the coach accompanies passengers on the ferry or Le Shuttle crossing so there is no need to disembark with luggage at the port. Most Eurolines services do not carry hostesses or provide refreshments, as regular meal stops are included on long journeys.

Fares structures
On most services, there are reduced priced fares for children, for young people under 26 years, and for senior citizens of 60 years and over.

Ferry crossings
Eurolines (UK) Ltd's services from the UK to continental Europe and Ireland use a variety of ferry crossings operated by P&O European Ferries and Irish Ferries. In addition, the company offers one service a day to Paris using Le Shuttle. A similar Express service operates daily to Amsterdam during the summer peak season.

Short breaks
Eurolines (UK) Ltd has negotiated special rates for its passengers at over 60 hotels belonging to the French Ibis and Campanile chains in destinations throughout Europe. In addition, Euro Breaks is a short-break programme offering competitively priced short-breaks inclusive of coach travel and hotel accommodation in Paris, Amsterdam, Bruges, Budapest, Lille, Cologne and Poitiers, which has the Futuroscope theme park nearby.

Competition
Eurolines (UK) Ltd competes with smaller companies which offer fortnightly and weekly services from the UK to a few continental Europe. In contrast with such operators, Eurolines is able to provide a comprehensive and high-frequency service with connections to 250 destinations across Europe.

Eurolines (UK) Ltd also faces competition from Eurostar on the Paris and Brussels routes, which has reduced its passenger volumes on these routes and put pressure on fares. However, as the parent company's 1996 Annual Report pointed out, this effect was countered by good growth in volumes on other newer routes, particularly services to Bratislava, Budapest and Vienna (NEG 1997). On the whole, Eurolines (UK) Ltd has benefited from lower cross-Channel ferry costs, brought about in part by competition from the Channel Tunnel.

PROSPECTS FOR EUROPEAN COACH TRAVEL

Coach travel remains a low-priced mode of tourist travel in the EU, and price remains the most important selling point. Nevertheless, customers are generally sensitive to issue of 'internal comfort' (receiving a comfortable ride and a pleasurable on-board experience) and 'external comfort' (limited waiting times, reliability of services and direct services rather than connections at interchanges).

One of the main problems facing all coach operators in Europe is related to this issue of external comfort. The absence of high-quality coach interchanges in many European capitals negatively impacts upon customers' perception of this market. However, transport authorities are aware of the problem and some steps to improve the situation were taken during the 1990s. For example, Victoria Coach Station in London underwent a £3 million programme of investment and Paris announced plans to develop a central coach station under cover, in order to improve customer provision.

In general, Page (1994) is optimistic about the future of coach services in Europe. He points in particular to Eastern Europe, which has provided a new focus for the EU coach industry, as it offers a hitherto untapped market for inbound and outbound travel. Yet, he maintains that this is no solution to the highly regulated nature of the coach industry in many EU countries. Even with the development of high-speed train services in Europe, the coach will maintain its highly competitive role as a mode of transport for tourists and day-trippers.

However, according to Page, the real potential for the European coach transport industry is in the development of a greater inter-urban express coach service in EU countries.

> If coach operators are able to identify the potential market for different types of services, a period of growth may lead to the natural development of coaching throughout Europe. However, if this is accompanied by a large number of new entrants into the market, aggressive price competition may result in different countries, thereby leading to mergers and acquisitions in line with the experience of deregulation of the UK coach market. Yet in the long-term, this will lead to a virtual monopoly of service by the large operators.

Whether this is in the best interests of the consumer remains to be seen. (Page 1994)

COACHES AND THE ENVIRONMENT

The growth in coach transport in Europe during the 1990s has not come about without a marked environmental impact. Some day-trip destinations, for example, are now so overwhelmed by coaches (Canterbury in the UK, for example, receives as many as 200 coaches a day in the peak season) that cities are being forced to look at visitor management strategies, to manage both the coaches and the visitors they bring (see Davidson and Maitland 1997).

Historic towns in particular suffer from the presence of vast numbers of coaches, and many destinations throughout Europe have adopted increasingly restrictive policies against the circulation and parking of such vehicles. The threat of the total banning of coaches from certain towns and cities is never far away, as their residents become more vociferous in their opposition to what they regard as a growing threat to their general quality of life. Professional organisations such as the IRTU the Universal Federation of Travel Agents' Associations (UFTAA) and the International Hotel Association (IHA) have had to respond to such threats by publishing, in their own defence, information chosen to place coach transport in a favourable light, compared with private car transport. Figure 4.6 shows figures which have been selected to argue in favour of coach transport.

The IRTU has also issued a list of ten recommendations, which, it claims, would improve the functioning of coaches used for tourism:

1 Strict equality of treatment between all tourists must be established everywhere, regardless of the means of transport used by them, so as to guarantee free access to tourist sites.
2 Non-discriminatory access to culture and to tourism must be respected for all and the social character of coach tourism must be retained.
3 Infrastructures must be set up or improved and adequate access provided for coaches to tourist sites, together with an adequate number of

Selected figures

TRANSPORT CAPACITY
1 coach = 35 private cars
(in urban traffic)

SURFACE OCCUPATION
Coaches' use of space is twice as efficient

with full quota of passengers
(speed 10 km/h):
$\quad$ 3.1 m²/passenger
private car under same conditions:
$\quad$ 6.2 m²/passenger

SAFETY
Coach travel: 11 times safer than the private car

Number of accidents, in thousand million passenger-kilometres:
Coach: $\quad$ 0.81
Private car: $\quad$ 9.08
Rail: $\quad$ 5.94
Air: $\quad$ 5.93

INTERNATIONAL TOURISM
Private motoring aside, coach touring plays a significant role in holiday travel

Germany:
10% against 11% for rail travel
Belgium:
11% against 8% for rail travel
Spain:
20% against 10% for rail travel
France:
8% against 10% for rail travel

Netherlands:
12% against 5% for rail travel
United Kingdom:
19% against 11% for rail travel

ENERGY SAVINGS
Coaches consume far less fuel per passenger/km than cars:

A touring coach consumes 29 litres per 100 km, i.e. based on average occupancy of 50 passengers: 0.58 litres.
A private car consumes 7.1 litres per 100 km, i.e. based on average occupancy of 2.3 passengers: 3.08 litres.

GASEOUS EMISSIONS
Coaches are the least polluting in g/km per passenger/km

CO: $\quad$ 0.5 against 4.4 for private cars
CO_2: $\quad$ 56 against 127 for private cars
Other emissions:
$\quad$ 1.5 against 2.4 for private cars
From 1986 to 2010, emissions will decrease by 34%

NOISE
Coaches, as all other heavy vehicles, are becoming increasingly silent

In db(A)*: $\quad$ 88 in 1985,
$\quad$ 84 in 1991,
$\quad$ 80 in 2000
• 3 decibels correspond to a decrease of 50% in noise level

Figure 4.6 Coach travel compared with other forms of transport
Source: International Road Transport Union (I.R.U.)

parking spaces at reasonable prices, while respecting the needs of the environment.

4 Traffic conditions must be improved, in particular through better road signs and better information for drivers.

5 Interfaces must be created between the major modes of tourist transport, whenever this is necessary (aircraft–trains–coaches–boats), in particular by building multi-modal hubs.

6 Account must be taken of the real performance of coaches with regard to environmental protection, energy savings and road safety.

7 Local or national economic spin-off, which

promotes employment, must be safeguarded where it is directly or indirectly generated by coach tourism and diminishes the seasonal nature of tourism.

8 The creation of an awareness and sense of responsibility among coach company directors, drivers and passengers must be developed and continued everywhere.

9 A genuine policy for the reception of coaches must be put in place so as to consolidate the image of tourist countries and regions.

10 An interactive policy must be developed for consultations between coach operators and

other professionals in the tourist sector, local authorities and their administrations, before a decision is taken on any definitive policy which introduces changes (IRTU 1997).

Rail travel

INTRODUCTION

For over a century, it was Europe's rail network which provided the most comfortable means of travelling to tourism destinations both near and far. But with the advent of other modes of transport, rail travel was eclipsed by the glamour of flying and the independence and convenience of the private car.

However, although the use of rail for leisure and business travel had remained comparatively low in Europe since the arrival of mass tourism, there was, by the 1990s, growing evidence that rail travel was set to expand its market share. This was only partly due to the previously discussed congestion on Europe's roads and capacity constraints in the air transport sector. As this section of the chapter indicates, significant advances in rail transport technology and the support of EU policymakers have also set the scene for a railway renaissance in Europe.

A 1990 survey by Signal International and Cleverdon Steer, cited by Page (1993) pointed towards a revival of rail travel in the 1990s, with a steady rise in the rail travel market for business journeys of between 500 and 1,000 km. According to this report, the key factors likely to promote this growth were the development of a pan-European high-speed rail network, the opening of the Channel Tunnel, and a greater potential for journeys involving both air and rail.

These three themes will be explored in this section of the chapter. However, it is first necessary to examine in more detail the market for passenger rail services in Europe.

THE MARKET FOR RAIL TRAVEL IN EUROPE

Figure 4.7 shows the various segments within the European rail travel market. While this qualitative assessment of the market for rail travel is some-

---

SEGMENTS OF THE RAIL TRAVEL MARKET

- business travellers seeking a high-quality, efficient and regular city-to-city service;
- young people without a car or drivers licence ('the youth market');
- the elderly who wish to avoid road congestion and retain the independence afforded by the opportunity to travel by scheduled services;
- people who prefer to travel by the most economical method of transport, since rail transport is one of the most competetive forms of travel over a long distance;
- train enthusiasts and special interest tour operators who organise holidays and day excursions by train;
- tourists and day trippers in Alpine regions where adverse climatic conditions may hamper road and air transport (e.g. ski resorts);
- tourists and day trippers travelling to urban areas who prefer the convenience and accessibility of rail services direct to the heart of most European cities;
- tourists who choose the most scenic rather than the fastest mode of travel to their destination and who are not time-sensitive;
- passengers transferring from airports and sea ports to gain access to city centre locations and to continue their journey to destinations not served by air or cost-effective road transport; and
- suburban commuters.

Figure 4.7 Segments of the rail travel market
Source: M. Kosters *Tourism by Train: Its Role in Alternative Tourism*, quoted in Page, S. (1993).

---

what descriptive, it highlights some of the reasons why people are likely to choose rail for tourist and recreational travel.

In quantitative terms, the general trend in rail passenger traffic in Western Europe overall has been one of extremely gradual growth throughout the 1980s and 1990s. The number of passenger kilometres in the EU and ETFA countries rose from a total of 261 billion in 1980 to 277 billion in 1995 (UIC 1996a and UIC 1997). The general upward trend continued into 1996. During the first nine months of that year, rail passenger traffic in the fifteen countries of the EU rose by 1.2 per cent compared with the equivalent period in 1994 (UIC 1997).

Exactly how much of this rail travel is linked to tourism, as opposed to simple commuting, is difficult to estimate, although research into European rail travel undertaken by the Economist Intelligence Unit at the end of the 1980s suggested that 15 per cent of the total railway business in Europe was directly associated with the tourism industry (Travel and Tourism Analyst No. 5, 1988).

What is clearer is that, in terms of rail passenger kilometres, the European rail market is dominated by four countries, which between them account for almost three-quarters of all rail passenger kilometres. In 1995, out of the total 277 billion rail passenger-kilometres for the EU and the EFTA countries, Germany accounted for 22 per cent, France 21 per cent, Italy 18 per cent and the UK 10.5 per cent. (UIC 1997). The relative importance of national markets in Europe is shown in diagrammatic form in Figure 4.8.

Regarding the relative national/international rail traffic proportions in Europe, the vast majority of journeys made by train are domestic. Page cites Community of European Railways (CER) figures which show that, towards the beginning on the 1990s, of the 94 billion passenger kilometres travelled by citizens of Germany, Belgium, France, Italy, Luxembourg, the Netherlands, Austria and Switerland, 79 per cent were national traffic and only 21 per cent international in origin. The explanation given was that many existing international services at that time were over long distances, slow and therefore less competitive on time than air and road transport (Page 1993).

But the 1990s saw the extension in many European countries of high-speed train networks which included the first cross-frontier links, making international high-speed train travel a reality for Europeans. While precise Europe-wide statistics on the use of international rail travel for tourism are unobtainable, the UIC's 1995 Annual Report mentions that a major trend that year was the increasing proportion of international rail traffic for *freight*, not only in Western Europe where, that year, increases ranged from 19.2 per cent for France and 17.9 per cent in Portugal to 14.6 per cent in the Netherlands, but also in Central and Eastern Europe, where there was an overall increase of 21.8 per cent.

THE EU POLICY FRAMEWORK FOR THE RAILWAYS

A number of steps have been taken by the European Commission to support the rail mode within the EU. Before examining these, it is worth asking the question: why is the EU so supportive of rail travel, as opposed to other modes of transport?

Part of the answer lies, no doubt, in the efficacy of the various lobby groups promoting the expansion of rail travel in Europe. Most important among these is the Community of European Railways (CER) mentioned above. This organisation is responsible for representing the railway

Figure 4.8 Relative importance of national markets for rail travel

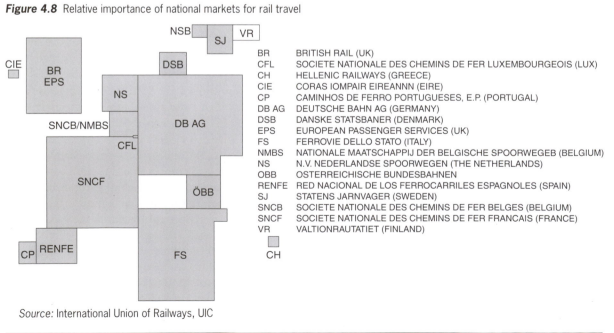

BR	BRITISH RAIL (UK)
CFL	SOCIETE NATIONALE DES CHEMINS DE FER LUXEMBOURGEOIS (LUX)
CH	HELLENIC RAILWAYS (GREECE)
CIE	CORAS IOMPAIR EIREANN (EIRE)
CP	CAMINHOS DE FERRO PORTUGUESES, E.P. (PORTUGAL)
DB AG	DEUTSCHE BAHN AG (GERMANY)
DSB	DANSKE STATSBANER (DENMARK)
EPS	EUROPEAN PASSENGER SERVICES (UK)
FS	FERROVIE DELLO STATO (ITALY)
NMBS	NATIONALE MAATSCHAPPIJ DER BELGISCHE SPOORWEGEB (BELGIUM)
NS	N.V. NEDERLANDSE SPOORWEGEN (THE NETHERLANDS)
OBB	OSTERREICHISCHE BUNDESBAHNEN
RENFE	RED NACIONAL DE LOS FERROCARRILES ESPANOLES (SPAIN)
SJ	STATENS JARNVAGER (SWEDEN)
SNCB	SOCIETE NATIONALE DES CHEMINS DE FER BELGES (BELGIUM)
SNCF	SOCIETE NATIONALE DES CHEMINS DE FER FRANCAIS (FRANCE)
VR	VALTIONRAUTATIET (FINLAND)

Source: International Union of Railways, UIC

companies of the EU Member States and of Switzerland and Norway in dialogue with the Community institutions: European Commission, European Parliament, and the Economic and Social Committee. Its task is to ensure that the point of view of Europe's railway companies is taken into consideration during the drafting of EU transport policy and railway policy by the various bodies of the European Union.

What are the CER's main arguments in favour of rail transport?

Advantages for the environment

Travel by train is presented as one means of providing Europe's population with sustainable mobility compatible with the constraints of environmental conservation.

It is argued, for example, that new high-speed railway lines require considerably less space than a motorway. Generally speaking, the breadth of a double-track line is 13.7 metres for a capacity equivalent to a four to six–lane motorway which, at 30 to 36 metres wide, needs more than twice the surface area. The savings in land-take are demonstrated by the CER, claiming that for the construction of the first two new high-speed lines in Germany, 3.3 ha/km were needed by comparison with the 9.3 ha/km required for the construction of German motorways (UIC/CER 1995).

Lower pollutant emissions are also emphasised by the rail transport lobbyists. Pollutant emissions are directly dependent on the level of energy consumption. The low level of friction between wheel and rail means that rail's energy consumption is substantially less than that of road vehicles. The energy consumption of high-speed trains per passenger/kilometre is between 30 per cent and 50 per cent that of car energy consumption, as shown by the chart in Figure 4.9.

High safety standards

Each year, nearly 60,000 people are killed on the roads in Western Europe, but the railways have managed to improve their safety record: in the mid-1970s, there were 1.6 passenger fatalities per billion passenger kilometres (pkm), but twenty years later this figure had fallen to 0.4.

Litres of petrol per 100 pkm

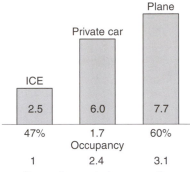

Figure 4.9 Comparison of primary energy consumption per 100 pkm. Example: Hamburg–Frankfurt/Main, approx, 500 km, 1992
Source: International Union of Railways, UIC

The International Union of Railways (UIC) itself puts this progress down to: wheel/rail system reliability, rigorous operating procedures and application of state-of-the-art technologies for traffic control and communication.

Low external costs

Rail lobbyists also claim that, as a result of the foregoing factors, the overall external costs (the costs generated by factors such as accidents, noise, air pollution and climactic change) of train travel are lower than those of other modes. To demonstrate this, the UIC commissioned in 1993/4 a Europe-wide study from consultants IWW in Karlsruhe and Infras in Zürich. The study showed that in 1991, the total volume of external costs ascribable to transport in seventeen European countries (the fifteen members of the EU plus Norway and Switzerland) amounted to ECU 272 billion. Of these, 92 per cent of external costs were caused by road traffic and only 1.7 per cent by rail traffic. A series of four effects were examined for each of the transport modes, and the results are shown in Figure 4.10.

For cars, the average external costs were 50 ECU per 1,000 pkm. The external costs for road coaches were a lot lower at 20 ECU per 1,000 pkm, as were those attributable to rail, with 10 ECU per 1,000 pkm – one-fifth of the figure for cars.

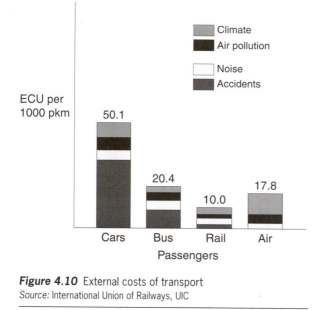

Figure 4.10 External costs of transport
Source: International Union of Railways, UIC

For many years, the UIC has lobbied for the external costs of transport to be 'internalised', or in other words, charged to the user (i.e. motorists, coach, airline and rail passengers), claiming that this would create 'a level playing field' between all modes of transport, which would cater to the need for environmental protection and would be in keeping with market imperatives.

The lobbying seems to have paid off and the EU appears to have been convinced, or at least interested in this idea. In December 1995, the European Commission published a Green Paper, *Towards fair and efficient pricing in transport*, on the internalisation of the external costs of transport. The Green Paper, which sets out to foster the development of those transport modes that are least harmful to the environment, recognises the railway's strengths in this respect. It also points to ways of achieving *internalising of external costs* without theatening the competitiveness of Europe's economy as a result.

Rail deregulation

In most EU countries, rail transport and rail networks are state-owned and they receive subsidies to assist with the operation of uneconomic services. By the mid-1990s, most of Europe's rail-ways were running massive deficits. For example, in France in 1995, the rail system generated US$10 billion worth of revenue, but it cost US$16 billion to run. Similarly, in Switzerland, the rail deficit rose from US$134 million in 1991 to US$337 million in 1995 (IRF 1997). But the close relationship between the management of railways and the interests of national governments has meant that in the past policymaking for European railways has been largely inward-looking and focused on national rather than EU-wide concerns.

Page (1993) cites a study by R. Gibb and C. Charlton, *International Surface Passenger Transport: Prospects and Potential*, which demonstrates the extent of the EU's inability to affect rail transport policy due to the vested interests of national governments in their own rail networks. The authors identify two principal objectives of EU rail transport policy:

1 the desire to liberalise rail transport to achieve liberal free-trade policies in the move toward the European Single Market;
2 the need to harmonise the conditions of competition in rail services in pursuit of social intervention policies.

The 1991 EU Directive 91/440 embodied both of these principles and was aimed at revitalising Member States' railway systems at a time when rail travel was losing market share in many Member States and some European railway companies had debts amounting to three to five times their annual turnover. This directive proposed rail deregulation as the principal means of resolving the railways' problems in the areas of service quality, productivity and finance. It aims to boost rail transport in Europe by introducing a measure of competition and liberalisation into the running of train services, with a view to their commercialisation and eventual privatisation.

To this end, the directive proposes two main developments: a complete overhaul of the financial systems of Member States' railways and, in each country, a clear division between those who exercise regulatory powers over the railways (normally the state) and those who provide rail services – a measure aimed at boosting management autonomy. These changes clearly imply an end to the highly regulated environment in which most state-managed railway enterprises were traditionally operated.

The second main aim of Directive 91/440 is to ensure that the Community's railways develop beyond their original national boundaries. It therefore seeks to introduce open access to European railway infrastructure on the basis of charging operators (railway companies) for running services. The application of this provision of the directive means that new forms of railway company can be set up to run services on the European network.

Thus, by adopting Directive 91/440, which entered into force in 1993, EU Member States agreed to:

- management independence of the railways;
- separation between the provision of railway operations and the ownership of rail infrastructure;
- improving the financial structure of railways;
- access to their railway infrastructures by certain operators.

Progress towards the actual implementation of the Directive 91/440 (and the directives complementary to it) was, however, very gradual. The three Member States which acted relatively promptly to implement the directive were Germany, Finland, and the UK:

1 In 1994, German Railways (DB AG) became a holding company. A year later, company directors affirmed that the objectives of improving the competitiveness of rail transport in Germany and the lightening of the load on the Federal budget had been achieved in full, with DB AG recording a 2.2 per cent increase in turnover. In 1995, in application of the European Directive, DB AG also published the tariffs for use of its infrastructure.

2 Finnish Railways (VR) became a joint stock company in July 1995, splitting into two separate organisations: VR Group Ltd for the commercial operation of transport services and the Finnish Rail Administration (RHK) with responsibility for infrastructure.

3 In the United Kingdom, in 1994, a public administration with responsibility for infra-

structure management, Railtrack, was created, and the rolling stock leasing companies were put up for sale. Negotiations on the franchising of passenger services to new outside operators followed, and on the 4 February 1996, the first private train, belonging to the coach company Stagecoach, ran between Twickenham and Waterloo Station, London (UIC 1996a). Railtrack is responsible for the provision and maintenance of track and signalling, and private operators such as Stagecoach run services on the system, based on an infrastructure access contract with Railtrack.

But by the beginning of 1997, a number of Member States, had still not fully translated into action the four key requirements of the directive.

Their reluctance to do so is, in many cases, partly due to their reservations concerning the consequences of full implementation of Directive 91/440. For example, one of the worries expressed by some commentators about open access to Europe's rail tracks is that of 'cherry picking'. One of the forms which this may take is that operators select only the relatively profitable routes (such as that between London Victoria and Gatwick Airport, for example), leaving the incumbent – usually the national railway company – with only the less profitable routes.

This poses a problem where the existing structure of train services is designed to allow for cross-subsidisation – i.e., using gains from the more profitable routes to subsidise the less profitable routes. 'Cherry picking' of this kind could mean that the incumbent is left with no excess profits to distribute, which in turn means either that less profitable routes have to be closed entirely or more explicitly subsidised through the Treasury – which may be less politically acceptable in some countries.

Local passenger train transport, although more important for commuter traffic than for tourism, is another form of service which requires heavy subsidy in most Member States. The usual argument given to justify such subsidy is based on the congestion that would be caused if all such traffic switched to private cars. But such routes are also threatened if the possibility of using cross-subsidisation is lost and if the new commercialisation of rail operations requires individual route viability. At present, the position of local passenger traffic seems to be secure, with most countries committing themselves to continuing to explicitly subsidise these services – for the short-term at least (Bowers 1995).

Another of the aspects that most worries the critics, and some of the supporters, of railway reforms is the question of coordination: the difficulty of organising the railways as a network rather than sets of isolated lines where different agencies operate the services. Such a system raises questions over issues such as network coordination, timetable organisation, connecting trains, links between franchises and the availability of tickets across franchises. There are also potential difficulties concerning the marketing of the product, especially national/international services which cross several franchises: who pays and who benefits? For example, will DB AG be willing to advertise its international services if the French and Dutch railways are significant suppliers of the services and may also reap considerable benefit from DB AG's campaign? (Bowers 1995).

It remains to be seen whether the anticipated efficiency gains and improved market orientation deliver the railway renaissance which the EU has envisaged for twenty-first century Europe. But an early reaction to railway reforms in the UK, one of the first Member States to privatise rail services, was not encouraging. The 1997 Carlson Wagonlit Travel/MORI survey of UK business travellers showed that most of those felt that the promise of increased competition, lower fares and higher standards had not been fulfilled. Of those interviewed, 62 per cent felt that privatisation had scarcely brought about greater competition and only 5 per cent felt that it had led to lower fares. Moreover, only 12 per cent of companies considered that services and standards were better and 8 per cent that reliability had improved, compared to 60 per cent of companies in Carlson Wagonlit's 1996 survey who believed that better service standards were likely and 48 per cent who thought that privatisation would lead to greater reliability.

In that earlier survey, 63 per cent thought that privatisation would lead to higher fares and 73 per cent to a smaller national network, while 57 per

cent thought that through ticketing would be reduced. By 1997, almost 50 per cent of those surveyed had still not yet made up their mind as to the real benefits and costs of privatisation. Commenting on these results, the Commercial Director of Carlson Wagonlit UK Limited observed that:

> Obviously, it is early days yet but one would have hoped competition would have been more forthcoming. The railways really do need to get their act together and create an effective 'interline' booking system. How the industry will do business with 25 denationalised railway organisations without such a system is difficult to imagine! (Carlson Wagonlit 1997)

It is generally accepted that very little real competition has emerged as a result of rail privatisation in the UK. In reality, the system operates through a number of local monopolies on the vast majority of routes.

Further gloomy news followed in August 1997, with the publication of the results of a survey showing that rail travel in the UK was the most expensive in the world, with fares at three times the world average. This was said to be the result of fare rises applied following the privatisation programme. The report notes that one year before privatisation of the UK's railways, they ranked alongside Swiss railways as the most expensive in the world. But by 1997, following two years of privatisation, a standard class ten-mile journey in the UK cost £35, while the same length of trip in Switzerland cost only £22. In reply to these comparisons, UK train operators maintain that increasing competition on railways will hold down and possibly even reduce prices over the years ahead (Times 1997b). Opponents of privatisation claim that tourists in the UK stand to suffer from such fare rises more than those using trains to travel to work. For although government ministers have traditionally prevented train companies from introducing above-inflation fare increases on commuter routes, operators have been free to impose substantial increases on long-distance and off-peak journeys. Such increases make the prospect of travelling around the UK less attractive and make the dispersal of overseas visitors much more difficult to achieve.

Introduction

Czech Railways (Ceské Dráhy) has been called Europe's biggest open-air museum, a reflection of the antiquated state of its trains and infrastructure following many years of neglect and under-investment during the years of Communist rule. In 1996, the rail operator made a loss of £151 million and had £64 million in overdue debts (Times 1997c). Unfortunately for the company, some of those debts were with the electricity board, who, in August 1997 decided to cut off power supplies to the head office of the loss-making state railway because of unpaid bills. Following the power cut (which did not affect operations), the Czech government approved a long-term railway privatisation plan. However, the plan to slow the railway's losses was conceived long before the headquarters fell dark. This case study examines the plan to prepare Czech Railways for the twenty-first century.

The Czech Railways and the network

The company came into existence in 1993 after the division of Czechoslovak Railways, which came about as a result of the political separation of the former Czechoslovakia into the Czech and Slovak Republics. At that time, all moveable state assets were split between the two new countries in proportion to the number of their inhabitants, namely 2:1 in favour of the Czech Republic, while real estate was divided on the territorial principle, with the Czech and Slovak Republics becoming the owners of the state property located on their respective lands. As a state enterprise, the rail network of the Czechoslovak Republic was split on the basis of the territorial principle, with the result that the Czech railway network now amounts to 9,441 km, of which 2,640 km are electrified, while the Slovak railway network consists of 3,665 km, of which 1,457 km are electrified. Given the higher density of the Czech railway network, the length of railway lines is 2.56:1 in favour of the Czech Republic.

Comparisons with neighbouring countries reveal the relative density of the railway network in the Czech Republic: while in that country there are 91cm of railway line per head of population, in the Slovak Republic there are 68 cm, in Germany 50 cm, and in Italy only 28 cm. When the length of rail network per km^2 of the surface area of the state is calculated, the figures are 120, 75, 113 and 53 respectively. It has been suggested that this high-level density rail network in the Czech Republic (and the Slovak Republic) means that it would be very difficult for the two successor railways to uphold operations on all lines, given the high maintenance costs compared to individual line profitability.

Czech Railways provide the major part of both rail passenger and rail freight services in the Czech Republic and, at the same time, acts as manager of the Czech railway infrastructure. Regarding passenger transport, the main problem facing Czech Railways is the decline in the volume of traffic as a result of, first, competition from buses (for example, on the main Prague–Brno route) and, secondly, the division of the former Czechoslovakia.

Despite these problems, Czech Railways was determined to overcome the disadvantages facing it and to offer high quality services, especially on main corridors.

The first Eurocity train started operations in June 1991, linking the cities of Prague and Vienna. Since then, the number of Eurocity trains has substantially increased and these high quality services are now provided between Prague and several other European cities, including Budapest, Warsaw, Berlin, Hamburg, Munich and Dortmund.

The modernisation programme

As far as railway infrastructure is concerned, the major modernisation projects include four main Czech railway corridors which have been chosen in line with the major European railway routes passing through the Czech Republic, as shown in Figure 4.11. The most important (and first to be modernised) is the corridor connecting Berlin, Prague, Vienna and Bratislava and Budapest (on Czech territory, the Decin–Breclav section via Ceská Trebovâ). The part of this corridor situated on Czech territory is 454 km long and its modernisation began in 1993. Work is due to be finished by the year 2000.

continued

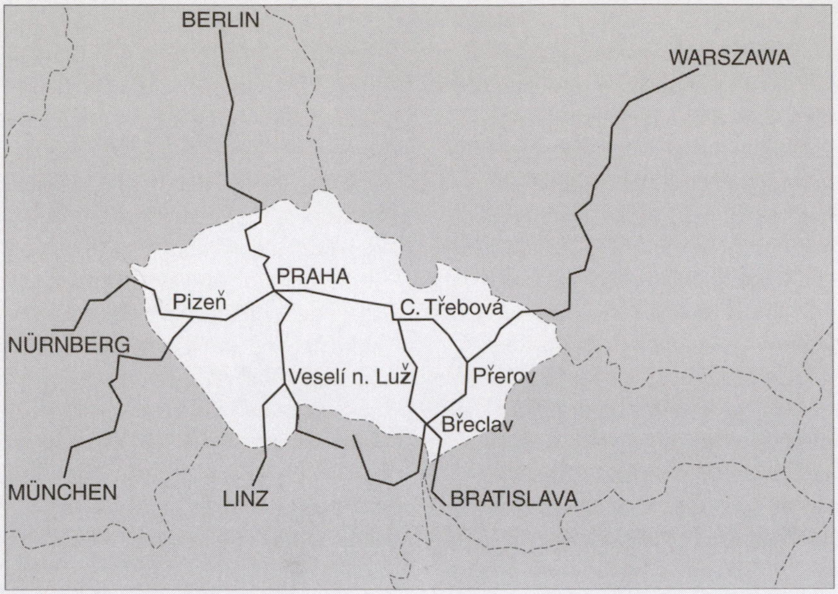

Figure 4.11 Czech railway corridor modernisation
Source: Rail International

All modernisation work is planned for a maximum line speed of 160 km/h. The main goals of Czech Railways' modernisation programme are:

- Shorter travel time (between Berlin and Vienna by approximately three hours by comparison with the pre-modernisation EC and Intercity trains).
- Higher passenger safety standards – fewer level crossings and the construction of new platforms.
- Reliability – higher quality route management, better information systems for passengers on connecting trains and on the possibilities offered by other transport modes.
- Greater passenger comfort, with the advent of new trainsets. Czech Railways has ordered ten tilting train units for providing services on the corridor.
- Access for the disabled in selected stations and special coaches.

The next route to be modernised is the link between Warsaw and Vienna, on Czech territory between Petrovice u Karviné and Breclav. This modernisation process also includes the link between the corridor already mentioned above and the north-south corridor between Ceskâ Trebová and Prerov. Its length is 215 km and modernisation has already been prepared.

Reconstruction work will proceed until 2003. The technical parameters of this corridor are identical to those of the previously described corridor.

The corridors which are already under reconstruction correspond to the main Central and Eastern European corridors approved at the pan-European Conference in Crete (Corridors 4 and 6). In the case of the Berlin–Vienna (Budapest) link, this applies in full, whereas, in the case of the Warsaw–Vienna link, full incorporation of this route into Corridor 6 will depend on approval being obtained at the pan-European Conference in Helsinki in 1997. Preparatory negotiations took place between the Czech, Slovak, Polish and Austrian Railways in 1995 in Warsaw and all the participants agreed terms and produced a common declaration of intent.

Modernisation of the corridors mentioned has been approved by the Czech government and is to be financed on the basis of a combination of State budget, commercial and non-commercial (development) credits.

The possibility of running high-speed operations on Czech Railways was also being considered.

continued

Preparations for EU membership

From the political viewpoint, the Czech and Slovak Republics now act as two separate sovereign states, whose activities are aimed at the fastest possible integration into European economic structures. In 1997, the Czech Republic's application to join the EU was accepted.

Long before then, in anticipation of full EU membership, all the branches of the Czech economy were endeavouring to bring their conditions as closely as possible into line with EU requirements. In the field of rail transport, efforts to fulfil these requirements took the form of preparing for the full application of EU Directive 91/440 and subsequent EU directives and regulations relative to the railway business.

By 1997, the situation regarding fulfilment of the principal requirements of Directive 91/440 was as follows.

Relations between state and railway: railway autonomy

Czech Railways was established in 1993 as a state organisation by the Czech National Council. It acts as an individual business entity, while being a state-owned organisation. Public services (passenger transport) are subsidised by the state to a certain degree. The amount of this subsidy is not, however, permanently fixed and is negotiated each year between Czech Railways and the state, in relation to the state budget.

There is no contract between the state and the railways in respect of public services, a factor which continues to undermine the position of Czech Railways in this connection. Moreover, Czech Railways acts as manager of the railway infrastructure of the Czech Republic. The cost of this management and maintenance is included in the budget of Czech Railways, as is the cost of some infrastructure investment. Major investment in railway infrastructure is financed either from the special funding programme approved by the government (for example, modernisation of the main corridors for the speed of 160 km/h) or some additional limited subsidies from the State budget (in addition to the passenger transport subsidy) are provided.

By 1997, work was in hand on a project to transform Czech Railways. The basic issues of this project concerned:

1 The size of the Czech Republic railway network and the extent of rail services on it. Given the density of the system, as described earlier, Czech Railways believed that the State and the regions needed to express very clear ideas about whether or not they could afford to retain the network and the services offered on it.
2 The business strategy of Czech Railways, which would have to be supplemented by the requirements of the state and the regions as far as public services are concerned.
3 The issue of public service funding and the state/railway contract.
4 The issue of state responsibility for the construction and maintenance of railway infrastructure.

Czech Railways intended presenting a number of alternative proposals for comparison, in order that the best one might be chosen to enable the railway to become a standard commercial company with clear relations with the state.

Separation of infrastructure and operations

By 1997, operations and infrastructure had already been separated within the framework of Czech Railways. The existing Czech Railways structure enables completely separate accounts for infrastructure. The infrastructure division charges a fee for the use of infrastructure both to the Czech Railways operating division and to other operators.

Writing off past debts

Czech Railways finances are burdened by the weight of past debt, placing the company in a situation very unlike that of, for example, Germany Railways–where, as part of the transformation into a joint stock company, previous debts were written off. How much of these debts will be written off remains to be seen.

Access to infrastructure

Czech Republic legislation already allows for the possibility of more railway operators providing their services on the national railway infrastructure, and this

continued

possibility has already been put to use. Licences are being issued by the Railway Administration, an independent body established and managed directly by the Ministry of Transport.

Time will tell whether the preparatory moves to mould Czech Railways into better shape are enough to enable the company to make a break with the past. But in 1997, Jirí Havlícek, Director of the International Department of Czech Railways, wrote:

Despite four decades of Communist rule, with all its negative influences, Czech Railways are playing a significant role within the international railway community, and are already prepared, together with other branches of the Czech economy, to accept all the obligations connected with full EU membership and to play an active role in the railway part of pan-European dialogue.

THE EUROPEAN HIGH-SPEED RAIL NETWORK

In the 1960s, high-speed rail services – generally speaking taken to refer to rail passenger services operating at speeds above 200 km/h – began to take shape in Japan, with the Shikansen trains. These 'bullet trains' were followed by the arrival, two decades later, of high-speed rail services in Europe. This was the second of two innovations influencing European rail travel in the second half of the twentieth century, the first being the Trans European Express (TEE) service created in the 1960s. The novelty of the TEE was the possibility it offered of a seamless journey across the continent on an express train.

Whereas TEE trains ran on conventional lines, high-speed train services required new lines specially designed for this type of traffic, or the major upgrading of existing lines. Although this meant capital-intensive investment for the railway companies, many of them became quickly convinced of the advantages of high-speed services. High-speed trains have the potential to offer attractive products for journeys up to 1,200 km in day traffic and, in the years to come, 2,500 km for overnight travel. They are therefore well suited to the continent of Europe, where many inter-city links fall into this category.

Through the development of high-speed rail services, several European railways have radically improved their product range and have, as a result, substantially increased their market share of certain routes. Through such improvements in service quality, the railways have acquired considerable numbers of additional customers. In many European countries, high-speed train load factors are reaching remarkable levels and demonstrating the attraction for the customer of this combination of speed, comfort, safety and convenience.

In 1995, Europeans travelled a total of 33 billion km on board high-speed trains, which represented approximately 12 per cent of total rail traffic in Western Europe. (However, this figure should be compared with the situation in Japan, where high-speed traffic is almost two times greater for a population a third of the size) (UIC/CER 1995). Figure 4.12 shows the development of high-speed rail traffic in Europe.

It clearly emerges from this figure that France and Germany are Europe's leaders in high-speed rail travel. But, by the end of the 1990s, a number of other countries were also developing their own high-speed networks, as the following review of European high-speed rail links demonstrates.

France

Travelling at a maximum speed of 300 km/h, the network for French TGV (*train à grande vitesse*) trains was launched in 1981. It now accounts for half of all long-distance rail traffic in France and more than half of all travel by European high-speed rail services.

The French high-speed rail system is now centred around three main corridors. The original Paris–Lyons line has been extended south to Valence, with extensions planned to Marseilles and Montpellier by the year 2000. By then, these two cities will be a mere three hours away from Paris. The Atlantic TGV has linked Paris to many

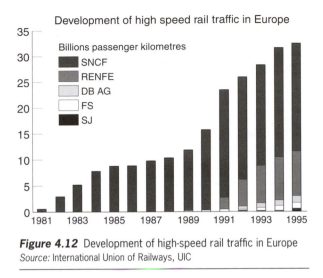

Development of high speed rail traffic in Europe

Figure 4.12 Development of high-speed rail traffic in Europe
Source: International Union of Railways, UIC

destinations in the west and south-west of France since 1989 and 1990, putting Nantes and Rennes two hours from Paris, and Bordeaux less than three.

In 1993 the 333 km section of the French part of the new line for the North European TGV was opened. This new infrastructure enabled journey times between Paris and Lille to be cut to one hour. This section now forms one of the links between Paris and the Channel Tunnel, as well as part of the Paris–Brussels–Cologne–Amsterdam link. In 1994, the TGV by-pass around Paris became operational, linking the North European and South East TGVs, with halts in the Greater Paris region (Roissy–Charles de Gaulle Airport and Disneyland Paris). Now, travellers arriving from the United Kingdom and other northern European countries have the choice of avoiding the need to change trains and stations in Paris by changing in Lille in order to travel directly to destinations such as Burgundy, the Loire and the Côte d'Azur. One consequence of these new links is that a growing number of British visitors to Disneyland Paris now visit the theme park without setting foot inside the city of Paris itself.

Demand in France is so great that, in 1996, TGV rolling stock was supplemented by new 'Duplex' (double-decker) models on busy services such as Paris–Lille and Paris–Lyons–Marseille. By comparison with the single-decker TGVs, these offer 45 per cent more seating capacity.

Germany

Train travel is steadily increasing in popularity in Germany. Between 1988 and 1996, German rail travel in general rose by 14 million passenger kilometres a year. Much of that increase was due to the advent of high-speed trains.

In Germany, high-speed operations began in 1991 with the launch of the InterCity Express trains (ICE) and the Mannheim–Stuttgart and Hanover–Würburg new lines. ICE services, which are phased with InterCity IC trains, form a mesh of regular-interval services. Since 1993, ICEs have also been serving Berlin, bringing the capital into the system. ICE services also cross the Swiss border to provide international through services such as Zurich–Frankfurt.

The development of the German high-speed network is considered by many to be of the utmost importance from a pan-European point of view, whether it be Cologne–Rhine/Main, Hanover-Berlin or Karlsruhe–Basle. Implementation of these projects is regarded as vital, both to release necessary capacity on particularly congested traffic corridors and for international transit along the north-south routes such as Scandinavia-Switzerland–Austria–Italy or east-west between the Benelux countries and the Paris basin towards Scandinavia, Poland, the Czech Republic, Austria, Hungary and south-east Europe. The demand for east-west travel has naturally been stimulated by German re-unification, and in order to respond to this demand, the German government has developed a 'gap-closing' programme (*Luckenschlussprogramm*) to re-link east and west through rail connections. The main aim of this scheme is to reinstate pre-Second World War arterial routes between the former East and West Germany. A number of these links will be high-speed.

In September 1996, a new timetable ICE2 was launched: a half-a-train concept to serve towns that do not justify the full-length high-speed trains, and with 'tilt body' technology (see page 134).

Italy

In Italy, high-speed traffic has branched outwards from the Rome–Florence *Direttissima* line, 262 km long and running along the backbone of the penin-sula. Passenger services run at a maximum speed of 250 km/h.

Since 1988, these trains have been operated not just on the *Direttissima* line but also to Genoa, Milan, Venice, Turin, Bari and Naples. By the year 2000, it is planned to open to traffic the Turin–Milan–Bologna-Florence and Rome–Naples new lines, making a major corridor with a total length of 898 km including the section already in use. (Planning, funding and execution of these high-speed projects is the task of a specially created company, Treno Alta Velocità (TAV), 40 per cent of whose capital is held by Italian railways with the remaining 60 per cent made up of private capital, in an interesting form of public-private partnership.)

A proposed trans-Alpine link between Lyons and Turin will join the French and Italian net-works. This link will include Europe's longest train tunnel, a 51 km stretch under the Alps between Italy and France, almost 2.5 km longer than the Channel Tunnel. This tunnel will take fifteen years to complete. The importance of this link for inter-national traffic cannot be overestimated since it connects major cities like Rome, Venice, Milan and Turin to Lyons, Marseilles, Paris, Barcelona, Valencia and Madrid. Used for the transporting of passengers and freight, the new link will also ease pressure on the main France–Italy road connection and the Mont Blanc tunnel. Thirty years ago this road was used by 53,000 lorries a year. By the end of the 1990s, 800,000 lorries were passing through this route annually, despite protests from environ-mentalists that exhaust fumes had turned much of the Alps into semi-desert (Guardian 1997b). (A number of other trans-Alpine road links, such as Basle–Milan via the Gotthard Pass, Munich–Verona via the Brenner and Vienna–Venice via the Tarvisio, will also help put an end to Italy's relative isolation on the other side of the Alpine barrier.)

Scandinavia

Sweden's high-speed train service, the X2000, mainly operates between Stockholm and Gothenburg. Such has been its success, with train traffic on that route rising from 30 per cent to 52 per cent at the expense of air and car, that it now extends from the capital as far south as Malmo, west to Arvika, north to Harnosand and northwest to Mora (Sunday Times 1996).

Moreover, the projects aimed at linking Scandinavia to the rest of Europe include the construction of major combined tunnel-bridge infrastructure. In 1995, a US$680 million contract to build the first direct road and rail link between Sweden and Denmark was awarded to a consor-tium of European companies. The Øresund bridge and tunnel between Malmo and Copenhagen will link Scandinavia with mainland Europe. The tunnel section, claimed to be the largest in the world, is intended to carry a two-lane motorway and a railway track in each direction (European 1995).

Spain

The high-speed era in Spain began in 1992 with the launch of the AVE (*Alta Velocidad España*) train between Madrid and Seville, which covers the 445 km in 2 hours 15 minutes with a punctuality record of 99.6 per cent. (Full fare refunds are made if the train is more than five minutes late.)

In 1995, the success of the Madrid–Seville line was confirmed, with an 8.7 per cent increase in the number of passengers and a 12.3 per cent increase in revenue over the previous year, the trend con-tinuing into 1996 (UIC 1997). One highlight was the increase in speed to a maximum of 300 km/h on certain sections of this line.

Unlike the rest of the Spanish network, this line was built to the international gauge of 1,435 mm, as a result of which all the high-speed lines built in Europe now have the same gauge, thereby opening the way for future interconnections with the Iberian Peninsula.

The next step, scheduled for the beginning of the twenty-first century, is the construction of a new line between Madrid and Barcelona and the French border. A link-up to the new line on the French side connecting the border to Perpignan and Montpellier and the connection to be estab-lished with the South-East TGV will then enable the Spanish network to be fully integrated with Europe. Another link across the Basque country will be established later to connect with the French high-speed network in Bordeaux.

A pan-European high-speed train network

Most high-speed lines, like their conventional counterparts, were planned with national travel considerations foremost in mind. Until recently, national governments' anxieties over international cooperation and management of their rail networks limited the large-scale realisation of cross-border international rail service opportunities.

However, it clearly emerges from the above review that although the first European projects were developed for priority routes at national level, the most recent plans for new high-speed train links include many cross-frontier lines. The new lines which are being progressively commissioned must therefore be seen from a dual point of view: while they contribute to improvements in services and mobility at national level, they also represent the basic components of a future pan-European network and will only assume their full value once the necessary interconnections have been completed.

By the mid-1990s, a number of truly international high-speed train services were starting to link the main centres of Europe, through the growing number of cross-border connections. In the summer of 1996, for example, the TGV-style Thalys service, a subsidiary of three national railways, French, Belgian and Dutch, came into operation between Paris and the Low Countries. The Paris–Brussels travelling time by rail was cut from 2 hours 50 minutes to 1 hour 58 minutes, with hourly departures and some trains continuing to Antwerp, some to Liège. Four trains a day link Paris and Amsterdam in 4 hours 50 minutes. It was expected that by 1998 Thalys trains would reduce the travel time on the Paris–Brussels route to a mere 1 hour 20 minutes, with the completion of the high-speed line between Antoing and Brussels.

In this way, Thalys will dominate the northern European rail scene, spear-heading a new generation of high-speed train travel *sans frontières*.

EU SUPPORT FOR HIGH-SPEED RAIL TRANSPORT

Proposals for a pan-European high-speed rail network, initially based on national projects, took shape in several stages. First, the European railway operators put together the report 'Proposals for a

European high-speed network' within the CER, a group comprising the railways of the EU Member States. This was submitted to the European Commission at the end of 1989, where it was given a favourable reception. On this basis, the Council of Ministers created a high-level Working Party for 'High Speeds', including Member States' representatives, railway companies, industry and other partners.

In 1990, this Working Party submitted a Master Plan for high-speed railway services (time horizon: 2010) to the Council of Ministers, proposing the construction of 9,000 km of new lines, the upgrading of 15,000 km of existing lines, and the development of fifteen key links to improve the degree of connectivity in the network. The Master Plan gained the approval of the Council of Ministers and as a result fourteen priority corridors for rail travel were identified across the EU. Figures 4.13 and 4.14 show the projected growth of the high-speed rail network, with the actual routes expected to be in service by 2002.

The total cost of the network is estimated at ECU 207 billion, for the whole of the EU plus Switzerland. Within this total, the cost of the key links is set at an estimated ECU 70 billion. To fund these amounts, it is necessary to call on both financial markets and the public purse. Although these sums seem substantial in absolute terms, the CER has pointed out that to fund such a network requires annual outlay in infrastructure investment

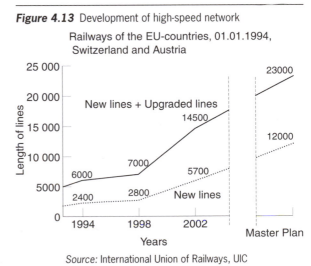

Figure 4.13 Development of high-speed network

Source: International Union of Railways, UIC

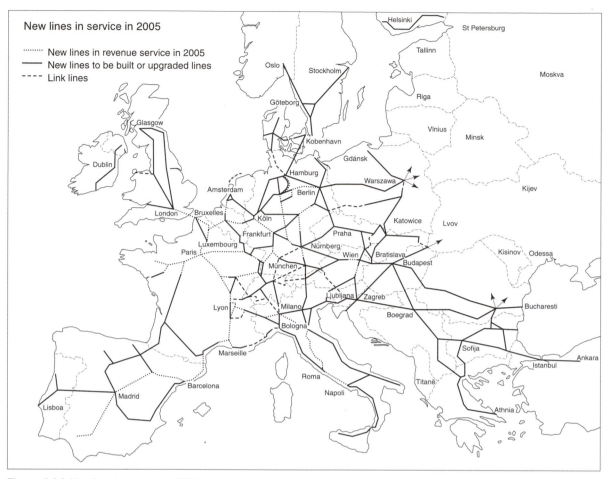

Figure 4.14 New lines in service by 2005
Source: Mission GV/International Union of Railways, UIC

of only 0.1 per cent of the gross domestic product of the countries concerned.

Of the fourteen major transport infrastructure projects acknowledged to be of top priority at the December 1994 Summit in Essen (see page 62) nine were rail projects, of which eight belonged to links on the high-speed network.

However, as discussed elsewhere in this chapter, the funding for such projects had, by the late 1990s, still not been forthcoming. In its annual report for 1997, the International Union of Railways (UIC) lamented that 'pressures on the European Union and state budgets are such that it has been impossible to release the necessary funds for injection into the budget for trans-European networks' (UIC 1997).

Combined transport networks: high-speed trains and air travel

A further element of EU transport policy involving Europe's train systems is that of promoting combined transport networks (CTNs).

This represents a departure from the conventional view of regarding high-speed train services and air services as being in direct competition with each other – something which has grown more acute with each new advance in rail technology. In that particular competition, high-speed trains have many advantages on their side:

- New tracks and better scheduling mean that there is now little difference between the door-to-door journey time taken by these two forms of transport between many European cities.

- In most cases, travel by high-speed train is more economical than travel by air to the same destination.
- Increasing congestion at Europe's airports and on its roads also spell a bright future for the fast train. Congestion on the ground at many airports and in the air make rail a more attraction option over medium distances. The launch of new rail services can lead to a reduction in the number of short-haul flights (as happened when the Paris–Lyons high-speed link was built), releasing capacity for use by the airlines on other routes.
- Rail travel also allows more usable time for work or rest, in a single chunk instead of broken up by waits at check-in, before take-off and in-flight.

These advantages of trains over planes are especially marked when travel times lie below three hours and distances under 800 km.

Nevertheless, rail travel does not always come out on top. City centre railway stations are not always convenient for travellers. In particular, those living near airports and those business travellers visiting the growing number of firms which have relocated out of town to be close to the airport may find it more convenient to leave from or arrive at an airport than a railway station. Moreover, business travellers are not cosseted by the railways to the same extent as they are by the airlines. There are few executive lounges or frequent traveller schemes in operation for rail travellers.

But CTNs stress the *complementarity* between these two forms of travel, rather than the competitive nature of the relationship that can exist between them. Train/plane synergies are already playing a key role in the development of the European passenger transport market, and this role seems set to grow. This synergy exists in different forms. For example, express airport shuttle services, such as that which transports passengers from London's Victoria Station to Gatwick Airport, have proved very successful for both air and rail operators. This indicates that cooperation rather than competition can benefit each operator financially, as well as pleasing customers. This is particularly the case where airline check-in facilities are provided at mainline stations.

But rail–air complementarity has gone further than this, with the growing trend towards combining rail journeys with medium or long-haul flights, through interconnections between premium mainline rail services and airports. Such interconnections already exist in Frankfurt, Zurich, Geneva, Amsterdam, Paris–Charles de Gaulle, and Lyons–Satolas. The growing trend towards integration of major airports in the European high-speed network is an example of how the railways are cooperating with other modes of transport in order to increase the efficiency of the system as a whole.

The importance of CTNs for EU transport policy is emphasised in the Maastricht Treaty, which makes provision for the development of trans-European networks. As far as rail travel is concerned, the basic idea is to develop the European high-speed and combined transport networks, designing them for optimum connections with conventional rail services and those of other modes.

Criticisms of high-speed rail services

Despite the general enthusiasm of governments and many passengers for high-speed rail travel, this form of transport is not without its critics in Europe.

There is, in particular, growing concern among transport analysts that the capital investment required for high-speed services may be at the expense of conventional, provincial rail services. In spatial terms, critics claim, the existing plans for investment in high-speed services in the EU are likely to lead to a greater concentration of rail traffic in transport corridors, thereby marginalising peripheral areas.

Lundgren is among those commentators who believe that the trans-European networks will only benefit strategically positioned cities, leaving more peripheral centres by the wayside.

> The costs of the TGV system make it very 'hub-dependent' in its future growth, which would in turn exclude expansion in certain directions – northeastern and eastern Europe come to mind. Thus, the high capital investment, combined with

the need to produce substantial revenue on a sustained basis will produce a spatially quite rigid high-speed train system favouring inter-city tourism on a continental scale. (Lundgren 1992)

The problem is seen in France, where critics have accused the state-owned SNCF of neglecting traditional lines by overspending on TGV tracks (Guardian 1996). The high-speed train system in that country has divided populations, which have either fiercely resisted new lines – notably in Provence – or actively lobbied for TGVs in the hope of stimulating local economies. This ambivalent attitude may be expected to be reproduced elsewhere in Europe as the high-speed network advances.

Technological advances

What will be the impact of future technology on rail travel? With some commentators predicting even faster trains early in the twenty-first century, the acceleration process was already underway in the 1990s, in the quest to satisfy the need to speed. 'The maximum operating speed in European high-speed lines is 300 km/h but France has plans to run trains at up to 360 km/h on its new route east of Paris. Speeds of up to 500 km/h will be possible and may well become the norm within twenty years, according to some rail engineers' (Batchelor 1996).

Rail engineers have two main technological advances at their disposal: tilting trains and magnetic levitation.

Tilting trains

There is a major problem associated with expanding high-speed train services and it lies in the nature of high-speed trains themselves. For, despite their high-tech image, such trains represent a technological compromise: they can go very fast, but they can only travel in virtually straight lines, and thus require special purpose-built tracks.

Not only is the building of such track very costly, but in some cases, new lines may not be feasible because of environmental constraints. For this reason, rail operators are increasingly looking to maximise speeds over conventional or only slightly modified track. In the 1990s, 'tilting trains'

emerged as an attractive solution. These can provide a high-speed service on existing tracks, because, tilting into the bend on corners much like motorcyclists, they can maintain higher speeds than traditional trains, cutting 20 per cent to 30 per cent off journey times.

In 1996, it was reported that, despite the fascination of successive French governments with the super-speed TGV rail network, France was looking with interest at the possibility of using an alternative technology based on the tilting trains principle of the British Advanced Passenger Train. This would allow TGVs to run on existing lines at about two-thirds of their top speed of more than 300 kph. In 1996, the British-owned GEC-Althsom, which builds the TGV, said the tilting train prototype would be developed by the end of 1997 and could be in service by 2000. But the company admitted that some technology may have to be bought from Germany and Italy, where the tilting principle that improves cornering on traditional tracks was perfected (Guardian 1996).

In 1997, the International Union of Railways reported that tilting body rolling stock was increasingly in use as a means of making radical improvements in journey times on a number of major European corridors:

1   In autumn 1996, direct 'Pendolino' tilting train services were launched between Italy and France (Milan–Turin–Lyons) in conjunction with through TGV services between Paris, Turin and Milan.
2   In 1996, there was an extension of the number of routes and services worked with the X2000 in Sweden.
3   In the same year, plans were made to create a new tilting train service in Finland, and to build a link between Helsinki and St Petersburg.
4   1996 also saw the introduction of the Cisalpino between Switzerland and Italy (Milan–Basle and Milan–Geneva).
5   Even the United Kingdom, where the first experiment with high-speed tilting trains was considered far from successful, has shown a revived interest in this form of technology. A British Rail prototype tilting train developed in the early 1980s and dubbed the 'Queasy Rider'

had to be scrapped because its tilt mechanisms made passengers feel sick and spilt their drinks. However, in 1997, Great North Eastern Railway, the private company running trains between London and Edinburgh, bought two tilting trains, which, it was predicted could cut the journey time on that route to 3 hours 30 minutes within three years (Times 1997a).

In the search for a compromise between large-scale expansion of Europe's high-speed train network and the status quo system of traditional *trains à petites vitesses*, tilting trains look increasingly like the most likely solution. Commentators have been quick to recognise their significance and their complementarity with high-speed links: 'Tilting trains . . . are expected to make an even greater contribution to high-speed travel than specially built high-speed expresses. Together, the two technologies are expected to improve the attractions of rail as a means of travel for business and leisure (Batchelor 1996).

Magnetic levitation

The idea of travel by magnetic levitation ('maglev') dates back to the late 1800s, but has yet to be used on a large scale as a means of rail transport in Europe. Unlike conventional trains, whose speed is limited by the structural limits of the steel rails on which they ride, maglev trains float over a metal guideway, lifted by powerful electromagnets. Since they create almost no friction, the trains are capable of speeds of up to 500 km/h, far faster than even the swiftest trains in existence today.

Europe has taken a commanding lead in the race to develop maglev, thanks largely to government support for infrastructure projects. In 1997, the German government gave the go-ahead for one of the most advanced of these projects – a US$5.8 billion scheme called Transrapid. Construction of the Transrapid is scheduled to commence in early 1999 and the first trains are due to start gliding between Hamburg and Berlin at speeds of 450 km/h in 2005. As conceived, the Transrapid will travel the 292 km between these two cities in one hour, including three stops, with departures every 20 minutes, a journey which takes about 2 hours 30 minutes using the traditional train service. Of the estimated US$5.8 billion, US$3.6 billion is being provided by the German government to build the guideway and US$2.2 billion will come from a private consortium, to build the rail cars and install the electrical systems.

Although Transrapid promises to be much less polluting than planes or cars, and quieter than other high-speed trains, the project has met resistance from the state government of Schleswig-Holstein, through which it passes. The Green Party also opposes the train on both environmental and economic grounds, claiming that the maglev will mean the end of the existing railway network, due to lack of traffic, and that the area through which the Transrapid passes will get no benefit from it.

Nevertheless, proponents of the system are hoping that maglev trains will find a niche for high-speed transport in Europe over distances of less than 1,000 km, where present train travel times are often considered too long and travel by air too expensive and congested (Time 1997a).

Demand for high-speed rail services

With expansion of high-speed rail continuing apace, the question necessarily arises: does sufficient demand exist to justify such a network?

One answer to this question (predictably affirmative) is supplied by the results of a study entitled *Traffic and Profitability of a Western European High-speed Rail Network*, commissioned by the UIC/CER and the European Commission in 1994. This established traffic forecasts and potential rates of return for high-speed rail network operators for the year 2010 (UIC/CER 1995). Based on moderate economic growth prospects and taking into account expected motorway and air service developments in Europe, the study estimated that, between them, all European railways operating high-speed services by the year 2010 could be running an extra 140 billion passenger kilometres each year. This represents relative growth of 73 per cent in 15 years for those operators, with 29 per cent of the additional traffic being newly-generated and 71 per cent shifting from other modes of transport (40 per cent from the roads and 31 per cent from the airlines).

Assuming the construction of a high-speed train network and key links in the rail infrastructure, the report estimates that the rail market share for all long-distance passenger transport (over 80 km) should grow from 14 per cent to 23 per cent approximately (in terms of passenger kilometres). High-speed trains would then account for 65 per cent of long-haul rail passenger kilometres, compared with only 7 per cent in the absence of high-speed infrastructure improvement (UIC/CER 1995).

Whatever the accuracy of these predictions, it is almost certain that leisure travel from EU core areas to peripheral tourist destinations (e.g. the Mediterranean) is unlikely to be diverted from air to high-speed rail. Business and tourist travel between the main European capitals will be the main beneficiaries of the forecast growth in high-speed travel by rail.

The Channel Tunnel

Of major significance in the northern section of the emerging European high-speed rail network is the Channel Tunnel fixed link between continental Europe and the UK.

It is a remarkable fact that despite a series of seemingly overwhelming difficulties and bad publicity, the Channel Tunnel, in the space of only a few years, has developed into an accepted and well-appreciated part of the infrastructural landscape of Europe.

Eurotunnel is the name of the private company that owns and operates the tunnel's physical infrastructure. The company was financed through a public flotation in November 1987 and subsequent refinancings as total costs rose. Eurotunnel's many problems have been well publicised. The operating company has often been described as 'a financial disaster zone'. Not only did building the tunnel take two years longer than planned, but at £10 billion, it cost double its original budget (as well the lives of ten construction workers). In the early 1990s, Eurotunnel came close to financial collapse before the Channel Tunnel had been completed. Then, once the tunnel had opened for business, the company found itself stuck with debts it could not afford to service and was obliged to settle a number of complex financial deals with its creditors in order to stay afloat.

It is clear with the benefit of hindsight that many of the financial problems which continue to confront Eurotunnel are endemic to the whole project itself and its private-sector status. Vickerman sums up the problem as follows: 'What is very clear is that governments all over the world have learned that there is no easy fix by which the private sector can simply substitute for the public sector in such major projects' (Vickerman 1995).

Added to these financial problems were the project's technical difficulties. The inauguration of services was delayed, partly due to Eurotunnel's problems in commissioning the tunnel, and partly to problems with the technically complex rolling stock – Eurotunnel's own Le Shuttle trains, the Eurostar trains and the Class 92 freight locomotives. Then just when things seemed to be going smoothly, fire broke out on a freight shuttle on 18 November 1996.

But the tunnel's difficulties are only part of the story. Seen from another angle, the Channel Tunnel's construction is a triumph of twentieth century technology and a monumental tribute to the imagination and determination of those who made it possible.

The statistics give some idea of the scale of the enterprise. It is the longest undersea passenger tunnel ever built. At peak capacity, the railway lines will be the busiest in the world. The trains that run on them are the heaviest ever built. The wiring on each is as complex as on a passenger jet and each train consumes enough electricity to power a small town.

What became evident very quickly was the Channel Tunnel's success with the travelling public, if not with the shareholders (the vast majority of whom are French). The ambivalent nature of the Channel Tunnel's success has been eloquently summed up as follows: 'Contrary to the usual pattern of free-enterprise endeavour, this massive investment pays enormous dividends to its users, while its shareholders remain among the most disgruntled in the marketplace' (Sunday Times 1996).

The 'dividends' which the Channel Tunnel offers its users are the theme of this section of the chapter. What value does this highly sophisticated system add to Europe's transport network? Why has the Channel Tunnel become so popular so quickly with such a major section of Europe's cross-Channel travelling public?

Some of the answers to these questions are linked to the nature of the Channel Tunnel system itself. This will be examined first.

THE CHANNEL TUNNEL SYSTEM

The Channel Tunnel transport system linking the UK and France comprises three tunnels which are each 50 km in length, about 38 km of which are under the Channel, at a maximum depth of 45 metres below the seabed. Two of the tunnels are for railway traffic (each is operated on a one-way basis, one tunnel being used for each direction of travel), and these are connected every 375 metres to the service tunnel, which is used for maintenance and safety purposes. The system transports road vehicles on board special shuttle trains and the tunnel is also used by the national railways' through trains, operating under the name of Eurostar. The fixed link is open 24 hours a day, 365 days of the year.

The tunnel's two terminals are served by direct access to and from the motorway networks in both countries. The locations of those terminals are such that, in fact, users of the Channel Tunnel might be forgiven for forgetting that France and England are still separated by the sea. For there is no point during the journey in either direction from which the sea is visible. In England, the Channel Tunnel terminal is sandwiched on a narrow plain between the last high ridge of the North Downs and the outskirts of Folkestone. In France, the tunnel emerges nearly three miles inland in a tangle of new motorways and flyovers by the village of Coquelles, near Calais. Figure 4.15 shows the locations of the Channel Tunnel termini.

The system can carry 30 trains and shuttles per hour in each direction, at peak periods. In all, it is designed to be used, on an alternating basis, by four different types of railway traffic:

Figure 4.15 The Channel Tunnel

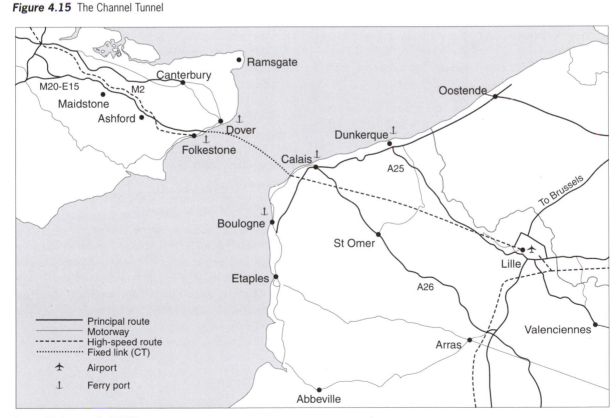

Source: Vickerman, R. (1995)

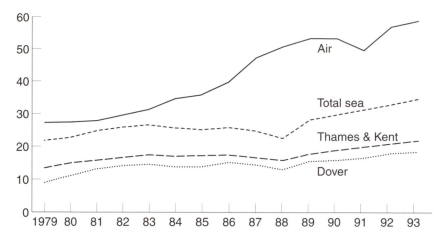

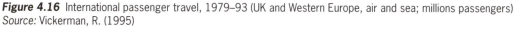

Figure 4.16 International passenger travel, 1979–93 (UK and Western Europe, air and sea; millions passengers)
Source: Vickerman, R. (1995)

1 Services operated by Eurotunnel:
   • passenger-vehicle shuttles for the transport of cars, coaches, caravans, minibuses, motorcycles and bicycles;
   • freight shuttles for the transport of heavy goods vehicles.
2 Services operated by the national railway companies:
   • Eurostar cross-Channel high-speed trains;
   • freight trains.

Freight services, provided by both the Shuttle and direct train services, are a vital part of the market for the Channel Tunnel. But as they lie outside the scope of this book, they will not be described in detail here.

An examination of the tourism-related services offered by the Channel Tunnel follows an analysis of the state of the market which the tunnel was built to serve.

The cross-Channel market

Eurotunnel's entry into the cross-Channel market practically doubled capacity on the short sea-routes and provided a totally new service with the Eurostar trains.

There is general agreement that this is a market which, in the years immediately leading up to the opening of the Channel Tunnel, was already displaying strong growth. This is confirmed by the data contained in Figure 4.16. The data present a picture of overall growth in the market for passenger travel between the UK and Western Europe by air and sea, and shows, in particular, the growth in that segment of the market most likely to use Eurotunnel's shuttle services – traffic through the Thames and Kent port group and through Dover.

Vickerman comments that this growth may have reflected a number of trends of those times: a switch in the market for tourist travel from the air package to car-based travel; growth in additional tourist travel, such as for extra short break holidays; and strategic marketing by ferry companies with spare capacity on bigger ships, while also trying to develop a cushion against the impending arrival of the tunnel (Vickerman 1995).

The Channel Tunnel's success will depend on what share of this market it can persuade to use its own services, as well as the extent to which the tunnel itself stimulates new business. Market research undertaken by Eurotunnel suggests that there will be a significant number of additional cross-Channel trips taken, with existing travellers crossing more frequently, along with passengers who will be stimulated by the introduction of a fixed-link (Garnett 1993).

The shuttle service

Eurotunnel markets its transport services to motorists under the name of Le Shuttle. These ser-

Figure 4.17 The Shuttle service
Source: @ Eurotunnel

vices operate around the clock, on a 'turn-up-and-go' basis, with no reservations required. For the road vehicle user, the Shuttle service therefore offers a streamlined, relatively interruption-free journey. The no-reservation, turn up and go system increases flexibility (Figure 4.17).

Le Shuttle service moves passengers and cars between the tunnel's two terminals at Folkestone and Calais. This service effectively provides a link between the M20 motorway in Kent and the A16 and A26 autoroutes in France. On arrival at the terminals, vehicles pass through the toll area and then complete the frontier controls for both countries, prior to departure. Before reaching the frontier controls, Le Shuttle customers have the opportunity of stopping at the passenger amenity building for duty and tax-free shopping (until 1999, at least). Placing frontier controls at the entrance to the tunnel allows a control-free exit at the other end, bringing down the total transit time. On arrival, customers are free to continue their journey immediately. The journey time, from platform to platform, is 35 minutes, of which about 26

are spent actually travelling through the tunnel. Eurotunnel's target is a 75-minute motorway-to-autoroute time, allowing for check-in, loading, the 35-minute tunnel transit and unloading.

By 1997, for passenger-vehicle shuttles, there were up to four departures per hour at peak times, up to three departures per hour at other times, and one departure per hour during off-peak night hours. The shuttles' maximum speed is 140 km/h and each can transport 120 cars and 12 coaches.

Competition with ferry services

Crossing the sea rather than going under it is still a viable mode of transport between the UK and the continent, and one which is exploited to the full by ferry operators, Le Shuttle's main competitors.

The impact of the Channel Tunnel on cross-Channel ferry services was felt long before its opening. Ferry operators responded to the prospect of competition by upgrading the quality of their services and applying more competitive pricing policies during the 1980s and early 1990s.

Passengers travelling on the 'new-look' ferries found themselves in air-conditioned interiors more like a luxury hotel than a cross-Channel ferry. Deep-cushioned chairs and deep-piled carpets, shopping malls, playrooms and even cinemas featured in the ferries' advertising which did everything possible to make them sound like cruise liners (see Peisley (1990) for further details).

More importantly, perhaps, increased frequency, faster loading times and shorter turnrounds all contributed to reducing the critical motorway-to-autoroute time. Faster conventional ships and the gradual reduction in frontier controls, which helped smooth travellers' passage through ports, brought typical crossing times down to 75–90 minutes. Although this was still longer than the time taken by Le Shuttle, the ferry companies attempted to turn this into an advantage, by marketing their slower transit time as an ideal opportunity to take a rest or meal-break in a journey. But, as Vickerman (1995) points out, it is important to take into account the wishes of passengers who want to take meals elsewhere, and not when they are in transit across the Channel. Indeed, fast ferries, such as hovercraft, which do not offer much in the way of meal-break facilities, have maintained a reasonable share of the cross-Channel market. Perhaps of greater importance is the extent to which passengers wish an opportunity to leave their cars and walk around, which, in the case of Le Shuttle service, is minimal.

In addition, the ferry companies were assisted in their efforts to out-compete the tunnel by two developments: the delayed opening of the Tunnel and the extension of duty-free until 1999 (Jefferson 1992).

The ferries' efforts intensified after the opening of the Channel Tunnel. For example, in 1996, Hoverspeed announced that it was planning to double its fast-craft fleet based at Dover in a direct challenge to Eurotunnel in preparation for the summer of 1997. The company planned to add two Seacats to its existing hovercraft and introduce first-class cabins in an aggressive attempt to boost passenger numbers. After bucking trends in 1996 by holding on to its 10 per cent share of the cross-channel market, the company was aiming to take share away from the car-carrying Le Shuttle service

by offering up to 24 departures a day on the Dover–Calais route the following summer, cutting crossing times to 35 minutes, the same as Le Shuttle (Times 1996).

Vickerman rightly predicted that, regarding pricing policy, there would be little initial attempt to make price competition a major feature in the battle between operators to attract customers. Due to an understandable reluctance to experiment with price, the marketing strategy of all the operators, including Eurotunnel has been to try to maintain the status quo on prices. A comparison of the fares of Le Shuttle and a number of cross-Channel ferry operators showed that no one operator had a consistent price advantage over the others, as each had chosen different means of presenting their fares structure (Vickerman 1995).

In general, all operators are intent on seeing the establishing of a 'level playing field'. The ferry companies have campaigned in an attempt to ensure that no special favours are granted to Eurotunnel, such as subsidies to rail services. Eurotunnel has campaigned against duty-free sales on board ferries, although without great success, and in favour of imposing equivalent safety standards on ferries. This latter issue is a source of considerable concern for ferry operators, as it could require the fitting of bulkheads or other measures to increase stability. The net effect would be threefold: an additional investment burden on the ferry companies; longer loading, unloading and turnaround times; and reduced capacity. All three effects would benefit Eurotunnel's revenues both through greater time advantage and less downward pressure on prices (Vickerman 1995).

EUROSTAR PASSENGER TRAINS

With the opening of the Channel Tunnel came the start of high-speed direct Eurostar rail services directly linking London, Paris and Brussels, thus ushering in a new era of international train travel in the north of Europe. Operated by the British, French and Belgian railway companies, the Eurostar services were launched in November 1994, to carry passengers between the three capital cities.

By 1996, Eurostar were operating fourteen return trips per day between London and Paris and seven per day between London and Brussels. That year, Eurostar traffic represented 58 per cent of the market on the Paris–London route for both rail and air combined (UIC 1997). At the same time, on the London–Brussels route, Eurostar had won 45 per cent of air/rail traffic (Telegraph 1996).

The tunnel has quickly come to be a vital link in the north European rail network linking Paris, Brussels, Cologne, Amsterdam and London. London is the biggest traffic generator in this network. With medium-term projections of 10–15 million passengers a year using the rail link through the tunnel, this makes it one of the most heavily used international links in the whole European transport network and on a par with many of the major national links (Vickerman 1995).

Two important planned developments will add to the attractiveness of Eurostar services. First, there are to be daily through services on the east and west coast main lines from Glasgow/ Edinburgh and Manchester/Birmingham to continental destinations; and the service will be further extended to include night sleeper services from a variety of points including Glasgow, Manchester, Swansea and Plymouth, to Paris, Amsterdam and Basle. Secondly, rail travel between the UK and the continent will also have an increasing advantage as the extension of high-speed lines in several countries brings a growing number of destinations into the network.

Naturally, one of the longest-awaited links still to be built is in the UK itself: the dedicated high-speed link between London and the tunnel. The delay in building this all-important link, which was first planned in 1986 may be explained by the refusal of the then British government to fund the high-speed rail link out of public funds. This was a direct consequence of the government's policy of prefering to involve private enterprise in the funding of major infrastructural projects at the time.

A solution was reached when, in early 1996, a consortium, London & Continental Railways, was awarded a contract to build the (US$4.6 billion) high-speed rail-link connecting London and the Channel Tunnel. The line will cut train travel time from the UK to Paris by 30 minutes, to 2 hours 30 minutes when it is completed in 2003. Trains will be able to run at a top speed of 270 km/h, the current speed on the Calais to Paris leg of the journey. Current speed in the UK is around 130 km/h.

London & Continental Railways received a British government subsidy of £1.4 billion to build the 109 km link from London's St Pancras station to the Channel Tunnel and the consortium itself is responsible for raising the rest. In return for its investment, the consortium gained ownership of European Passenger Services, the high-speed Channel Tunnel train company that holds a 999-year concession on the service.

COMPETITION BETWEEN RAIL AND AIR

The advantages of the Eurostar service over its airline competitors are similar to those of high-speed trains in general (see page 133). The benefits of Eurostar are presented to the travelling public as being: direct city centre to city centre trips, rapid travelling times, more personal space and uninterrupted journeys rather than *ad hoc* combinations of trips by plane with train/taxi/car/coach journeys at either end. In reality, how do the Eurostar services compare with air travel for the same routes?

On *time*, Eurostar services between London and both Paris and Brussels appear to show a clear advantage over their airline rivals in terms of city centre to city centre times, as shown by the data in Table 4.2.

The situation may not, however, be so clear-cut. Once it is assumed that at both ends of their trip, passengers have to travel from their home or place of work to the point of departure of their chosen mode of transport, the advantages become blurred. It may be at least as convenient for some passengers to travel to the airport as to a central railway station.

Also, one downside of the Eurostar service which has been highlighted (Telegraph 1996) is the fact that, with the one-hour time difference between the UK and France, those travelling from London to Paris for a 10am appointment have to catch the 05.08 train from Waterloo. (However, an inventive compromise solution is available to those travelling between London and Paris, in the form of a link between Eurotunnel and the air carrier,

Table 4.2 Comparison of rail and air times for London–Paris,[1] 1995

	Air	Rail
Access to airport	1 hour 0 min	–
Check-in	30 min	20 min
Journey time	1 hour 10 min	3 hours 0 min
Access to city	1 hour 0 min	–
Total journey time	*3 hours 40 min*	*3 hours 20 min*

Note: [1] City centre to city centre
Source: Vickerman, R. (1995)

British Midland. This provides the option of flying out and taking the train back – or vice versa, for those with late afternoon meetings in Paris.)

The comparison of the *level of service* offered by both transport modes depends on frequency as well as comfort. Eurostar's service frequency has been slow to develop, and this has led to a slow build-up of patronage. Until the planned (at least) hourly service is in operation, the frequency of air services will appear much superior and this will continue to enhance the attractiveness of air travel.

Price is particularly difficult to compare. The proliferation of special offer fares, including the availability, through consolidators, of air fares at below published prices makes it very difficult to effect a comparison. There is therefore no conclusive answer to the question of which mode of transport is cheaper. What is clearer, however, as has already been mentioned, is that all sides are keen to avoid a price war. There is general recognition of the fact that a price war between the tunnel and the ferries or between train and plane would only give short-term benefits to consumers, since the usual outcome of such a war is to destroy the competition and ultimately enhance the monopoly power of the remaining operator.

THE CHANNEL TUNNEL'S FINANCIAL PERFORMANCE

Generally, the Channel Tunnel's financial results appear to be going in the right direction. By 1997, Eurotunnel was able to announce 'favourable' financial results, with total revenue for 1996 up from £299 million for the previous year to £448 million. More than 13 million people travelled through the tunnel in 1996, compared with 8 million in 1995, the tunnel's first complete year of opening (Eurotunnel 1997).

There is no doubt, however, that the fire of 18 November 1996 was a serious incident, leading to extensive damage to the rail tunnel. Nevertheless, in the event, the service tunnel which runs between the two rail tunnels, provided the safe haven for the lorry drivers and train crew to escape, just as it had been designed to do. Following an investigation undertaken by Eurotunnel with the aid of outside specialists, the company decided to improve some equipment, modify and simplify some procedures, and enhance the training of all the staff who operate the system.

When the tunnel reopened to passenger traffic in December 1996, priority was given to Eurostar, which resumed with 90 per cent of departures. But tunnel capacity remained restricted due to the repair works and as a result, Eurotunnel was only able to offer half the normal service on Le Shuttle Tourist, and no service at all for Le Shuttle Freight. By June 1997, full service had been resumed in time for the summer traffic. The operating company's objective was to reach, by the end of 1997, the share of the cross-Channel market which it enjoyed before the fire incident.

Figure 4.18 shows the growth in Le Shuttle Tourist traffic between 1995 and 1997. In the first six months of 1996, such traffic had almost doubled, and by August of that year, more vehicles had been carried than in the whole of 1995 – over

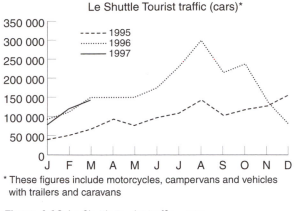

Le Shuttle Tourist traffic (cars)*

* These figures include motorcycles, campervans and vehicles with trailers and caravans

Figure 4.18 Le Shuttle tourist traffic – cars
Source: Eurotunnel

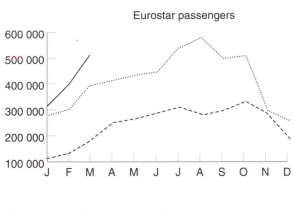
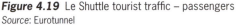

Eurostar passengers

Figure 4.19 Le Shuttle tourist traffic – passengers
Source: Eurotunnel

2.1 million tourist vehicles. Business was helped by a reduction and a simplification of tariffs in May 1996, and by Eurotunnel's decision to reduce the duty-free prices on goods on sale in its shops in both terminals. By the end of 1996, Eurotunnel's duty-free sales totalled just under £100 million, particularly as a result of the growth in coach traffic using Le Shuttle (Eurotunnel 1997).

Figure 4.19 shows the increase in the number of passengers carried by Eurostar between 1995 and 1996. By the end of 1996, Eurostar had carried a total of almost 5 million passengers, an increase of 67 per cent over 1995. Growth was helped by increases in the number of Eurostar departures per day and by the introduction, in June 1996, of direct services between London and Disneyland Paris. Growth continued into 1997. In June 1997, Eurostar carried 524,520 passengers, an increase of 20 per cent over the same month in 1996. As a result, Eurotunnel was able to make a modest (£7 million) operating profit for the first time, although, as financiers rightly pointed out, this was wiped out by interest charges of £330 million (Times 1997c).

The business segment

The 1996 Carlson Wagonlit survey revealed an increase in the UK business community's level of demand for Channel Tunnel services operated by both Eurostar and Le Shuttle. The same survey also suggested that the fire in the Channel Tunnel

had not dampened enthusiasm for its use by the business community. Those decision-makers interviewed just after the fire were found to be just as likely to use the service as those interviewed before. Similarly, the survey appeared to show that the attitudes of business travellers themselves had not been affected by the accident. Of those interviewed before the fire, 93 per cent said that they would use the service again compared to 91 per cent interviewed after the fire.

There was also an upward trend in the number of companies that said they would take Eurostar to destinations beyond Brussels and Paris (39 per cent in 1996, compared to 34 per cent the previous year), indicating a growing interest in the advantages of the intra-European rail network in the business community (Carlson Wagonlit 1997).

In 1996, Eurotunnel introduced Club Class for business customers using its Le Shuttle service. Such customers make up 25 per cent of Le Shuttle's customers. The service offers priority boarding and unloading, specialised catering and duty-free facilities as well as the use of telecommunications services (fax, telephone) in a reserved lounge prior to boarding.

To raise its appeal, in particular to business travellers, Eurostar launched a frequent traveller scheme in 1996. Under this scheme, card-holders earn 50 points for a one-way standard crossing. With 500 points, they can claim a free standard return (Telegraph 1996).

Looking to the future, poll evidence from Mori

suggests that more than one in three business travellers would support Eurostar services operating beyond Paris and Brussels. Most business interest has centred on Bordeaux (8 hours from London) and Lyons (5½ hours), changing at Lille; and Cologne and Amsterdam (each 6½ hours), via Brussels. There is also demand for trains to Europe from cities outside London. At present, there is one train a day from Manchester and Edinburgh to Waterloo, to connect with Eurostar departures. From April 1997, direct Paris services were due to start from Birmingham (5 hours), Manchester (5¾ hours) and Edinburgh (8¼ hours).

It is envisaged that direct sleeper services trains will leave every night from Glasgow, Carlisle, Swansea and Plymouth, arriving in Paris at breakfast time (Telegraph 1996).

The leisure market

Le Shuttle lost no time in linking up with motoring holiday operators to have its services packaged in their programmes, as well as setting up its own inclusive tour operations programme, Le Shuttle Holidays, which offers holiday packages both from the UK and from the continent. Before the opening of the Channel Tunnel, it was estimated that overall, about 20 per cent of Le Shuttle's traffic would be travelling on inclusive tours of one kind or another (Garnett 1993).

Much has been made of the part played by the Channel Tunnel in encouraging the British to take short breaks on the continent and its potential to make Britain a much more attractive short break destination for continental visitors. Short breaks acquire their popularity through their convenience and speed of journey, which allows maximum time in the chosen destination. The short-break growth is particularly strong in the winter or off-season, and the weather-resistant nature of Le Shuttle will also come into play in persuading the short-break decision-maker to book self-drive short-break holidays (see Chapter 7).

CONCLUSION

Within a very short space of time, the Channel Tunnel has provided an essential transport service in Europe. It has changed the relationship between the UK and continental Europe and has become a key feature in the economic and social development of South East England and the Nord-Pas-de-Calais region of France.

Given time, the Channel Tunnel could bring further advantages. As it uses rail travel, it has the potential to improve the balance of traffic between more and less environmentally friendly modes; and it could also have significant impacts on the long-term process of European integration.

Whether Eurotunnel has the time to secure these benefits remains to be seen. Considering the outlook for the Channel Tunnel system, Vickerman has written: 'The indications are that this complex system is inherently viable, but in reality whether it achieves viability and how soon depends on a complex mixture of economic, financial and market factors, the outcome of which has yet to be determined' (Vickerman 1995). Clearly, a key element in forecasting demand for cross-Channel travel in general is the assumption made about the future growth of the European economy, and more particularly that of the UK, since the greatest share of passenger traffic is of UK origin. Income growth is the major explanatory factor in the long-term growth of the cross-Channel market. The extent to which the Channel Tunnel succeeds as a transport system will, in effect, be a direct reflection of the performance of the European economy as a whole.

UPDATE

Undertake your own research to find out the answers to the following questions:

- In the debate over motorway expansion which side has been more successful in persuading the EU that its approach is the right one: the pro-motorway lobby or the environmentalists?
- How has the European high-speed rail network developed?
- To what extent has EU Directive 91/440 been successful in revitalising Member States' railway systems?
- Who is winning the battle to increase their share of the cross-Channel tourism transport market: the Channel Tunnel or the ferries?

References

AIT (1996) *Evolution of Tourism and the Automobile*, International Touring Alliance, Geneva.

Batchelor, C. (1996) 'A high-speed future', *Financial Times*, survey, 15 February, p. 4.

Bowers, P. (1995) 'Commercialisation, local and international access on the rails', *Public Transport International*, No. 1, pp. 25–9.

Carlson Wagonlit (1997) *Carlson Wagonlit Travel/Mori 1996 Business Travel Survey*, Carlson Wagonlit/Mori, London.

CEC (1996b) *The Citizens' Network-fulfilling the potential of public passenger transport in Europe*, European Commission, Brussels.

Davidson, R. and Maitland, R. (1997) *Tourism Destinations*, Hodder & Stoughton, London.

European, The (1995) 'The Øresund Bridge contract', 21–27 July.

Eurotunnel (1997) *1996 Annual Report and Accounts*, Eurotunnel, Folkestone/Paris.

Garnett, C. (1993) 'Impact of the Channel Tunnel on the tourism industry', *Tourism Management*, December, pp. 436–9.

Guardian, The (1996) 'End of the line for TGV', 3 October.

Guardian, The (1997) 'Kinnock seeks Euro-wide cut in speed limit and safer cars', 10 April.

IRF (1995) *Eurovia: The Advanced Integrated Motorway System in Europe*, International Road Federation, Geneva.

IRF (1997) XIIIth IRF World Meeting, Advance Press Briefing, International Road Federation, Geneva.

IRTU (1997) 'The coach and tourism in towns', International Road Transport Union, Geneva.

Jefferson, A. (1992) Speech in *Proceedings of the 1992 Tourism in Europe Conference*, Centre for Travel and Tourism, Houghton le Spring.

Lundgren, J. O. J. (1992) 'Transport Infrastructure Development and Tourist Travel – Case Europe', in *Proceedings of the 1992 Tourism in Europe Conference*, Centre for Travel and Tourism, Houghton le Spring.

NEG (1997) *1996 Annual Report*, National Express Group, Birmingham.

Page, S. (1993) European rail travel, in *Travel and Tourism Analyst (1)*, Travel and Tourism Intelligence, London.

Page, S. (1994) The European coach travel market, in *Travel and Tourism Analyst (1)*, Travel and Tourism Intelligence, London.

Peisley, T. (1990) 'The UK–Europe ferry industry and strategies for the 1990s', *Travel and Tourism Analyst*, **No. 2**, EIU, London.

Scard, I. (1993) 'Transport Changes in Europe – a time for hubbing?', *Insights*, March issue, English Tourist Board, London.

Sunday Times, The (1996) 'Back on track', 25 August.

Telegraph, The (1996) 'Eurostar leads the way into a new railway age', 21 November.

Times, The (1997) 'The coming rail revolution', 16 June.

Times, The (1996) 'Hoverspeed plans a high-speed boost', 3 October.

Times, The (1997a) 'New trains take tilt at record time', 29 January.

Times, The (1997b) 'Rail travel in Britain is most expensive in world', 28 August.

Times, The (1997c) 'Tunnel makes its first profits', 23 September.

UIC (1997) *Annual Report 1996*, International Union of Railways, Paris.

UIC/CER (1995) 'High speed rail: mobility on the right track', International Union of Railways/Community of European Railways, Paris and Brussels.

Vickerman, R. (1995) The Channel Tunnel – a progress report, in *Travel and Tourism Analyst (3)*, Travel and Tourism Intelligence, London.

5

Theme parks in Europe

KEY OBJECTIVES

Reading this chapter will enable you to:

- Understand how theme parks fit into the full range of Europe's tourist attractions.
- Familiarise yourself with the distinguishing features of Europe's theme parks: supply and demand.
- Know what makes Disneyland Paris different to all other European theme parks.
- Be aware of current trends in the supply of and demand for theme parks in Europe.

Introduction

THEME PARKS AS VISITOR ATTRACTIONS

Traditional visitor attractions, including monuments, castles, churches, religious shrines and the great art collections, were the original motors of tourism in Europe. Visiting historic and cultural attractions was the prime motivation behind the pilgrimages, the Grand Tours and, later, the sightseeing holidays undertaken by those curious to see Europe's rich heritage for themselves. Despite the development of mass markets in other forms of tourism, such as sun/sea/sand/ and ski-ing holidays, visits to historic and cultural attractions still remain a vital part of many full-length holidays, short breaks and city visits, school trips and incentive trips (Jenner and Smith 1996).

But although the traditional attractions continue to draw large numbers in visitor volume terms, they are now being challenged by another category of attractions, Europe's growing number of theme parks.

The visitor attractions market now falls into two fairly distinct parts. On the one hand there are the cultural/historic attractions, often inherently associated with the destination itself. Thus, for example, tourists visiting Rome for the first time will almost certainly want to see the Coliseum, while tourists in London will expect to visit places such as the Tower of London and the British Museum. Many of these attractions have become such strong images that they have effectively come to symbolise the destination, for its own residents as well as for foreigners. Monuments such as the Arc de Triomphe, the Little Mermaid and Barcelona's Sagrada Familia have become powerful icons, widely used by tourism industry marketeers because of their ability to evoke instantly associations with the places where they are situated. Regarding the structure which would appear to be the favourite candidate for the position of the monument best symbolising not only the country where it is situated but the entire continent of Europe, there would appear to be a clear winner, – see Figure 5.1.

However, such established and instantly recognisable European attractions have now to compete for the attention of tourists with the second category of visitor attractions, that of theme parks. While the supply of cultural and historical monuments is more or less fixed, theme parks have proliferated in Europe, during the last forty years. This chapter examines the reasons for theme parks' popularity in Europe and traces the development of this type of attraction.

Question: Of the following European monuments, which are the two which, for you, best symbolise the whole continent?

(Answers in percentages)

	ITALIANS	BRITISH	SPANISH	GERMANS
The Eiffel Tower	**50**	**62**	**59**	**39**
The Acropolis	20	14	11	12
Big Ben	13	**49**	14	12
The Alhambra	3	2	**36**	5
Mont St Michel	2	1	–	4
Leaning Tower of Pisa	**31**	20	24	16
The Brandenburg Gate	8	16	8	**57**
Château of Versailles	19	11	8	21
NONE	36	12	24	13

Source: Société Nouvelle d'Exploitation de la Tour Eiffel (Survey carried out between 15 March and 2 April 1996. Approximately 1,000 visitors of each of the four nationalities were questioned at the entrance to the Eiffel Tower)

Figure 5.1 The Eiffel Tower – the symbol of Europe
Source: Société Nouvelle d'Exploitation de la Tour Eiffel

THE THEME PARK CONCEPT

The concept of theme parks is one which is not easily defined. It is generally agreed that all theme parks are concerned with entertainment and physical experiences, provided by a backbone of varied rides and attractions (McEniff 1993). The Tussauds Group, the UK's leading theme park operator, defines the term 'theme park' as: 'Visitor attractions offering permanent rides and entertainment. Ideally these are in uniquely themed settings providing something for the whole family, usually by paying one price for unlimited access to all rides and attractions in a fun and secure environment' (CWA 1997).

The main identifying characteristics appear to be the huge scale of such attractions, with a range of attractions including state-of-the-art thrill rides, and what may be termed 'constant customer experience'. The visitor is continually bombarded with sensory stimuli, visual and aural. Even when queuing for rides, the visitor's attention is never allowed to lapse into abstraction or, worse, boredom.

Theme parks provide all of the services required for the visitor, including a wide range of retail outlets selling food and souvenirs. POP – 'pay one price' – admission is another distinguishing feature of theme parks. This system, by which admission charges include access to all rides as well as the car park, is based on the premise that visitors prefer not to have to pay up for each separate facility used during their visit to the theme park.

Theme parks are distinguishable from fairgrounds or other similar leisure attractions by an overall themed experience which runs through most of the attractions. However, what constitutes a 'theme' is not always clear. Some parks have multiple themes spread across different segments of the park; others may simply have a mascot. In Europe, a much looser interpretation of the term is used, than in the USA (McEniff 1993).

HISTORICAL BACKGROUND

Several attractions claim to have pioneered the theme park concept in Europe. The idea may be traced back to the 'pleasure parks' which were constructed in many European capital cities at the end of the nineteenth century: for example, Vienna's Prater Park and the Tivoli Gardens in Copenhagen. Recently, another, more novel, contender for the title of the theme park prototype has been suggested. D'Hautesserre (1997) maintains that the first theme park in the Western world was built at the end of the 1200s by Robert II of Artois at Vieil Hesdin, in the north of France. Sounding strangely modern in its design, the park, according to the author, 'included a revolving castle, a grotto within which rain or snow could be willed, animated marionettes, collapsing bridges, as well as exotic plants and animals that symbolised paradise. Charles V destroyed the park 300 years later'.

In any case, what seems less controversial is Europe's claim to be the birthplace of the modern theme park concept, three years before Disney pioneered the theme park in the USA. Despite the public perception of Walt Disney as the inventor of the theme park, De Efteling can lay claim to be the first of its kind, having opened its park in southwest Holland in 1952, based on the theme of European fairy tales. Modern theme parks began to develop in Europe in the 1960s and 1970s, fostered by growth in leisure time, rising disposable incomes and the increased mobility of consumers through rising car ownership. Nevertheless, they developed at a much slower pace and on a much more modest scale than their North American counterparts.

Why, despite being the birthplace of the theme park concept, did Europe lag behind the USA in terms of park development? It has been suggested that part of the answer at least would seem to lie in the USA's lack of historic sites and, by way of contrast, Europe's great richness in these. As car-ownership spread in Europe, there may have been a perceived obligation on the part of a newly mobile generation of tourists to visit those places where their continent's heritage was to be found. As Jenner and Smith (1996) observe:

> For families from the 1950s to the 1970s, at least, sightseeing meant art, culture and being (however reluctantly) 'educated'. That sense of obligation to 'do' the important sites is now gone for many families. For the generation brought up on videos and computer games, sightseeing means not the most historic but the very latest.

The general level of prosperity also certainly played a role in delaying the development of theme parks in Europe. One aspect of this is the difference between levels of car ownership in Europe and in the United States, with North Americans entering the age of widespread car ownership much earlier than Europeans. By 1970, for the inhabitants of the fifteen countries which now constitute membership of the EU, private car transport represented 77 per cent of all travel undertaken in those countries, while by then, in the USA, transport by private car accounted for 90 per cent of all travel (Eurostat 1997).

GEOGRAPHICAL SPREAD

Most of the great classical sightseeing attractions are in the south of Europe, where they remain as monuments to the grandeur of Roman, Greek and Moorish civilisations: the Alhambra, the Coliseum, the Forum and the Acropolis being among the most notable examples.

The newer theme parks, by contrast, tend to be in northern Europe, far from Europe's Mediterranean playground with its migratory millions of annual visitors. What are the reasons for the great concentration of Europe's theme parks in the cooler northern countries of the continent?

The fact is that theme parks are targeted not so much at people on holiday but at people resident within a catchment area that makes a large number of day visits possible. Theme parks have been described as the 'heavy industry' sector of the tourism industry, due to the huge investment required to build and maintain this type of business. For a theme park to have favourable chances of making this level of investment pay dividends, it must be within easy reach of its potential market. It has been estimated that there must be 20 million residents within two hours' drive of the park, or that the park should be within one hour's drive of major holiday destinations and two hours of 5–6 million residents (McEniff 1993).

Thus situated, the theme park's potential market will be composed of those inhabitants who enjoy a level of leisure time and prosperity which enables them to pay the (fairly substantial) price of a family outing to an attraction of this kind.

For this reason, the great concentration of

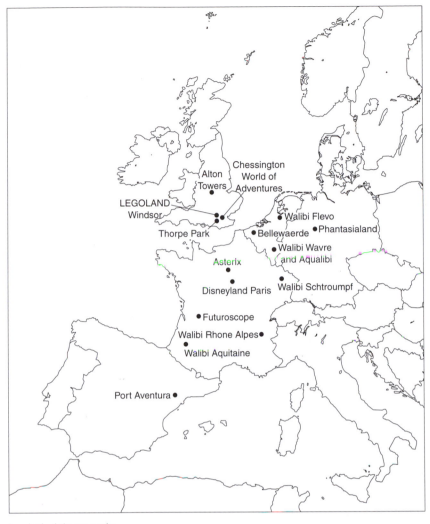

Figure 5.2 Europe's principal theme parks

major European theme parks lies in the highly industrialised, densely populated and relatively wealthy triangle based on Paris, the northern Rhine and the North Sea, including parts of Germany and France, as well as most of Belgium, the Netherlands and Luxembourg. Figure 5.2 shows the location of Europe's principal theme parks.

Germany has more major theme parks than any other European country and the sector is well established and relatively stable in terms of the number of parks and attendance levels. (In 1992, out of a total membership of 101 parks, the Europarks association of European theme parks,

had 44 individual German member parks.) Table 5.1 shows attendance levels at theme parks in the principal European countries for this form of visitor attraction.

The north of Europe offers a number of other advantages for theme park location. It lies far enough away from the Mediterranean beaches which, with their long summer season and comparatively inexpensive recreation opportunities, might present competition for theme park's potential market. Also, in the north of Europe there is a greater tendency for mothers to have jobs outside the home than there is in Mediterranean countries. Not only does this provide a second

Table 5.1 European theme park attendance 1994

Region	Visitors (millions)
France	15
UK	12.6
Germany	12
Netherlands	6.7
Scandinavia	6
Belgium	4
Italy	2.8
Total	59.1

Source: Theme Parks – UK & International Markets, 1995; Tourism Research and Marketing

salary for the families concerned, thus increasing their level of discretionary income, but it also means that parents, having generally less time available for their children, have a greater tendency towards occasionally indulging their offspring and paying for the type of lavish treat which a trip to a theme park represents.

However, the geographic distribution of the industry is to some extent influenced by park size. Although large parks are generally located a short distance from major urban concentrations for the reasons already mentioned, Europe also has a substantial number of smaller parks providing an important part of flanking attractions in traditional resorts, some of which are in the south of Europe.

Theme parks which rely on a market basically composed of holidaymakers find themselves in a business that is necessarily seasonal. In the same way, of course, theme parks in northern Europe also tend to be seasonal, as a result of the weather.

McEniff notes that estimates from IAAPA (International Association of Amusement Parks and Attractions) indicate that seasonality is more evident in Europe than in parks elsewhere in the world, reflecting the northern European climate. One consequence of this is the high level of seasonality in theme park employment in Europe (McEniff 1993).

The advantage of locating in a densely populated area, however, is that theme parks doing so avoid the risk of linking fortunes with a tourism destination whose future cannot be known for certain.

The theme park market in Europe

DEMAND FOR THEME PARKS

Quantitative

Both Europarks and the IAAPA provide data on major theme parks. IAAPA estimate that annual attendance at all Western European parks was around 110 million in 1995, but the total is somewhat higher when non-affiliated parks are included. Economic Research Associates, a UK consultancy, estimate that just under 16 million people visited Europe's top two theme parks in 1995 and the top eight parks attracted around 30 million visitors.

North America, where total attendance numbers for theme parks exceed those of all major sports events, is the standard reference point for international comparisons of theme parks. The USA continues to dominate the worldwide theme park market. In Europe, attendance figures are much lower than in the USA, as is expenditure, as shown in Table 5.2.

Clearly, the highest growth in theme park attendance is evident in the developing markets of China, South East Asia and Australia, where high levels of GDP growth and general prosperity in the Asia Pacific region in general has provided a sound customer base for such products.

But even in the mature marketplace of Europe, there are some positive signs. Richards (1996) points out that spending is rising faster than growth in the number of admissions (particularly in the UK). As he remarks:

> With the levels of investment required for the 'theme park game' being continually raised – most notably in the cost of new attractions but also in increased marketing and infrastructure costs – European parks will be hoping that the trend of growth in revenue can be sustained or perhaps improved upon.

Table 5.2 Estimated international theme park admissions and spending, 1994

	Attendance (millions)	% Change 1993/4	Spend £m	% Change 1993/4
UK	12.6	+5	170	+20
Other Europe	46.5	+1	910	+8
USA	94.0	+2	1,795	+5
Japan	31	+7	860	+7
SE Asia	12	+20	107	+18
China	4	+25	9	+20
Australia	3.5	+17	36	+19
South America	3.0		9	
Total 1994	206.6	+6	3,896	+7
Total 1993	195	+10	3,628.5	+4
Total 1992	177		3,484	

Source: Theme Parks – UK & International Markets, 1995; Tourism Research & Marketing

Another difference between North American theme parks and those in Europe is the level at which admission prices are set. Research undertaken by the IAAPA shows that general admission prices in Europe in 1992 were the highest of all world regions, as shown in Table 5.3.

But higher admission prices have done little to dissuade the expansion of the theme park market in Europe. Attendance at European theme parks rose by 9 per cent in 1995. In the same year, by comparison, US theme park attendance grew by 7 per cent (Wall Street Journal Europe 1996).

There is clearly room for the amusement park industry to grow in Europe. In the USA, the 265 million annual visitors to the country's amusement parks nearly equals the total population, but in Europe, only one in three Europeans each year visits a theme park (Parker-Pope and Calian, 1996). As is the case for many types of tourist activity, the demand for theme park visits, paid for out of the discretionary income available to families, will depend partly on the general level of prosperity in Europe, which in turn is closely linked to the performance of the European economy as a whole.

Qualitative

Mainly domestic visitors

The market for theme parks in Europe is overwhelmingly a domestic one. Unlike some of the most well known of Europe's historical and cultural visitor attractions, European theme parks are tourism products where domestic visitors are generally much more in evidence than their international counterparts. The smaller theme parks in Europe attract a clientele mainly resident in the region where the park is situated. Larger parks may manage to have a national catchment area, particularly if they offer something unique, such as the high-technology, cinema-based attractions of France's Futuroscope.

However, the international attraction potential of European theme parks varies from attraction to attraction. A number of parks do generate substantial cross-border visits in their own right, particularly if they are situated close to frontiers. Disneyland Paris clearly leads in this respect. Just as in the US, where the Disney theme parks have been successful in attracting long-haul visitors, the company's European park draws over 60 per cent

Table 5.3 Global comparison of admission prices and attendance growth,[1] 1989–92

	Attendance growth (% per year)				Admission prices (US$, 1992 prices)	
	1989	*1990*	*1991*	*1992*	*Adult*	*Child*
Europe	2.0	2.0	2.0	–	12.99	10.23
Canada	} 1.0	–	–1.0	3.0	10.83	7.17
Pacific Rim		6.0	9.4	4.0	7.91	4.38
USA	8.0	–3.0	3.9	3.3	9.66	7.64
All regions (average)	–	1.0	6.8	1.5	10.04	7.60

Note: [1] Survey-based, therefore can only be regarded as a general guide to growth trends
Source: McEniff, J. (1993)

of its visitors from outside France. But the nearby Asterix Park, with only 15 per cent of its visitors coming from outside France, is a more typical European theme park in terms of its predominantly domestic market.

Many argue that the majority of small and medium-sized theme parks in Europe depend for their continuing success on the ability to develop a loyal core of customers who may sample other theme parks but who will ultimately continue to visit their favourite or 'local' attraction. This is particularly true of strong regional parks such as, in the UK, Chessington World of Adventures in the south-east (where 40 per cent of visitors return year on year) and Drayton Manor Park in the English Midlands (CWA 1997).

Mainly a day-trip market

By way of contrast with the USA, European theme parks have a market predominantly composed of day-trippers. As many Americans take only two weeks holiday a year, all-in-one holiday packages including hotel and theme park hold much appeal for them. Europeans, on the other hand, tend to spend the greater part of their more generous holiday entitlement at a single resort, or touring, keeping theme parks for additional day-trips taken throughout the year. (Once again, this observation must be qualified by mention of the Disney exception.)

A family market

Theme parks depend for their success on appealing to all members of the family. Although the 'white knuckle' rides which appeal to teenagers and young adults tend to dominate the headlines and are given the limelight in the parks' advertising campaigns (especially when they are new), most parks also offer a range of other attractions, from gentler 'pink knuckle' rides for young children, to more sedate attractions such as parks and gardens for visitors seeking a measure of relaxation.

In seeking to explain the growth of theme parks in Europe, some analysts have cited a tendency among baby-boom families to seek out family-orientated excursions: 'There is a generation of people who want to do things with their kids, and this is a way to do it', says Panmure Gordon analyst Lorna Tilbian in London (Wall Street Journal Europe 1996).

However, the theme parks as family entertainment idea can be over-played, especially in respect of families with young children. In fact, for many theme parks, the proportion of young visitors is much lower than might be expected. At Futuroscope, France's high-tech 'European Park of the Moving Image', for example, only just over one-third of visitors are children. Some themes hold considerable appeal for older children and adults. Indeed, some theme park attractions are closed to young children on safety grounds.

THEME PARK SUPPLY

Much of the increased demand for theme parks in Europe is supply-driven, as experienced at the macro level by the opening of new parks, and at the micro level by the strong promotion of the new state-of-the-art rides which are considered necessary to create repeat business.

New parks

Theme parks require very substantial capital investment, and the huge sums of money that have been spent on building new theme parks in recent years exclude all but the biggest players. Table 5.4 shows the start-up costs of a number of European theme parks constructed in the 1990s.

To take the UK as an example, theme park activity in the 1990s has been remarkable. Following the success of their park in Denmark, the Legoland Corporation opened their second theme park on the site of Windsor Safari Park, just west of London, in March 1996. The park, specifically aimed at younger children, does not feature a thrill ride – although as Richards (1996) points

Table 5.4 Start-up costs of major European theme parks (US$ millions)

Park	Location/opening	Cost US$
Disneyland Paris	France/1992	3,150.0
Walibi Flevo	Netherlands/1994	12.7
Port Aventura	Spain/1995	458.7
Warner Bros. Movie World	Germany/Spring 1996	243.8
Legoland Windsor	UK/Spring 1996	130.0
Sega World	UK/Summer 1996	68.8
Warner Bros. Movie World	UK/1999	344.0

Note: Park construction costs only; costs have been converted from the original currency at current exchange rates
Source: Wall Street Journal Europe (1996)

out, it is rumoured that a rollercoaster has been planned should visitor numbers decline after the novelty has worn off. The Sega World 'virtual' theme park opened in London's Trocadero Centre, and a number of other proposals were being put forward for new UK theme parks, whose construction could be under way before the end of the decade: the Warner Brothers Studio, the re-awakening of the Battersea Power Station, and a Tussauds/BBC project for a theme park at Greenwich were among the proposals being considered by the mid-1990s.

New rides

The cost of most new rides, in particular the 'white-knuckle' rides is often almost as breathtaking as a ride on the attraction itself. One single ride, The Galaxy, at the German theme park Phantasialand, cost £13 million in 1994 and the park's new ride for 1996, the Colorado Adventure, cost £11 million. At Parc Astérix near Paris, the 1995 'Menhir Express' attraction, an aquatic rollercoaster, cost FF45 million and took 80 tonnes of wood to build. The trees came from Albertville, cut down to make way for the ski-runs for the 1992 Winter Olympics held in that town (Le Figaro 1995).

Yet this level of investment is often being made simply to maintain existing volumes and revenues at theme parks the world over. Theme park operators understand that the existence of desirable fun rides is an important demand determinant when it comes to the market choosing between different theme parks. Theme parks opening a new ride, especially when it is more hair-raising than those of its competitors, know that this creates a wave of valuable publicity for the park and serves to differentiate it from other similar attractions.

THEME PARK OWNERSHIP

Although corporate ownership is relatively common in the UK, most theme parks in Continental Europe are privately owned (McEniff 1993). One advantage of corporate ownership is the possibility of creating a strong brand. Disney is the master in this respect, but in Europe, other theme park 'chains' have formed, which although

Table 5.5 Europe's three major theme park operators, 1995

	Euro Disney SCA	Tussauds Group	Walibi Group
Number of sites	1	8	10
Theme parks	1	3	7
Theme park attendance (mn)	10.7	7.2	3+
Total attendance (all attractions) (mn)	10.7	12[1]	47 BFR mn
Profit	114 FF mn (£15 mn approx.)	£18.3 mn	(£1 mn approx.)

Note: [1] Not including The London Planetarium which was closed for refurbishment until June 1995
Source: Jenner, P. and Smith, C. (1996)

small by comparison with the US corporation, may nevertheless signal the beginnings of a trend in theme park ownership.

The operating companies

Jenner and Smith (1996) describe the European theme park business as being dominated by three companies: the Tussauds Group, the Walibi Group, and Euro Disney SCA. This is a situation which dates back to the early 1990s only. In 1990, Disneyland Paris had yet to open and the Tussauds Group and Walibi Group were smaller and less international. The emergence of a 'big three' underlines the enormous investment muscle that is now necessary to compete in this sector. Table 5.5 shows the respective financial weights of these three operators:

The Tussauds Group

The Tussauds Group is a wholly owned subsidiary of the entertainment division of Pearson plc, the international media group. Attractions in the group brought in an all time record total of 12,334,000 visitors in 1996, compared to 11,964,000 in 1995, which was also a record year.

Although these global figures surpass Disneyland Paris' visitor numbers, only three of the Tussauds Group sites strictly count as theme parks: Alton Towers, Chessington World of Adventures (both UK) and Port Aventura, Spain,

with a combined attendance of 7,415,000 in 1996. (The company also operates Madame Tussaud's, The London Planetarium, Rock Circus, Warwick Castle and Madame Tussaud Scenerama in Amsterdam.)

Alton Towers

This theme park in Staffordshire, in the north west of England, has been a Tussauds Group attraction since 1990. Since 1992, Alton Towers has been the UK's number one paid-for attraction, narrowly beating its stablemate Madame Tussaud's in London. The park attracted 2,749,000 visitors in 1996, compared with just over 2.7 million in 1995. However, Alton Towers had 3 million visitors in 1994. Jenner and Smith (1996) note that the 1995 decline in the visitor numbers occurred despite a two-year investment programme which included the construction of two new thrill rides, Nemesis and the Energiser, and against a background rise of 2 per cent in visits to British attractions. In the attempt to boost its visitor numbers at least back to 1994 levels, Alton Towers responded with a £20 million investment for 1996, most of which was devoted to the construction of the Alton Towers Hotel, 'the UK's only themed hotel', which opened in the spring of that year.

The 175–room hotel, the first on the site, was built in response to the growing demand for two-day visits to the theme park: by 1996 representing 17 per cent of all visitors. Jenner and Smith reported the company's conviction that with this hotel, Alton Towers would position itself in the short breaks market, attracting a higher percentage of visitors from the wealthy south-east of England and from abroad (Jenner and Smith 1996). By 1997, the Tussauds Group was able to confirm that encouragingly high occupancy levels had contributed to a very successful year for the hotel. The Divisional Director of Marketing summed up the investment in the following upbeat statement:

> The hotel was a strategic investment reflecting Alton Towers' new focus on the increasingly important short breaks market and increasing our accessibility and attractiveness to our far markets (those over a two-hour drive time). The first season has been a phenomenal success with over 100,000 guests and an occupancy rate of around 85 per cent. In addition, our levels of re-booking for 1997 are already very high, which is proof that we were successful in bringing the magic of Alton Towers to this unique hotel. (CWA 1997)

In 1997, new developments at Alton Towers included a £2.5 million Ripsaw-themed ride and an indoor interactive attraction in association with the children's satellite television channel Nickelodeon.

Chessington World of Adventures

Chessington Zoo opened in 1931. Following the takeover of Madame Tussaud's by the zoo's owner, Pearson plc, the Tussauds Group was formed and the zoo was relaunched as Chessington World of Adventures in 1987, following a £18 million investment – a small sum by today's standards. Situated 12 miles south of London, it attracted 1.77 million visitors in 1995, a record year. In 1996, increased competition, notably from the new Legoland theme park near Windsor, led to the number of visitors falling slightly, to 1.7 million (although actual visitor spending rose). Nevertheless Chessington World of Adventures still maintained its position as the south of England's number one theme park for the fourth year in succession.

For the 1997 season, Chessington World of Adventures joined forces with the toy manufacturer Hasbro UK to create a new attraction, Action Man's Critical Mission, aimed at four to nine year-olds.

CASE STUDY: Port Aventura

Opened in 1995, Port Aventura is one of Spain's largest private sector investments since the 1992 Olympic Games, with the overall development cost estimated at £300 million.

The first major theme park on the Mediterranean, Port Aventura is located in the Solou-Vila-seca area of the Costa Dorada on the north-east coast of Spain, just over an hour's drive from Barcelona. The Costa Dorada is one of Europe's most popular holiday regions, which receives about a quarter of all visitors to Spain. It is two hours' drive from the equally popular Costa Brava. The Solou-Vila-seca area is served by three airports: Reus, 15 km from the park, handling mainly charter flights; Barcelona, one hour's drive away; and Girona, less than two hours' drive away. There is a regular train service to Barcelona, Valencia and Tarragona. The Port Aventura site covers 115 hectares, with 6,000 parking spaces.

The Costa Dorada has around 300 hotels and 175,000 apartments along its 200 km coastline. Its major attractions are its sunny climate, plentiful beaches, numerous golf courses and historic sites such as the monasteries of Poblet, Santes Creus as well as Vallbona de les Monges, the Roman city of Tarragona and the national parks of Deltebre, Sierra del Monsant and Mont Caro. There are a number of marinas at eleven ports along the coast.

Ownership

The driving force behind Port Aventura was the American multinational, Anheuser–Busch, which has a 19.99 per cent share in the park. Although best-known in Europe as the manufacturer of Budweiser beer, Busch Entertainment Corporation is one of the leading operators of theme parks in the United States, with nine major parks, attracting over 20 million visitors between them in 1995. The manager of the park is the Tussauds Group, which owns a 40.5 per cent share. The Spanish savings bank La Caixa has a 33.59 per cent share, and Fecsa, a Spanish utility, holds 5.92 per cent.

continued

Attractions

The theme of Port Aventura has been described as 'a voyage of discovery to exotic lands'. For Richards (1996), the park offers a kind of 'virtual tourism', with its five adventure travel areas: a typical Mediterranean port, a Polynesian village, a Chinese fishing port and Imperial Palace, the dense jungle of the lost Mayan Empire and the nineteenth century Wild West town of Penitence. Each area features rides, gifts, shows, plants and foods themed to its geography.

Rides

The park features 30 rides in total, including four large-scale 'white knuckle' rides. A park opening for the first time in 1995 would be expected to have the most advanced rides, and Port Aventura's Dragon Khan gained a place in the Guinness Book of Records for its eight loops on a 1,285 metre circuit which reaches a height of 45 metres and on which the cars run at speeds of up to 110 km/h.

Said to be the world's biggest looped rollercoaster, or, as the British press would inevitably have it: 'roller *costa*' (Daily Express 1995), the Dragon Khan was the star attraction during the park's first year of opening. Intriguingly, however, the rollercoaster has exposed a significant southern European cultural trend, identified by analysts studying visitor behaviour at Port Aventura. According to London-based *Tourism Research and Marketing*, observers say few Spanish men are riding the eight-loop Dragon Kahn rollercoaster. The men, the consulting firm reports, prefer 'to watch from the sidelines rather than risk exposing any symptoms of fright' (Wall Street Journal Europe 1996) Figure 5.3.

The presence of such high-profile rides as the Dragon Khan and the Tutuki Splash (where Polynesian boats are pulled up to the heart of a volcano and sent soaring down at over 55 km/h into the lake below) have been instumental in earning the park favourable reviews from consumer surveys and the press. For example, the Rollercoaster Club of Great Britain were 'impressed and particularly liked Port Aventura' (Richards 1996).

But a key element in Port Aventura's philosophy is the deliberate intermingling of children's and adults' rides, unlike many parks where the gentler rides are

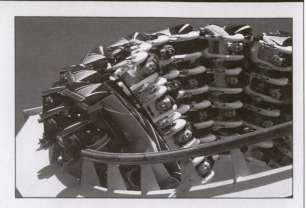

Figure 5.3 The Dragon Khan
Source: Port Aventura

reserved for a separate children's area. The idea is that families should be able to stay together when they play together.

Shows

Port Aventura also emphasises 'family entertainment', with many live shows. In the Far West, visitors can enjoy a Wild West Show, a Country Music Show or a Saloon Show. In China, they may visit the special effects magic theatre or the 1,200-seat theatre for a twenty-minute display of Chinese acrobatics. A fifteen-minute Mexican dance show is performed in La Cantina, allegedly the world's largest restaurant (Richards 1996).

In all, there are 70 choreographed street performances and live shows every day, all geographically themed, according to which of the five 'countries' they are staged in.

Catering

It has been recognised for some time that the fast-food fare offered at US theme parks also is not so popular in some European countries. In an interview given to Parker-Pope and Calian of the Wall Street Journal Europe (1996), Michael Jolly, chairman and chief executive of Pearson's Tussaud's Group, suggested the reason for this: 'One big difference is that the Spanish and the French like to interrupt their day for a more serious lunch. A large proportion of our catering is in sit-down, waitress-catering and fine-dining.'

Like everything else in Port Aventura, the food on

continued

offer follows the park's geographical themes, from Chinese Xim Pang in baskets to guacamole and nachos in the 1,000-seater Mexican Cantina. There are stalls with fresh fruit and iced water.

Most importantly, the management have aimed to keep the catering costs in their fifteen restaurants, fifteen cafeterias and fifteen food stalls within a relatively low price range, and have not found too much difficulty in pleasing all the varying European tastes. Richards (1996) notes that a reviewer on the 'Summer Holiday' TV programme in the UK was also impressed and drew attention to the favourable price comparisons with Disneyland Paris as a whole, especially in relation to the cost of on-site catering.

Shopping

The sales outlets in Port Aventura also closely follow the theming of the park and help to clearly differentiate the different 'lands'. As well as the usual range of inexpensive souvenirs, visitors can buy hand-crafted merchandise, such as Polynesian shawls, Chinese costumes, drums made by Cherokee and Pawnee Indian tribes and Mexican jewellery.

Clientele

Target market

Port Aventura's philosophy regarding its target market is different from most other European theme parks in that it expects to derive its audience more from tourists than residents of the catchment area. It is certainly situated in one of the continent's most visited regions. Jenner and Smith note that in its publicity, The Tussauds Group states that 'the region receives over 20 million visitors a year'. But they believe that this would be rather to overstate the 'region' that Port Aventura can call on:

> The immediate Tarragona area has approximately 1 million tourists, slightly weighed in favour of Spanish people. Barcelona receives about 2.5 million visitors, divided fairly equally between Spanish and foreigners. Adding in the Costa Brava and the Costa Azahar as far south as Valencia, a more realistic total seems to be closer to 7 million. Most of the publicity has been within

Spain, with the park relying heavily on tour operators to capture the foreign tourist. In the UK, for example, Port Aventura is featured in the brochures of Thomson, Airtours, First Choice, Cosmos and many others. (Jenner and Smith 1996)

In any case, there is little doubt that for the Costa Dorada, the theme park is a valuable and much-needed additional asset.

> Port Aventura has filled a yawning gap in the entertainment market for the nearby Spanish resorts. With little else but the beach, swimming pool and nightly drunken excursions to the barbecue in the hills, there was a vast market willing and able to spend money to be entertained. The most interesting aspect of this new development was that it tapped a new market for theme parks – the Spanish population – nobody had offered them this style of sophisticated entertainment before. (Richards 1996)

Performance

In its first year of operations, 1995, the park attracted 2.7 million visitors, against a target of 2.5 million. This generated an income of £62.6 million for the park.

Over 1 million of its visitors were Catalans, from the region in which Port Aventura is situated. In its second season, the visitor numbers rose to 3 million, of which the vast majority (89 per cent) had already made the decision to visit the park before travelling to the region.

In all, 80 per cent of visitors are Spanish, and these are followed by visitors from the UK and France. Significantly, the park's visitors include a considerable number of Russians: over 35,000 in 1996, making them the fourth largest nationality to visit the park. Such has been the success of the park with Russians that a guide to Port Aventura has been produced in their own language. Appropriately enough, the park's rollercoasters are said to be the main attraction for the Russian visitors. (The Russians are said to have created the first such rides, in the fifteenth century, using ice tracks, and the Spanish word for rollercoaster is still *montaña rusa*, Russian mountain.)

continued

Moreover, the Russians are among those who take the longest holidays in the region – on average, twelve days (Vanguardia 1996a).

Port Aventura's impact

Regarding the park itself, Port Aventura provides much-needed employment opportunities for the region. During the busiest months of the year, the park employs 2,800 people, the majority of whom are under 25. This number shrinks to 170, out-of-season during the winter (Vanguardia 1995).

But the park's economic impact on the surrounding region is even more considerable. In its first year of opening, Port Aventura was reported to have brought 20,000 million pesetas to the five local authorities immediately surrounding the park. Most of this sum came in the form of spending in the local hotels, restaurants, transport companies and shopping (Vanguardia 1996b). The same source noted that the opening of Port Aventura had also made possible the extending of the holiday season in that region, stretching it to begin in March and end in October. Finally, Port Aventura was found to be attracting a new profile of client, with more spending power and originating from parts of Spain which had hitherto prefered other destinations.

'Tourist authorities . . . consider that Port Aventura has brought about a unique opportunity for the surrounding area to modernise and to adapt what it has to offer to the demands of new markets. In particular, the sector which has most benefited from the impact of Port Aventura is the hotel business. The establishments of Salou, Cambrils and Vila-seca have registered extremely high occupancy rates during eight months of the year' (Vanguardia 1996b).

In 1996, the president of the local hoteliers' association confirmed that Port Aventura had generated new types of visitor to the area, namely school groups and weekend family visitors, which had filled hotels during the months leading up to the summer season. Between mid-June and mid-September 1996, hotel occupancy rates reached 95 per cent and stood at 80 per cent for the other months of the season (Vanguardia 1996a).

However, this degree of success must be seen in the context of changing trends regarding visits to the Costa Dorada by the Spanish. Whereas the region in the past was a traditional destination for Spanish holidaymakers, by the 1990s, their visits to the resorts of the Costa Dorada had been reduced to a period of somewhere between three and five days. The municipal councillor in charge of tourism for Salou was quoted as saying that two-week holidays taken by the Spanish in that destination were a thing of the past (Vanguardia 1996a).

The task therefore facing tourist authorities is to provide complementary attractions in order to persuade those visiting the Costa Dorada to go to Port Aventura, to prolong their stay in the area by an extra day. Visitors to the region will, in any case find no shortage of accommodation. In time for the 1997 season, the central zone of the Costa Dorada, which includes La Pineda, Salou and Cambrils saw the number of 4-star hotels increase by three. The majority of the 60 establishments in this zone are 3-star, and many of these had carried out extensive refurbishment the previous winter, basically redecoration and installing in air-conditioning, in order to adapt to the demands of the new higher-spending visitors who are coming to this region. Three hotels had invested sufficiently in renovations and new facilities to acquire 4-star status (Vanguardia 1997). Finally, in 1996, the Pearson group announced its own plans to build hotels at its Port Aventura park (Sunday Times 1996).

Perspectives

In March 1997, Port Aventura opened its gates for its third season, with the objective of consolidating the 3 million visitors it received in 1996. For this season, the park had invested more than 1,500 million pesetas, 1,200 million of which had gone towards the construction of the new rides. The park was expecting a significant increase in the number of visitors it receives from the UK, Russia and the south of France, following extensive advertising campaigns in those countries (Pais Cataluña 1997).

Among the thrills awaiting visitors was a new 'white knuckle ride', Stampida, the world's first twin-track 'racing' wooden rollercoaster. Costing £7.5 million to build, the ride uses a record-breaking 7,700 feet of track. Trains on parallel tracks compete to get to the

continued

end first, reaching vertical 'g' forces equal to those experienced by space shuttle astronauts and hurtling down drops of up to 80 feet at a maximum 50 miles an hour. The outcome of the race was said, by Port Aventura's own publicity, to be 'just one of the surprises in store for riders, who will also be treated to a top secret, unexpected encounter of the thrilling kind along the way'.

Following its policy of combining 'white knuckle' with 'pink knuckle rides', Port Aventura added a 'junior track', the Tomahawk, to the Stampida ride. Joining the race towards its end, this third mini-track gives younger visitors the opportunity to savour the excitement and compete against the more grown-up members of their families riding Stampida.

For the park's third season, one of the main objectives was to raise the proportion of foreign visitors from 18 per cent to 25 per cent of the total number of visitors (Vanguardia 1997).

Contrasts with Disneyland Paris

By 1996, Port Aventura was calling itself the second theme park in Europe, in terms of the number of visitors.

Port Aventura is distinct from Disneyland Paris in many significant ways, the climate of the location being the most obvious: the Costa Dorada has only four days' rain every season, as compared with the much more changeable weather of Marne-la-Vallée.

But the differences go much further than that. From the beginning, Port Aventura targeted much lower visitor volumes than Disney, aiming for 2.5 million visitors in its first year. Also, unlike Disneyland Paris, the Spanish park will not remain open all year round. It receives visitors between March and October, and stays open until midnight or later between mid-June and mid-September, to take advantage of the local climate. The unlimited leisure time of nearby holidaymakers, combined with the Spanish habit of staying up late, keep the park bustling at night.

The scale of investment of the two parks is another marked contrast between them. Disneyland Paris is a £2.2 billion resort. Port Aventura is a £300 million park. Correspondingly, the break-even points of both parks are far apart. At the opening of the Spanish park, its managing director described the situation as follows: 'They need 10 million visitors a year; we can make a profit with 2.65 million' (Mail on Sunday 1995).

Entrance fees for Port Aventura are lower than those for the Parisian park: £21 for adults and £16.40 for children (1997 prices). Night tickets, for holidaymakers who want to visit the park after a day on the beach, and two/three-day tickets are also available.

But one of the most marked contrasts for visitors to both parks may be the attitude of the staff. A journalist trying out Port Aventura for the Daily Express found the young staff extremely cheerful, and quoted the park's general manager's explanation for this: 'You don't have to tell the Spanish to smile' (Daily Express 1995). There is some temptation to make an easy comparison between this attitude and that which was reported to characterise park employees in Marne-la-Vallée in Disneyland Paris's early days: 'Day after day, the Disney University labours to turn out smiling employees from the glum-looking ranks of French job applicants' (Sunday Times 1993). But Port Aventura has not been entirely beyond reproach in respect of its staff's customer relations skills. The same Daily Express reporter, for example, found that the park needed more English-speaking staff, to prevent the kind of misunderstanding and frustration he experienced during his visit.

Conclusion

After a promising start, can Port Aventura go on to make a success out of offering theme park entertainment to visitors to the Costa Dorada? Traditionally, wisdom has had it that theme parks can only prosper in the wealthier northern countries of Europe, where the density of the resident population guarantees a ready market for this type of day-visitor attraction. This wisdom seemed confirmed when, at the end of the 1990s, the Zygofolis theme park near Nice closed down with losses of FF300 million after only two unhappy years of operations. Can a theme park prosper in the Mediterranean area relying mainly on holidaymakers as its market? The theme park industry is watching Port Aventura with interest.

THE WALIBI GROUP

Expansion

The Walibi Group was founded in 1975 by Eddie Meeus, when he created his first theme park at Wavre, close to the Brussels-Namur motorway. Since then, Walibi has grown to become a household name in Belgium (where 25 per cent of the population visit a theme park each year) as well as the third largest European operator in the theme park market. A second park between Lyons and Chambery in France was established in 1982, when Walibi took over Avenir Land, which had opened in 1979. In 1989, the park was renamed Walibi Rhone-Alpes and a Radja River ride was installed.

Back at Wavre, the company built a completely new Aquatic Park called Aqualibi, which could be visited on a joint ticket with Walibi or on its own. Further expansion by acquisition came in 1991 with the takeover of Bellewaerde, a park founded by the Florizoone brothers at Ypres, Belgium in 1954, and of Le Nouveau Monde des Schtroumpfs (the New World of the Smurfs), which had opened in 1989 near Lorraine, France, and had run into trouble and gone bankrupt. The park was renamed Walibi Schtroumpf.

In 1992, Walibi opened Walibi Aquitaine and acquired Oceade, Brussels. In 1994, the group opened Walibi Flevo in the Netherlands, the star of which is El Condor, a ride which drops passengers head downwards into 'nothingness' (Jenner and Smith 1996).

By 1997, the Walibi group owned six theme parks, two tropical swimming pools and one miniature park, in Belgium, France and the Netherlands. Such rapid expansion had not come cheaply, and in particular the Walibi Aquitaine, Walibi Schtroumpf and Walibi Flevo parks had required substantial financing (1.6 billion BEF) over five years in order to bring their infrastructure and attractions up to the level of the other parks in the group (Walibi 1997).

Performance

As the group has expanded, visitor numbers have grown, as shown in Figure 5.4a and 5.4b.

In 1996, attendance at all of the group's parks was down by 8 per cent compared with 1995, although the improvement in average receipts per visitor of 3 per cent nevertheless managed to limit the fall in turnover to 5 per cent. The fall in visitor numbers was blamed by the group's management on the general economic gloom which had settled over Belgium and its neighbours during the year, and on the growing number of new parks opening up.

One distinguishing characteristic of most parks in the Walibi group is that their geographical positions near frontiers enables them to attract both domestic visitors and visitors from bordering countries, as highlighted by Figure 5.4 (b). Clearly, the percentage of visitors from neighbouring countries varies from park to park, but in the Bellewaerde park, for example, half the visitors are French (Walibi 1997).

Receipts at each of Walibi's parks originate from three sources: the sales of entry tickets (68 per

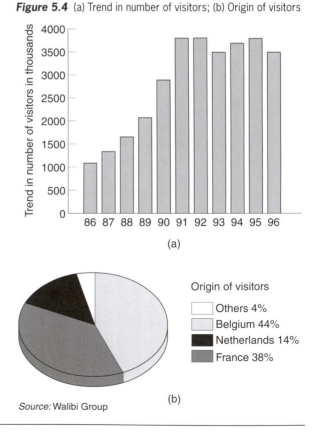

Figure 5.4 (a) Trend in number of visitors; (b) Origin of visitors

(a)

Origin of visitors

☐ Others 4%
☐ Belgium 44%
■ Netherlands 14%
▨ France 38%

Source: Walibi Group

(b)

cent of turnover), catering (26 per cent) and the sales of souvenirs and receipts from amusement arcade type games (6 per cent). In recent years, in the attempt to improve profitability, the Walibi group has taken back into its own operations many of the activities, such as points of sale, which it had previously outsourced to operators external to the group. (This also has the advantage of giving the group better control over the service provided.)

Measures such as this, combined with a new pricing policy, and a more active marketing approach based mainly on joint promotional campaigns with a number of carefully chosen partners, gave the Walibi group grounds for believing that they could look forward to more prosperous years leading up to the new century.

EURO DISNEY SCA

Euro Disney SCA is the operating company of the Disneyland Paris Theme Park and Resort. At the end of September 1995, it was 39 per cent owned by EDL Holding Company, a wholly owned subsidiary of The Walt Disney Company, and 24 per cent owned by Prince Alwaleed of Saudi Arabia.

Operating at a single location 30 km to the east of Paris, Euro Disney SCA is the top theme park operator in Europe. On a single site of 56 ha (and a further 1,300 ha undeveloped) Disneyland Paris attracted almost as many visitors in 1996 as did the Tussauds Group from its three theme parks and five other sites.

Before examining the characteristics of Disneyland Paris itself and its performance over its first few years of operations, it is worth asking the question: why Europe and why Paris?

In its early Annual Reports, the company gave its reasons for choosing to locate in Europe and in Paris. The choice of Europe was to give the company access to a market of 350 million potential customers, almost one and a half times the size of the population of the United States. It was believed that a European park would enable Disney to take advantage of the growth of European short-break holidays, together with the growth in numbers and in sophistication of tourists in Europe, two marked trends of the 1980s and 1990s. The other factor encouraging Disney was the apparent popularity of its existing products on the European market. The products division of Disney Company was receiving 50 per cent of its worldwide revenues from Europe. Fifty-five million copies of the *Mickey* magazine are published every year in Europe (including, now, a Russian version), as compared to only 30 million in the US (D'Hauteserre 1997).

The two other main contending countries besides France were Spain (for its sunshine) and the UK. The UK's geographic detachment from the continent of Europe put it at a clear disadvantage, even with the opening of the Channel Tunnel in perspective. But how was the Disney Company persuaded to choose a location in the cooler north of Europe, with its unpredictable climate, as opposed to the sunny Penedes hills near Barcelona?

The Marne-la-Vallée site is located in one of the three major poles of population concentration in Western Europe, the other two being London and the Rhine Valley, and it is the most accessible from the other two. Spain and the UK would have been more peripheral locations. The Paris basin is at the juncture of Northern and Southern Europe, and is a thoroughfare between the two halves of the continent. The Disney Company also recognised that, as one of Europe's most attractive cities, Paris had been successful in attracting visitors in excess of 20 million a year.

D'Hauteserre explains why the Marne-la-Vallée site, in particular, was eminently suitable to the Disney Company's requirements:

> [The Disney Company] also realised that its projects needed a minimum critical mass to allow them to function as resorts. They were thus looking for a site whose size would allow them to plan the final project right from the beginning, a site that would guarantee the land area needed, not only for its theme parks (a total of three are planned into 2017) but also for the hotels, restaurants, residences, offices that would be built because of the demands generated by the parks . . . Spain had offered the Walt Disney Company a better deal than France, but was not able to put together a large enough parcel of land.
> (d'Hauteserre 1997)

Thus, Disneyland Paris was not only to be a theme park but a large urban development, supported by major developments in the transport network financed by the French government.

pened in 1992, as Euro-Disney, the entire ppment comprised six hotels, a ranch, a golf course, the Festival Disney entertainment centre, as well as the theme park itself. The theme park, like many others, is divided into 'lands': Main Street USA, described as 'small town America at the turn of the century'; Frontierland, 'a Far West boom town during the gold rush era'; Adventureland, 'the crossroads for all adventurers'; Fantasyland, 'the land of fairy tales and make-believe'; and Discoveryland, 'the land of the future'. But, in almost every other aspect of its operations and performance, the Disney park is very different to all of Europe's other theme parks.

What makes Disney different?

Visitor numbers

Emphasis on Disneyland Paris' well-publicised initial problems has tended to obscure the remarkable scale of its achievement. Virtually overnight, it has come to rank with the major tourism sites of Europe, as shown in Table 5.6.

Disneyland Paris beats all other paid entry attractions in terms of volume of visitors, and, even as Europe's most expensive theme park to visit, it stands alongside the continent's classic free attractions. Even in a country as rich in historic and cultural attractions as France, Disneyland Paris has come out on top, attracting 11.7 million visitors in 1996, more than the Eiffel Tower, the Louvre and the Château of Versailles put together (Echo Touristique 1997).

Disneyland Paris also attracts three times more visitors than the next three most successful European theme parks put together.

Scale of investment

Regarding the investment required to create Disneyland Paris, nothing on the same scale has been seen before or since, in European theme park development. As shown in Table 5.4 (see page 153), Disneyland Paris cost approximately ten times the amount required to build an 'average' European theme park.

But in the attempt to understand why Disneyland Paris attracts such vast numbers of visitors, it is all too easy to cite the scale of its development and overlook the other important factors.

Total management

Disneyland Paris is involved in just about every aspect of attracting visitors. For example, it developed its own hotels along with the theme park. But the scale of the vision regarding hotels is completely different to those of Europa Park, De Efteling and Alton Towers, with only one each, compared to Disneyland Paris's seven fully themed hotels.

Unlike all other European theme parks, Disneyland Paris can genuinely claim to be a complete holiday resort destination, and is sold through the travel trade as such. A potential customer can walk into almost any travel agent in Europe and buy an off-the-shelf package that includes transport, hotels, meals and entrance tickets to Disneyland Paris. It even has its own in-house tour operator, Disney Vacances. Parks such as Efteling and Alton Towers have finally caught on to all-inclusive holidays, but are well behind Disney. In fact, according to Euro Disney SCA, 60 per cent of its foreign visitors come to France exclusively to visit Disneyland Paris.

Partnership

Another element that differentiates Disney is its involvement of other companies as 'participants', for example, American Express, BNP, Coca-Cola, Esso, France Telecom, Hertz, IBM, Kodak, Mattel, Nestlé, Philips and Renault. All of these play a part in raising the profile of the park and may be involved in sponsoring specific attractions within the park, a marketing technique now emulated by Futuroscope, Efteling, Legoland and, as mentioned above, the Walibi group.

Regarding the distribution of Disneyland Paris-based packages, all of the major leisure distribution networks in France have entered into partnership with Disney Vacances, the tour operating arm of Disneyland Paris. French travel agents now make as much commission from selling trips to Disneyland Paris as they do from car hire or winter sports: 25 million FF in 1996. Of French visitors to the park, 20 per cent book through the travel trade, which sells altogether 30 per cent of the nights spent in the park's hotels.

Table 5.6 Selected major European attractions, 1995

Attraction	Visitors (000)	Free[1] paid[2]
Disneyland Paris, France	10,700	195 FF adults
		150 FF children (low season 150/120 FF)
Notre-Dame de Paris, France	10,000	Free
Blackpool Pleasure Beach, England	7,300	Free
Mont-St-Michel, Brittany, France	7,000	Free
British Museum, London, England	5,746	Free
Tivoli, Copenhagen, Denmark	3,800[3]	Paid
Cologne Cathedral, Germany	3,500	Free except DM4 for guided tours
Alton Towers, Staffordshire, England	2,707	£17.50 adults; £13.50 children
Port Aventura, Costa Dorado, Spain	2,700	Ptas3,900 adults; Ptas3,000 children
Tower of London, England	2,537	Paid
LEGOLAND, Billund, Denmark	1,300	Paid
Neuschwanstein, Bavaria, Germany	1,267	DM10 adults; DM7 children
Meli Park, Adinkerke-De Panne, Belgium	710	595 BFR adults; 595 BFR children
Cirque of Gavarnie, Hautes Pyrenees, France	600	Free

Note:
[1] Admission is generally free but some visitors may pay for guided tours, for access to restricted areas, may make a voluntary donation and may make expenditure on related services and goods
[2] Admission prices, where quoted, are for 1996
[3] 1994
Source: Jenner, P. and Smith, C. (1996)

Most French travel agents were registering impressive growth in their sales of the Disneyland Paris product in the mid- to late-1990s. For example, the Afat chain's sales increased by 65 per cent in 1995, 54 per cent in 1996, and 50 per cent in the 1996–97 winter season. Similarly, Selectour saw their sales of Disneyland Paris packages rise by 64 per cent in 1994–95, 40 per cent in 1995–96 and 45 per cent during the first four months of 1996–97. During the same period, Selectour's sales of holiday packages in general rose by 5–6 per cent a year, on average (Echo Touristique 1997).

Nevertheless, Disney Vacances has kept the lion's share of bookings for itself, well ahead of all its partners. Particularly since 1995, when the Disney tour operator began selling fully inclusive packages including transport, tour operators such as Visit France, which had previously held exclusivity in selling air travel-based packages, saw their sales fall dramatically (Echo Touristique 1997).

Entertainment

A third element of the Disney package is the emphasis on theatrical-type entertainments: free shows in restaurants, squares and auditoria. In three years, for example, 2 million spectators have been to Buffalo Bill's Wild West Show, an evening dinner entertainment at Festival Disney. Some other European theme parks have become almost as inventive as Disney in this respect. (For 1996, Parc Astérix staged what it claims to be the largest live-action show at any European theme park, inside a 2,000–seat theatre with a 50-metre stage. The twenty-minute 'stunt' show was entitled 'Main Basse sur la Joconde' (The Great Mona Lisa Caper). Phantasialand and Walibi Rhone-Alpes also offer live theatrical entertainment on a large scale.

The problems

Despite all of the above assets, however, Disneyland Paris has been described as 'a FF36 billion experiment that went almost terminally wrong' (Sunday Times 1995). The problems began even before the parks opened the gates to the Magic Kingdom.

Public image

During the construction phase, a negative image of Disneyland Paris was diffused by the press, 'based on its American cultural attributes, its business of selling false reality for pleasure and its bullyish negotiating tactics with the French government and later with private companies and labour' (D'Hauteserre 1997). Some of the French criticism was particularly sharp, describing Euro Disney as a 'cultural Chernobyl' (McEniff 1993).

Imported US working practices contributed negatively to the company's image, as presented to the public by the French press. The left-wing French newspaper *Liberation* stingingly described the park as 'Mousewitz', in reponse to stories of Disney's alleged 'brainwashing' of staff and its insistence on their conforming to its rigorous standards of appearance and behaviour (Sunday Times 1993). France, it appeared, was not ready for the America corporation's ferocious work ethic and near manic attachment to in-house values.

Miscalculations

The financial problems of Disneyland Paris have been well publicised. When the park opened, it was already saddled with construction-cost overruns and a mountain of debt.

This problem was exacerbated when the park attracted neither the numbers nor the spending which had been forecast. Many are of the opinion that the admission fees were pitched unrealistically high, at FF 225 for adults and FF 150 for children under 11 years old. The characteristic Parisian climate also played a part. Disney is thought to have miscalculated the deterrent effect of the weather, which, in the depths of winter, can make Marne-la-Vallée a truly bleak place to spend the day. Off-season attendances were consequently well below expectations.

Spending on Disney merchandise in the park was also well below expectations. Such spending accounts for about a third of income for Disneyland in the USA, whereas for European theme parks, for example, the average is not much over 10 per cent (Jenner and Smith 1996). Part of the problem is that European customers have not been able to take some of the products seriously. Disney cuddly toys are well understood by Europeans, but not expensive clothes bearing the Disney name.

But, perhaps the greatest disappointment for Disney was the way in which Europeans' use of the hotels was so far below that of Americans in the Orlando parks. The occupancy rate of Disneyland Paris' hotels (5,200 rooms) remained far below Orlando's rate of 79 per cent, even if it did increase from 55 per cent in 1992 and 1993 to 61 per cent in 1994 and 68.5 per cent in 1995 (D'Hauteserre 1997). As has already been stated, Europeans do not base their longer holidays on a visit to a theme park as Americans tend to do, and the perception of Disneyland Paris as a resort destination has been slow to establish itself in European thinking. Moreover, many found the Disney hotels in Marne-la-Vallée to be overpriced by European standards (particularly in the country which invented the hotel room at FF 100 per night). As a result, a substantial proportion of Disneyland Paris' visitors chose to lodge in family-run 2-star hotels in the centre of Paris and travel out to the park each day.

To make matters worse, after barely reaching, in its first year of opening, the 11 million visitors it needed annually in order to break even, Disneyland Paris's visitor numbers followed a downward trend, dropping to just over 5.5 million visitors in 1994. (In 1995, however, the park registered a 21.5 per cent increase in visitor numbers.)

But many of Disney's problems stemmed, not from its own miscalculations but from a generally unfavourable economic environment, far beyond its control. The recession of the early 1990s killed its short-term property development ambitions; and currency turmoil, which resulted in the French franc being very strong against other currencies, made the park far more expensive for British and southern European visitors.

The solutions

The cuts

In the winter of 1993, Euro Disney and its 60 banks began rescue talks that culminated in a £725 million rights issue in June 1994, and brought on to the share register Prince Al-Waleed of Saudi Arabia. In March 1994, a restructuring agreement, designed to enable Disneyland Paris to generate profits, was reached between all parties.

The financial restructuring was accompanied by a frantic overhaul of operations. Every facet was scrutinised and revised as part of the project codenamed Challenge 1994. The park's name was changed to Disneyland Paris for marketing reasons, including closer identification with the destination, Paris, although the debt-burdened operating company stayed as Euro Disney.

The marketing was redrawn and repitched, the workforce was trimmed by 5,000 to 12,000, and entry prices were cut.

The FF 225 entrance fee was set at FF 195 for the high-season, and a low-season price of FF 150 was introduced. A lower-priced admission for those arriving after 5pm, was also made available, aimed at encouraging more Parisians to visit or return to the park. Despite the price cut, Disneyland Paris in the high season remains the most expensive attraction of its kind in Europe. Most commentators agree that Disneyland Paris stands alone in being able to demand entrance fees at this level – and equally clear that it cannot charge more. For most other theme parks, the ceiling seems to be around £20, although, as was seen in the example of Port Aventura, some are creeping above this threshold.

The rates at the resort's hotels were also reduced, with cheaper room rates in the off season.

New attraction

The turnaround in the fortunes of Disneyland Paris certainly had something to do with Space Mountain, which was opened in 1995. The 'white knuckle ride' cost FF 600 million to build, the price of a single Ariane launcher. Despite being far from Europe's most knuckle-whitening experience, the ride was a useful hook on which to hang Disneyland Paris' new marketing approach and its reputation spread fast. It is now the park's most popular ride.

The compromises

Finally, the management of Disneyland Paris was obliged to compromise on a number of points, if only to make a gesture towards acknowledging that corporate America could not dictate in Europe as it has grown accustomed to in the US.

Wine is now served in selected restaurants, breaching a 40-year tradition of prohibition in the Disney parks, but also ending the agonies of French men and women confronted with the prospect of washing down their *croustade aux fruits de mer* with tumblers of Diet Coke. The park also now (reluctantly) allows women 'cast members' to wear non-approved shades of lipstick, nail varnish and hosiery.

The results

It would be far from the truth to describe the Disneyland Paris venture as a failure. It is certainly the case that with less financial muscle behind it and with lesser reputations riding on it, the park might otherwise have been left to collapse in the wake of other spectacular French theme park disasters, such as Myrapolis and Zygofolis. In reality, the overall Disneyland Paris achievement has been an impressive one.

Following the above changes, attendance figures bounced back from 8.8 million in 1994 to 10.7 million in 1995. Although theme park spending per visitor declined by approximately 10 per cent that year, total theme park revenue went up by 8 per cent to FF 2,468 million as compared with takings in the 1994 financial year.

Some 11.7 million people visited the park in its fiscal year ending 30 September 1996, up by 9 per cent on the previous year, making it the most popular tourist attraction in France. Net profits rose by 77 per cent to FF 202 million from FF 114 million a year earlier. Disneyland Paris' seven hotels also achieved a record operating performance in 1996, with an average occupancy of 72 per cent and turnover exceeding FF 2 billion.

The parks hotels were increasingly attracting conferences and business meetings, which accounted for revenues of 160 million FF and 100,000 bed nights in 1996. This sector was expected to grow further in 1997 as a result of Disneyland Paris' new conference centre opening that year in the Newport Bay Hotel (TIM 1997).

With happier days having finally arrived, Euro Disney SCA by 1997 was once again able to contemplate an investment programme for the park. A multiscreen Beaumont cinema, a Planet Hollywood restaurant and a second convention centre were planned as additions to the existing attractions and facilities in Marne-la-Vallée.

The operators were even daring to talk again about Phase 2 of the development. The Magic Kingdom was to have been the springboard for a second theme park to open in 1996, which would have added a further 8 million visitors, taking the projected 1996 total to 21 million visitors. But the pace of subsequent development had been slowed dramatically, following the park's initial poor performance. But by 1997, plans for a vast new park next door with a cinema theme, similar to Hollywood's Universal Studios were back on the drawing board.

The impact of Disneyland Paris on other European theme parks

Before the gates of the Magic Kingdom were thrown open in the heart of Europe, there was widespread optimism in the European attractions sector that Disney's presence there would enhance theme parks' image, help improve standards of presentation and raise consumer expectations and their willingness to pay.

Writing during the year of the park's opening, Varney suggested three positive effects of Disneyland Paris:

1 *Quality standards*: Disney's high standards will impress a growing market for leisure activities and encourage both greater penetration of the theme park market and frequency of visits; this will benefit venues matching these standards and lead to a shake-out of poorer quality attractions.

2 *Market growth*: theme park and other attrac-tions, particularly in the vicinity of Disneyland Paris, will benefit both from the specific effect of greater awareness of theme parks as a leisure attraction and from the centring of a large holiday market around the Disney park.

3 *Pricing*: the Disneyland Paris entry price is almost twice that of Alton Towers and as the clear market leader, Euro Disney will establish terms of reference for what constitutes value for money in tourist attractions. Those operators who meet the quality standards should find it easier to institute price increases, which they need to reinvest in their product (Varney 1992).

Nevertheless, the same author stressed that the impact of Disneyland Paris was not likely to be wholly beneficial:

> The threat from Euro Disney, on the other hand, is as relevant to other parts of the tourism industry as it is to theme parks, in that short-break destinations will suffer from an influx of visitors to Euro Disney. The greatest threat is the as-yet unquantifiable impact of Euro Disney's planned expansions. Data from the USA indicate that the cumulative impact of adding EPCOT and then MGM Studios to the Magic Kingdom in Florida has been to negate many of the second- and third-day visits to other attractions, as Disney increasingly offers sufficient activities for an entire holiday (Varney 1992).

To what extent have Varney's predictions been bourne out by events?

McEniff (1993) indicated that the initial impact of Disneyland Paris did not adversely affect the industry. Reflecting the positive impacts mentioned above, major parks suffered little immediately following Euro Disney's opening, despite the recession in Europe at that time.

As might be expected, Parc Astérix, located closest to Disneyland Paris, was one of the few parks which had a substantial fall in attendances. But, there, the drop in visitors was short-lived, as attendances rose again in 1993. Astérix's recovery was such that in 1995, the park received 1.8 million visitors, as compared with the 1.35 million it had in 1989, the year of opening. It may owe much of this continuing success to Disneyland Paris. D'Hauteserre (1997) cites Saffarian, who reports that under the influence of Disneyland

Paris, Asterix Park began a five-year refurbishment programme in 1992, and points out that the park had also been forced to define its product more clearly. Later, Parc Astérix's management was to frankly acknowledge the extent to which the Disney impact on other European theme parks had been positive: '[Disneyland Paris] created the demand and we benefit from it' (Le Figaro 1995).

Moreover, it appears that it is not only the major theme parks in Europe which have been galvanised into improving their product in response to the extra competition. The Wall Street Journal (1996) observe that 'the surge in US-style theme parks (in Europe) has forced some of the smaller existing parks to invest in new attractions. The UK's Drayton Manor last year spent £750,000 on a new Wild West roller coaster ride, and Lightwater Valley spent £1 million on the Falls of Terror, a kind of aquatic roller coaster.'

Indeed, Varney's prediction that other European theme parks would benefit from the increased awareness of this form of attraction after the opening of the Disney park appears to have been bourne out. In the year Disneyland Paris opened, Alton Towers actually experienced a substantial increase in attendances, topping the UK's list of most-popular admission-charging attractions for the first time ever.

McEniff (1993) quotes from two surveys of that time, carried out by the EIU and *Park World* magazine, showing that over Europe as a whole, the opening of Euro Disney did not have a damaging impact. Combining the two surveys, attendances data for 1991 and 1992 show that out of a total of 36 theme parks in the main countries affected by the Disney park – Belgium, France, Germany, the Netherlands, and the UK, decreases were recorded in only ten parks, with substantial falls in only five cases – Parc Astérix, Efteling, Chessington World of Adventures, Phantasialand and Walibi Wavre.

France's theme parks may, in fact, have benefited more than any others country's from the Disney affect. For example, in the mid-1990s, French tour operators, having established a substantial customer base composed of those interested in theme park-based short breaks through their experience of offering the Disney product, broadened their range of such products to include

packages at other French parks, such as the Walibi parks, Futuroscope and Park Asterix. The tour operator Episodes (see page 219) has gone as far as to publish a special theme park brochure, containing packages based on eleven parks in France and Belgium (Echo Touristique 1997). This includes joint visits to Disneyland Paris and Asterix Park.

Trends in European theme parks

In general, there is a great deal of optimism in Europe over the future prospects of the theme park sector. The arrival of Disney in Europe has been seen by many as a sign of the maturity of the European theme parks market. With Port Aventura open and a number of other large parks planned, the theme park is alive and well in Europe.

In this section a number of specific key issues likely to shape the development of the European theme park industry in the future are examined.

CONTINUING INVESTMENT

Theme parks must reflect the constant evolution taking place within a sector susceptible to rapid changes in both technology and consumer tastes.

While the ageing of the European population has seen some emphasis shift from 'white knuckle rides' towards more family orientated entertainment, most parks recognise the need to continue to provide bigger and more exciting rides and market them strongly, on a continuing basis. Constant replacing of rides and other attractions with more recent and more thrilling replacements remains the primary, and increasingly costly, method of keeping the appeal of theme parks fresh (McEniff 1993).

This means that the best parks are undergoing a process of continual evolution in order to meet the demands of their target markets. This necessitates an on-going commitment to investment in the park (in new rides and attractions and also in improving the quality of basic levels of service such as food, toilets, etc.) and a clearly differentiated marketing campaign to ensure that existing and potential visitors are regularly reminded about what is on offer. An on-going question is whether the high returns demanded from the investment in new parks and rides are achievable. A 'rides war' – the highest, fastest, longest, etc., is not in the industry's long-term interest as it serves merely to encourage short-term shifts in admission numbers rather than market growth (CWA 1997).

Richards (1996) predicts that although Eastern Europe is still without a major theme park, this may be set to change, as the second-hand rides from the more popular West European parks are passed on.

EXTENDING THE LENGTH OF VISITS

With the aim of benefiting from the trend towards more short-break holidays, Europe's major theme parks are increasingly positioning themselves as overnight destinations or fully-fledged resorts. The strategy adopted by many parks has been twofold: provide more attractions in order to give visitors a reason for prolonging their stay; and, despite the mixed performance of the Disneyland Paris hotels, provide accommodation on or nearby the park.

An example is that of De Efteling in the Netherlands, which, in the 1990s, added an eighteen-hole golf course and its own hotel, while announcing future plans for a self-catering complex. At the same time, while some theme parks have added accommodation, others have entered into arrangements with hotel groups. For example, the UK Legoland links up with nearby Marriott hotels.

The UK holiday and short-break market, with its traditional of extensive travel overseas is heavily targeted by continental theme parks eager to attract staying visitors. Consequently, a number of theme parks (Futuroscope, Disneyland Paris, Parc Astérix, Legoland (Denmark), Phantasialand, and Europa Park) are being promoted by UK tour operators.

EXTENDING THE SEASON

An interesting development to follow into the twenty-first century is that involving theme parks' efforts to extend the season. With the exception of Disneyland Paris, all European theme parks close during part of the year, meaning that a valuable resource goes completely unused during several months.

The increasing popularity of indoor attractions has widened the possibilities for extending the season (as well as for extending opening hours during the main season). This development is both demand- and supply-driven. A theme park such as Futuroscope, the European Park of the Moving Image, where most of the attractions are cinemas can remain open during a relatively long season, as it operates more independently of climatic conditions.

Fortunately for theme park operators, their moves to stretch the season for this type of attraction has coincided with increased demand in Europe for off-peak short breaks (see Chapter 7). Some parks have tested the market with Christmas and New Year opening periods (CEC 1996).

Many theme park operators are also turning to the corporate sector to boost demand during off-peak periods by offering corporate hospitality packages and special events for companies. These include family fun days, tickets for incentivising staff and venue hire for product launches and other events. Specific special events (for the general public) are another successful product extension and growth area for some parks. Alton Towers has had particular success with both classical and pop concerts (CWA 1997).

INCREASING SECONDARY SPEND

Investing in new rides and attractions, as well as accommodation, encourages visitors to increase their length of stay in theme parks and consequently presents an opportunity for increasing their secondary spend, on food and merchandising. The authors of a 1997 report published by Chessington World of Adventures stated that:

> The most successful parks will be those that achieve incremental income by delivering higher per capita secondary spend. This is particularly important when parks are busy, as secondary spending can not only distract the visitor from queues but also relieves the pressure to fill the park beyond comfortable levels in order to boost revenue. (CWA 1997)

Emerging merchandise trends indicate a strong move towards offering products linked to visitors' experiences. For example, visitors who enjoy Chessington World of Adventures' new attraction for 1997, Action Man's Critical Mission, had the opportunity to buy Action Man merchandise from a unique Action Man shop in the park. Legoland Windsor also relies heavily on sales from its outlets stocking Lego.

It is generally recognised, however, that parks must, however, be sensitive to over-commercialising or exploiting their customer base.

SPONSORSHIP

A notable trend identified by several commentators is the move towards sponsorship of rides and attractions. This delivers strong benefits to both the theme park operators and the linked brands. The theme parks achieve incremental revenue while the brands are offered a unique opportunity to be presented outside their usual marketing environment.

Returning to the example of Action Man mentioned above, the Marketing Director of Hasbro UK justifies his involvement in the theme park partnership thus:

> Licensing and sponsorship play a critical role in building long-term brand equities as it allows consumers to 'live' the experience. The Action Man Critical Mission attraction at Chessington World of Adventures does exactly that – by giving children and adults alike the opportunity and pleasure of experiencing action and adventure and 'live' the 'World of Action Man', as Action Man. (CWA 1997)

MIXED DEVELOPMENTS

There appears to be general agreement that the combination: theme park + retail development is a promising one which may attract growing investment in the future. Shopping malls with theme park-type attractions have already succeeded, for example in the West Edmonton Mall in Canada and the Metroland development in Gateshead, UK. Indeed, the *Travel and Tourism Analyst* report (No. 2, 1990) argued that mixed-development proposals would find it increasingly easy to secure investment finance relative to those totally dependent on the leisure market. Moreover, technological developments such as virtual reality (see below) will make it increasingly easy for mall developments to incorporate theme park-style attractions in their limited space.

There is also considerable scope for integrating theme parks into other type of visitor attractions. A number of zoos have reoriented their operations into theme parks over the past decade, although such changes are now also occuring in the opposite direction. Increased emphasis on education and nature themes is resulting in aquaria, sea mammal shows, pet zoos and botanical gardens becoming more common in theme parks.

THEME PARKS AND NEW TECHNOLOGIES

New technology is the life blood of theme parks, which have been quick to incorporate the very latest techniques (robotics, holograms, lasers, etc.) into their attractions. Now, much attention is being focused on the potential which virtual reality offers the theme park sector (see Williams and Hobson 1994 for a full and entertaining treatment of this subject).

It is certainly the case that virtual reality and simulation technologies are increasingly being directed at leisure applications, reflecting a fall-off in demand from military sources. (There was a degree of satisfaction and not a little irony when, in 1996, it was announced that an Italian armaments factory had converted to the production of high-tech hardware for theme parks.) This synergy between theme parks and technology took another unexpected turn when, in 1997, a real Russian Mir station became a major attraction at Germany's Europa Park.

However, as yet, there has been no large-scale application of virtual reality technology in theme parks, although this can only be a question of time. Disney have promised to use virtual reality technology in their proposed historical America Park outside Washington DC. As the senior vice-president of Walt Disney Imagineering has pointed out: 'We can make you a civil war soldier . . . We can make you feel what slavery was like during that period, and what it was like to escape on the underground railroad' (Williams and Hobson 1994).

Meanwhile, Sega's 'urban theme park' indoor development, Segaworld, at the Trocadero in London is often cited as a forerunner of what virtual reality-based theme parks will be like. In reality, Segaworld is a combination of mainly 'old-tech' rides and computer games arcades, far removed from what is normally understood by interactive virtual reality. In addition, some argue that, as an indoor attraction, which does not deliver the real outdoor 'wind in the hair' experience, Segaworld does not in fact fit most definitions of a theme park (CWA 1997).

Amid all the anticipation of how virtual reality will enhance the experiences offered by theme parks, some voices are warning that the impact of new technology on the theme park market may not be wholly positive. The threat comes from the possible use of home-based entertainment based on this technology. In 1993, McEniff warned that 'For all recreation parks, however, home-based consumer electronic entertainment systems will provide an increasingly sophisticated and relatively cheap form of competition, (McEniff 1993); while others have commented that 'It is conceivable, however, that one day such new technology could also sound the death knell of the theme park. Who will need to go to a theme park when a virtual reality headset (perhaps connected to a motorised chair) will be able to recreate the same sensations in the living room?' (Jenner and Smith 1996).

More optimistically, some have predicted that the fact that new technology has a tendency to isolate individuals at home means that people will increasingly need to get together as a family or with friends, for organised social interaction:

> Tele-working, tele-banking and the Internet, to name a few examples, are becoming increasingly commonplace. This reduction in everyday human interaction creates a need for shared experiences which theme parks can help provide. In addition, the increase in computer-shopping will reduce the amount of leisure time occupied by trips to the shops. (CWA 1997)

In order to compete successfully with home-based entertainment, theme parks may have to adapt their marketing strategies to emphasize certain aspects such as the fresh air, human animation and the opportunity to meet others.

COACH TOUR OPERATORS

Increasingly in Europe, coach tour operators are working with attractions such as theme parks to put together customised packages that will appeal to their customers and fill up their coaches. This symbiotic approach means that not only are theme parks acquiring more business from tour operators but also tour operators are acquiring more business from theme parks through both excursions and private hire. In the UK, the Tussauds Group has been particularly active in developing this market. Each of the group's attractions employs a sales force specifically dedicated to this sector, producing their own promotional material with the objective of helping coach operators to sell their trips. It has also established a unique award scheme – the Tussauds Group Coach Operator of the Year Award – which seeks to recognise and reward those coach operators who consistently visit a variety of the Tussauds Group's attractions.

THEME PARKS AND THE EDUCATION MARKET

McEniff (1993) drew attention to the fact that in the USA in particular, but also in Europe, there is an on-going switch in emphasis from pure entertainment to entertainment plus education, in many cases seeking participation from customers. Quoting Chris Gratton of Tilburg University, a leading analyst of the theme parks sector, he writes that 'continued growth in theme park attendances will require operators to increase the 'skill level' of attractions'. He gives as an example of a higher skill level attraction the traffic school at Legoland, where children can take a twenty–minute mock driving test.

Educational themes associated with culture and nature are becoming increasingly common in theme parks, while some cultural attractions are boosting their appeal by resorting to activities more at home in theme parks: the use of interactive shows, virtual reality, etc., to 'dynamise' cultural attractions and allow visitors to 'experience' simulations of historical and cultural events.

Consequently, many parks now offer complete educational packages including teacher talks and workbooks linked to school syllabi. Chessington World of Adventures, for example, has a dedicated education facility, employs a full-time teacher and offers a package of educational talks and workbooks based on aspects of the park – particularly the animals – which are tailored to various stages of the National Curriculum.

Richards (1996) describes 'edutainment', a word coined by the Disney Corporation, meaning a combination of education and entertainment. He writes that many surveys of visitors to leisure attractions and general visitor feedback has indicated that the public's number one expectation from leisure facilities is that they should contain some educational element which enables visitors to broaden their horizons in some way.

Theme parks, of course, do not have the monopoly on 'edutainment' but are in competition with other attractions. For example, several 'Discovery Centres' such as the Bristol 'Exploratory' centre and Halifax's 'Eureka' centre in the UK have sprung up in a number of European countries during the 1990s. One of the most recently opened being La Cité de l'Espace near Toulouse, which also bills itself as the European Space Park. A Discovery Centre is a 'science-based tourist attraction aimed at the younger educational market and charging admission'. It is generally promoted as an interactive learning experience as opposed to the passive 'science museum', although the centre may well be associated with an established science museum or institution (Richards 1996).

Discovery parks may act as a spur to encourage theme parks to develop educational and interactive features of their own. However, as Richards insists,

theme parks must remember that they are places of leisure visited in holiday time, and that the largest queues are to be found snaking around the 'white knuckle rides'. While new technology, such as audio-animatronics, hands-on computer displays and simulation technology may help to make the education 'fun', the educational element must always be subordinate or incidental to this entertainment. Effectively, the move towards 'edutainment' must be a change of the presentation rather than the content of the park' (Richard 1996).

This is confirmed by an observation by McEniff (1993), who quotes from a survey in *Park World*

magazine that year, indicating that rollercoasters and other thrill rides still remained the most popular of all theme park attractions.

At the same time, as Richards writes, diluting or distorting culture and history to make them more accessible or entertaining also leaves theme parks open to charges of trivialisation. In the US, Disney's plan to build 'Disney's America' was challenged successfully by a group of intellectuals who accused the company of creating 'synthetic history by destroying real history'. He therefore concludes that 'parks seeking to provide "edutainment" have a minefield in front of them. On the one hand, they must not allow education to overshadow the entertainment, and on the other, the educational content must not be vulnerable to accusations of superficiality' (Richard 1996).

The EU and theme parks

With its powers to regulate on a number of issues, the EU has the potential to impact quite considerably on the operation of theme parks in Member States. With regards to the regulatory environment in which theme parks function, EU legislation is relevant in a number of areas, including food hygiene, employment, consumer protection and competition policy. Three of the most important are examined below.

EMPLOYMENT

Employment in the theme park sector is highly seasonal, and EU moves to improve entitlements for seasonal and part-time workers so that they are equal to those of their full-time counterparts will have a major impact. (All large parks keep a minimum permanent staff all year round, but generally employ between two and five times as many additional workers in the peak season, Disneyland Paris being the exception.)

But in a number of northern European Member States, work conditions for theme park employees are already relatively high and there is little concern about the impact of existing and proposed EU legislation (CEC 1996).

THE ENVIRONMENT

Large parks may have a range of negative impacts on the environment, including noise pollution (Euro Disney fireworks displays have led to complaints from Marne-la-Vallée residents), scenic intrusion, and attracting a high volume of motorised transport. In addition, the theme park sector is land-intensive, requiring space for attractions and parking.

As McEniff notes, with increasing environmental concern among consumers reflected in planning legislation and in the EU requirement for environmental impact assessement for major projects, the time-lag from designing major theme parks to their construction is considerable and lengthening. Many parks recognise that meeting strict environmental standards is in their own interests and that a sympathetic landscape surrounding the approaches to theme parks is a major benefit.

VAT

Theme parks are included on the list of products and services upon which Member States can levy a reduced rate of VAT. French and Belgian parks benefit from relatively low rates of VAT, 5.5 per cent and 6 per cent respectively, in comparison with competitors in Germany (15 per cent), the Netherlands (17.5 per cent), and the United Kingdom (17.5 per cent). Where parks lie close to national boundaries which can be easily crossed by pleasure seekers, those parks with low rates of VAT have a competitive advantage. This is of particular concern to the Dutch parks, which lose out to Belgium (Richards 1996). Rates in Spain, Portugal and Italy are also relatively low, but their distance from the high-VAT North European Member States reduces distortionary trade impacts (McEniff 1993).

VAT is another contentious issue surrounding Disney's arrival in Europe. It is alleged that one inducement offered by the French to Euro Disney was the preferential VAT rate of 5.5 per cent, less than most other Member States.

Europarks

In dialogue with EU institutions on issues affecting theme parks in Member States is the trade association Europarks.

Europarks, the European Federation of Amusement and Leisure Parks, has as its members eight national theme park trade associations (from the United Kingdom (BALPPA, see below), Germany, France, the Netherlands, Belgium, Sweden, Spain, and Italy) and a number of individual European theme parks from countries without national organisations (Denmark, Finland, Norway and Portugal).

Europarks was founded in 1981 by two national associations, the British Association of Leisure Parks, Piers and Attractions (BALPPA) and the German association, VDFU. Europarks now represents more than 150 European theme parks, attracting over 130 million visitors per year, and employing approximately 35,000 men and women (25 per cent permanent and 75 per cent part-time or seasonal). Based upon global figures, the gross turnover of these parks amounts to some ECU 1,500 million.

One of the main objectives of Europarks is to convince European politicians and organisations of the importance, for Europe, of developments in the theme park industry.

Its priorities are:

- Furtherance of the realisation of European safety standards on fairground and amusement park machinery and structures.
- The implications of VAT harmonisation for the European tourism industry. (Application of the reduced VAT rate on *all* the sectors of the industry, including recreation, is a logical consequence of this harmonisation process that tries to avoid unfair competition between individual European Member States.)
- A simplification and harmonisation of the rules, regulations and taxation on part-time and temporary work.
- Awareness of the importance of the environment for this industry.

On this last issue, Europarks maintains that the (auto) mobility of the tourist has to be guaranteed as long as there are no real alternatives, but is also trying to reduce the negative impact of car-based visitors to theme parks by cooperating to improve public transport options for access to parks.

References

CEC (1996) *Panorama of European Industry*, European Commission, Brussels.

CWA (1997) *The Business of Fun: Theme Parks – Moving Towards the Millennium*, Chessington World of Adventures, Chessington.

Daily Express, The (1995) 'Spain's roller Costa reaches new highs', 29 April.

D'Hautesserre A-M (1997) 'Disneyland Paris: A permanent economic growth pole in the Francilian landscape', *Progress in Tourism and Hospitality Research*, Vol. 3, pp. 17–33.

Echo Touristique (1997) 'Disneyland Paris réveille le marché des parcs de loisirs', 11 April.

Eurostat (1997) *EU Transport in Figures*, Eurostat/DG VII, Brussels.

Figaro, Le (1995) 'Mickey, Astérix et les 101 techniciens', 12 September.

Jenner, P. and Smith, C. (1996) 'Attendance trends at Europe's leisure attractions', *EIU Travel and Tourism Analyst (4)*, Travel and Tourism Intelligence, London.

McEniff, J. (1993) 'Theme parks in Europe', *EIU Travel and Tourism Analyst (5)*, Economist Intelligence Unit, London.

Mail on Sunday, The (1995) 'Enter the Dragon', 26 March.

Pais Cataluña, El (1997) 'Port Aventura quiere consol-idar los tres millones de visitantes anuales', 17 March.

Richards, B. (1996) 'The future for theme parks', *Insights*, May, English Tourist Board, London.

Sunday Times, The (1993) 'EuroDismal', 22 August.

Sunday Times, The (1995) 'Smiles return to the Magic Kingdom', 12 November.

Sunday Times, The (1996) 'Asterix and Obelix head for Londinium', 21 July.

TIM (1997) 'Attractions', *Travel Industry Monitor* April Issue, Travel and Tourism Intelligence, London, pp. 18–19.

Vanguardia, La (1995) 'El 25 per cent de los clientes de Port Aventura visitó el parque temático más de una vez', 1 November.

Vanguardia, La (1996a) 'Port Aventura se consolida como el segundo parque de Europa al cierre de la temporada', 27 October.

Vanguardia, La (1996b) 'Port Aventura aporta 20,000 millones anuales a los municipios de su entorno', 3 December.

Vanguardia, La (1997) 'La reapertura de Port Aventura avanza el inicio de la temporada turística en el Costa Daurada', 16 March.

Varney, Nick (1992) 'EuroDisney and the UK Tourism Industry: Friend or Foe?' *Insights*, May issue, English Tourist Board, London.

Walibi (1997) *1996 Annual Report*, The Walibi Group, Wavre.

Wall Street Journal Europe, The (1996) 'Thrills and tills: New UK theme park follows trend to tap Europe's fun-seekers', 14 February, Dow Jones & Company, Inc.

Williams, A. P. and Hobson, J. S. P. (1994) 'Tourism – the next generation: virtual reality and surrogate travel, is it the future of the tourism industry?' in Seaton et al. (eds), *Tourism: The State of the Art*, John Wiley, Chichester.

6

Business tourism in Europe

KEY OBJECTIVES

Reading this chapter will enable you to:

- Understand the value of business travel and tourism in Europe.
- Distinguish the four main sectors of the business travel and tourism market and their specific characteristics.
- Identify the principal current trends in each of the four sectors as well as the impact of the EU on all four.

Introduction

This chapter is concerned with the European market (supply and demand) for travel and tourism which is directly related to the traveller's professional activity. The various segments of this market are examined in turn: general business travel – for example, people travelling to visit customers, suppliers and business contacts; meetings and conferences; incentive trips; exhibitions and trade fairs.

The benefits of business tourism for Europe are considerable. Overall, business tourism in Europe represents an economic sector of immense importance, which is expressed in the direct and indirect benefits which the various segments or sub-sectors bring in terms of turnover, employment and tax revenues. Furthermore, the business tourism sector covers a large range of activities for which the main objectives include the transfer of knowledge and expertise, networking and the exchanges of goods and services. In this way, the sector contributes

directly and continually to the process of European integration.

Nevertheless, despite the widespread recognition of its ability to bring important economic and social benefits to communities, the business tourism market is poorly documented and under-researched in Europe. A reason suggested for this is that, traditionally, business tourism was considered to be more resistant to the economic cycle and exchange rate fluctuations than leisure travel, and had also proved resilient to political change. Thus the travel industry took it for granted that travelling for business would continue to represent a dependable and unwavering sector (Rockett and Smillie 1994).

But the combined effect of the Gulf War and recession in Europe, following fast on the heels of the high-spending 1980s, altered this perception and demonstrated the rollercoaster fortunes of business travel and tourism at their most extreme highs and lows.

The 1980s ended on an up-beat note of confidence for business tourism in Europe. After the remarkable liberation of Eastern Europe, the continent seemed set for a new era of prosperity and peace, leading up to closer European cooperation and the completion of the Single Market. Demand was generally buoyant for all sub-sectors of the business tourism market.

Almost overnight, the Gulf War dramatically changed the situation, as across the globe, meetings activity involving travel was abruptly thrown into reverse. International travel in particular was affected. Fear of flying became endemic as companies demanded that their staff keep both feet on the ground, and meetings were cancelled, postponed,

Table 6.1 Business tourism turnover in the EEA, by sector

Segments		Turnover	% of sector
Individual business trips	115,000	million ECU	70.8
Conferences/Congresses	5,450	million ECU	3.3
Business meetings	20,420	million ECU	12.6
Incentive trips	3,900	million ECU	2.4
Exhibitions/fairs	17,700	million ECU	10.9
Total	162,470	million ECU	100.0

Source: CEC (1996)

or kept in-house. Hotels suffered extensive cancellations, as many professional conference organisers saw their clients lists sadly depleted; and airlines pulled out of routes and laid off staff (Davidson 1992a).

In the event, the conflict was sharp and short, but it was followed, in Europe, by a damaging recession which stubbornly set in to cloud over the economy of every European country until the middle of the 1990s.

It is now clear that business travel and tourism can be affected by the fortunes of the national/world economy as a whole, just as much as the market for leisure travel is vulnerable to changes in the levels of financial well-being of individuals. But although it is true that spending fell abruptly during the recession, it is not the case that the end of that economic slump has been followed by a corresponding increase in business tourism expenditure in Europe.

The quality of information on business tourism in Europe advanced considerably in 1994, when the European Commission Directorate General XXIII commissioned a study of business and conference tourism. The objective of the exercise was to conduct a quantitative and qualitative evaluation of the supply of, and demand for, this form of tourism in the European Economic Area (EEA), which is composed of the Member States of the EU, together with Norway and Iceland.

The results of the survey, commonly known as the Horwarth Axe study, after the consultants who carried it out, were presented at ITB tourism trade fair in Berlin in March 1996. At that time, the study estimated the value of business travel and tourism in Europe at around ECU 162 billion ECU, broken down as shown in Table 6.1.

In addition to this volume of direct turnover, business tourism in the EEA has considerable induced effects and generates a large number of ancillary activities linked to conferences and exhibitions. In total, this induced activity is estimated at 1.5 to 2 times the direct turnover of the sector (CEC 1996).

The rest of this chapter examines the four main sectors of the business travel and tourism market:

1 general business travel
2 meetings
3 incentive travel
4 exhibitions and trade fairs.

Nevertheless, it is important to recognise that a distinguishing characteristic of this market is that the different categories often merge into one another, blurring the distinctions between them. Many conferences are accompanied by an exhibition on the same theme – for example, medical conferences often include an exhibition of pharmaceutical products. Similarly, when a conference is held in an attractive destination, such as Monaco or Nice, for example, an employer, in selecting a member of staff to attend, may also be using the event partly as a form of incentive for outstanding performance in the workplace. Finally, exhibitions often include conferences featuring high-profile speakers as a way of attracting more visitors.

General business travel

DISCRETIONARY AND NON-DISCRETIONARY BUSINESS TOURISM

Three out of the four types of business tourism listed above – meetings, incentive travel and exhibitions – may be considered to be 'discretionary'. This means that the choice of where such events are to be held is open to negotiation and that the organiser or planner of these forms of business tourism can use some discretion in choosing a venue. As a result, all potential destinations which could serve as venues for conferences and other meetings, incentive trips, exhibitions and trade fairs are in competition with each other to attract these events. As the venues for these types of event are negotiable, those with responsibility for choosing the venue are usually open to being persuaded by effective marketing by the destinations or by the lobbying of potential delegates or clients.

General business travel, on the other hand, is principally non-discretionary. It involves trips taken within the normal framework of professional activities, by commercial travellers, for example, or by those who travel to meet clients or to provide a service as a routine part of their working lives.

General business travel is considered to be non-discretionary as it is practically impossible to influence the final destination of such trips. If the contract to be signed or the customer to be visited is in Hong Kong, for example, then no amount of marketing or lobbying will persuade the business traveller to fly to Monaco instead. It is also very difficult for the tourism industry to influence the amount of general business travel, as this is primarily demand-led, being determined by the pattern and volume of economic activity which is outside its control. (Nevertheless, efforts are being increasingly made by the tourism industry, for example, to persuade business travellers to extend their trip by adding on a 'leisure weekend' and/or to bring their spouse/partner on the trip.)

THE VOLUME OF EUROPEAN GENERAL BUSINESS TRAVEL

The European Business Travel and Expense Management Report 1993 published by American Express (1994) ranked Europe as the world's foremost business travel market, outspending the United States and Asia. In the ten European countries surveyed (Belgium, France, Germany, Hungary, Italy, the Netherlands, Spain, Sweden, Switzerland and the UK), there were over 94 million people in the private sector workforce alone. In 1993, the last year for which the survey was undertaken, private sector expenditure on T&E (travel and entertainment) amounted to US$141 billion or 2.5 per cent of the total GDP of the countries involved. Some idea of the magnitude of the private sector's spending on T&E is given by the information contained in Table 6.2.

Of the six countries' T&E, 31 per cent is spent on international travel, primarily by sales staff and management.

Table 6.2 Principal European business travel and expense markets

	T & E (US$ billion)	% of GDP on T & E	% of T & E spent abroad
Germany	38.8	2.5	24
United Kingdom	30.3	3.5	38
France	25.3	2.2	24
Italy	16.0	1.9	28
Spain	8.8	1.9	23
Sweden	6.8	3.8	60

Source: American Express (1994)

TRENDS IN EUROPEAN BUSINESS TRAVEL

More for less

For the mid-1990s, the Horwarth Axe survey identified an increase in the number of European business trips, but a reduction in the average spend per trip. Part of the explanation given for this phenomenon was that the development of faster modes of transportation increasingly allows the possibility of a return day trip within Europe, where previously it would have been necessary to spend a night in a hotel as part of the trip. A decline in the number of nights spent in hotels as a result of destinations being served by high-speed trains, for example, is a phenomenon which has been observed in Europe ever since the Paris–Lyons TGV connection was built. For this reason, the consultants claim, the European programmes to develop the transportation infrastructure (including the high-speed train network) may have a notable influence on the number and nature of business trips in Europe. However, they add that the impacts of those programmes on European business travel are not likely to be measurable before the years 2005 to 2010 (CEC 1996).

The principal reason for lower spending on business travel per trip is that many of the buyers of business travel and tourism have remembered the cost-saving lessons they learnt from the dark recession days of the early 1990s and have continued to follow the same spending patterns. The various measures taken by European companies to control their travel costs, as described by Davidson (1994a) have increasingly become institutionalised: trading down on class of travel for trips made by air and rail; implementing formal company travel policies to control spending; and using the centralised purchasing of travel and accommodation in order to negotiate special discounts and corporate rates.

As early as 1993, some commentators were predicting that the cost-consciousness made necessary by the recession would not automatically diminish with the return to more prosperous times. Among them was O'Brien, who maintained that 'The Gulf War educated the corporate sector as to the amount of non-essential travel expenditure incurred in previous years . . . The 1990s will witness the advent of the responsible, cost-con-

scious business traveller. Travel preferences will become less important to the corporate client as the benefits of cost reductions will increasingly outweigh them' (O'Brien 1993). Echoing this point one year later, Verchère wrote that:

> Even an economic rebound . . . is unlikely to shake off this quest for value now demanded of airline, hotel, car rental and travel firms by their corporate clients. Where once extravagance reigned, large and multinational corporations now exert the biggest squeeze on the budgetary and travel fronts. (European 1994)

By the mid-1990s, Europe had witnessed a dramatic recovery in business travel – at least in terms of numbers of people travelling. In 1996, the Daily Telegraph in a special report was able to report that: 'Business travel in Europe has never been more diverse or more competitive. Driven by the economic upswing and the liberalisation of air routes, passenger traffic is at record levels with an unprecedented choice of carriers and fares' (Daily Telegraph 1996).

But, as forecast, actual spending on general business travel was far less buoyant. Even by 1996, despite steady increases in the volume of people travelling on business, there were no signs of a return to the pre-recession spending levels. Taking as an indicator air travel budgets for business travel, the IATA Corporate Air Travel Survey for that year reported that these remained 'essentially unchanged despite the recovery of economies around the globe. Where a change has been noted, 18 per cent saw some reduction in budgets while 10 per cent reported increases' (IATA 1997).

Carlson Wagonlit's annual business travel survey for 1996 was launched with the heading: 'Business travel trends reflect increased economic optimism' (Carlson Wagonlit 1997). The survey confirmed the general increase in the number of business trips being made: 38 per cent of those interviewed for the survey expected to make more business trips over the following 12 months, as opposed to 28 per cent at the time of the previous survey, a year earlier.

The importance to companies of managing their travel costs was also underlined in the survey, which highlighted a slight increase in the number of companies prepared to trade down in class of travel, and a greater increase in the number of companies operating formal travel policies (from 60 per cent to 77 per cent of the companies interviewed).

Moreover, the moves towards more Spartan levels of comfort for business trips appear to have the support of the travellers themselves, as predicted by O'Brien, above. The demands of business travellers regarding their means of transport, as identified by Carlson Wagonlit, were summed up by the phrase: 'No frills, speedy service and keen pricing.' As an indication of this attitude, around 81 per cent of travellers, decision-makers and travel bookers agreed that they would be happy to travel on less expensive, no-frills flights on short-haul routes within Europe, a rise of 5 per cent over the previous survey published in January 1996.

Ample space in which to work was only considered important when travelling long distances by train or on long-haul flights. From a list of travel extras and facilities, speed of service, including rapid check-in, was felt to be the most important factor when travelling by Eurostar, 'Intercity' trains or on short-haul flights (Carlson Wagonlit 1997).

More women business travellers

Verchère, writing in the European (1993) quotes American Express research showing that an increasing proportion of those travelling on business are women. Over Europe as a whole, according to American Express, the average proportion of women among business travellers is around 13 per cent. Most countries are close to this figure, but the UK has the greatest proportion of businesswomen on the move, due to the high ratio of UK business travellers who are women working in the financial and service sectors.

Nevertheless, Europe has still a long way to go in order to match the situation in the USA, where 40 per cent of business travellers are women. But, commentators generally agree that as European economies continue to shift away from manufacturing towards the service sector, where most women business travellers are concentrated, the situation seems set to change. The question which the various sectors of the business tourism industry is currently asking itself is how best to cater for this growing market?

Regarding hotels, policies range from providing a host of special facilities for female guests – an approach used by chains such as Thistle Hotels, who offer 'suitable toiletries and magazines . . . a communal ladies-only table in the restaurant, and secure floors' (Daily Telegraph 1996) – to the lighter touch used by chains such as Hilton International, who, although keeping a close watch on the interests of their female guests 'through a discreet mixture of gender diplomacy and customer research' (European 1993), claims to have no special agenda for female corporate clients. This would appear to be the policy favoured by Heather Blaseby, European managing director of Utell International, who claims that women travellers do not want to be segregated on separate hotel floors but treated the same as their male counterparts. She believes that highlighting the female traveller makes them a 'sitting target' (European 1993).

SUPPLY-SIDE INCENTIVES

As the market becomes more demanding and more cost-conscious, the business travel industry has had to find more effective ways of winning and keeping customers. Following the principle that it is cheaper to keep existing clients than to attract new ones, hotels, airlines and other forms of transport are increasingly offering incentives to woo their most loyal customers. Hotels, in particular those belonging to national and international chains, have launched their own loyalty programmes for frequent travellers, emphasising the savings in time and money which membership of such schemes can bring. For example, the late check-out or early check-in facilities offered to certain cardholders can avoid the expense of paying for an extra night's accommodation, while express check-in/check-out facilities can make for valuable time savings. Free room upgrades, discounts on laundry and telephone surcharges, and free nights' accommodation at weekends are among the other perks offered by hotel chains in their efforts to attract and keep business clients.

But perhaps the best-known of all incentives are the airlines' 'frequent flyer programmes'

(FFPs). During the 1990s, European air carriers followed the example of their North American competitors and offered FFPs as a means of encouraging regular business travellers to book with them. The principle is that the passenger travelling on an airline earns points, or air miles, which can be accumulated and eventually exchanged for free flights or other benefits, such as upgrades to business or first class on the airlines.

The popularity of such schemes in Europe – at least with the business travellers themselves – was shown as early as 1993, when the November survey of such travellers conducted by Official Airline Guides showed that 70 per cent of those interviewed said that, given a choice of carriers on a route, they would choose the one to which their FFP belonged (Financial Times 1993). The fact that, in the vast majority of cases, the actual cost to the airlines was minimal, since the 'free' seats were merely using spare capacity on their aircraft, added to the apparent win-win aspect of such programmes.

By 1996, however, a number of problems had emerged which indicated that the appeal of FFPs was less than universal. Objections arose from two sources. First of all, those actually paying for the tickets, the business travellers' employers; and secondly, the tax authorities. Companies were increasingly voicing the opinion that FFPs were responsible for inflating travel costs (because their employees tended to choose the flight offered by the airline to whose FFP they belonged, which was not always the cheapest on offer for the journey to be undertaken) and even for encouraging employees to make unnecessary or circuitous trips in order to earn bonus points. A 1996 poll of 'travel decision makers' carried out by MORI for Carlson Wagonlit Travel showed that 64 per cent of them said that FFP benefits should go to the company and not the individual. But according to another survey by American Express, only 9 per cent of companies required FFP benefits to be handed over to them by employees (European 1996).

Nevertheless, the growing unpopularity of such schemes with many companies is clear. In Sweden in 1996, for example, more than 50 companies, including Electrolux, Volvo and Saab pressed the national airline SAS either to abandon its EuroBonus FFP or to award the benefits directly to them rather than their employees. If this becomes part of a growing trend and companies increasingly claim FFP benefits for themselves, that would not only be bad news for their employees, it could be very bad for the airlines themselves: if companies use the 'free' air miles to fly their executives around the globe, instead of buying tickets in the normal way, this would represent a substantial loss of revenue for Europe's airlines.

Another factor calling the future of FFPs into doubt is the attitude of some countries' tax collectors. In Canada in the mid-1990s, an auditor from the government's revenue department reassessed the incomes of two executives to take account of free airline tickets they had received through FFPs. In a landmark legal ruling, the court decided that the value of the tickets was their actual market value on the particular flight taken, rather than the (minimum) incremental cost to the airline of filling what would otherwise have been an empty seat. Following this case, there were growing signs that some European governments were also considering taxing such perks.

Nevertheless, even if such moves mean that FFPs lose their appeal as incentives, the airlines have no shortage of other incentives designed to entice business travellers and, to as great an extent as possible, keep them in business and first class compartments. Davidson (1994a) describes the inducements ranging from limousine transfers to airports and executive lounges to on-board telephones and air-to-ground teleconferencing facilities. Time will tell whether tendencies towards belt-tightening or, more likely, 'political correctness' in the business travelling community grow to the extent that such luxuries are no longer acceptable in the current climate of cost-consciousness in Europe.

THE IMPACT OF THE EU

In an expanded EU, the business travel market will grow in importance. The right of any business based in a Member State to establish itself in any other Member State of the EU means that companies will increasingly have branches in different European countries. Consequently, the need to travel internationally to meet colleagues will grow. In addition, as companies expand in this way, they will no doubt seek to strengthen their trade links and their presence in the regional and global marketplaces, and reach out more often to their partners in business in other European nations. All of this means more business travel, in particular, intra-European.

Meetings

DEFINITIONS

Most professionals agree that in collecting and analysing data and statistics relating to meetings and conference activity, a consensus on terminology is a basic and urgent requirement. But poor definition of the individual market segments means that there is still no clear agreement on the terminology used in the meetings sector, which may include conventions, conferences, seminars, symposia, congresses, colloquia and so on.

Those events commonly referred to as conferences and conventions constitute the best-documented segment of business tourism because they assemble a large number of participants in one place and generally over a period of a few days. Seminars are much harder to identify than conferences because they are generally of smaller scale (frequently 20 to 50 participants) and shorter.

Regarding the market for the meetings industry, it is customary to make the distinction between the corporate sector and professional and voluntary associations. The corporate sector consists of companies, whose main reasons for holding meetings are commercial: sales and marketing conferences, new product launches and training sessions for staff. Professional associations' meetings bring together those who are active in the same occupational field, usually to bring themselves up to date with developments in their specialist domain, while voluntary associations cover the entire range of human experience outside work: people's leisure activities and interests, their faith, beliefs and ethical aspects, for example.

SUPPLY

There is a great diversity of facilities designed to serve the European conference market. The supply of venues comprises a large number of varied facilities (for example, purpose-built conference centres, convention centres, hotels, universities and multi-purpose venues) that compete on both the national and international level.

Conference centres

In most European countries, the majority of these are built from public funds, often as loss leaders, in an endeavour to bring high-spending delegates to the destination. Few make a true profit, taking into account the cost of construction, interest on capital, and so on.

In 1995, the supply of major European conference centres of an international standard comprised 261 facilities, distributed by country as illustrated in Table 6.3.

The evolution of the supply of European conference facilities is partly characterised by a progressive upgrading of the existing facilities, in order to satisfy the growing requirements of clients in terms of what they require from facilities – especially flexibility of areas, of services and on prices. In particular, the possibilities offered by new information technology (i.e. tele-conferences) are now considered to be essential equipment for international facilities.

This constant upgrading of the European supply of conference facilities is considered essential to face the fierce competition which has developed in destinations of the Asia-Pacific region (CEC 1996). Cities such as Hong Kong, Jakarta and Singapore have recently developed state-of-the-art facilities competing favourably with established centres in Europe and North America.

Parallel to moves to improve the quality of Europe's conference centres, the quantity of such facilities has also increased. After the waves of conference centre development throughout Europe in the 1980s, it is now widely recognised that the supply of conference facilities has reached an oversupply situation in certain areas.

The increase in numbers of meetings has not kept up with the growth in numbers of conference centres in Europe. Consequently, many new conference centres are in reality multi-purpose buildings.

Table 6.3 Number of conference centres and the national seating capacity in the EEA, 1995

	Germany	Austria	Belgium	Denmark	Spain	Finland	France	Great Britain	Greece
Main conference centres	30	7	13	8	24	7	94	14	2
National seating capacity	50,000	64,200	18,400	15,700	40,000	25,500	90,000	79,500	2,800

	Ireland	Iceland	Italy	Luxembourg	Norway	Netherlands	Portugal	Sweden	Total
Main conference centres	0	1	32	1	3	13	4	8	261
National seating capacity	0	4,000	85,000	1,550	10,200	24,500	4,150	23,000	538,000

Source: CEC (1996)

They may have been planned and designed as meeting places, but as soon as they open, they compete for audiences of every conceivable nature – for exhibitions, indoor sports such as tennis, boxing, wrestling, running etc., dances, concerts, opera and ballet, and much more mundane occasions such as writing examination papers. (EFCT 1996).

Moreover, old habits of accepting the loss-making attributes of facilities are increasingly queried. In its review of conference activity in Europe in 1996, the European Federation of Conference Towns notes that 'managements are under pressure, often for the first time, to achieve operational profits for congress centres, mostly in the public area. The hotel sector, where a majority of meetings takes place, has, of course, always been based on this' (EFCT 1997b).

Hotels

It is not necessary to go very far back in time to return to an era when many hoteliers in Europe regarded conferences as a useful source of income in the slack period, but something of a nuisance in busy months. With the realisation that conferences represent a lucrative all-year-round market, the attitude of Europe's hoteliers is now very different. Far more conferences, seminars and other meet-ings take place in Europe's hotels than in its confer-ence centres. Most major European hotel groups, and many individual properties, now offer meet-ings packages which include the services of special-ised professional conference staff.

On the European-wide scale, seminars and other business meetings are estimated to represent an average of about 15 per cent of total activity in hotels, or a volume estimated at more than 160 million bed nights per year. This market segment is estimated to generate a turnover of approximately ECU 20 billion on accommodation in hotels in the EU member countries alone (CEC 1996).

Dedicated residential conference centres

Throughout Europe in the 1990s, entrepreneurs identified a gap in the market for small, business-orientated residential conference venues, which were different from hotels in being free from the distractions of holidaymakers and children. They responded by providing purpose-built venues ded-icated to the unique requirements of conference clients, as alternatives to the facilities of hotels and other multi-function venues.

In Europe, the concept of the dedicated man-agement training and conference centre with accommodation, built for commercial purposes, is probably most developed in Scandinavia and the

UK (with growing interest in France). Such centres are now estimated to number between 60 and 75 in both countries

Typical of these is Sedgbrook Hall, near Northampton in the UK, which opened in 1992, in a Victorian country house converted into meeting rooms, with an added new wing containing 60 4-star standard bedrooms and hotel-type catering facilities. Sedgbrook Hall's client list is drawn from the top 100 companies and its core business is training and management meetings. The general manager attributes the centre's success to 'its provision of a businesslike environment which facilitates communication and learning. For example, a common request from companies booking rooms for training purposes is for plentiful natural light. Specialist management training centres frequently score better on this point than hotels, which have often been designed with evening social functions in mind' (Financial Times 1993).

The dedicated, or purpose-built, residential conference centre is therefore based on the creation of a 'total meeting environment' for conferences. This sets it apart from hotels in that the facility is designed specifically to serve the requirements of the meetings industry and to offer accommodation under the same roof. The service and technology employed, as well as the volume of meeting space available, are the principal elements which help to set such centres apart. However, it is interesting that few UK and Scandinavian facilities have emulated the resort orientation of many of the residential conference centres in the USA, which manage to integrate leisure facilities, such as golf courses, into the work environment without it becoming counter-productive to the principal objective.

OTHER VENUES

Spurred on by the conference business's love of novelty, a growing variety of venues throughout Europe have been entirely converted to meetings facilities or have diversified by adding meeting rooms to the range of services they provide.

For example, Europe's ample supply of country mansions, chateaux and castles have for many years been eager players in this sector, often emphasising their historical and cultural connec-tions as a unique selling point. But more recently, other categories of venue have been added to Europe's supply of meetings facilities. This trend is well illustrated by the example of the UK, where 'there is a trend towards unusual venues for conferences and hospitality. Sports grounds are investing millions in meetings facilities. Kempton Park race course is rebuilding its conference and exhibition space, while Murrayfield in Edinburgh is building ten boxes and sixteen suites, each seating between fourteen and 40, for hospitality and small meetings. In Huddersfield, the Alfred McAlpine Stadium, one of the most advanced in the country, has been granted £5.2 million of lottery money for a new stand which will include a hi-tech conference suite. Scotland's largest conference venue, the Glasgow-based Scottish Exhibition and Conference Centre, is building a new £30 million conference facility alongside the main building which will seat up to 600. Edinburgh, meanwhile, has some unusual venues for press launches or events: 'if the Scotch Malt Whisky Society's private club is too staid, the Deep Sea World aquarium will do press events in an underwater perspex tunnel with sharks circling above' (PR Week 1997).

Universities, too, have emerged in recent years as major venues for conferences, following considerable investment in upgrading of their facilities, including the standard of student accommodation. Traditionally, European universities have succeeded best in two niche markets: high attendance, low budget conferences, and the smaller training and management seminar type of events. But, more recently, many have moved upmarket by opening their own year-round management centres for meetings of up to 200 people. Whether purpose-built or converted, the centres are usually fitted out to at least 3-star standard. And, unlike most university conference centres, availability is not limited by the academic timetable. By the mid-1990s, there were at least 30 such centres, with more due to open (Financial Times 1993).

Even Europe's ferry operators have established themselves in this market. Many large ferries, first in the Baltic Sea then elsewhere have been equipped with conference rooms. For example, the ferry operator Stena Sealink offers a one-day

Table 6.4 Number of international congresses held by continent, 1989–93

	1989	1990	1991	1992	1993	% market share 1993
Africa	356	355	368	399	446	5.1
America	1,665	1,642	1,547	1,762	1,802	20.4
Asia	1,024	1,008	985	1,018	1,138	12.9
Australasia	175	186	187	149	162	1.8
Europe	4,945	5,225	5,107	5,299	5,269	59.8
Total	8,165	8,416	8,194	8,627	8,817	100.0

Source: Rockett, G. and Smillie, G. (1994)

conference on board a ferry plying the Harwich–Hook of Holland line. Guests go on board in the morning, and by the time the ship sets sail at 11.30 am, the conference can be underway in the purpose-built auditorium seating up to 230 delegates. Before disembarking the next morning, delegates have the added opportunity (until 1999) of stocking up in the ship's duty-free shop.

DEMAND

Little has changed since the early 1990s when Smith (1991) lamented the continuing absence of reliable statistics for the European meetings industry.

Practically the only widely accepted statistics for this sector in Europe are published by the Brussels-based Union of International Associations (UIA), which has provided figures on the meetings industry for more than 40 years. Even then, their annual survey is representative of only a fraction of the overall meetings and conference activity: the market for major *international associations*' congresses.

Traditionally, Europe holds the top position in the world for the hosting of such events, as shown in Table 6.4. For 1995, the UIA listed a total of 8,802 international conferences, of which 58 per cent were held in Europe, 20 per cent in America, 14 per cent in Asia, 5 per cent in Africa and 3 per cent in Australasia (EFCT 1997a).

These figures clearly indicate that Europe is considerably ahead of other continents in respect of hosting this type of meeting, but is nevertheless losing market share to other world regions. Keeping business from defecting from Europe to other regions is as difficult for the conference sector as it is for the leisure travel sector, and for the same reasons, in many cases: cheaper long-haul flights, lower rates, and the novelty value of holding an international conference in Ho Chi Minh City or Shanghai.

Regarding individual destinations for international associations' conferences, the order of popularity does not change dramatically from year to year. In 1995, the top country for international conferences was, as always, the USA, with 1,004 events, followed by France, the UK, Germany, Italy, the Netherlands, Belgium, Austria, Switzerland and Spain. The leading city was Paris, with 332 congresses followed by Vienna, London, Brussels, Geneva, Singapore, New York and Amsterdam.

Although many European capitals succeed in this sector, France is a perennial favourite location for this type of conference – partly for the same qualities which make it a favourite holiday destination, but also due to the fact that a great number of major international organisations have their headquarters there. Paris alone has over 1,000 such associations, out of a world total of between 6,000 and 7,000, with UNESCO and the OECD being among the largest generators of this type of meeting.

Nevertheless, international events can also give a country a temporary advantage. For example

Spain moved from the tenth to the fifth busiest country for international congresses in 1992, when it hosted the Summer Olympics in Barcelona, the World Exposition in Seville, and Madrid held the title of the Cultural Capital of Europe. Similarly Portugal also emerged as a popular conference (and incentive travel) destination in 1992, partly due to the overall perception of this country as a 'safe' destination in the aftermath of the Gulf War, and partly due to the fact that an incentive to the Algarve did not appear particularly extravagant during a period of belt-tightening in European companies.

In recent years, two former Eastern bloc cities – Prague and Budapest – have emerged as favourite destinations for this type of meeting. Also of note is the rise of Barcelona, showing the city's higher profile resulting from the 1992 Summer Olympiad (Rockett and Smillie 1994).

It must be remembered that the above figures represent only one part of the vast conference scene in Europe. To these must be added domestic demand for national and regional conferences as well as the vast corporate sector, which, between them account for approximately 80 per cent of the number of events (CEC 1996). At the same time, it would be wrong to play down the importance of international congresses too much. Although they are a minority of the total market in terms of actual numbers of meetings, these are the events for which many conference centres were designed; they last longer and bring many side benefits, such as focusing the spotlight of international attention on a host city (EFCT 1997a).

TRENDS IN THE EUROPEAN MEETINGS INDUSTRY

Steady growth but tougher competition

Each year, the EFCT produces a report on Europe's progress in the international meetings world, through scrutiny of over 70 leading conference towns and cities, all of them EFCT member destinations. The introduction to each report gives an interesting overview of the state of the continent's meetings business for that particular year.

The assessment of 1995 was indicative of the mid-1990s as a whole:

generally increasing growth, against a background of tough competition and a user demand for always higher standards and value for money, allied with concern about security and environmental factors.

Europe's economic recovery, though patchy, continues, and is reflected in both association and, particularly, corporate meetings.

The extended Common Market continues to stimulate meetings activity in line with the freedom of movement for capital, goods, services and people across the borders of the fifteen Member States – however imperfect these freedoms may sometimes seem. (EFCT 1996).

The same report shows that the bigger cities, such as Paris, Lyons, London, Berlin, Helsinki, Oslo, Dublin and Trieste, mostly showed an increase in the number and quality of meetings, but stressed that this trend was not confined to the big population centres, and popular destinations. For example, Brighton, Eastbourne, Bergen, Valencia, Reykjavik and many others also had a successful year.

In east/central Europe, Budapest, St Petersburg, Riga, Varna, Prague, Ljubliana and Zagreb are attracting meetings from around our global village. The end of the Bosnian War should enable Belgrade, Dubrovnic and eventually, we hope, Sarajevo to regain their past prominence on the congress map. (EFCT 1996)

Overall, taking into account all sizes of meetings, the picture which emerges is one of steady growth in Europe as a whole. The European Federation of Conference Towns' 1996 Report on Europe suggested that after a long period of recession, the conference business in Europe was returning to a degree of stability and increasing prosperity. The member towns' reports of how they fared in 1996 once again painted a general picture of 'continuing growth and increasing facilities against a background of tough competition' (EFCT 1997a).

Fewer large meetings

The Horwath Axe survey of business and conference tourism undertaken for the European Commission found that, at the European level, as on the worldwide scale, there was, by the mid-

1990s, a relative stagnation in the number of large events. This almost certainly reflected the downward trend in the worldwide number of international association meetings. The 47th Union of International Associations' survey covering 1995 reported a 2.99 per cent decrease over the previous year in international meetings and national meetings with large international participation. Counting only meetings organised by international associations, the figure fell -3.59 per cent compared with the previous year. Only Asia and Australasia recorded an upward trend.

Correspondingly, there has been an increase in the number of smaller meetings (to the benefit of hotels). In parallel, the average duration of events is shortening, and the content becoming increasingly scientific and technical (CEC 1996).

Shorter lead times

Lead times, the length of the period from the booking of the venue until the date of the event, have been shrinking since the early 1990s, as buyers attempt to have more negotiating power with venues increasingly desperate for business. Buyers realise that, with the over-supply in Europe's stock of conference and meetings venues, they can safely take the risk of finding all venues fully booked for the required dates.

Most of the professional conference organisers (PCOs) interviewed for an EIU study undertaken by Rockett and Smillie identified booking lead times as the area of most dramatic change that has occured in the market for meetings and conferences over the past few years.

> It used to be taken for granted that the meetings business would book some six months to a year before the event date, but booking time has shrunk considerably. One of the PCOs interviewed for this study reported arranging a meeting in Vienna for 500 delegates four weeks before the event. (Rockett and Smillie 1994)

Less ostentation

Most observers note permanent changes in spending levels and client expectations, as many of the practices brought about by the recession continue to characterise buyers' patterns of behaviour in

Europe. The UK trade body, the Meetings Industry Association, for example, sees organisers 'still negotiating aggressively' over accommodation, facility and meal rates, and prepared to spend more time than before in selecting the right venue (Financial Times 1996a).

Summers, in the same *Financial Times* article (1996a), also quotes the general manager of a conference hotel: 'It is doubtful if there will ever be a return to three-course lunches with wine. Meetings remain short and provide as much impact as possible. Delegates only stay overnight if it's essential.'

Ostentation and entertainment and travel for their own sake went out of favour during the recession and remain so. 'Nobody wants to be associated with anything that could be seen as a jolly, holiday or freebie' (*ibid.*). More business and less tourism would seem to be the order of the day throughout the European business community.

More technology

An increasing requirement for specialised audio-visual equipment and information systems equipment is a further noteworthy recent trend in the meetings and conference sectors. It has been explained by the fact that the consumer has become more sophisticated in terms of technology and therefore has more sophisticated needs in the meetings environment. Facilities throughout Europe are becoming much more sophisticated, with increasing emphasis on the provision of communications equipment and services as part of the tenancy 'package'. The concept of the venue as an empty black box is losing its appeal, largely because customers have demanded certain features as standard, for example good sound and lighting, effective simultaneous interpretation equipment and – most of all – venue staff who are trained in the provision of meeting facilities.

But Summers quotes the managing director of the UK-based Event Organisation Company, who echoes the belief of many buyers and suppliers in this sector, in maintaining that the importance of face-to-face contact will continue to sustain the conference and meetings industry, as well as the exhibition sector. 'Video-conferencing, E-mail or the Web will never replace physical networking' (Financial Times 1996a).

Eastern Europe

In the 1990s, several East and Central European countries became active competitors in the international meetings markets, offering a range of new facilities to attract conference organisers and other decision-makers.

The Ljubljana (Slovenia) contribution to the European Federation of Conference Towns 1996 annual report is representative of the kind of progress made by many Central and East European cities in the conference business, during the 1990s:

> The gradual growth of the conference business in Ljubljana has been favoured by the strengthening of Slovenia's identity, its progressive inclusion in international, intergovernmental and professional organisations, the opening up of the Slovenian economy, and the country's political, economic and social stability . . . Due to a growing interest in 'new' Central European destinations and the active participation of local scientists in international associations, Ljubljana has good bookings in the forthcoming years, including conferences previously organised in top European convention cities.
>
> New developments in the hotel infrastructure include a 280-room 5-star Sheraton, under construction alongside the World Trade Centre, with multi-purpose conference and banqueting facilities. Its opening is planned in late summer 1998. As a complement to the existing meeting facilities, this will make the World Trade Centre district the second largest conference venue in the city. (EFCT 1997b)

Easy access is an important asset in the international meetings market, and so for Slovenia, establishing regular air links with the rest of Europe has been a matter of the utmost priority. Within six years of the country's independence, national carrier Adria Airways, a feeder airline to both Lufthansa and Swissair, has developed a network of regular scheduled services to major European cities.

Outlook

The outlook for conference activity in Europe's cities is on the whole a positive one. Three main factors justify this measured optimism.

1 In spite of a strong increase in competition from destinations in the Asia-Pacific region, prospects for the European market are helped by the fact that 80 per cent of current demand for meetings in Europe is domestic (CEC 1996). Jakarta is simply not a contender in the competition for which venue the Lytham St Anne's Rotary Club will choose for its annual general meeting and dinner and dance. Europe has a buoyant captive market composed of association and corporate events at this level.

2 Physical travel throughout Europe has become easier and faster in many cases, aided by the opening of the Channel Tunnel and the development of high-speed train services linking many of the main business centres in Europe. Where time is money, the speed and ease with which business travellers can get to and back from their meetings is a powerful argument in favour of face-to-face interaction as opposed to conducting business by fax, phone and teleconferencing.

3 The impact of the EU. According to the European Federation of Conference Towns (EFCT), the EU 'has boosted the European conference scene. The freer movement of people, capital, goods and services across the fifteen participating nations has simpified many aspects of meetings marketing and management' (EFCT 1997b). The level of EU interest in this sector is considerable, and further evidence of the European Commission's involvement is discussed at the end of this chapter.

Background

It is indicative of the degree of fragmentation which exists in business tourism that each market sector is represented by its own association, and often by more than one. In the meetings industry alone, a confusing proliferation of international organisations and alliances exist, including, for example:

- EFCT: European Federation of Conference Towns
- AIPC: l'Association Internationale des Palais de Congrès
- IACC: International Association of Conference Centres
- ICCA: International Congress and Convention Association
- IACVB: International Association of Convention and Visitor Bureaux (Rockett and Smillie 1994)

Smith (1991) describes the role of each of these organisations in detail. This case study examines the role of the European Federation of Conference Towns (EFCT).

The Federation was inaugurated in 1964 by a far-sighted group of Europeans as a focal point for the European meetings industry and to promote Europe as a conference destination. It also had the objective of helping meeting planners to find the right destination for them anywhere in Europe, for their next event.

Now with members in 33 countries, the EFCT has become a prominent international trade association and the centre of a network playing a significant role in the international meetings world.

EFCT activities

- Support of its members in international competition
- Worldwide publicity by means of joint brochures and actions
- Exchange of information on past and future events, of experience and ideas, of studies and publications on conferences, exhibition and incentive travel
- Collaboration with international authorities, associations and institutions
- Advance training of relevant specialists through the organisation of courses and exchange visits
- A professional advisory service to meeting planners, incentive travel and exhibition organisers and other users

Conditions of membership

The European conference cities and towns that comprise the EFCT have gained membership through satisfying a number of strict criteria. They must be able to show that they:

- have conference facilities which can accommodate at least 300 participants, with proper equipment and providing the usual services;
- have satisfactory hotel accommodation for at least 300 participants;
- are able to provide the latter with necessary transportation;
- have a team of experts in conference organisation;
- can furnish proof that they have hosted in a satisfactory manner at least five international conferences during the previous three years;
- are in a country to and from which freedom of travelling is assured.

Members

There are three different types of member of the EFCT:

1. *Full members*: European conference towns which fulfil the conditions for membership
2. *Affiliated members*: A national association of conference towns of which at least five cities of its country are full members
3. *Associated members*: Non-European towns which fulfil the conditions for membership.

Sales support

One of the principal benefits which membership brings is a range of services in the form of sales support. The main services are:

The EFCT Directory

This annual publication goes to over 10,000 meetings planners around the world. It lists every member town and outlines the various facilities and services they provide. Using this, organisers can personally contact the key people in conference centres in member towns and cities in Europe.

EFCT on the Internet

EFCT's new directory of European destinations is now

continued

available through the Internet and can be exploited 24 hours a day. Anyone connected can call up the Directory and search for EFCT cities (http://www.efct.com).

Trade shows

Cooperative booths are arranged at trade shows such as Confex, EIBTM, etc. These enable members to be present at a lower cost than if they were to have their own exhibit. EFCT also provides back-up by directing buyers to members who do have their own exhibits or are part of a national presence.

Marketing clinic

This is open to all members and enables them to make contact with any sort of marketing problems they may have. It is frequently used by members who need a language or editorial check for new publications.

The EFCT and EU tourism policy

EU legislation has the potential to exert an important influence on the development of the conference industry in Europe, for good or for bad. For this reason, forthcoming EU legislation needs to be carefully and constantly scrutinised by those who could be affected by it. As the EFCT states: 'The EU seldom legislates with our industry in view, but what does emerge can often inhibit conference activity' (EFCT 1996).

Over the years, the EFCT has developed a close relationship with the EU institutions in Brussels, Strasbourg and Luxembourg. In 1994, a permanent EFCT Liaison Office was created in Brussels, dedicated to close contact with the EU in all its facets and especially with DGXXIII.

This office has enabled the EFCT to look at pending legislation and to make representation to avoid aspects that might hinder the conference business. It does this in collaboration with other professional bodies including the International Association of Professional Conference Organisers, the International Congress and Convention Association and Meetings Planners International, through a joint forum, the European Meetings Industry Liaison Group (EMILG).

The EMILG has been able to provide advice and guidance on specific industry matters. For example, they were leaders in the movement against the draft EU legislation concerned with Distance Selling. This was a consumer protection measure essentially designed to protect those purchasing items from catalogues, by telephone, etc. However, due to the wording of the original draft legislation, the directive could have left operators in the business tourism and leisure tourism sectors extremely vulnerable to unscrupulous clients claiming refunds. The onus would have been on the tour operator or conference centre management, for example, to prove that the client had had a satisfactory holiday or conference. This was considerably amended as a result of pressure from organisations representing sectors of the tourism industry, including the EFCT.

The EFCT has, however, in common with many other trade associations in the tourism industry as a whole, registered a number of disappointments with the lack of recognition for this sector within the EU. It supported the campaign for tourism to be accepted as a competency of the European Union, for example; and in its Report on 1996, the EFCT regretted the fact that the EU's proposed Philoxenia programme, which would have provided the leisure and business tourism industries with marketing and promotional support of 25 million EUROS over several years (see page 69) had not been approved (EFCT 1997b).

Incentive travel

THE USE OF INCENTIVE TRAVEL

In the increasingly competitive global marketplace, Europe's executives and sales staff constantly need to be urged on to make extra efforts in order to perform to their full capacity. A useful management tool, incentive travel is widely recognised as an effective means of rewarding and motivating employees. Its effectiveness can be partly explained by its popularity with the 'award-winners' themselves: it would appear that no matter how frequently participants travel on business as part of their job, for them incentive travel ranks with cash bonuses and other motivational tools such as performance/profit-related pay as a highly desired reward for achieving higher sales figures or reaching/exceeding a performance target.

Incentive travel is essentially composed of memorable and enjoyable trips paid for by the traveller's company. Although such trips may have the external appearance of leisure holidays or short breaks, they count very much as business tourism due to the very specific, work-related purpose which lies behind them. Incentive travel has been defined by the Society of Incentive Travel Executives as: 'A modern management tool used to accomplish uncommon business goals by awarding participants an extraordinary travel experience upon their attainment of their share of these goals'. This form of business tourism often takes the form of group travel, participants travelling with other award winners, with or without their spouses/partners. The trip may also involve a seminar or conference, or at the very least, a 'pep-talk' from the managing director. Those on incentive trips are particularly targeted by the destinations and tourism facilities because they generate a significantly higher spend per head than other business tourism sectors, in the order of ECU 400 to ECU 800 per day per participant (CEC 1996).

The use of travel as an incentive to motivating employees began in the US at the beginning of the twentieth century, but only gained a foothold in Europe in the 1970s, first in the UK, then around ten years later in continental Europe. Market estimates suggest that the West European incentive travel market was worth ECU 1.4 billion in 1995, a figure which accounted for less than 5 per cent of all European business travel expenditure (O'Brien 1997).

However, progress in the growth of incentive travel in Europe has not been rapid, and it was fairly devastated by the Gulf War recession of the early 1990s, when major companies pared their travel and promotion budgets, causing many small incentive travel organising companies to go out of business. The incentive travel market was also affected by the recession of the early 1990s, but by 1993, this sector had begun to show signs of recovery as big corporations across Europe found new budgets and regained confidence in prize travel as

an essential staff motivator. Since then, it has been growing by around 3–4 per cent a year.

INBOUND INCENTIVE TRAVEL TO EUROPE FROM OTHER CONTINENTS

(*Note*: Much of the following information on the characteristics of the incentive travel market is based on the market study *Incentive Travel Usage and its Impact on the UK and Ireland* (October 1996) conducted jointly by Travel Business Consulting and the Gordon Simmons Research Group for the British Tourist Authority, English Tourist Board, Northern Ireland Tourist Board, the Scottish Tourist Board, the Wales Tourist Board and Bord Failte Eireann, and as reproduced in the Travel and Tourism Intelligence report on the West European Incentive Travel market (O'Brien 1997). Survey data were collected from 215 interviews with British, German, Italian, Irish and US companies which purchase incentive travel as well as interviews with a sample of incentive travel houses. Data source references to this study are abbreviated in the text to the *1996 Incentive Travel Usage and Impact study*.)

The European incentive travel sector is heavily dependent, for business, on the US market – still the largest incentive travel market in the world. According to the Howarth Axe survey, US companies generate about 5.7 million incentive trips per year, compared with 1.5 million for European businesses. Europe benefits from this market, since it has been the primary international destination for US incentive groups since the 1960s. The US outbound incentive travel market accounts for close to half of all incentive travel visitors to Western Europe (O'Brien 1997).

The attractions of the incoming incentive travel market are the relatively high spending characteristics of incentive visitors from the USA and other long haul destinations. These visitors to Europe mainly use 4- and 5-star hotels and stay for an average of seven days.

But, it would appear that during the 1990s, even the US market has become more cost conscious. While at the end of the 1980s it was not uncommon for massive incentive programmes to bring over 500 visitors to Europe at a time, ten years later the average group size for US incentive trips to Europe was between 100 and 200 people. And although their employers still pay for all aspects of the incentive trip, 'it is noticeable that costs are being reduced by allowing visitors to have more free time to do their own shopping' (ibid.).

For the US market, Europe is perceived as a luxury, top-end of the market destination. Incentive travel organisers therefore seek venues which offer quality facilities and which will create a memorable experience for award-winners. The major cities of Europe are popular venues – most notably, for the US incentive travel market, London, Edinburgh, Paris, Amsterdam, Madrid and Dublin – and many historic castles, country manors, spa resorts and casinos across the continent also compete effectively in this market.

INTRA-EUROPEAN INCENTIVE TRAVEL

The *1996 Incentive Travel Usage and Impact Study* (O'Brien 1997) enables us to draw a number of interesting comparisons between the US market for incentive travel and the short-haul intra-European incentive travel market. The most notable characteristic of the latter is that although the trips are still regarded as a reward for performance, European companies do not tend to regard incentive travel as an out-and-out perk. Rather, European companies attempt to obtain maximum value from the trip. Hence, 3- and 4-star accommodation is more often booked than 5-star hotels; many trips take place at the weekend, in order to minimise disruption at work; the average European incentive trip lasts four nights (typically Thursday to Sunday), with a budget of around ECU 930 for accommodation and ground arrangements but excluding transport costs; European incentive groups also tend to be smaller, averaging 40–50 people. Unlike the US market which is dominated by visits to core cultural and heritage attractions, European incentives are often based on sports and hunting types of programmes and a greater emphasis is placed on the composition of activities during the incentive trip, rather than on the type and cost of accommodation provided. Those activities are also increasingly likely to include non-leisure elements such as a conference or visit to a factory, site or business, since a growing number of European companies deliberately build in work elements in order to achieve better value from their incentive travel budgets (O'Brien 1997).

In Europe, the incentive travel market is dominated by the UK, France, Germany and Italy. However, the Scandinavian countries, Austria, Belgium and Spain are rapidly developing as incentive travel generating countries. (In the Scandinavian countries, as the author of the 1997 Travel and Tourism Intelligence survey of incentive travel in Western Europe points out, the elitism implied by incentive travel goes against the work ethos, especially in Sweden. Where travel is awarded, it tends to be offered to practically everybody in the company, and as a result, incentive travel is closer in nature to a company outing than a US-style incentive trip.)

Table 6.5 details the size of the main European markets for incentive travel, together with an estimate of the total Western European market.

THE MAIN INTRA-EUROPEAN MARKETS

One contrast which emerges from Table 6.5 is that between the extent of domestic incentive travel in the UK and that of the other three major markets. UK companies tend not to regard the home market

Table 6.5 Size of domestic and outbound incentive travel markets, 1995

Country	Ecu mn	Proportion of incentive market spend on domestic travel (%)
UK	424.46	7
Germany	385.92	40
Italy	274.47	45
France	164.36	40
Rest of Western Europe	132.28	na
Total West Europe	1,381.49	na

Source: O'Brien, K. (1997)

as an appropriate destination for their award-winners, instead prefering to send them to overseas destinations in France, Germany, Spain and Italy. Long-haul destinations favoured by UK companies for their high achievers are the US and the Caribbean, although interest in Far Eastern destinations is growing rapidly.

In Germany, despite the impact of the cost of re-unification and the recession, expenditure on incentive travel remained buoyant throughout the 1990s. However, the recession did restrict incentive travel budgets and force German companies to run more incentive programmes within Europe, and particularly within Germany itself (two-thirds of German companies include the home country as an option when considering a number of incentive travel destinations). Another characteristic of the German market is that a high proportion of incentive travel arrangements are handled internally by the company, rather than via third parties such as travel agents and incentive travel houses. Both the Italian and the French markets are characterised by strong domestic markets, followed by other European destinations. However, by the mid-1990s, there were signs of moves towards shorter incentive trips being sought by Italian companies, as well as a degree of trading down on hotel accommodation. Regarding the French market, it is thought that the value of this might be understated, as French companies tend to play down their involvement in the incentive travel market for reasons of tax avoidance (O'Brien 1997).

Throughout Europe, the major buyers of incentive programmes remain as they always have been, the automotive, financial services, pharmaceutical, office equipment, electronics and consumer durables sectors (European 1995) – all extremely competitive sectors, where maintaining or increasing market share demands constant exhortations to greater efforts on the part of the salesforce and management.

At the level of individual companies, in 44 per cent of the businesses surveyed for the *1996 Incentive Travel Usage and Impact Study*, company chairmen/women and director-level personnel were found to be the most important decision-makers in the selection of the destination for the incentive programme. Sales, marketing and commercial managers selected the destinations in a further 33 per cent of companies. Incentive travel budgets tended to be allocated from either the sales or marketing departmental budgets. Hence, incentive travel programmes – along with other motivational tools, most notably cash bonuses and profit-related pay schemes – compete internally for budgeting against other competing calls on the sales and marketing budgets (O'Brien 1997).

INCENTIVE TRAVEL DESTINATIONS

How are destinations for incentive travel programmes selected? For the European market, budget and cost consideration have been found by the Travel and Tourism Intelligence survey to be the most important determinants in the decision process, being mentioned by 34 per cent of companies. Exotic destinations were the second most mentioned influence (by 8 per cent of respondents), followed by the availability of sports/recreational facilities (6 per cent), climate and ease of transport (5 per cent each). In comparison, the US incentive travel market places less emphasis on programme cost but more on geographical considerations such as climate (67 per cent), the availability of recreational facilities (67 per cent), sightseeing and cultural attractions (58 per cent).

The USA and Europe remain the key geographic destinations for incentive travel, while the Far East, Australia, Eastern Europe and the Caribbean all attract consideration as potential incentive destinations within the selection process. Table 6.6 shows the prefered European incentive destinations of the companies taking part in the *1996 Incentive Travel Usage and Impact Study*.

THE EU AND INCENTIVE TRAVEL

The Directive on Package Travel has had an impact on the organising of incentive travel. Whereas previously, hoteliers were free to put together and market incentive packages, they now have to be bonded (see page 50) if they offer two or more components, for example, accommodation and a day's golf or clay pigeon shoot. Alternatively, hoteliers can leave the actual packaging up to incentive agents and other professional organisations (Caterer and Hotelkeeper 1993).

Table 6.6 Destination ratings for the top incentive travel destinations, 1996

Attractiveness of destinations in Europe for incentive trips	Ratings[1]
London	7.5
Paris	7.2
Vienna	7.2
Rome	7.0
French Riviera	6.9
Venice	6.8
Switzerland	6.6
Athens & the Greek Islands	6.6
Barcelona	6.5

Note: [1] Ratings are scored out of 10
Source: Source: O'Brien, K. (1997)

TRENDS

Cost consciousness

As is the case for the conference and general travel sector of the business tourism industry, incentive travel buyers' cost-conscious attitudes have continued even after the end of the recession of the early 1990s.

One indicator of this is the trend in choice of destinations for incentive trips. According to the Horwath Axe business and conference tourism survey for the European Commission, European companies' incentive trips, having favoured long-haul destinations in the 1980s, were returning to the European and, in particular, Mediterranean regions (short or medium haul trips) by the mid-1990s. The survey report noted that due to the costs incurred and the economic context of recession, companies tended to favour less prestigious and expensive destinations, putting emphasis, instead, on the quality of the organisation and content of the programme. To this end, the European destinations have had the opportunity to reposition themselves in this market segment (CEC 1996).

These findings were echoed by Sarah Webster,

executive director of the London-based Incentive Travel and Meetings Association: 'one trend is companies being more prudent with their incentive spend, compared with the pre-recessionary 1980s . . . The long-haul market has shown no real sign of growth, but many more companies are providing incentives either domestically or within Europe to a broader range of staff rather than just the very top achievers' (European 1995).

Nevertheless, as the 1997 Travel and Tourism Intelligence survey of incentive travel in Western Europe notes, both flight and accommodation costs associated with long-haul travel, for example, to the Asia-Pacific region were falling by the mid-1990s, making long-haul travel, for all purposes, an increasingly competitive product: 'In the long term, larger aircraft offering both lower seat rates and faster journey times will make the long haul markets more competitive in incentive travel, but this will not occur before 2001' (O'Brien 1997).

More generally, the same survey noted that even although the incentive travel market was still growing by an estimated 3–4 per cent a year in Europe by the mid-1990s, this growth had been achieved 'against a background of tighter negotiations with suppliers to drive down average travel costs. As a result, the European incentive travel market is growing significantly, but corporate belt-tightening in Europe, particularly in France, Germany and Italy, is influencing the market. Tougher supplier negotiations and selective reductions in the standard of accommodation mean that there are more European incentive travellers but that average rates per traveller are falling' (O'Brien 1997).

Market growth

Webster's point above, concerning the extension of incentive travel awards to include a wider range of employees, is worthy of note. Elaborating on this point, she adds that: 'Incentives such as luxury spa weekends are also being geared more towards women as premier prize winners. Women will soon represent up to 50 per cent of the market.' Companies appear to be increasingly aware of the importance of motivating not only those 'out in the field' selling their products, but also those on whom their sales staff depend for support, back at base. It will be interesting to see whether, indeed, this trend towards awarding incentive trips to secreataries and administrative staff, for example, will continue in the face of a general squeeze on spending.

The 1997 Travel and Tourism Intelligence survey of incentive travel in Western Europe also forecast growth in the market from other European countries, such as Austria, the Benelux countries and Spain, which it considered were set to join the UK, Germany, France and Italy as major generators of demand for this form of business tourism. The same survey estimated that ten years after its publication, Eastern Europe would also represent an important market for incentive travel (O'Brien 1997).

Another possible source of growth is thought by many to be the USA incentive travel market, as a rising number of US companies look to hold more of their incentive trips abroad. Time will tell how much of this market Europe can capture, but by the mid-1990s, a number of European Destination Management Companies specialising in the US market were reporting that group sizes were increasing again, and Europe was set to host a number of major incentive events involving groups of up to 500 participants in the period up to 1998 (O'Brien 1997).

Changing trends in destinations for incentive travel

Apart from the general trend towards European companies selecting cities and resorts nearer home for their award-winners, a number of other changes have been identified regarding their choice of destinations.

Eastern Europe

At the beginning of the 1990s, Eastern Europe was considered by many to be the part of Europe showing the greatest potential for expansion as an incentive travel destination (Davidson 1992a). However, although many parts of Eastern Europe did succeed in establishing themselves as incentive travel destinations, towards the end of that decade, commentators were predicting that the popularity of Eastern Europe as an incentive travel destination may soon wane . . . In the past, Eastern Europe was regarded as an exciting new destination and allowances were made for the lack of tourism infrastructure there because of the (then) new economic and political circumstances. However, Eastern Europe has become an expensive incentive travel region and one that will find it increasingly hard to justify its high costs given that it can no longer be considered a new destination. (O'Brien 1997).

New destinations

Choice of destinations for incentive travel is influenced by many factors, including the all-important one of novelty value. New destinations and types of incentives are important in order to revitalise the concept of incentive travel. Given, also, that award winners are often people who travel extensively for work-related purposes, incentive travel organisers are constantly on the look-out for new destinations or new ways in which to package well-known places.

An example of the latter is the use of the Channel Tunnel, which as a novel form of transport, was incorporated into many incentive travel programmes in the few years following its opening. The 1997 Travel and Tourism Intelligence survey of incentive travel in Western Europe noted, in particular, that the fixed link had created the phenomenon of the one-day incentive for Belgian, French and UK groups, adding that, while this was unlikely to last, it was indicative of how a new transport system can itself stimulate an incentive event.

Another, more enduring focus for incentive trips, also identified by the 1997 Travel and Tourism Intelligence survey is the cruise market, which, it is claimed, is increasingly regarded by West European buyers of incentive travel as a competitive destination option for this form of employee motivation:

The rise of cruising as an incentive travel option for the west European market (it has been popular with the US market for many years) stems from the economic benefits that cruising offers. It is now possible to block-book capacity on cruise ships twelve months ahead of the incentive programme and at guaranteed rates. The fact that all participants are ship-bound enables better coordination of both the incentive and any other company-sponsored events, and costs can be carefully controlled because food and beverages are usually contained within the negotiated rates. (O'Brien 1997)

However, as the author of the report points out, within five years, as cruising becomes more of a mass-market activity, the incentive travel industry may avoid the cruising sector, as it will no longer be perceived as exciting, new or interesting for incentive travel participants.

Finally, a number of long-haul destinations have begun targeting the European incentive market, including Australia and South Africa. The latter also offers business potential for European destinations, since it is now considered as a new incentive travel generating market, with particular interest in the UK. The Asia-Pacific incentive travel market does not yet extend to Europe, since most incentive trips offered by companies in that region tend to be short in duration (typically three days) (TTI 1997).

Outlook

It is generally acknowledged that while incentive travel in the USA is nearing maturity in marketing terms, in Europe, the market is still in the growth cycle. There is broad acceptance in the industry that Europe remains a huge potential market for this form of business tourism. As the Horwath Axe survey of business tourism in Europe said of incentive travel: 'Europe currently constitutes a considerable demand-generating resource, which remains significantly under-exploited' (CEC 1996).

Naturally, external factors play a major part in determining the volume of incentive travel undertaken in Europe. For the inbound US market, in particular, the purchasing power of the dollar against European currencies is a key consideration; while the size of European company budgets available for expenditure on intra-European incentive travel is largely determined by the state of the economy in general.

However, one commentator sees the incentive market as being under threat from two internal factors relating to employee performance and company expenditure. First, Gold (1996) points out that the incentive market is driven by clients' conviction that their employees 'could do better', or in other words, that they are not working to their full capacity. The theory behind incentives of any kind is that employees can be urged on to even greater achievements on behalf of the company if they are inspired or rewarded by travel products. But, he claims, in the increasingly competitive world of modern commerce, where employees are under more and more daily pressure to achieve better results, higher sales figures and so on, it is no longer the case that there is a great deal of unused potential in the system. As a growing number of those in employment are finding that they have to work flat-out just to hold on to their jobs, the incremental returns from sending staff on incentive trips may diminish to the extent that such awards are no longer cost effective.

Secondly, the same author predicts that companies may choose to invest in other means of making their employees more productive. He maintains that one problem with incentive travel is the short-lived nature of the benefits it brings. Accordingly, he sees the greatest threat to incentives coming from in-service staff training, which company managers increasingly consider the most effective way of increasing their employees' productivity (Gold 1996).

Exhibitions and trade fairs

THE USE OF EXHIBITIONS AND TRADE FAIRS

Exhibitions, which may also be called trade fairs or trade shows, may be defined as 'presentations of products or services to an invited audience with the object of inducing a sale or informing the visitor'. They are generally recognised to be a cost effective way of communicating information between buyers and suppliers. Without this form of communication, the efficiency of trade would be severely diminished. As an advertising medium, exhibitions play a vital role in the marketing of goods and services. They encourage domestic trade, and when foreign visitors attend them, they also promote exports.

Exhibitions are attractive to both exhibitors

EMECA Venues Economic Impact	
Gross direct expenditure 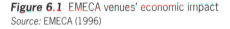	ECU 7,783 million
Visitors	44%
Exhibitors	56%
Retained income to the region	ECU 2,733 million
Jobs supported in the region	155,500
Comparators	
Average income retained per 1,000 m² of exhibition space	ECU 1,197,700
Average jobs supported per 1,000 m² of exhibition space	68

Figure 6.1 EMECA venues' economic impact
Source: EMECA (1996)

and visitors because they offer face-to-face contact in bringing together exhibitors and potential buyers. They also represent a form of 'three-dimensional' advertising where, in many instances, the product can be seen, handled, assessed by demonstration and (depending on the product) even smelled and tasted.

From the point of view of the tourist industry, the advantage of exhibitions is that they stimulate travel for two different groups of people: the exhibitors who travel to the venue and the exhibition visitors, or audience, who, except in the case of consumer shows, are most likely to be attending for work-related reasons. Both groups create a high level of demand for travel services, catering and accommodation.

THE SUPPLY OF EXHIBITION FACILITIES

Each year in Europe, over 3,000 trade fairs are staged, attracting hundreds of thousands of exhibiting companies and many millions of visitors (EMECA 1996). Compared to other types of business tourism, the exhibition market is one sector for which the supply is relatively easy to identify because of the size of facilities and the heavy investment required.

The Horwath Axe study found that countries in the EEA have, in all, about 130 exhibition complexes offering on average more than 10,000 square metres of rentable surface area – the size generally required to attract events of an international stature. Most of the overall supply is concentrated in Germany, Italy and France (CEC 1996).

The considerable economic impact of exhibition activity in Europe was highlighed by a study undertaken in 1995 by the consultants KPMG on behalf of an association of Europe's leading exhibition venues, the European Major Exhibition Centres Association (EMECA). At the time of the study, EMECA's fifteen members were exhibition centres in Barcelona, Basel, Birmingham, Bologna, Brussels, Frankfurt, Leipzig, London, Lyons, Madrid, Milan, Paris (two centres), Utrecht and Verona. Since then, Düsseldorf and Nuremburg have also entered the association.

Only EMECA members' activities were included in the study, which was, in addition, restricted to the exhibition centres' trade fair programmes only, leaving aside the many other types of events (congresses, entertainment events, etc.) also hosted by such venues. Figure 6.1 shows the results of this study.

The appraisal undertaken by KMPG reveals the economic benefits of exhibitions on regional economies, showing the aggregate impact of EMECA-related exhibition activity on the fourteen regions where EMECA members are situated. During 1995, the fifteen EMECA venues attracted gross direct expenditure of ECU 7,783 million to their regions. Of this 44 per cent was generated by visitors and 56 per cent by exhibitors. After allowing for leakages, retained income for the fourteen regions was ECU 2,733 million, which was estimated to support 155,500 jobs. This employment creation includes jobs based at the exhibition centres themselves as well as in hotels and transport services.

Naturally, the economic spin-off effects of centres' exhibition activity is not limited to the surrounding region. Most notably, exhibitions generate considerable tax revenues for governments (VAT, corporate tax, etc.), which, for the purposes of the KPMG study were included as 'leakages' outside the host regions.

THE MARKET

The European market for exhibitions and fairs corresponds to about 19 million square metres rented per year, that is between 70 per cent and 80 per cent of the world's total capacity. The total number of exhibitors is estimated at over 420,000 and the number of visitors is estimated at around 50 million (CEC 1996)

The revenue associated with exhibitions and fairs in Europe is considerable, resulting from direct expenditure of visitors and exhibitors during their stay, but particularly from the spending linked to the hire of equipment and services for exhibition stands.

Figure 6.2 shows the main meetings and exhibitions regions of Europe.

The bar chart in Figure 6.3 shows the largest exhibition centres in Europe by volume. As Figure 6.3 indicates, exhibitions and trade fairs represent one sector of the tourism industry where German dominance is undisputed. Germany has three of the world's five biggest exhibition centres and claims to host two-thirds of the 150 leading international fairs. Apart from the three leading cities, every major German town boasts its exhibition centre (*Messe*) and local economies often move to the rhythm of big fairs.

In 1995, German trade fairs attracted record numbers of exhibitors and visitors, partly because several big fairs coincided. Exhibition centres had revenues of DM3.2 billion (US$2.2 billion) and generated another DM 11 billion or so in business for hotels, taxis, restaurants and shops in host cities, according to the Association of German Fairs.

Part of the secret of Germany's success is that, under the current arrangements, most fairgrounds are owned by city and state governments, who carry most of the property costs and employ their own fair organisers. This means that the exhibition centres are not under pressure to reap financial rewards from ticket sales or the amount of space they rent, but instead are recognised as important instruments for boosting the local economy. That helps Germany to out-compete France and Britain, where property owners expect a decent return.

Table 6.7 shows the top ten German trade fair venues for 1995, by turnover and visitors.

New and bigger fairgrounds are on the way. Rentable space in Germany grew by 17 per cent between 1990 and 1995, and was expected to increase by a further 7–10 per cent in the five years leading up to the year 2000, as *Messen* planned to invest more than DM5billion in new buildings and modernisation (Economist 1996).

Leipzig, once the showcase of East European industry, opened a DM1.3 billion exhibition centre in April 1996, replacing the old fairgrounds located near the centre of the city which, under the Communists, had for years hosted two annual fairs, attracting mostly East European enterprises. Like Germany's other trade and conference centres, it benefited from generous financing by the city and state authorities. About DM500 million of the construction costs were raised from selling off part of the old fairgrounds. Ownership of the new fairground is shared between the city and the state of Saxony, who also shared the remainder of the construction costs as well (Financial Times 1996c).

In 1996, *The Economist* reported that Berlin's fairgrounds were to expand capacity by 60 per cent before the end of the century, and that some DM800 million was to be spent in upgrading the *Deutsche Messe* in Hanover, the world's biggest, and the services around it, in order to prepare for the EXPO 2000 exhibition. (The Hanover exhibition centre has a dedicated high-speed train link to Würzburg in the south.)

In expanding to this extent, exhibition centres insist that they are merely responding to the

Figure 6.2 Meeting and exhibition industry in Europe
Source: CEC (1996)

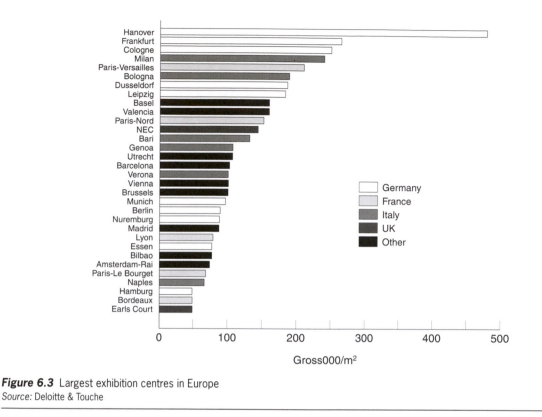

Figure 6.3 Largest exhibition centres in Europe
Source: Deloitte & Touche

market. The leading fairs are demanding more space; fairgrounds that fail to provide it risk losing business to other cities. Berlin, for example, claimed that it could have rented 30 per cent more space than it had available for the 1995 *Funkausstellung* (a biennial fair which bills itself as the world's biggest consumer electronics show for the general public). But the problem is that constructing extra space for such blockbuster exhibitions leaves the exhibition centre with spare capacity which, to be profitable, has to be filled by other events as well.

The Economist (1996) reports that one solution to this problem being used in Germany is that of poaching events from other exhibition centres. Therefore, despite generous support from the city and state, Germany's fairs are beginning to compete with each other for exhibitors, visitors and profits. For example, the article reports, Berlin hopes to snare an international car show from Frankfurt, and Stuttgart wants to win back a toy fair from Nuremberg once it expands.

However, it is clear that such beggar-my-neigh-bour tactics cannot enrich the whole business. Another answer is to fill the space with new fairs. Berlin hosted five new events in 1996, including one for kindergartens and another for the food and hotel industry, featuring a culinary Olympics for big-name chefs.

But as Dempsey (Financial Times 1996c) points out, an uncertain future hangs over fairgrounds in Germany because the cities and states may soon be no longer able to afford to continue to subsidise or own them and thus insulate them from genuine competition. Germany's towns and cities expected an overall deficit of DM11.9 billion in 1996. At the same time, they were being pressed by the federal authorities in Bonn to privatise or contract out certain services, from refuse collection to the maintenance of swimming pools and playgrounds. There is no reason to suppose that exhibition centres will not be subject to the same discipline. Trade fairs are beginning to realise the pressures they will have to face increasingly in the near future.

Germany's fairs are changing in another way as

well. The days when each fair could flag itself as the annual event for toys, furniture, cars or computers are over. With budgetary restrictions being the order of the day, exhibition centres are beginning to diversify and come up with more ideas to generate an income and make space earn a living. It is no longer the case that one place can be synonymous with one event, leaving the facilities unused for most of the year. Consequently, Leipzig's 1996 programme included as usual its international automobile fair in April, but this was followed by nineteen other events, on themes ranging from multimedia to the conservation of old buildings (Financial Times 1996c).

Figure 6.4 shows that Germany is not only the European country with the greatest supply of large exhibition centres – more than its nearest two rivals, France and Italy put together – but that it is also the country where the greatest demand for this form of business tourism exists.

TRENDS

Sustained growth

During the recession in Europe, and throughout the Western world, in 1993 and 1994, almost all sectors reduced their level of expenditure on exhibitions. However, the vast majority continued to participate, confirming their trust in this form of communication (EMECA 1996).

By 1996, the exhibition and fairs market was found to be experiencing sustained growth, greater than the growth of tourism as a whole (CEC 1996). Figures for the fifteen EMECA members shown in Figure 6.5 indicate the progression made between 1993 and 1995, in terms of numbers of exhibitions, numbers of exhibitors, numbers of visitors and gross exhibition area rented.

While the number of trade fairs at these exhibition centres increased by 3 per cent between 1993 and 1995, the number of exhibitors and visitors rose by 9 per cent and 12 per cent respectively. Between 1995 and 1996, growth for the EMECA members' business continued, with the number of exhibitions rising from 874 to 1000 (EMECA 1997).

Table 6.7 Top ten German fairs, 1995

	Turnover (DM mn)	Visitors (mn)
Düsseldorf	450	1.8
Frankfurt	420	2.4
Hanover	380	2.3
Cologne	363	1.3
Munich	273	2.3
Berlin	211	1.3
Stuttgart	158	1.4
Leipzig	90	0.7
Nuremburg	81	1.3
Hamburg	60	1.2

Source: © The Economist, London, 20 January 1996

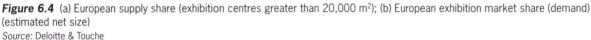

Figure 6.4 (a) European supply share (exhibition centres greater than 20,000 m²); (b) European exhibition market share (demand) (estimated net size)
Source: Deloitte & Touche

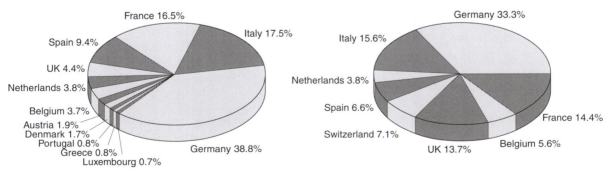

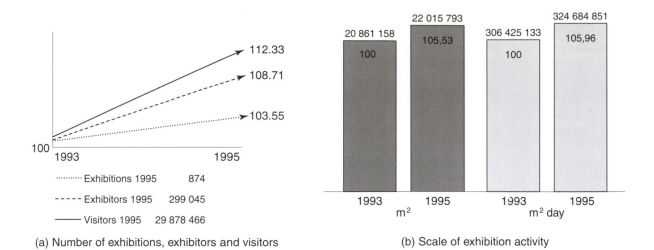

(a) Number of exhibitions, exhibitors and visitors

(b) Scale of exhibition activity

Figure 6.5 (a) Number of exhibitions, exhibitors and visitors; (b) Scale of exhibition activity (gross exhibition area rented by centres (base=100... 1993)
Source: EMECA (1996)

Eastern Europe

Will growth in the exhibitions market lead to an increase in demand for such events in Eastern Europe? Investment in the necessary infrastructure and transport systems would appear to be just as essential a prerequisite for success in this sector, as in the other tourism sectors, in the emergent democracies of Eastern Europe.

Summers (Financial Times 1996a) quotes the chairman of Reed Exhibition Companies, who expressed the belief that Eastern European markets were showing promise, but that there were still many obstacles to be overcome. 'For example, it may be difficult to establish security of tenure in halls and there can be confusion over who owns or is in charge of renting out space. In a number of cases, the condition of the halls themselves leaves a lot to be desired.' Nevertheless, according to their chairman, Reed expects to be in 'one, possibly two significant Eastern European markets in the next one to two years'.

New types of exhibition centre

Could the future signal an end to German dominance of this sector? Recent trends suggest that the massive exhibition centres, which were the key to German supremacy in this sector of business tourism, may be in the process of becoming increasingly unsuitable for the type of exhibitions which are now being held in Europe. In their survey of the exhibitions industry, consultants Touche Ross noted that it was no longer the case that exhibition activity was concentrated in so-called 'blockbuster' exhibition centres in central Europe: 'In future, quite the opposite trend is likely to prevail, with a focus on quality rather than quantity, and on specialisation rather than volume, with central Europe threatened to be left with an oversupply of very large, inefficient, inflexible, exhibition centres.' The consultants also noted a fundamental change in the nature of exhibitions, with 'a trend towards niche marketing, the integration of other media, and the need for exhibitions to become more involved in buyer education, as product life-cycles reduce. This requires a new type of exhibition centre designed for flexibility of use and integrated with conference and seminar facilities' (Touche Ross 1994). Their findings are particularly relevant to the following case study.

The UK as an international exhibitions venue

As a venue for international exhibitions, the UK has some outstanding advantages. English, as the language used worldwide for multicultural business negotiations, is a strong asset for the UK, particularly for North Americans wishing to base themselves there for an event. Travel by air is straightforward, given the UK's position at the world's largest airline crossroads, while the Channel Tunnel has improved communications with Continental Europe. Cultural, historical, rural and 'heritage' attractions add to the UK's appeal for business visitors who combine their trip with some time-off for leisure pursuits, and these play an important part in the promotion of the UK as a business tourism destination. On the other hand, in general, the UK is not a favoured location for international events, because of its position away from the geographic centre of Europe.

Nevertheless, many professionals argue that, compared with its EU partners, the UK has been slow to invest in exhibition facilities, and that this is most evident in London, where facilities for world-standard events remain extremely limited by comparison with those available in other European capitals.

Among these is the chairman of Reed Exhibition Companies, a division of the Anglo-Dutch publisher Reed Elsevier, who in 1996 described as a 'scandal' the fact that the capital had not, until recently, 'got behind a plan that will deliver a major purpose-built venue'. The consequence, he added is that the UK was 'in terms of quality and size of space, way behind continental Europe and America' (Financial Times 1996b).

Compared to many of their European counterparts, UK exhibition venues are generally quite modest in scale. There are only a handful of venues with more than 10,000 m^2 of space and the market is dominated by the National Exhibition Centre, Olympia and Earls Court. Most exhibition centres are multi-purpose, hosting a wide variety of sporting events, product launches, pop concerts, conferences and other spectator activities (Beioley 1991).

One reason for this difference between the UK and the rest of Western Europe is no doubt political. In Continental Europe, there is a greater acceptance of the notion that exhibition centres are justified through their ability to generate jobs and significant regional income, rather than as fully commercial entities in their own right. Such beliefs account for the high degree of public sector investment in such facilities and, in many cases, the provision of on-going financial support. During the 1980s and much of the 1990s, such an approach was incompatible with the political climate in the UK.

Supply and demand in the UK

In 1994, the London Docklands Development Corporation commissioned consultants Touche Ross to conduct research into the supply and demand of exhibition space in Europe viewed from a UK perspective. This was to be carried out with a view to assessing the extent of the potential demand for an exhibition centre located at the Royal Victoria Dock, East London.

The research revealed the following characteristics of the demand for exhibitions in the UK:

1 Currently the total demand (per capita) for exhibitions in the UK is comparable with that of other countries in Western Europe, with the exception of Germany, where demand is higher.
2 The demand for exhibitions in the UK shows a high degree of correlation with the growth or decline of the economy. Demand in the UK declined by around 25 per cent between 1990 and the mid-1990s, although this should be viewed in the context of a market which doubled between 1983 and 1990. (The consultants predicted that as the UK economy moved out of recession, it could be expected that demand would pick up again and that, by the late 1990s, there would be a shortage of exhibition space.)

Concerning the supply of exhibition centres in the UK, the Touche Ross researchers reported that:

1 The UK has only a 4.4 per cent share of the European supply of large exhibition centres, but represents 13.7 per cent of European demand for

continued

exhibitions and trade fairs (see Figure 6.4, page 199).

2 The imbalance between demand and supply in the UK exists at all levels, but is less marked among the largest exhibition centres (greater than 100,000 m^2) and among the smaller centres (less than 20,000 m^2). The imbalance between demand and supply is therefore most significant in the 'middle' sized range, where the market opportunities are consequently greatest.

The major UK venues for exhibitions and trade fairs are shown in Table 6.8:

At almost 160,000 m^2, the National Exhibition Centre (NEC) in Birmingham is a large centre, by European standards, but it hosts relatively few international events compared with continental European venues of a similar size.

On the other hand, few exhibition centres of less than 20,000 m^2 in Europe achieve a genuine return on investment. Though there may be a demand for these smaller centres from a public amenity point of view,

the consultants advised that any such development in the Docklands would need to accept that public amenity rather than profitability was the primary purpose. (It was on this basis that a previous scheme, the London Dome project was put forward, but failed to secure sufficient funding.)

Touche Ross' conclusion was that there was a particular shortage of supply of exhibition centres in the UK of between 50,000 m^2 and 100,000 m^2. There is only one exhibition centre in the UK which can satisfy the demand for exhibitions in this size range: Earls Court. Moreover, the Touche Ross research indicates that exhibition revenue, per m^2, in larger centres is around three times the equivalent of that in smaller halls.

Recommendations

Consequently, the Touche Ross recommendation was to build an exhibition and conference centre of 60,000 m^2 of gross letting capacity with the potential of increasing the capacity to 80,000 m^2 at some later stage. The consultants advised that the centre should be integrated, offering exhibition, conference, seminar, retail and catering facilities, thereby creating a complete 'destination'. A 300-room hotel was also included within the recommended facilities.

Regarding location, the prime determinant of success, the report pointed out that anywhere in or around London was well located for the distribution of potential visitors and would benefit from the capital's international status. The site at the Royal Victoria Dock, less than 10 km east of the City of London, benefits from many advantages, arising from the massive investment in local infrastructure made during the 1990s: improved road access from the north and west, a new light railway system and direct connection to London's West End via the underground's Jubilee Line extension (due for completion by 1999). London City Airport, situated nearby, offers flights to a number of UK and European cities.

But the consultants also pointed out that the lack of road crossings from the south of the River Thames could cause congestion, and that for this reason another river crossing was desirable if the site was to reach its full potential.

Nevertheless, the report conceded that exhibition

Table 6.8 The supply of exhibition facilities in the UK

Exhibition centre	Approx gross lettable capacity 000 m^2
National Exhibition Centre	157
Earls Court Exhibition Centre	61
Olympia Conference and Exhibition Centre	41
Scottish Exhibition and Conference Centre	19
Wembley Exhibition and Conference Centre	17
G-Mex (Manchester)	13
Harrogate	12
Brighton (Metropole Hotel)	12
Total	332

Source: Deloitte & Touche

continued

organisers, who are the first level of decision-maker in the 'buying chain' for an exhibition centre, consider that the optimum location for a new exhibition centre in the UK would be somewhere near the M25 on the west side of London. But it was the consultants' belief that any project to build an exhibition centre in that part of the capital was unlikely to go ahead, since the environmental drawbacks (increased traffic congestion and the need for vast areas for car parking) would not be adequately compensated for by the increased regional economic benefits which an exhibition centre would bring to that already prosperous area. By way of contrast, the opposite situation applies in the east of London, where a comparative lack of development and higher rate of unemployment means there is potential for increased regional economic benefits.

ExCeL

The solution proposed to remedy London's deficiency in the exhibitions sector, as identified by the Touche Ross research, was a new international exhibition and conference centre, ExCeL, situated on a 100-acre site on the north side of the Royal Victoria Dock, in London's Docklands area.

Figure 6.6 shows a model of Phase 1 of the ExCeL development.

ExCeL (Exhibition Centre London) is also the name of the consortium put together to design and promote the new exhibition centre.

Figure 6.6 New exhibition centre, Royal Docks
Source: ExCel (Mr Hamish McFall)

The project has the support of the London Docklands Development Corporation (LDDC), who are both the landowner and the planning authority for this part of London. The British government gave the project Private Finance Initiative status in 1993 and in 1994, the London International Exhibition Centre Ltd (LIECL), a consortium established specifically to develop the exhibition centre, was selected by the LDDC as the prefered developer.

Originally, the intention was for the first phase to be completed in 1998, providing 47,000 m² of lettable exhibition hall space, at a cost of around £120 million. A second phase of the project would provide 110,500 m² of lettable exhibition space.

The full development, in addition to the lettable exhibition space, will also include:

- hotels, providing a total of 1,000 rooms;
- twin conference/banqueting suites, each with a 500-seat capacity;
- a 3,000-seat conference centre;
- a trade centre;
- conversion of historic warehouses on the site for exhibition-related uses, and;
- a variety of shops and restaurants.

Economic impact

In a second report linked with the development of ExCeL, the consultants Touche Ross (1995) provided an assessment of the exhibition centre's potential economic impact. The assessment of potential visitors and exhibitors to the centre was based on comparisons with existing major exhibition centres across Europe and available statistics on the UK market. The consultants' conclusion was that a total of almost 1 million visitors and exhibitors were likely to be attracted to the exhibition centre each year for the Phase 1 development, rising to about 2.8 million people per year when the overall scheme was completed.

In total, the net expenditure likely to be generated each year by the centre's visitors and exhibitors was estimated to be £146.4 million for Phase 1 of the development and £407.6 million for the end state, broken down into the categories shown in Figure 6.7.

Regarding the local economic benefit (the benefit to the London Borough of Newham and the

continued

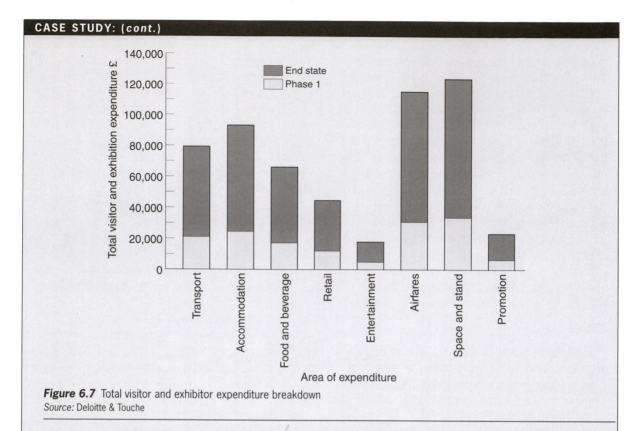

Figure 6.7 Total visitor and exhibitor expenditure breakdown
Source: Deloitte & Touche

immediately adjoining boroughs), Touche Ross estimated that this would amount to £35.4 million for Phase 1, rising to £272 million for the full end-state development.

At the same time, it was estimated that £94 million of regional benefit would accrue to the rest of Greater London, as a result of Phase 1, and that this figure would rise to £159 million for the end-state scenario.

Finally, concerning jobs created by the development, the consultants predicted that approximately 1,066 'person years' of employment would be generated by the construction of the centre, over fifteen years; 1,180 local permanent job opportunities would be generated from Phase 1, rising to about 9,000 for the completed development; and 3,133 jobs would be created for the rest of Greater London, with a total of about 5,300 regionally when the development was in its finished state (Touche Ross 1995).

Competition: go west?

ExCeL's main competitor came in the form of a proposal from Earls Court Olympia, owned by P&O, the shipping group, which in 1995 began pursuing its own development of a site for an international exhibition centre near Heathrow airport in west London. That year, the group's Communications Manager told the Financial Times (1996b): 'For the last 20 years, the cry from the exhibition organising community has been that any new exhibition centre in London needs to be built near the main international airport.'

The rival Earls Court Olympia's plan was for a first phase of 60,000 m², to be completed by 2000, and consisting of three interconnected halls of 20,000 m² each, at a cost of £141 – £172 million. In 1996, negotiations were taking place on land acquisition, and the project had the support of the local authority, Hillingdon Council and was in partnership with the British Airports Authority.

By 1997, however, Hillingdon Council had withdrawn its support for the P&O proposal for an international exhibition centre near Hayes, Middlesex, following a lack of progress on the idea since it was first put forward (Sunday Business 1997).

continued

Funding

Following a number of abortive funding attempts during 1996 and 1997, funding for the ExCeL development was finally within sight in January 1998, when a Malaysian Company, Country Heights, was expected to invest £120 million in the development. But, despite the length of time it took to find a suitable investor, the promoters were in no doubt as to the level of demand for the exhibition centre.

In 1996, the chief executive of ExCeL was able to announce that, 'The responses we have received confirm the strong demand for a modern exhibition facility in London. Out initial expectations have been exceeded by the large number of firm bookings that have been made already by a wide range of significant international exhibition organisers. Demand is so strong that we are now planning to accelerate the start of the second phase of ExCeL' (ExCeL 1996).

More specifically, the following year, it was reported (Sunday Business 1997) that National Boat Shows, organisers of the Earls Court Boat Show, had been in discussion with ExCeL and were ready to switch the lucrative consumer show from west London to the Docklands if construction of the exhibition centre began by March 1998. As well as the Boat Show, exhibitions such as the Motor Show and the Ideal Home Exhibition were also believed to be in ExCeL's sights.

General Outlook

The Horwath Axe report concludes that regarding the future development of business tourism in general, a majority of professionals anticipate a good outlook or growth of the market, without being able to quantify it with precision.

Overall, it has been estimated that the outlook for the business tourism sector will grow globally at a superior rate to that of the tourism market in general, for which, according to the World Tourism Organisation, a 2.7 per cent average rate of increase is forecast in the years up to 2000/2005.

This optimism is based on major trends observed in the market over the last few years; these include:

- A significant growth in the need to exchange information.
- An increasing specialisation and professionalism of activities, which results in a growth in training needs and the necessity for permanent updates.
- International companies face fierce competition from the non-European markets, which requires an increased cooperation and strategic planning between the Europeans and worldwide players (CEC 1996).

The key question is: how well-placed is Europe to benefit from this general growth in business tourism activity? What are the strengths of Europe in terms of business tourism which will enable it to compete successfully with other world regions?

The main assets of the European supply, as defined by Horwath Axe, are:

- Its attractive diversity in terms of destinations and cultures
- Its level of market maturity, due to its historical position
- The expertise and professionalism of its specialists and the quality of the products
- The presence in Europe of many company head offices, institutions and associations, which generates an important need for meetings and exchanges of information.

Nevertheless, the European conference and exhibition industry must face up to structural and organisational problems and insufficiencies, which include:

- A real lack of statistics and information at all levels of the sector (local, national and European).
- A number of fiscal and legal barriers which hamper the activity within Europe and penalise the competitive position of the European offering in the international marketplace.
- A critical need for specialised skills training,

which are constantly evolving and which require an increasing level of professionalism from those involved.

- Scattered promotional programmes which poorly reflect the wealth and complementary nature offered by the numerous business tourism destinations in Europe.
- A lack of clarity in the definition of the business tourism activities compared with careers in traditional tourism sectors.
- The insufficient recognition of the sector as a whole and of the importance of the benefits that it generates for the region or country.
- A lack of development planning at national and European levels, which leads to an over-supply situation in several locations, detrimental to the overall sector. (CEC 1996)

The EU's solution to the European business tourism industry's problems, as described above, is to establish a common policy and global strategy to reach 'a coherent structuration' of this sector. This structuration, it is held, is necessary in order to strengthen Europe's market position, both on the European market area and in the international marketplace.

The strategy proposed by the EU, for action on a European scale, can be summarised in four main points:

1 Establish and/or reinforce coordination or partnership practices at all levels between the institutions, the representative professional organisations and the various operators of the sector.
2 Improve the structure and the activity pattern of a sector which is growing rapidly, improve its knowledge and its recognition at national and European levels.
3 Provide a coherent framework for the different actions taken by the European Union related to business tourism.
4 Modernise the existing supply to maintain its

competitiveness, revitalise its marketing and promotion in Europe and abroad, and stimulate demand to counter the competition, particularly that from North America and the Asia-Pacific region.

A European Action Plan for business tourism would be the instrument for putting this strategy into action. Regarding the administration of this Action Plan, a specific responsibility for business tourism could be created within DGXXIII, together with a permanent committee to favour exchanges and partnership between the Commission and the professional and institutional players in business tourism. It would be the role of such a committee to define the Action Plan and implement and monitor measures related to it.

The proposed strategy was welcomed by many of those operating in Europe's business tourism sector. But, as ever, the question uppermost in their minds was: would the plan ever make the transition from paper into practice?

UPDATE

Undertake your own research to find out the answers to the following questions.

- What has been the fate of frequent flyer programmes in Europe?
- Has Europe been able to hold on to its share of the conference market in the face of growing competition from the Asia-Pacific region?
- Is incentive travel still a growth market in Europe or has belt-tightening (or other factors) restricted growth?
- Have moves towards the privatisation/contracting out of exhibition facilities in Germany had any impact on this country's domination of the trade fair market?
- How successful has ExCeL been in its first years of operation?

References

American Express (1994) *European Business Travel and Expense Management Report 1993*, American Express, Brighton.

Beioley, S. (1991) 'Business tourism', in *Insights*, September, English Tourist Board, London.

Carlson Wagonlit (1997) *1996 Business Travel Survey*, Carlson Wagonlit Travel/Mori, London.

Caterer and Hotelkeeper (1993) 'That special break: making incentives work for you', 10 June.

CEC (1996) *Business and Conference Tourism in the European Economic Area*, European Commission, Brussels.

Daily Telegraph (1996) 'Detail is the order of the Thistles', 21 November.

Davidson, R. (1992) 'Business tourism in Europe since the Gulf War', *Insights*, September, English Tourist Board, London.

Davidson, R. (1994) 'European business travel and tourism', in A. V. Seaton et al. (eds), *Tourism: The State of the Art*, John Wiley, Chichester.

Economist, The (1996) 'Messe business', 20 January, pp. 71–2.

EFCT (1996) *1995 Report on Europe*, European Federation of Conference Towns, Brussels.

EFCT (1997a) *Directory 1997–1998*, European Federation of Conference Towns, Brussels.

EFCT (1997b) *1996 Report on Europe*, European Federation of Conference Towns, Brussels.

EMECA (1996) *Review of Business*, European Major Exhibition Centres Association, Paris.

EMECA (1997) *Review of Business*, European Major Exhibition Centres Association, Paris.

European, The (1993) 'Women force a five-star service', 19–25 November.

European, The (1994) 'Corporate high-fliers look for better value', 20–26 May.

European, The (1995) 'The executive love of the travel perk', 30 November–6 December.

ExCeL (1996) News release, 22 February, Tavistock Communications London.

Financial Times, The (1993) 'A world of locations', 22 February.

Financial Times, The (1996a) 'Face-to-face still beats the computer', 14 February.

Financial Times, The (1996b) 'Laggard is starting to catch up', 14 February.

Financial Times, The (1996c) 'Leipzig changes ways', 14 February.

Gold, J-P. (1996) 'Un marché en plein mutation', in *Tourisme d'Affaires*, Les Cahiers Espaces 45, February.

IATA (1997) 1996 Corporate Air Travel Survey, International Air Transport Association, Geneva.

O'Brien, K. (1993) *The West European Business Travel Market 1993–1997*, The Financial Times, London.

O'Brien, K. (1997) 'The West European incentive travel market', in *Travel and Tourism Analyst* (1), Travel and Tourism Intelligence, London.

PR Week (1997) 'Boom times for new centres', 28 February.

Rockett, G. and Smillie, G. (1994) 'The European conference and meetings market', in *Travel and Tourism Analyst (4)*, Travel and Tourism Intelligence, London.

Smith, G. (1991) Professional organisations in the European meetings industry, *International Journal of Hospitality Management*, Vol. 10, No. 2, pp. 119–26.

Sunday Business (1997) 'Triple boost for Docklands centre', 25 May.

Touche Ross (1994) *Royal Victoria Dock Proposed Exhibition Centre Demand: Specification Study (Executive Summary)*, Touche Ross & Co, London.

Touche Ross (1995) *Royal Victoria Dock Proposed Exhibition Centre: Economic Impact Study (Executive Summary)*, Touche Ross & Co, London.

7

Short breaks in Europe

KEY OBJECTIVES

Reading this chapter will enable you to:

- Understand the reasons for the growth in the taking of short breaks in Europe.
- Identify the main characteristics of short breaks and the features which distinguish them from longer holidays.
- Familiarise yourself with the supply of and demand for international short breaks in Europe.
- Compare the approaches of two tour operators, one French and the other British, both specialising in short break packages.

Introduction

During the 1980s, travel frequency – the number of overnight leisure trips taken each year by those Europeans who are part of the holiday-taking population – rose sharply in many national tourism markets. The explanation for this is provided by the growing numbers of Europeans who took several short leisure breaks throughout the year as well as their one main annual holiday.

Traditionally defined as trips of one- to three-nights' duration taken primarily for holiday purposes, short breaks were recognised as a dynamic and increasingly significant sector of the European tourism industry during the 1980s and 1990s. During the 1980s in particular, short breaks were generally held to represent the fastest growing sector of the entire European travel market. Faché (1994) cites a number of commentators from different European countries claiming that at the

end of the 1980s, the growth rate for the taking of short breaks in those countries was much higher than that found in other segments of the travel market.

Short breaks are now regarded as being indicative of a changing pattern of holiday-taking in Europe, where there is a marked trend towards the taking of shorter main holidays supplemented by a number of short breaks dispersed throughout the year – the 'fragmentation' of Europeans' holiday-taking. The classic holiday-taking schedule of an erstwhile typical French family – for example, a month by the Mediterranean in either July or August, with perhaps a week's skiing holiday in February – is becoming more and more of a rarity, as taking more frequent short breaks several times a year becomes increasingly the norm for a growing number of Europeans. The results of this trend may be seen, for example, in the fact that the length of the average stay with Club Méditerranée fell from almost nine days in 1985 to only seven a decade later. Moreover, as a reflection of an associated trend, the same tour operator found that in the same period, the proportion of visitors who book only five days or fewer before they want to go on holiday had doubled to 14 per cent (Economist 1995).

STATISTICS AND DEFINITIONS

Although the rise of the short-break trip is acknowledged to be a Europe-wide phenomenon of the 1980s and 1990s, information on this sector suffers from a number of definitional problems. The statistical evidence concerning short breaks in Europe is difficult to collect and not at all easy to interpret. One of the reasons for this is because there are different ways of defining short breaks. Faché (1994) notes, for example, that while some national surveys include both short breaks taken in commercially provided accommodation (for example, hotels, guest houses, self-catering establishments) and non-commercial accommodation (for example, VFR, caravanning or in other forms of accommodation owned by the person making the trip), others consider only short breaks taken in the former. Surveys undertaken in different European countries are, as a result, sometimes very difficult to compare.

Europe-wide studies of short-break activity being rare, very few attempts have been made to quantify the extent of all short break taking by Europeans. However, in 1990, a pan-European study undertaken by French consultants BIPE (quoted in Davidson 1993) estimated at 300 million the total number of short breaks taken annually at that time. The same study estimated that the annual rate of growth in this market was between 10 per cent and 20 per cent, according to the individual country.

One problem with statistics for this form of tourism is that, as those taking short breaks tend to forget them fairly quickly, figures are sometimes less than reliable, especially those on domestic short breaks – weekends away, and so on.

Short breaks taken abroad are, however, generally more memorable. The European Travel Monitor (ETM), the only regular pan-European survey of the outbound tourist market, is therefore a very useful source of figures on international short breaks taken by Europeans. ETM conducts interviews on average six times a year in eighteen countries in Western Europe and in key Eastern Europe markets, using a minimum sample base of 2,000 adults aged fifteen years and over. This generates a total of more than 60,000 reported cases of outbound travel each year.

ETM data indicates that in 1993, the European *international* short break market alone accounted for some 26 million trips a year, representing 17.5 per cent of the total international holiday market for Western Europe. That year, the total expenditure on such short-break travel by West Europeans was ECU 8.7 million (Potier and Cockerell 1995).

Reasons for growth

The 1980s saw unprecedented growth in the short-break sector in Europe. During that decade, travel frequency – the number of trips taken every year by those who travel for leisure – rose sharply as people increasingly took two, three or more shorter breaks instead of the traditional one main long annual holiday. This growth in the fragmentation of Europeans' holidays was the direct result of a number of demand and supply factors.

DEMAND FACTORS

Economic factors played a vital role in stimulating the growth of short breaks. Rising levels of disposable income, partly as a result of the growth in the number of working wives, meant that there was more money to spend on leisure pursuits in general. However, although an important factor, this development in itself does not explain why was so much of this increase in income was spent on travel and tourism rather than on other consumables. Other essential factors were at play.

Increases in annual leave entitlements for those in work also had an impact, as many European countries moved towards matching the generous annual leave allocated to employees in countries such as France. Additional public and national holidays gave growing numbers of Europeans the chance to go away for long weekends, and this opportunity was taken up by many, with great enthusiasm.

More flexible ways of working also played a part in stimulating demand for short-break holidays in Europe. Faché (1994) notes that working patterns are more and more flexible, resulting in greater variety in the actual timing of tourist patterns. He cites the increase in flexible hours for those in full-time employment and a distinct growth in part-time working and shared jobs as factors contributing to the rise in the number of long-weekend and mid-week breaks taken by Europeans. Clearly, when those in employment have the possibility of organising their working hours so as to be able to take a Friday or a Monday off, for example, this increases the likelihood of them taking long weekend breaks away from home.

But cultural factors may have been decisive in determining that most Europeans use their extra free time and money for travelling rather than for gardening, DIY or other home-based leisure pursuits. By the 1980s, the majority of West Europeans had made travel for leisure purposes an integral part of their lives. Growing curiosity about others' heritage and cultures, coupled with greater confidence in travelling meant that for many, the annual one-off holiday trip to a single destination was increasingly unable to satisfy their desire to explore other regions and other countries for leisure and pleasure. Short breaks provide a means of travelling more widely throughout the year, to a greater variety of destinations.

As many commentators have pointed out, frequent leisure breaks were also increasingly seen as a way of temporarily escaping from the stresses of daily life. For many of those in work, these stresses were not inconsiderable, during a decade characterised by pressure to be ever more productive, efficient and competitive, with the twin spectres of 'downsizing' and 'rationalisation' always present in the workplace.

Linked with this pressure at work, it has also been suggested that the fragmentation of Europeans' holidays is due in part to executives' and managers' growing fear of being away from work for too long at a single stretch. The explanation offered is that more and more employees are anxious about taking long periods away from their place of work, in case they come back to find that their authority has declined during their absence or even that they have been replaced! (Bertinchamps 1993).

SUPPLY FACTORS

Transport operators

In Europe, as early as the 1960s, short breaks were recognised as an effective way of filling seats on passenger transport at weekends. For example, Goumaz (1993) refers to the city breaks offered for many years by the German train company DB AG, similar to the popular 'train+hotel' formula proposed by the French national rail operator, the SNCF. He adds:

Hotels, especially those belonging to chains, offer very substantial price reductions at weekends, when there are no business clients. The same goes for the airline companies, who, by offering flights at very attractive rates, have contributed to the expansion of foreign short breaks. (Goumaz 1993).

Most European airlines are now heavily involved in the short break market, combining flights with hotel accommodation, often with dinner included in the price and the option of renting a car for the duration of the stay.

Goumaz also points out that, more recently, the advent of the airlines' frequent flyer programmes (see page 178) has also contributed to the growth in short breaks taken overseas, as travellers use their accumulated points to obtain free flights for weekend breaks in other countries.

Hotels

The off-peak marketing efforts of many hotel groups led to the concept of the 'commercial short holiday break', which Edgar *et al.* (1994) have defined as 'hotel packages of one to three nights which, for a single price, together with accommodation include one or more of the following: meals, transport, entertainment or a programme of activities'. The principle was that any room sold during off-peak periods was contributing to hotels' fixed costs, emphasising the importance of marginal pricing as a strategy to boost occupancy and increase profitability.

As the market matured, the off-peak concept developed into a market in its own right and companies actively attempted to compensate for low-season trade by offering short breaks to effectively extend their operating season (ibid.).

Holiday villages

The success of holiday villages such as Center Parcs is almost entirely based on short-break occupancy. The Center Parcs formula was developed in the Netherlands and successfully exported across northern Europe. The key elements include quality self-catering villa accommodation, attractive woodland and water settings, a large leisure pool inside a heated dome and a number of indoor and outdoor activities for adults and children. A holiday at a Center Parcs resort is not meant to be taken as an alternative to a main summer holiday, but as a complementary break in an attractive and easily accessible environment. Center Parcs' success has led others such as Sun Parks and more recently Oasis Villages (The Rank Organisation) to emulate the same formula.

Destination marketing

Cities, regions and resorts throughout Europe have made great efforts, either individually or in partnership arrangements, to market themselves as short break destinations. There have been many initiatives led by local authorities, local tourist boards or national tourist organisations, such as the English Tourist Board's *Let's Go* promotion of off-peak short-break holidays in England during the late 1980s. One example of a successful Europe-wide collaborative initiative is Art Cities in Europe, which was developed by the Federation of the European Cities' Tourist Offices (FECTO), partly sponsored by the European Commission and launched in November 1994. Through this initiative, some 30 European cities joined together to promote short-break holidays based on their cultural activities and other tourist services. The wide range of hotels and cultural events can be booked via the major computer reservation systems worldwide.

Infrastructure

Improvements in Europe's transport infrastructure made the prospect of taking a short break more attractive, as new motorways and high-speed rail services brought a growing number of enticing destinations within shorter travelling time of major markets. For example, Parisians, who since the advent of the train à grande vitesse (TGV) can travel to the Mediterranean coast in four and a half hours, are now much more likely to consider passing a weekend there than they were in the days when it took them twice that time to get to the south of France. The Channel Tunnel has also played an important part in stimulating short breaks between the UK, France, Belgium and the Netherlands (see Cresta case study, page 224).

The combination of these demand and supply factors has created the rapid and considerable growth in the short-break market. The off-peak image of short breaks has given way to the concept of year-round trips, domestic and international, taken regularly as part of the normal tourism consumption patterns of a growing number of Europeans.

Characteristics of short breaks

MAINLY DOMESTIC

Although the increase in short breaks has been generally welcomed by the tourism industry as a whole, it is clear that the destinations chosen for short breaks are not always the same as those associated with longer holidays usually taken in the summer, i.e. destinations often situated abroad, such as Mediterranean resorts or, increasingly, long-haul.

The widespread pattern which has emerged in many European countries, particularly in the northern markets is one of main holidays being taken abroad, supplemented throughout the year with short breaks taken in the country of residence. Even in relatively small countries, it would appear, the vast majority of short breaks are taken domestically. Faché (1994) quotes from statistical evidence showing that, for example, 83 per cent of Dutch people taking short breaks take them in their own country, while 63 per cent of Belgian short breaks are taken domestically. The same author concludes that because of the brief duration of short breaks, people mainly look to take them near to the places where they live.

The largely domestic nature of short-break destinations in Europe has led Gratton (1990) to argue that, on the national level, short-break holidays are likely to generate greater economic benefits and fewer economic costs than conventional tourism. For most northern European countries in particular, international tourism has an adverse effect on the balance of payments, since there is a net outflow of tourism expenditure. But since the major share of short-break holidays is domestic tourism, this has the potential to improve the adverse balance of payments implications of tourism as a whole.

Nevertheless, many market analysts have pointed to the growing trend towards the taking of international short breaks in the 1980s and 1990s (see below).

LESS SEASONAL THAN LONG HOLIDAYS

One of the most attractive features for the tourism industry of short breaks is that they do not show the same sharp seasonal peaks as long holiday travel. Indeed, as mentioned earlier in this chapter, short breaks present the various sectors of the tourism industry with an effective means of alleviating the problems caused by an over-concentration of holiday-taking at certain periods of the year. In a continent where seasonality presents the tourism industry with major difficulties, this characteristic of the short breaks market is a considerably appealing one. Figure 7.1 shows the relative monthly shares of short breaks and long holidays of four nights and more.

Short breaks are spread much more evenly thoughout the year than longer holidays are. Their importance in Europe, particularly in the shoulder months, is clear. As would be expected, there is a dip in the volume of short breaks taken in the summer months, when long holidays peak sharply.

Short break travel does not only contribute to easing seasonal peaks and troughs, but also provides a partial solution to the problem of periodicity – concentration of business in certain days of the week. Since short breaks are predominantly taken over weekends, in contrast with the largely Monday–Thursday business travel market, they have the potential to help the various sectors of the tourism industry balance their capacity on a day-to-day basis.

TRANSPORTATION

Given the fact that the vast majority of short breaks are taken within the home country, it is not surprising that the private car is by far the main means of transportation used for this form of tourism – as it is for longer holidays. Destinations which receive substantial numbers of tourists taking short breaks therefore must recognise that, as is the case for places attracting vast numbers of day-trippers, there can be implications for traffic flow and environmental problems in the locality.

TAKEN SPONTANEOUSLY AND INDEPENDENTLY ARRANGED

Patterns of planning and booking short breaks do not follow those for decisions concerning longer holidays. Decision-making as far as short breaks are concerned tends to be more spontaneous and more last-minute. The considerable self-confidence of a growing number of Europeans as a result of many decades' experience of travelling domestically and internationally, also means that the vast majority of short breaks are arranged independently.

The decision to take a short break may be prompted by a number of factors, ranging from a sudden change in the weather (usually a change for the better, but in some cases – for example, Center Parcs, a change for the worse), through financial reasons (such as a receiving a small windfall or simply feeling 'flush' at the end of the month) to mere impulse.

LARGELY TAKEN OUTSIDE THE COMMERCIAL ACCOMMODATION SECTOR

Most short breaks are taken in non-paid accommodation, such as friends' homes or in second homes. In France, for example, a substantial proportion of short breaks taken by the French themselves are taken in their own *résidences secondaires*. France has more of these pri-

Figure 7.1 Seasonality patterns

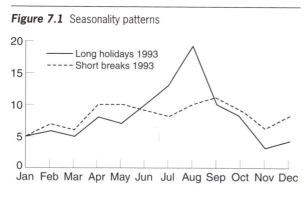

Notes: Short breaks = trips of 1–3 nights,
     Long holidays = trips of 4-plus nights
Source: Potier, F. and Cockerell, N. (1995)

vately owned holiday homes per head of population than any other country in the world. Even families on a fairly modest income level may own a holiday flat by the sea or a simple country cottage in which to spend long weekends and other short holidays.

Visiting friends and relatives (VFR) trips are included in most definitions of short breaks, excluding those taken for 'non-holiday purposes' – visiting the sick, or other family obligations, for example.

The situation is exemplified by the UK market, whose use of accommodation for short breaks is shown in Table 7.1.

A commonly held point of view among tourism analysts is that commercially accommodated short breaks – taken in hotels, guest houses, and other forms of paid-for accommodation such as self-catering establishments – while still a minority, are growing much faster than short breaks taken in non-commercial accommodation. This is almost certainly partly a result of hotels, and in particular hotel chains, in Europe offering incentives such as special weekend deals in order to deal with the problem of periodicity. This part of the accommodation sector has been extremely dynamic in Europe.

Furthermore, there is, according to Beioley (1991) evidence to suggest that commercial short break *packages* (i.e. commercially marketed packages including accommodation, meals and other

services at an inclusive price) were growing, in the UK at least, at rates of between 15–20 per cent per annum.

Profile of the short break taker

Faché (1994) emphasises the similarity between the profiles of short break takers in different European countries, pointing out the resemblance, for example, between the UK market, as described by Beioley (1991) and the former West German market. The following emerges from his analysis.

The market comprises mainly young and middle-aged travellers. The over 65s are under-represented, by comparison with their numbers in the population as a whole. This is in marked contrast to this age group's near proportionate participation in long holidays. Beioley notes that those buying commercial short-break packages are more concentrated in the 35–54 age group.

Regarding their socio-economic profile, those taking short breaks tend to come from the upper socio-economic groups. Short breaks are thus more unevenly distributed across the population than long holidays; for while the practice of long holiday-taking extends throughout most socio-economic groupings, the professional (AB) and clerical and supervisory (C1) groups dominate the market for short breaks.

Moreover, short break takers tend to be eager consumers of tourism products generally. Beioley (1991) maintains that short breaks are mostly additional holidays rather than substitutes for a main holiday, using as support for this hypothesis a study carried out for the Wales Tourist Board in 1986. In this study, it was found that frequent short break takers were more likely to have had a long holiday in the same year and more likely to have been abroad than those who did not take short breaks. Faché (1994) mentions research findings from the Netherlands which also support this hypothesis.

Moreover, concerning consumers' 'psychological attitude' towards taking a short break, research shows that the psychological threshold of the first-time short-break holiday is an important one to cross. Once people have actually experi-

---

Table 7.1 Accommodation used on short holidays (1–3 nights) in the UK by British residents

	(%)
Serviced	
Licensed hotel	12
Other hotel	5
Self-service	
Rented flat, cottage, etc	4
Camping, caravan	11
Non-commercial (homes of	68
friends or relatives, second homes, etc.	

Source: United Kingdom Tourism Survey (English Tourist Board, Northern Ireland Tourist Board, Scottish Tourist Board, Wales Tourist Board)

enced a short break holiday, they are much more open to the idea and continue taking short breaks (Faché 1994).

Definitional problems

Most national travel and tourism surveys use a traditional definition of a short break – that is, a trip of one- to three-nights' duration. This definition has been widely accepted since as long ago as the end of the Second World War, although it was only adopted by the World Tourism Organisation in 1992, after the Ottawa statistics conference – long after the definition had outlived its usefulness, according to many industry experts (Potier and Cockerell 1995).

However, at the present time, there is a move towards redefining and refining the definition of the short break. One solution would involve bringing in a new category of trip between 'long' and 'short' breaks: trips which last from four to seven nights. There appears to be general agreement that this would be a sensible move. Many trips are indeed undertaken for a single week (for example, during school half-term breaks). And it may well turn out on closer examination that trips lasting for four to seven nights actually have quite different characteristics from either longer holidays or short trips. On the other hand, some commentators suggest that trips of three nights have more in common with those of four or even five nights than they have with two-night trips. In either case, it would appear that a statistical redefinition of short breaks is now necessary.

The authors of the 1995 survey of *international* short-break trips taken by Europeans, based on ETM data argue in favour of a complete redefinition of the short break, widening the category to include trips of up to five nights in length. Such a redefinition, as well as adding to our understanding of the market, would also provide a neat solution to a certain statistical problem which has arisen concerning European short breaks.

Using the traditional definition of short-breaks, the results of the 1995 survey suggested that, following a boom in the 1980s, the international short-break market in Europe actually appeared to

go into *decline* in the early 1990s. The study estimated that the annual volume of leisure trips of one to three nights taken by West Europeans outside their own countries had actually fallen from a peak of around 29 million in 1991 to 25 million in 1994. However, as the report admitted, this conclusion was clearly at odds with industry perceptions – and industry performance, both of which suggested that the short-break boom was continuing.

The explanation offered for this apparent paradox is that, in fact, the length of a typical short break is growing and that it is the volume of international short breaks of four or five nights or longer which has increased sharply during the 1990s. This is supported by evidence showing that as a percentage share of total volume of holidays taken abroad by Europeans, trips of four to seven nights inclusive increased by 25 per cent between 1989 and 1993 alone (Potier and Cockerell 1995). Therefore, if a wider definition of a short break were to be used – say trips of between one and five nights – the sector would be found to be performing well, as indeed it is.

International short breaks

Despite the widely acknowledged need for a redefinition, most research is still undertaken using the traditional definition of short break. In this section, the one to three-night definition is the one used. A substantial part of the material presented here is drawn from the 1995 study of the European international short-break market undertaken by Françoise Potier and Nancy Cockerell (EIU 1995), using as their main source statistical data from the European Travel Monitor.

During the 1980s, domestic travel continued to account for the majority of short breaks taken in Europe. However, according to the ETM, the average annual increase in international short-break travel was in double digits by the end of the 1980s, resulting in an increase in the share of short breaks in the total outbound holiday market from 14 per cent in 1988 to 19 per cent in 1990. Even in 1991, when the European travel market was adversely affected by the Gulf crisis and by the

Table 7.2 Leading West European international short-break holiday markets, 1990–93

| Market | % share of total European short-break trips[1] | | % change in absolute no of trips |
	1990	1993	1993/90
Germany	33	35	−1
UK	8	10	11
Sweden	7	8	−2
Belgium–Luxembourg	11	6	−49
France	5	6	11
Italy	7	6	−27
Finland	4	5	25
Switzerland	4	5	44
Austria	4	4	−10
Netherlands	7	4	−46
Norway	3	3	35
Spain	5	3	−31
Other	3	5	n.a.
Total	100	100	

Note: [1] Holiday trips of one to three nights in length
Source: Potier, F. and Cockerell, N. (1995)

start of the economic recession, the number of international short leisure trips increased by 4 per cent.

MAIN MARKETS

Table 7.2 shows the leading west European international short-break holiday markets.

Germany leads by far, accounting for approximately a third of the total West European volume and generating three and a half times more short-break trips abroad than the UK, its closest contender in the volume ranking that year. Nevertheless, somewhat surprisingly in view of its island status, Britain stood in second place in this market that year. The top three countries, Germany, the UK and Sweden, between them account for well over half of all short breaks taken by West Europeans outside their own countries.

As the authors of the 1995 report note:

It is not surprising to see either Germany or Belgium among the European leaders for short breaks, nor for that matter, the Netherlands, Luxembourg, France and Austria, even if some of their market shares are surprisingly low. It is obviously easy for these continental Europeans to cross land borders . . . It is more surprising to see the British so high up the list, because they have to cross water to go abroad . . . This can be explained by the fact that the British generally have a higher propensity to travel abroad than many of their European neighbours and . . . the British seem much less prepared to give up their leisure pursuits because of economic constraints . . . than most other Europeans. (Potier and Cockerell 1995)

MAIN DESTINATIONS

In continental Europe, most international short breaks are between neighbouring countries with

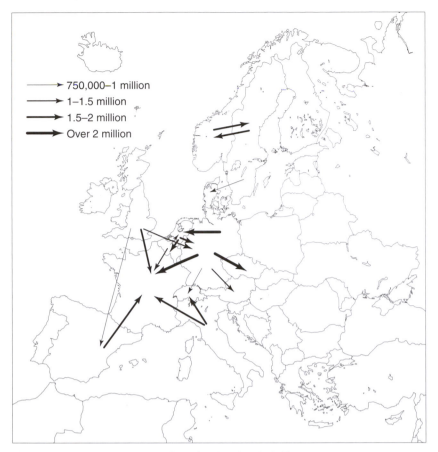

Figure 7.2 The main international flows for short breaks in Europe
Source: Françoise Potier and Nancy Cockerell, in *Cahiers Espaces 34*, Tourisme de court séjour, Dec. 1993

land borders. Figure 7.2 shows in diagrammatic form the main short break tourist flows between Western European countries.

The relative importance of different European countries as international short-breaks destinations is shown in Table 7.3.

According to these figures, the leading destination for European short breaks is France (18 per cent) followed by Austria (11 per cent). Much of France's popularity in this sector can be attributed to the continuing appeal of Paris, which has been added to by the opening of Disneyland Paris and the Channel Tunnel. But France also offers a wide range of other towns, cities and outdoor environments for short breaks. These are particularly appreciated by the British for whom France, and more particularly Paris is the top international short-break destination. Austria is particularly popular with the Germans and its tourism fortunes fluctuate

with the level of demand from that country. Like France, Austria is also a favourite destination with other nationalities for winter sports trips. There is also a significant volume of short-break travel for cultural reasons from Italy to Austria.

Regarding Eastern Europe, it is not surprising to note that since the collapse of the Iron Curtain, renewed interest in this region has led to an increase in the proportion of short breaks taken there. Eastern Europe's share rose from 6 per cent to 8 per cent between 1990 and 1993. Among city-break destinations, Prague and Budapest, in particular, have achieved some considerable success in attracting short break visitors from the West.

Eastern Europeans themselves have used their new-found freedom to travel in order to take short breaks in their own region as well as in Western Europe. Nevertheless, the ETM statistics shown in Table 7.4 indicate that the volume of short-break

Table 7.3 Major destinations for West European short breaks,[1] 1990–93

| Destination | % market share of short breaks[1] | | % change in absolute no of arrivals by destination 1993/90 | | |
	1990	1993	Short breaks[1]	Long holidays[2]	All holidays
France	18	18	−8	−4	−5
Austria	11	11	−4	3	1
Germany	11	8	−32	−6	−13
Netherlands	8	7	−24	21	2
Italy	7	7	−18	−19	−19
Sweden	4	6	21	34	28
Denmark	5	6	13	27	22
Belgium-Luxembourg	8	5	−39	−20	−28
Switzerland	5	5	−5	−8	−7
Spain	4	4	−6	−	−
UK	3	4	22	13	15
Western Europe	89	89	−10	−1	−3
Other Mediterranean	4	2	−46	−28	−29
Eastern Europe	6	8	23	17	19
Long haul[3]	1	2	42	30	30
Total	100	100	−8	1	−1

Notes: [1] Holiday trips of one to three nights in length, [2] Holidays of four or more nights, [3] Long haul=destinations outside Europe and the Mediterranean region. Figures have been rounded, which causes some distortion, especially regarding long-haul destination shares.
Source: Potier, F. and Cockerell, N. (1995)

trips fell between 1990 and 1993.

The authors of the 1995 report on international short breaks explain this by the fact that the initial euphoria felt by the residents of these countries for travel after the opening up of Eastern Europe rapidly gave way to severe belt-tightening as the realities of the change towards more market-driven economies hit home (Potier and Cockerell 1995). Western Europe accounts for some 56 per cent of all east European short breaks, with another 35 per cent taking place to Eastern Europe itself. The balance is made up by visits to other Mediterranean countries, notably Turkey. Among west European destinations, Austria leads the ranking with a 20 per cent share of all trips, followed by Germany with 15 per cent and France and Italy, each with 8 per cent.

TYPE OF TRIP

City breaks account for close to one-third of total trip volume. The popularity of urban short break tourism has almost certainly been boosted by the growth in the number and range of package programmes on offer since the beginning of the 1990s. Many of these are linked to special events, or cultural events. Following city breaks come international short breaks based on touring and sun and beach breaks. The latter appeal particularly to residents of Portugal, France and Spain, despite the fact that they have excellent sun and beach facilities in their own home countries.

Perhaps the best growth sector, alongside city breaks, has been the mini-cruise market, which has

Table 7.4 East European short break[1] travel, 1990–93			
	No. of trips (000)		Estimated % change
Market	1990	1993	1993/90
Bulgaria	110	100	−10
Czech Republic/ Slovakia	1,480	1,260	−15
Hungary	970	485	−50
Poland	850	380	−55
Romania	1,100	605	−45
Former Yugoslavia	660	n/a	n/a

Notes: [1] Holiday trips of one to three nights in length, [2] Estimated
Source: Potier, F. and Cockerell, N. (1995)

shown rapid growth in the 1990s, particularly in Scandinavia. The authors of the 1995 report suggest that this has come about as a result of an easing of restrictions on duty-free purchases made on mini-cruises within that region. If this is so, a fall in the popularity of short breaks based on mini-cruises can be expected following duty-free abolition in 1999.

TRANSPORTATION

Surface transport, and notably private car travel dominates with a 52 per cent share of the international short-breaks market. This is not surprising, as most trips are made to destinations in neighbouring countries. Coach travel comes in second place, with a 19 per cent share of west European international short-break trips in 1993. Nevertheless, this must be compared with a 24 per cent share in 1990. But if the use of coach travel for international short breaks appears to be losing some of its appeal, both air and rail travel are growing in popularity. As would be expected, preference for air travel for short breaks overseas is highest in island and peripheral European nations such as Ireland, Iceland, Greece and to a much lesser extent, the UK.

ACCOMMODATION

The share of international short breaks involving paid accommodation has remained steady at around 82 per cent, contrasting strongly with the much lower percentage of domestic short breaks in the commercial accommodation sector.

Discussing the use of hotel accommodation for international short breaks during the early 1990s, Potier and Cockerell highlight an important difference between business and leisure tourism patterns of consumption of those years:

> While there is no doubt that business travellers have been trading down in an effort to cut costs since the beginning of the 1990s, it would seem that leisure travellers – and perhaps more especially weekend travellers – have been able to take advantage of special weekend offers to fill what would be otherwise empty rooms. So, in effect, they have been trading up, helped perhaps by the tendency for hotels to discount prices during recession.

Within Europe, there are some considerable variations in the level of preference for hotel accommodation used for short breaks abroad. The Scandinavians are least likely to use hotels – partly due to their higher than average share of holiday homes abroad, but also due to the popularity of mini-cruises among these markets. The Irish also favour non-commercial accommodation for this form of tourism; this is perhaps in part due to the considerable proportion of Irish families who have a son or daughter working in another European country, who is able to provide free accommodation to visiting friends and other members of the family.

ORGANISATION

Almost half of Europeans' trips involve no pre-booking and are primarily car trips to people's second homes/holiday homes for the weekend or to stay with family and friends. But short breaks booked either through travel agencies or directly with the suppliers themselves – airlines or hotels, for example – rose between 1990 and 1993 from 11 per cent to 17 per cent and from 11 per cent to 18 per cent respectively.

However, fully-inclusive tour packages (ITs) fell in popularity during the same period from 32

...clearly unconvinced of the profitabilty of ...odes' short-break packages. The average ...Episodes product in 1990 was FF 1,000, ...at the travel agent's commission for selling ...ducts would be relatively low, for the work ... Moreover, they claimed, that time-wise there ... almost as much work involved in selling an ... package as there would be to sell, for ..., a cruise or a long-haul holiday at ten times ...ce – and ten times the commission. This would ...rtly due to the fact that the concept of short ... packages was a new one in France and would ... to be explained to potential clients.

...Since the Episodes product was not to be mainly ...tributed by travel agents, it was necessary for the ...mpany to find alternative ways of bringing the ...roduct to the attention of potential clients. In order to ...unch the product, advertisements were placed in ...national French magazines in order to establish the product on the market.

But as this type of operation is expensive and its effectiveness is difficult to assess, Episodes instead opted for a three-pronged strategy: the brochure, the Episodes Club and partnership.

The brochure

Three times a year, an attractive 50-page brochure showing all Episodes packages for that season is published. Instead of including photographs of the hotels, which in the majority of cases are in themselves not the client's main motivation for making the trip, Episodes puts the accent on photographs of the destination itself. At the same time, every month, Episodes publishes a series of leaflets advertising short breaks based on individual events (e.g. the annual Avignon drama festival, the Rembrandt exhibition) and giving details of special offers. These publications are distributed either through joint promotions with other partners, directly to potential customers who request them or through the Episodes Club.

The Episodes Club

Anyone who purchases an Episodes short break automatically becomes a member of the 'Club', which is, for Accor, a way of keeping in touch with their customers and creating repeat business. Members receive copies of the annual brochures and the above-mentioned special offers. This is the company's way of prompting their clients to take another short break with Episodes, and is also designed to give the company a dynamic and up-to-the-minute image.

Partnership

In conjunction with these direct marketing operations, Episodes also works in partnership with a number of other companies by, for example, using the partner's mailing list in order to distribute its short break brochures and leaflets. Sometimes Episodes pays for this service, but more often, the partners see such mailshots as being an additional service provided for their clients, and as such are pleased to be associated with Episodes, to whom no charge is made. Some recent examples of Episodes' partnership operations are:

- the promotion of Antwerp, the Cultural Capital of Europe 1996, in collaboration with the FNAC chain of stores and the Belgian National Tourist Office;
- the promotion of 'sports weekends' in the outlets belonging to the Décathlon chain of sportswear shops;
- an operation to distribute Episodes' leaflets through 700 French tobacconist shops.

Naturally, the synergetic relationship with the rest of the Accor group means that there are a number of joint operations conducted between Episodes and other subsidiaries belonging to the group. For example, the short break tour operator collaborates in joint marketing schemes with the hotels in the Novotel chain and with the seawater therapy centres which comprise Accor's Thalassa subsidiary; and Episodes' products are also sold through the group's Wagon-Lits Tourisme chain of travel agencies.

Company performance

By 1992, after its first two years of operations, Episodes had reached a total of 23,000 clients, representing 45,000 bed-nights and a turnover of FF 25 million (Bertinchamps 1993).

By 1996, the company had a turnover of FF 35 million, with 38,000 clients, of whom 70 per cent chose French destinations and 30 per cent went abroad to other European destinations. A significant

continued

---

per cent to 24 per cent, in line with the general trend towards less rigidly packaged tour programmes, witnessed particularly in the more mature northern European travel markets. In those countries – notably the UK, Germany, Switzerland and the Netherlands – travellers have increasingly been looking to tailor their own individual holidays and short breaks since the mid-1980s, choosing from a growing range of flexible mix-and-match programmes.

Regarding the supply of such programmes, the authors comment that:

> It is probably fair to say that the industry in some countries has been slow to respond to the demand for flexible programmes while in others there is a wide variety of different options, from full packages to '*à la carte*' options. This usually includes a choice of transport mode – those who want to travel by car can do so – plus an accommodation package, optional excursions, rental cars, theatre tickes and so on. One of the main attractions of these '*à la carte*' products is that they cater to individual tastes, but are easily

purchased on a one-stop shopping trip, for less than the price of putting together the different options oneself.

Regarding the flexible short-break package market, Potier and Cockerell make the following observation:

> It is increasingly noticeable that most of these new products are coming from suppliers rather than the travel trade, and noticeably vertically integrated groups, such as Accor, which are keen to increase the synergy between the different sectors of their operations. The danger for independent tour operators not linked to airlines or hotel groups is that they risk losing out on this potentially lucrative sector of the market, (Potier and Cockerell 1993).

The following two case studies examine two tour operators very active in the flexible short break market: the French tour operator Episodes, which is part of the vertically integrated group Accor; and the independent UK tour operator Cresta.

Figure 7.3 Episodes logo
Source: Episodes

Background

In 1990, the French hotel group Accor launched Episodes, billed as Europe's first tour operator specialising in short breaks in different countries across the continent. Until then, the Accor group, owner of chains such as Novotel and Sofitel, had concentrated on the business tourist market. Two main reasons were given for this policy: first, the business market was, generally speaking, considered to comprise a more loyal and therefore more stable clientele, and secondly, the business market for hotels, instead of demonstrating the same fluctuations as the leisure market, is more regularly spread throughout the year (Bertinchamps 1993).

However, one of the results of this policy was that while Accor's hotels enjoyed an occupancy rate of around 90 per cent from Monday to Friday, this fell to 30 per cent at the weekend, giving an average occupancy rate of around 70 per cent for the week as a whole. A further consequence was that at the end of the 1980s, the Accor group over Europe as a whole had a very strict 'business' image, which tended to drive away any leisure business from the hotels in the Accor chains.

In addition, the group had noticed a shortening of the week, as regards business tourism, as business

continued

clients were tending to end their week on Thursdays rather than on Fridays, as had been the case previously. Several factors contributed to this trend, including the developments in transport in Europe and the growing need for businesses to economise on the trips made by their employees. The added ease and speed of travelling by high-speed train and motorways meant that many trips could be made to the business traveller's destination and back in one day, avoiding the need to spend the night in a hotel; and, increasingly, the duration of seminars and conferences based in hotels was being reduced in order to cut costs.

Given the extent of Accor's investment in hotels for business travellers in Europe, the group decided, at the end of the 1980s, to target the weekend leisure market, in the attempt to fill its bed spaces during this normally quiet part of the week. Accor was encouraged in this strategy by its own research showing the growth in the number of short breaks to be one of the most significant trends in Europeans' holiday-taking patterns at the time.

For France, where the majority of Accor's hotels are to be found, the market was perceived to be particularly promising, since one-third of all international short-break trips made by non-French Europeans were found to have France as their destination. The Accor research highlighted other characteristics of the European tourism and leisure market:

- A growing preoccupation with the *quality* of life in general, including the environment and all products purchased for consumption.
- An increase in the importance of leisure in the family budget: even when households were cutting back on other expenses, they continued to spend money on holidays as usual.
- Confirmation of the trend towards going away on trips more often, breaking up the holiday entitlement into a number of different periods instead of just one long summer holiday.
- A willingness to try a greater variety of destinations, with the choice of destination often being dictated by fashion.
- A clear upsurge in the popularity of city breaks.
- The decision to go away for the weekend was being made at ever shorter notice, increasingly on

impulse: in 70 per cent of cases, the decision to take a weekend break was made during the seven days before the departure date.

- Increasingly, consumers were growing accustomed to shopping from home for products and services, using the telephone and/or viewdata systems. There was potential in using the same distribution networks to sell short breaks.

The Episodes product

In the light of these research findings, Accor created the subsidiary Episodes, to devise a product which would attract a leisure clientele to the group's hotels, thereby broadening the image of those chains to include weekend leisure breaks as well as business tourism products from Monday to Friday.

Further consumer research undertaken by Accor revealed the nature of the product which would best match the expectations of the French market regarding their short-break trips:

- More than half of those surveyed hoped to explore a new city or region during a short break.
- Most of the French wanted complete freedom to organise their stay according to their own wishes.
- Regarding the budget, the majority wanted to spend no more than FF 1,000 per person during the weekend (excluding transport).

As a result, Episodes devised a short-break product based on the following criteria:

- Their clients' need to take a break away from it all, to explore a new region or city, at their own pace and with no constraints.
- Their clients' wish to try some new sport or other activity or to be present at a specific cultural/sports event.
- An affordable price.
- Trips of one, two or three nights, available throughout the year.
- Trips made as a family, among friends or in groups.

The Episodes product comes in the form of a package, designed for maximum flexibility, and based around the hotel room (usually in a city centre location) and other hotel services such as meals, leisure facilities, etc. The choice of category of hotel (2-star to 4-star), number of nights, mode of transport, and the leisure activities undertaken during

continued

the short break are all left up to the client. For example, two activities are included in the package, out of a total of six suggested when the client arrives at the hotel.

Although there is a choice of different modes of transport, in reality the vast majority of trips are made by car within a radius of 200 to 300 km of the client's place of residence.

The client therefore designs the package according to his or her own needs or wishes. The strong selling point, according to Episodes, is the service provided by the company.

Pre-sales service

As the decision to take a weekend break is so often made at the last minute, a rapid and simple reservations system was vital to the success of Episodes. The telephone was chosen as the most effective means of allowing the client to book from home. Although this system is initially more costly for the tour operator than distributing the product through travel agencies (it requires the setting up of a specific structure, staff recruitment, training, etc.), the main advantage of a telephone reservation service is that it can operate outside the opening times of most travel agencies. Thus, Episodes' clients can book short breaks from 9am to 8pm Monday to Friday and from 9am to 6pm on Saturdays.

The tour operator's customers living in France can use an alternative means of booking, the Minitel service, a nationwide viewdata system. Twenty-four hours a day, seven days a week, those with this facility at home can book and pay for Episodes short-break products through the company's Minitel reservations service.

Once the booking has been made by either of these systems, the client receives from Episodes, by express mail, a Travel Pack. This is regarded as an essential element of the service provided by Episodes. The Pack contains not only the client's travel documents, hotel vouchers, maps and luggage labels, but also valuable information on the destination to be visited including the main attractions and places of interest to see, recommended restaurants, and so on. This is designed to help clients prepare their visit in advance, in order to save time during the short break itself.

After-sales

As people de minute often t somewhat unpre information on wh Episodes places m system of 'counsello destination, there is a for short break clients staff whose role it is to i destination's main attracti their stay in order to obtain it.

Originally, the job of opera Information Centres' in each hot clients was done by local tourism employed from Friday nights until M But later, the role of counsellor was receptionists, who were chosen accor knowledge of the region. By informing tourist assets of the destination, Episode active role in promoting the region or city hotels are situated, instead of a passive role previously been the case. Following the succe this operation, which lent Accor hotels an imag more geared towards leisure travel, Episodes employed 150 extra full-time members of staff, w received a special training for the job of informing only weekend leisure guests but also business clients on the local attractions.

Communication and distribution of the Episodes product

Even before the launch of Episodes, it was clear that travel agencies would not be the main distribution channel for Episodes' short-break packages. Not only was the telephone and Minitel service thought to be more suitable for the sale of short breaks, for the reasons given above, but also travel agencies presented two other disadvantages. First, in comparison with the inhabitants of northern European countries, the French make relatively limited use of travel agents. But the main reason was that in testing travel agents' reaction to their product, Episodes was confronted with a marked reluctance on the part of French travel agents' to sell their short breaks. Travel

agents were selling Episo cost of an meaning th such prod involved. would be Episode examp the pr be pa brea have

di c p

continued

proportion of French short breaks were based on visits to theme parks, in particular to the Astérix Park (in which Accor has a share), Episodes' best-selling product and one which sees sales rise each year.

In the future, Episodes is looking to increase its international business both into and out of France. Episodes packages are already responsible for a measure of inbound and outbound tourism in France. Two-thirds of the tour operator's sales for its city-break programme in 1994 were for destinations ouside France visited by French clients. In addition, demand for some 25 per cent of its packaged programmes for theme park weekends in France came from people living outside France, notably Belgium. Within France, the favourite destinations, for the French themselves as well as non-French clients, are Paris, Cannes, Nice and Avignon, Strasbourg, the Touraine region and the Atlantic coast.

The profile of Episodes' customers

They are most often:
- between 30 and 55 years old
- married, with one or more children
- managers or members of the professions.

They tend to:
- take a weekend break from twice to four times a year;
- stay in 2- or 3-star hotels;
- travel overseas for a holiday or short break twice a year;
- travel as a couple or with friends (64 per cent);
- travel as a family with children (30 per cent).

Product development

As regards competition, the Episodes' Director has been quoted as saying that there is very little in the way of direct competition for his company, as few other French tour operators have specialised in this domain; but the most major threat to the continuing success of Episodes lies in independently organised short breaks, resulting from customers' belief that they are perfectly capable of organising their own leisure breaks and can 'go it alone', setting off in the car and arranging their accommodation and activities as they go along.

The tour operator is therefore under pressure to constantly add attractive products to its existing

range. The following are some examples of Episodes' product extension.

Incentives and gift vouchers

Groups and incentive travel have been identified as additional markets for the short break products sold by Episodes. Under the name 'Passport', the tour operator now markets its weekend breaks as rewards for companies' high-achievers, using a gift voucher – *chèque cadeau* – system. These vouchers bear the name of the award winner and details of the prize: usually a weekend for two in a European city. The same vouchers are also sold as gifts for family members or friends.

Longer short breaks

By 1992, Episodes had expanded their range of products to include more 'classic' packages lasting one week. Such packages now account for 20 per cent of Episodes' products.

In an interview at the time (Echo Touristique 1992), the company's director claimed that such a development had been planned from the beginning: 'It is impossible to make a decent profit with a 17 per cent margin on packages costing on average FF 1,000. One-week packages bring larger profits.' More expensive packages also help get travel agents more interested in selling the Episodes product.

Greater variety of products

In response to the general move towards more flexible packages, the range of programmes and products has been expanded to include, in addition to city breaks in France and other parts of Europe, go-as-you-please type programmes covering different categories of hotels throughout France. New products also include packages based on visits to major European theme parks, and weekends centred around golf and other sporting activities, museums and art galleries, shopping, sightseeing, and wine-tasting through the vineyards of France.

Episodes has also made it its policy to develop the cultural aspect of its products by, for example, creating packages around the 1997 Braque exhibition at London's Royal Academy of Arts or the Delvaux retrospective at the Fine Arts Museum in Brussels.

The UK represents a substantial market for packaged overseas short break holidays, and the British, as an island race, are much more likely than most other European nations to book such products through the travel trade. Cresta Holidays is an example of a tour operator which has succeeded in this market.

Company background

Cresta Holidays is a leading UK-based tour operator for short breaks. Having started life as a travel agent in 1968, Cresta later began tour operating by offering holidays from Manchester Airport through travel agencies in the north of England. Since 1992, the company has been owned by the Belgian Group, Sun International, one of the largest travel groups in Europe, with interests in Belgium, France, Germany, the Netherlands and the UK. However, Cresta functions as a stand-alone business unit with commercial autonomy.

Product range

Cresta's product range includes two types of holiday: short breaks and longer stays, the former (defined as breaks lasting from nought to four nights) accounting for approximately 75 per cent of all holidays sold. Cresta's holidays are not pre-packaged in any way. Clients have the choice of any of the hotels in the Cresta programme (almost 1,000 in 1997, the majority of which were in continental Europe); they can stay for any length of time, and can select their means of transport: scheduled air or scheduled ferry/Channel Tunnel. Until the moment the travel agent or client contacts Cresta, the holiday, as such, does not exist. The tour operator then puts together the hotel bed (or apartment) of the client's choice with the scheduled travel of their choice, to create what is, in essence, a tailor-made holiday.

There are eight different types of product in the Cresta product range, each with its own themed brochure:

1 *Cities*: 66 destinations, 'from Amsterdam to Munich!'
2 *Paris/Amsterdam*: a wide range of hotels in these favourite destinations, by air, Eurostar, car or coach.
3 *Eurostar*: Paris, Lille, Amsterdam, Brussels, Bruges and other Belgian destinations, all by Eurostar.
4 *France*: a range of hotels from auberges to luxury châteaux, plus apartments, all with flexible travel arrangements, including Fly Drive.
5 *Disneyland Paris*: Cresta is a Selected Operator for Disneyland Paris, meaning that the company has guaranteed allocations at resort hotels.
6 *Golf in France*: comprehensive packages, including travel, accommodation and pre-booked tee times.
7 *Ireland*: packages including Dublin city breaks, self-catering cottages, golf breaks, horse-drawn caravans and river cruising.
8 *Italy*: short breaks to all the major destinations, Tuscany and Umbria villas, the Neapolitan Riviera, the Lakes and Sardinia.

Approximately 60 per cent of the short breaks sold by Cresta are city breaks. Figure 7.4 shows the top 20 destinations for 1996.

Paris and Amsterdam, in that order, are found at the top of the popularity ratings every year. In particular at the 'entry level' – the market composed of those taking an overseas short-break trip for the first time – Paris and Amsterdam continue to be the favourite destinations. The company explains this enduring popularity of these two cities for the UK market by the short travel time involved and by the wide choice of scheduled air travel from local airports (sixteen UK departure points each). In addition, Paris has benefited from continued interest in Eurostar since the opening of the Channel Tunnel.

Positioning

Cresta Holidays positions itself as the short-breaks tour operator market leader in the UK, in terms of range and choice of products it offers. In addition, the company also expected to be the market leader, from 1997, in terms of the actual number of packages sold that year. Until then, the only UK-based company selling more short break packages than Cresta was sister company the Bridge Travel Group, which focuses on Paris and Amsterdam. The company's other competitors in the city-based short break market include Travelscene, British Airways Holidays,

continued

1996 Cresta Top 20 (1995 positions in brackets)	
1 Paris (1)	11 Venice (12)
2 Amsterdam (2)	12 Madrid (11)
3 Rome (3)	13 New York (16)
4 Dublin (5)	14 Copenhagen (17)
5 Brussels (4)	15 Nice (15)
6 Prague (8)	16 Monte Carlo (new entry)
7 Barcelona (6)	17 Gibraltar (14)
8 Bruges (10)	18 Istanbul (13)
9 Vienna (7)	19 Lisbon (20)
10 Florence (9)	20 Reykjavik (new entry)

Figure 7.4 Cresta Top 20, 1996
Source: Cresta Holidays

Sovereign Cities, Crystal Premier Cities, and Time Off (now owned by Thomas Cook). Airtours and Thomson also offer this type of programme, but Cresta do not consider them as direct competitors as the majority of these two tour operators' products are based on using charter flights, which, Cresta claims, do not appeal to the mid- and upper-end of the market since they lack the flexibility and, in some cases, the quality demanded by their clients.

Company performance

Throughout the 1980s and 1990s, Cresta experienced consistent year-on-year growth in passenger levels, with some meteoric surges in key years. The company believes that the increase in business since 1986 was accounted for by two factors: first, by going national in terms of their brochure distribution and racking deals with UK travel agents, multiples and independent consortia; and, secondly, by general growth in the market for city-based short breaks, which the company was able to take advantage of.

In 1996, out of a total of 198,000 passengers carried by Cresta, 125,000 were short break clients. These figures represented a 4 per cent increase in passenger levels over 1995, a growth rate which was considered a relative disappointment by Cresta, following the much more substantial increases which they had experienced in previous years. However, the main reason for this comparatively disappointing performance was an internal one: in 1996, Cresta installed a new computer reservations system (CRS)

and management information system (MIS) computer, which, as well as bringing with it the usual technical 'hiccups', also meant that staff had to be retrained to deal with the new reservations system. This resulted in increased transaction times, which in turn led to considerable extra pressure on Cresta's telephones.

However, as mentioned previously, 1997 looked like being a record year for the company. Turnover for that year was expected to be £75 million, and by the summer of that year, booking levels overall were up 48 per cent compared to the same date in 1996, although this increase was expected to level out by the end of the year to +44 per cent.

Booking trends for the late 1990s

The impact of the Channel Tunnel

The 'Eurostar effect' has enhanced Paris' popularity. In fact, travel by Eurostar accounted for 74 per cent of all Cresta's London–Paris traffic between January–October 1996, taking some of the market share away from the airlines and at the same time bringing new clients into the short break market. This market growth occurred in spite of the French strikes and civil unrest during November and December 1995, which resulted in Cresta losing considerable custom during those two months and which had knock-on effects into 1996, as Paris got off to a slow start.

The 'Eurostar effect' also impacted on Brussels and, as a spin-off, Bruges, both of which continued to show increased business in 1996. However, the tour operator found that Belgium's low recognition factor among customers meant that a number of new destinations (Ostend, Namur and Tournai) introduced in their stand-alone Eurostar brochure failed to take-off, and as a result only Antwerp and Ghent were carried forward into the 1997 programme. Instead, Cresta has introduced Tours, Lyons and Bordeaux by Eurostar to Lille, then high-speed TGV to the final destination. Overall, travel by Cresta's clients using Eurostar increased by 48 per cent in 1996. Despite the Channel Tunnel fire on 18 November of that year, bookings recovered quickly and by 1997 the tour operator was able to report that it was satisfied that customer confidence had not suffered dramatically. The long-awaited advent of regional services from

continued

Manchester and the English Midlands will be much welcomed by Cresta.

According to Cresta's market data, the Channel Tunnel's Le Shuttle service has led to growth in the number of clients (up to 3–15 per cent) who decide to use their own car for short breaks in Amsterdam, Paris and Bruges, in addition to the large market for self-drive short breaks to Northern France.

By 1997, the tour operator was able to report that the opening of the Channel Tunnel and the resulting downward pressure on cross-Channel ferry prices had led to Cresta being able to reduce the majority of its French holidays by between 4–10 per cent on 1996 prices. At the same time, the company was able to offer an increased range of hotels in Northern France, which as a region had been moved to the front of Cresta's newly restructured brochure, reflecting its increased popularity with the UK market as a result of the fixed link (Figure 7.5).

Long-haul short breaks

In the maturing short break market, Cresta has detected a firm trend towards more long-haul and exotic destinations, as their loyal clients seek as many as two or even three new and different destinations each year. As a result, their long-haul destinations continued to perform well in 1996, encouraging the tour operator to introduce more cities in other continents, such as Rio de Janeiro, Montreal (following the company's success with Toronto since 1993), Boston, Chicago and Washington.

Eastern Europe

Another significant trend detected by Cresta has been the success of Eastern European destinations previously difficult to access under former Communist rule. Berlin, Prague and Budapest have been success stories since 1990 and in 1996, Cresta introduced Warsaw and Krakow into the programme, with considerable success. In 1997, Tallinn, the capital of Estonia, and Riga, the capital of Latvia, joined the tour operator's product range.

Product development

Destinations

In addition to the new destinations already mentioned, the Cresta portfolio was extended for 1997 to include a number of European and Mediterranean cities and islands: Guernsey, Madeira, Marrakech, Oporto, Salamanca and Toledo.

Clearly, the tour operator sees expansion possibilities for Spain, following the success of its existing Spanish destinations in 1996, when Madrid saw a 28 per cent increase in the number of Cresta clients choosing this city for a short break. This growth rate put Madrid in Cresta's top ten destinations in terms of their increase in popularity with the tour operator's customers between 1995 and 1996. At the top of that list came Dublin, with an increase of +119 per cent. The tour operator's explanation for this growth was that the Irish Republic capital benefited from the 'fashionability factor' as well as from greater exposure in Cresta's Ireland programme. Other destinations experiencing considerable growth in the number of Cresta Holidays clients they received in 1996 were: Cologne (+101 per cent), Reykjavik (+40 per cent), Berlin (+39 per cent) – with a new flight from Gatwick, Prague (+32 per cent) – benefiting from a new British Midland service from Heathrow and additional flights from Stanstead, New York (+28 per cent), Budapest (+27 per cent), Lisbon (+24 per cent), and Toronto (+23 per cent).

Conversely, in 1996, Cresta saw a decline in business to a number of destinations including Innsbruck, Salzburg and (to a lesser extend) Vienna, due to a perception of Austria as an expensive destination, with unfavourable exchange rates. Helsinki, Istanbul and Palma also experienced a drop-off in Cresta customers, in the case of Palma, because of competition from cheaper charters.

Activity/themed breaks

As a selected operator for Disneyland Paris, Cresta in 1997 reported an increase in 1996 bookings for this destination of +5 per cent over 1995. By the summer of 1997, growth in reservations for the theme park were up by over 50 per cent compared with the same period the previous year. The establishment of a regular Eurostar service direct to the park's gates was clearly a contributory factor. In addition, Cresta had also introduced coach travel as an option for packages including the theme park's Cheyenne and Santa Fe hotels as accommodation.

continued

Regarding golf short breaks in France and Ireland, Cresta sends approximately 5,000 clients each year to these destinations on organised packages complete with pre-booked tee times and pre-paid green fees. Furthermore, an unquantifiable number of Cresta's clients use standard packages as 'unofficial' golfing breaks, opting to take their clubs 'just in case', and selecting hotels close to golf courses.

Transport options

While continuing to offer its clients the choice of a wide range of scheduled flights from sixteen UK airports, Cresta introduced new transport options for 1997. For the first time, the tour operator introduced coach travel to Paris, Amsterdam and Disneyland Paris, using the scheduled services of Hoverspeed's CitySprint departures. The decision to extend their product range into short-break packages using coach travel was partly taken with the intention of enlarging Cresta's customer range to include clients on a modest budget. The coach travel option was therefore designed to bring Cresta's range of 2- and 3-star hotels in the two most important short-break destinations to a wider market. At the other end of the scale, Cresta also introduced into its Italy brochure short breaks in Venice, Verona and Rome using as transport option the Venice–Simplon Orient Express.

Day trips

Although beyond the scope of this case study, it is worthy of note that Cresta expanded this small but growing sector of its product range in its 1997 brochures, offering day trips by air to Paris and Amsterdam, and by Eurostar to Paris, Brussels and Lille. In addition, the tour operator noted a low but consistent level of demand for day trips from the UK to Disneyland Paris, often booked for birthday celebrations.

Outlook

By 1997, Cresta Holidays was looking towards the end of the 1990s and beyond with some considerable optimism. Due to their clients' high economic profile: A, B, C1, their short-breaks market was relatively unaffected by the adverse economic conditions of the

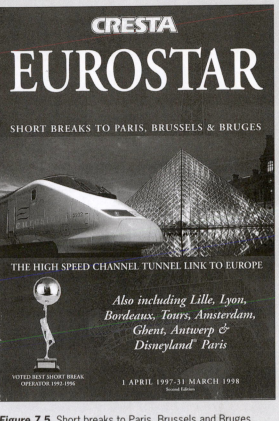

Figure 7.5 Short breaks to Paris, Brussels and Bruges
Source: Cresta Holidays

early 1990s. And as the end of the century came into sight, Cresta was reporting increasing evidence of the 'feel-good factor' which encourages customers in this sector to consume more.

Cresta's market data pointed to evidence that their clients were travelling on short breaks more frequently, tending to take more than one break per year, and that new clients were coming into the market in greater numbers than before. While many of these new customers had been introduced to the concept of overseas short breaks by the growing number of cut-price short breaks offered by charter operators using this business to fill aircraft in the winter, Cresta was of the opinion that, once in the market, such customers then tend to look towards the more established operators offering choice and flexibility on a year-round basis.

Short break trends

LONG-HAUL SHORT BREAKS

People have become much more adventurous in their choice of short-break destinations, and one result of this is the growth in long-haul destinations. Between 1990 and 1993, there was a rise of 42 per cent in the volume of long-haul short breaks taken by Europeans, compared with a 30 per cent increase in longer holidays to long-haul destinations. (Potier and Cockerell 1995)

At least half of Europeans' long-haul short breaks are taken in the USA. At the beginning of the 1990s, weekend shopping breaks to New York were considered a novelty and only likely to last as long as the US dollar remained weak.

> Since then, the dollar has fluctuated wildly, but cultural and shopping weekend breaks to a range of different destinations in North America have become part of a standard range of short break programmes from the airlines as well as tour operators, in an effort to help fill empty seats on aircraft at slack periods. (Potier and Cockerell 1995)

NEW PRODUCTS

The commercial sector, in particular, is booming. A number of specialist tour operators have entered the market in recent years (many claiming above-average growth rates) and where the variety of new products continues to expand. City breaks still dominate, but the variety of options is extensive, ranging from short breaks based on Europe's theme parks to anti-stress or fitness programmes at sea-water therapy centres (Potier and Cockerell 1995).

At the beginning of the 1990s, Beioley (1991) predicted a broadening of the demand for and supply of commercial short-break products, with:

- the increasing involvement of self-catering and holiday centre operators in this area.
- the development of more products aimed at families and younger age groups.

The same author also predicted growth in the short break market due to the growing number of over-65s who have both the income and the habit of taking short breaks: 'The coming generation of senior citizens may demonstrate different travel behaviour as part of a different lifestyle. They are more likely to be consumers of short break holidays than the present generation of over 65s.'

There may also be expansion possibilities arising through the opportunities presented by the business/leisure market, with packaged short-break products also appealing to those who choose to extend a business trip through a weekend, and who frequently take their spouses with them. As the authors of the 1995 survey of international short-break trips state, this is one sector for which more detailed research is essential, since current data do not provide sufficiently reliable indications of the volume or demand.

Finally, the trend towards growing segmentation in the short-breaks market is also noted by Faché (1994). He quotes Middleton and O'Brien, who identified a need for short-break programmes which appeal to specific market groups, for example, 'educational' breaks offering the chance to learn or improve a skill, such as painting or foreign languages, or health and fitness breaks.

NEW TECHNOLOGY

Developments in new technology have the potential to radically change the way in which short-break packages are distributed to customers, notably by enabling them to book directly with operators.

Direct booking accessibility for the public is likely to be one of the major factors influencing the future growth of the commercial short-break market – and the longer holiday market. As seen in the Episodes case study, in France, the 6.5 million households that subscribe to Minitel, the national viewdata system, are able to make firm reservations through the system direct from their living-rooms. Many of them also have the facilities to pay for bookings by credit card by using a separate card reader called Facitel to debit their accounts.

But whereas only certain countries have this type of national viewdata system, the ownership of personal computers (PCs) is much more widespread. A possible link-up between PCs and computer reservations systems (CRSs) could revolutionise the way in which short breaks are purchased. As CRSs have diversified from simple airline reservations into many other reservation functions such as car rentals, hotel bookings and train reservations, this product diversification has made the system appear more attractive to leisure travel agents in as far as they increase their competitive advantage and profitability. For short breaks, there have been some tentative experiments in Europe, in distributing these through CRSs: for example, the Art Cities in Europe (see page 211) used various CRSs to distribute its packages through travel agents.

But it has been predicted that in the near future, CRSs will begin to open up their information directly to customers. In the USA, Sabre has successfully introduced a PC-based on-line software package which gives travellers access to timetables and basic fare information. Galileo too is aiming to bring out a consumer application (Knowles and Garland 1994), enabling clients to consuct and book their leisure breaks directly.

Other possibilities are presented by the use of on-line technology. For Internet users, reservations facilities are already on offer in all sectors of the travel and tourism industry. By 1996, tourism information could be found in over 250 locations on the World Wide Web (Bentley 1996). For example, by using Netscape software, consumers can easily make an immediate reservation for a hotel room at a chosen destination and receive an e-mail confirmation within 24 hours. Hotel chains, airlines and car rental firms have wired themselves to the Internet, as a way of attracting extra business from the growing numbers of consumers who are drawn to this form of distribution. Once the public is reassured over security issues concerning transactions made on the Internet, this trend will be accelerated.

These developments will lead to a huge increase in suppliers offering their services direct to the market, encouraging consumers to by-pass the travel trade and put together their own leisure travel programmes, combining the different elements of transport, accommodation, and so on, into a tailor-made package. Given the spontaneous, last-minute nature of many people's decisions to take a short break, this means of making reservations may be seen as particularly appropriate.

Where does this leave Europe's travel agents? How should they prepare themselves for the day when they can no longer rely upon a generation on non-computer literate clients to use their services for the purchasing of short breaks and longer holidays?

Some believe that investment in the appropriate technology by travel agents could increase their usefulness and appeal to the market. One way of providing value-added service would be to provide 'cyberspace café' areas where customers would not only have the personal advice of the travel agency staff but also be guided through the fast-growing supply of multimedia software, to help them choose the best product for them. For example, with visual imaging made possible through the evolution of CD-ROM technology, potential customers can, for example, 'view' a hotel and its facilities before booking.

UPDATE

Undertake your own research to find out the answers to the following questions.

- Have there been any moves towards changing the accepted definition of the 'short break'?
- Has the commercial sector continued to make inroads into the short-break market?
- What new types of short-break products have come on to the market?
- Have any serious rivals for Cresta and Episodes emerged in their respective countries?

References

Beioley, S. (1991) 'Short holidays', in *Insights*, September, English Tourist Board, London.

Bentley, R. B. (1996) 'Information technology and tourism: an update', *Tourism Management*, Vol. 17, No. 2.

Bertinchamps, P. (1993) 'Episodes: le spécialiste des courts séjours', in *Les Cahiers Espaces*, No. 34, Editions Touristiques Européennes, Paris.

Davidson, R. (1993) 'The European short breaks market', in *Insights*, May, English Tourist Board, London.

Echo Touristique (1992) 'Episodes allonge ses courts séjours', 17 January.

Economist, The (1995) 'A place in the sun', 29 July.

Edgar, D. A., Litteljohn, D. L., Allardyce, M. L. and Wanhill, S. (1994) 'Commercial short holiday breaks – the relationship between market structure, competitive advantage and performance', in A. V. Seaton et al. (eds), *Tourism: The State of the Art*, John Wiley, Chichester.

Faché, W. (1994) 'Short break holidays', in A. V. Seaton et al. (eds), *Tourism: The State of the Art*, John Wiley, Chichester.

Goumaz, M. (1993) 'Le marché du court séjour: un atout à exploiter', in *Les Cahiers Espaces*, No. 34, Editions Touristiques Européennes, Paris.

Gratton, C. (1990) 'The economics of short break holidays', in W. Faché (ed.) *Short Break Holidays*, Center Parcs, Rotterdam.

Knowles, T. and Garland, M. (1994) 'The strategic importance of CRS, in the airline industry', in *Travel and Tourism Analyst (4)*, Travel and Tourism Intelligence, London

Potier, F. and Cockerell, N. (1993) Les courts séjours des Européens, in *Les Cahiers Espaces*, No, 34, Editions Touristiques Européennes, Paris.

Potier, F. and Cockerell, N. (1995) 'The European international Short-break market', in *Travel and Tourism Analyst (2)*, Travel and Tourism Intelligence, London

Index

theme parks (*continued*)
  extending season 168
  increasing secondary spend 168–9
  mixed developments 169
  new technologies 169–70
  sponsorship 169
  virtual reality 169–70
 Value Added Tax 172
 as visitor attractions 146
Three Packages, air transport liberalisation 81–2
tilting trains 134–5
timeshare directive 50
toll roads 109
trade fairs *see* business tourism: exhibitions and trade fairs
trans-European networks (TEN) 35, 59–61, 62–3
 airports 98–9
trans-European road networks (TERN) 110
transport 2
  see also air transport; coach travel; passenger transport; rail travel; roads
  European Union policy *see* European Union

short breaks 210, 212, 218
technological improvements 4
Treaty on European Union (Maastricht Treaty) 36
Tussaud Group 154–9
twenty-first century predictions
 air travel 23
 greater variety 22–3
 origin-destination flow shifts 23
 rail travel 23
 shorter holidays 22

universities, meetings and conferences 182

Value Added Tax (VAT)
 EU harmonisation 40–2
 theme parks 172
virtual reality, theme parks 169–70
visiting friends and relatives (VFR) 213

Walibi Group 160–1
World Travel and Tourism Council (WTTC) 72–3